Plays from Famous Stories and Fairy Tales

Royalty-free dramatizations of favorite children's stories

By

ADELE THANE

Publishers PLAYS, INC. *Boston*

Library of Congress Cataloging in Publication Data

Thane, Adele.
  Plays from famous stories and fairy tales.

  Summary: Twenty-eight short plays based on the works of Hans Christian Andersen, the brothers Grimm, Charles Perrault, and other well-known tales and stories.
  1. Children's plays. [1. Plays] I. Title.
[PN6119.9.T48 1984]   808.82'041   83-23039
ISBN 0-8238-0262-0 (pbk.)

Manufactured in Canada

Contents

PLAYS FROM FAMOUS STORIES
and
FAIRY TALES

The Emperor's Nightingale

by Hans Christian Andersen

Characters

GONG-BEARER
STAGE MANAGER
PROPERTY MAN
THE EMPEROR OF CHINA
TU CHIN, *his sister*
CHAN TUNG, *his Lord-in-Waiting*
YU LANG, *the kitchen maid*
THE NIGHTINGALE
THE TOY NIGHTINGALE
TWO COURT LADIES
THE IMPERIAL DOCTOR
THE IMPERIAL NURSE
THE IMPERIAL WATCHMAKER

TIME: *Long ago.*

SETTING: *The Emperor's garden. A throne is at center with a tea tray on a stand beside it. At left center is a garden bench. A large lacquered box containing properties is down right.*

AT RISE: *The* GONG-BEARER *is standing on a platform up left. He strikes his gong, and the* STAGE MANAGER, *carrying a fan, enters from left. He walks sedately to the*

3

center of the stage and bows to the audience. The gong is struck again.

STAGE MANAGER: O most revered audience (*Bows*), your humble servant begs your worthy attention. If your gracious spirits should be moved to tears or moved to laughter, deign to let us know, O honorable audience. (*Bows*) I am the Stage Manager and this is the stage. O venerable stage! (*He turns and bows to the stage, then faces the audience again.*) In a moment, several actors will come here and act out a play. The name of the play is *The Emperor's Nightingale.* Now I am going to introduce you to a very important person, the Property Man. (*Claps his hands and calls off right*) Props! (PROPERTY MAN *enters, and goes to* STAGE MANAGER.) This is the Property Man. Bow! (PROPERTY MAN *looks blank and* STAGE MANAGER *taps him on top of the head with his fan.*) Bow! (PROPERTY MAN *and* STAGE MANAGER *bow to each other and then to audience.*) As you can see, he is dressed all in black. That makes him invisible, so that when he puts out the props, you are not supposed to see him. Understand? He will also be the sound effects: he will moo like a cow and croak like a frog. (PROPERTY MAN *moos and croaks, and* STAGE MANAGER *taps him on head again with his fan.*) Quiet! Not yet, later. Are all your properties ready? (PROPERTY MAN *nods vigorously.* STAGE MANAGER *glances up right and points with his fan.*) The willow tree—where is the willow tree? (PROPERTY MAN *blinks and grins sheepishly, then goes to property box for the willow tree. He places it in position up right and looks anxiously at* STAGE MANAGER, *who nods.*) Very well. (*They bow to each other.* PROPERTY MAN *returns to property box and sits on the floor beside it.* STAGE MANAGER *addresses audience again.*) The first scene of our play takes place in the garden of the Emperor of China. (EMPEROR *enters from left.*) This is the Emperor. (*They bow to each other.*) He is young in years, but old in ancestry, and his palace is the wonder of the world. (EMPEROR *turns and bows toward the palace off left, raising his hands in a gesture of wonder.*) So is his garden (EMPEROR *struts about.*)—which stretches away down to the deep blue sea. (EMPEROR *shades his eyes with his fan and gazes off right, then goes to throne and sits. As* STAGE MANAGER *continues,* PROPERTY MAN *brings* EMPEROR *a cup and saucer and teapot, pours a cup of tea, then retires down right.* EMPEROR *sips the tea daintily.*) In his garden, unknown to the Emperor, there lives a nightingale who sings so sweetly that even the poor fishermen stop to listen. From the four corners of the earth travelers have come to the Emperor's city and then gone home to write books about the palace and garden. But, most of all, they have written about the nightingale—and presently, O worthy audience, you shall hear what they had to say, because the Emperor's favorite sister, Tu Chin (TU CHIN *enters right*), is going to read aloud to the Emperor (PROPERTY MAN *bows and hands* TU CHIN *a book which she accepts with a bow.*) while he is drinking his afternoon tea. (TU CHIN *crosses to bench, sits, and opens book.* STAGE MANAGER *bows to audience and stands down left.*)

TU CHIN (*Reading*): "The palace of the Emperor of China is the most beautiful palace in the world." (EMPEROR *nods in agreement.*) "It is built entirely of the finest porcelain and is so fragile that it can be touched only with the greatest care." (*Looks up.*) Oh, that reminds me! One of the servants broke a balcony this morning while she was dusting it.

EMPEROR (*Frowning*): That makes the second one this week.

TU CHIN (*Contritely*): I know.

EMPEROR: If this keeps up, we won't have a roof over our heads. Please continue.

TU CHIN (*Reading*): "There are most extraordinary flowers in the garden. The prettiest ones have little silver bells tied to them which tinkle all the time." (PROPERTY MAN *comes forward and gives* EMPEROR *a paper flower hung with tiny bells.* EMPEROR *smells the flower, shakes it gently so that the bells tinkle softly.*) "But more wonderful than the porcelain palace, more wonderful than the garden, more wonderful than the flowers with silver bells is—the Nightingale."

EMPEROR (*Startled*): The Nightingale?

TU CHIN (*Looking closely at book*): The Nightingale.

EMPEROR: What's a Nightingale? Something to ride in?

TU CHIN (*Running her eye down page*): No—it's a bird.

EMPEROR: A *bird*? Called the *Nightingale*? I know nothing about it.

TU CHIN (*Pointing to book*): Well, that's what it says here. Capital N-i-g-h-t-i-n-g-a-l-e. (EMPEROR *rises.*)

EMPEROR: Let me see! (*He takes book.*) Capital N-i-g-h-t-i-n-g-a-l-e. (*Looks up in amazement*) Can there be such a bird in my kingdom, and I not know of it? Imagine my having to find out from a book! It's preposterous! (*He shuts book with a bang and slams it down on seat of throne.*)

TU CHIN (*Nodding*): Quite preposterous!

EMPEROR (*Clapping his hands and calling off right*): Chan Tung!

TU CHIN (*Contemptuously, as she rises*): You don't expect Chan Tung to know anything about the Nightingale, do you?

EMPEROR: Who else, if not my Lord-in-Waiting?

TU CHIN: Humph! He will only say "*Q!*"—which means nothing at all.

EMPEROR (*Crossly*): He won't say "*Q!*" to me. (*He claps his hands again.*) Chan Tung! (CHAN TUNG *hurries in right.*)

CHAN TUNG (*Bowing low*): Most excellent son of heaven! (*He remains bent over.*)

EMPEROR (*Sharply*): Look here, Chan Tung! *What* is a Nightingale?

CHAN TUNG (*Snapping upright in surprise*): *Q!* I mean, no! I mean, I *don't* know!—Your Imperial Majesty. (*His voice dwindles away as he meets the* EMPEROR'S *furious glare, and he bows to the floor.*)

EMPEROR: Well, they say there's a most remarkable bird in this kingdom called the Nightingale.

CHAN TUNG (*Gaping up at* EMPEROR, *still in bowing position*): Bird?

EMPEROR: They say it's the best thing in all my empire.

CHAN TUNG (*In a whisper*): Best?

EMPEROR: Why haven't I been told about it? (*He hits* CHAN TUNG *on the head with his fan, and* CHAN TUNG *scrambles to his feet.*)

CHAN TUNG (*Stuttering from fright*): Who-who-who's they?

EMPEROR: What do you mean—who's they?

CHAN TUNG: You said *they* say. (EMPEROR *picks up the book and shakes it under* CHAN TUNG'S *nose, driving him upstage around the throne to left.*)

EMPEROR (*Shouting*): The learned men who write books, you idiot! They, they, *they!*

CHAN TUNG: Your Imperial Majesty must not believe everything that is written.

EMPEROR: This book was sent to me by the Emperor of Japan! (*He backs* CHAN TUNG *onto bench.*)

CHAN TUNG: Nevertheless, Your Majesty—

EMPEROR: Nevertheless, poppycock! (*He shoves book into* CHAN TUNG'S *hands.*) *Where* is this Nightingale?

CHAN TUNG (*Cowering*): I've never heard it mentioned before. It hasn't been presented at court.

EMPEROR (*Bending over him*): Then I command that it *be* presented at court! This very evening! And it must *sing!*

CHAN TUNG: Of course, Your Majesty, of course. I will go and look for it right away. I will find it.

EMPEROR: If it's not here by sundown, I will have the whole court punished immediately after supper!

CHAN TUNG: Q! (*Runs off right*)

TU CHIN: "*Q!*" *He* will find it! Not likely! (YU LANG, *the kitchen maid, enters from left and bows low. She stands humbly.*)

EMPEROR (*Impatiently, to* TU CHIN): Who's that?

TU CHIN: Yu Lang, the kitchen maid. She has come to clear away the tea things. (*To* YU LANG) You may take them, Yu Lang. (YU LANG *clears away quietly, carrying the things to* PROPERTY MAN, *who puts them in box.*)

EMPEROR (*Sitting on bench*): The whole world knows my possessions better than I do! Why is it this Nightingale is well known every place except at home? I *will* hear it sing! I *insist* on hearing it!

TU CHIN (*Calmly patting his shoulder*): Yes, brother—but first it must be found. (*She notices* YU LANG, *who has come over and is standing timidly with bowed head.*) What is it, Yu Lang?

YU LANG: Most gracious lady— (*Hesitates*)

EMPEROR: What does she want?

TU CHIN: Yes, Yu Lang?

YU LANG (*Bashfully*): Most gracious lady, I heard His Majesty the Emperor speak just now of the Nightingale.

EMPEROR (*Suddenly interested*): Do you know this bird?

YU LANG: Oh, yes! I know the Nightingale!

EMPEROR (*Peevishly, to* TU CHIN): There! You see? Even the kitchen maid knows of it, while her Emperor remains in ignorance. (*To* YU LANG) Can it sing, this bird?

YU LANG: Like temple bells at evening.

EMPEROR: Where have you heard it?

YU LANG: In Your Majesty's garden—down by the sea. Its song brings tears to my eyes. I feel as if my mother were kissing me.

EMPEROR: Little kitchen girl, you shall be Imperial Pot-Walloper, with the privilege of watching me dine, if you will take me to the place where the Nightingale sings.

YU LANG: Gladly, Your Majesty. But it's not necessary for you to travel so far. The Nightingale sings here, too, in the willow tree.

EMPEROR (*Amazed; rising*): Here? In my willow tree? (*Moves to tree*)

YU LANG (*Following him*): Yes, Your Majesty.

EMPEROR: Then why haven't I ever heard it?

YU LANG (*Gently*): Perhaps you haven't listened, Your Majesty.

EMPEROR (*Sharply*): What's that?

TU CHIN (*Hastily going to* EMPEROR): You may have been in another part of the garden.

YU LANG: If Your Majesty will wait here and keep very, very quiet, I'm sure you will hear it.

TU CHIN: Don't you think we—

EMPEROR: Shh! (*As they assume listening attitudes,* CHAN TUNG *rushes in right, out of breath.*)

CHAN TUNG (*Bowing and bellowing*): Most glorious—

EMPEROR: Shh!

CHAN TUNG (*In a loud whisper*): Most glorious light of

day! The entire court is looking for the Nightingale, because no one wants to be punished after supper.

EMPEROR (*Hissing*): Well, they can stop looking and eat their rice. The Nightingale has been found.

CHAN TUNG: *Q!* Where?

EMPEROR: Where any fool but you would have expected to find it. Right here in my own garden.

CHAN TUNG: You don't say! Is it going to sing?

EMPEROR: Yes! Be still! (*After a moment of silence the* PROPERTY MAN *moos like a cow.*)

CHAN TUNG: There it is! What a powerful voice for a bird.

YU LANG: No, no! That is a cow. Listen again. (PROPERTY MAN *croaks like a frog.*)

EMPEROR: I hear it! Beautiful, beautiful! Just like the great bell of Peking.

YU LANG (*Shaking her head*): No, Your Majesty.

EMPEROR (*Disappointed*): No?

YU LANG: That is a frog in the pool. (EMPEROR *fidgets impatiently.*) Patience, Your Majesty. We shall hear it soon. (*The first notes of the* NIGHTINGALE *are heard from offstage.*) That's it! Listen! (*All listen intently to the* NIGHTINGALE. EMPEROR *is very moved, and at the end of the song he walks slowly to his throne, sits and bows his head.*)

CHAN TUNG (*Craning his neck, searching the treetops overhead*): Where is it?

YU LANG (*Pointing off right*): Over there! Don't you see? That little gray bird on the wisteria vine. (*They look offstage.*)

CHAN TUNG: *Q!*

TU CHIN: Is it possible?

EMPEROR (*Quietly*): Well, I never would have thought it looked like that! How—unassuming.

CHAN TUNG (*His nose in the air*): How *common!*

EMPEROR (*To* YU LANG): Ask it to come here.

Yu Lang (*Calling off right*): Dear Nightingale, our gracious Emperor wants to speak to you. Won't you come here? (Nightingale *enters and bows before* Emperor.)

Emperor: You have just been singing to the Emperor of China. Did you know?

Nightingale (*Happily*): Yes, I knew.

Emperor: Will you sing again tonight to the Imperial household?

Nightingale: Gladly, my Emperor.

Emperor: Yu Lang, you may stand behind the door and listen. (Yu Lang *bows.*)

Nightingale: I shall sit on the highest branch of the willow tree and sing to the rising moon.

Emperor: Oh, no, Nightingale. (*Loftily*) Tonight you are to sing in the Court of my Ancestors.

Nightingale: But my song sounds best in the trees.

Emperor (*Pointing to his foot*): I will give you my golden slipper to wear around your neck as a reward.

Nightingale: Thank you, my Emperor, but I have already had my reward.

Emperor: What was it?

Nightingale: When I sang just now, there were tears in your eyes. That is reward enough for me.

Emperor (*Gently strokes the head of the* Nightingale): Sing to me again, my precious Nightingale, but sing to me in the Court of my Immortal Ancestors. Come. (*He exits left, followed by* Nightingale, *who commences to sing, and* Tu Chin, Chan Tung, *and* Yu Lang. Stage Manager *walks to center and bows to audience.*)

Stage Manager: The next scene of our illustrious play takes place in the same garden. A week has passed. The Nightingale has given a concert every evening in the Court of the Emperor's Ancestors and the whole city is talking about the marvelous bird. The court ladies practice singing all day, hoping to sound like the Nightingale. (STAGE MANAGER *bows and retires down left. Two* COURT LADIES *enter from left. Each one tries to imitate the song of the* NIGHTINGALE. *They sit on the bench.*)

1ST LADY (*After trilling a phrase*): I can do it!

2ND LADY: I don't think you have the trill quite right. Listen. (*She throws her head back and does a trill.*) There! Try it. (1ST LADY *does so, and together they trill a duet.* CHAN TUNG *enters from right, carrying a jewel-studded casket.* LADIES *rise.*)

CHAN TUNG (*Bowing*): Night!

LADIES (*Bowing*): Gale! (*All sigh sentimentally.*)

CHAN TUNG: Have you heard the latest news?

1ST LADY: No, what is it?

2ND LADY: Tell us!

CHAN TUNG: Eleven silk weavers' children have been named after the Nightingale, and they haven't a voice among them.

LADIES (*Disapprovingly*): Tsk, tsk, tsk!

CHAN TUNG: And now the bird is to have twelve footmen.

1ST LADY: Twelve? The very idea!

2ND LADY (*Speaking behind her fan*): I have heard that the Emperor's Siamese cat is terribly jealous. (GONG-BEARER *strikes his gong.*)

CHAN TUNG: Shh! Here comes the Emperor! (CHAN TUNG *stands right of the throne. The* LADIES *stand behind the bench. All bow as* EMPEROR *enters and sits on the throne.*)

EMPEROR: Where is my precious little Nightingale?

CHAN TUNG: It is swinging on the Moon Gate, Your Majesty.

EMPEROR (*Smiling indulgently*): What a child it is!

CHAN TUNG: May it please Your Majesty to inspect the gift now?

EMPEROR: Gift? What gift?

CHAN TUNG: From the Emperor of Japan.

EMPEROR (*Delighted*): *Another* gift from the Emperor of Japan? Is it a book about the Nightingale?

CHAN TUNG: I don't think so, Your Majesty, but I'm sure it's something for the Nightingale. (*He holds out the jeweled casket.*)

EMPEROR (*Taking it*): Naturally, something for the Nightingale. (LADIES *move in for a closer view of the casket.* EMPEROR *opens it and finds a key.*) A key! Now, what can that be for? (PROPERTY MAN *hurries over with a key-tag and gives it to* EMPEROR *with a jerky bow.* EMPEROR *reads.*) "For the Nightingale." Hm, but why?

CHAN TUNG (*Pointing inside the casket*): There is a scroll also, Your Majesty. Perhaps that will explain.

EMPEROR: I don't see any scroll.

CHAN TUNG: There should be a scroll. (*He glares at* PROPERTY MAN.)

STAGE MANAGER (*Speaking across the stage to* PROPERTY MAN *in an angry hiss*): Where is the scroll? (PROPERTY MAN *searches frantically inside box and finally produces a small scroll which he brings to* EMPEROR, *bowing abjectly.* EMPEROR *unrolls it and reads.*)

EMPEROR: "The Emperor of Japan's Nightingale is very poor compared to the Emperor of China's. It awaits Your Majesty's pleasure in the Court of Politeness." (*Excitedly, to* CHAN TUNG) Chan Tung, go immediately to the Court of Politeness and bring this bird here. (CHAN TUNG *bows and hurries out right.* EMPEROR *muses over the scroll.*) "The Emperor of Japan's Nightingale." I didn't know there was another one in the whole world.

1ST LADY: It can't possibly come up to Your Majesty's Nightingale for absolute pitch.

2ND LADY: It won't have any more voice than the silk

weavers' children, you wait and see. (CHAN TUNG *enters right, pushing a draped figure ahead of him. He places it right of the throne. The others stare at it curiously.*)

EMPEROR (*Impatiently, to* CHAN TUNG): Well, take off the covering! (CHAN TUNG *removes the drapery and reveals the* TOY NIGHTINGALE, *gilded and studded all over with precious stones. All gasp with delight.*) Why, this is wonderful!

1ST LADY: How it sparkles!

2ND LADY: Oh, it's much prettier than the real one!

EMPEROR: Can it sing? (*To* TOY NIGHTINGALE) Can you sing? (TOY NIGHTINGALE *does not respond.* STAGE MANAGER *gets* EMPEROR'S *attention and pantomimes winding up a clock.*) What do you want?

STAGE MANAGER (*In a loud whisper*): The key, Your Majesty, the key!

EMPEROR: Oh! Oh, yes! (*He hands the key to* CHAN TUNG *who proceeds to wind up* TOY NIGHTINGALE *while the* PROPERTY MAN *provides the sound effect by twirling a clacker.* TOY NIGHTINGALE *sings a little monotonous tune until it runs down and stops.* EMPEROR *applauds.*) This is a *marvelous* Nightingale!

CHAN TUNG: Shall I wind it up again?

EMPEROR: Certainly. No—wait! (*To* 1ST LADY) Call in the other Nightingale. (1ST LADY *bows and exits left.*) They must sing together. What a duet that will be!

2ND LADY: Oh, dear! I wish I had my writing tablet with me. I want to set down the tune. I want to be the first to sing it. (1ST LADY *enters left with* NIGHTINGALE.)

NIGHTINGALE (*Bowing*): My Emperor wishes to speak to me?

EMPEROR: Yes, little Nightingale. (*He indicates* TOY NIGHTINGALE.) See here! A bird exactly like yourself—

except, of course, that it is more handsomely dressed.

NIGHTINGALE (*Aghast*): *That*—like me?

EMPEROR (*Frowning*): Do you doubt it? It can sing. Stand over there beside it.

NIGHTINGALE: Yes, Your Majesty. (NIGHTINGALE *bows and crosses to* TOY NIGHTINGALE.)

1ST LADY: How *very* gray it is! (EMPEROR *nods to* CHAN TUNG *who winds up the* TOY NIGHTINGALE. PROPERTY MAN *twirls his clacker*.)

EMPEROR: Now—sing a duet.

NIGHTINGALE: But, my Emperor, I sing whatever comes into my head. (*The* TOY NIGHTINGALE *starts to pipe its mechanical tune*.)

EMPEROR (*In a commanding tone*): Sing! (*The* NIGHTINGALES *sing together, but the duet turns out badly, as the* TOY NIGHTINGALE *keeps strictly to the beat, and the melodies are entirely dissimilar.* EMPEROR *marks time furiously with his hands, rising and shouting to the* NIGHTINGALE.) Keep to the beat! Keep to the beat! One, two—one, two! (NIGHTINGALE *tries to continue, but finally breaks down miserably and hangs its head in silence.*) Why do you stop? *Sing!* One, two—one, two! (NIGHTINGALE *hides its head in its wing and flees off right.* TOY NIGHTINGALE *runs down and stops singing.* EMPEROR *looks after* NIGHTINGALE *with a puzzled expression.*) Now, what made it do that, I wonder?

1ST LADY: Look, it is flying away.

2ND LADY: What an ungrateful bird!

CHAN TUNG: I never did think much of that bird.

EMPEROR: It shall be banished from the kingdom, and in its place, this magnificent creature shall sit on a cushion beside my bed. It shall be called "Grand Imperial Singer-to-Sleep-of-the-Emperor."

1ST LADY: Oh, do let's hear it sing again.

EMPEROR (*To* CHAN TUNG): Wind it up as tightly as you can. (CHAN TUNG *does so.* PROPERTY MAN *twirls his clacker.*)

2ND LADY: Let's start learning the tune right away. (TOY NIGHTINGALE *begins to sing as before and all join in, nodding their heads and beating time with their hands.* LADIES *try to imitate the trill.* EMPEROR *sways back and forth, doing a little dance step. Suddenly the* TOY NIGHTINGALE *stops singing and collapses. The others break off, staring at the* TOY NIGHTINGALE *in consternation.*)

EMPEROR: What is it? What's wrong?

1ST LADY: A spring must be broken.

CHAN TUNG: Let me look. (*He examines the back of the* TOY NIGHTINGALE *and turns the key several times, but nothing happens. He shakes his head mournfully.*) It is broken, Your Majesty.

EMPEROR: Well, don't just stand there! *Do* something! Get the Imperial Doctor! (CHAN TUNG *runs off right.*) Get the Imperial Nurse! (LADIES *run off left.*) Get the Imperial Watchmaker! (*He looks about and sees that no one is left to carry out his order.*)

STAGE MANAGER (*Stepping forward and bowing*): Your Majesty, *you* will have to get the Imperial Watchmaker yourself.

EMPEROR: I?

STAGE MANAGER: Yes, Your Majesty.

EMPEROR: Oh, all right! Which way? (STAGE MANAGER *points right and* EMPEROR *starts off at a gallop, colliding with* CHAN TUNG *who is returning with the* IMPERIAL DOCTOR. EMPEROR *bellows at* CHAN TUNG, *pointing off right.*) Get the Imperial Watchmaker!

CHAN TUNG (*Bowing hastily*): Q! Your Majesty—I mean, yes! (*He scampers away.*)

EMPEROR (*Showing* DOCTOR *the* TOY NIGHTINGALE): Doctor, you must operate at once.

DOCTOR: Very well, Your Majesty. (*To* PROPERTY MAN) Knife! (PROPERTY MAN *brings a carving knife, which the* DOCTOR *takes with a grand flourish. He pretends to cut an opening in the* TOY NIGHTINGALE'*s back. A large wire coil springs out and* DOCTOR *holds it up.*) Here's the trouble.

LADIES (*Running in left with the* IMPERIAL NURSE): Here is the Imperial Nurse, Your Majesty.

NURSE: Where is the patient? Ah, I see. (*She hurries over to* TOY NIGHTINGALE *and tries to straighten its body, but cannot.*)

EMPEROR: Try it again! We *must* save my Nightingale. (NURSE *repeats action with the same result, as* CHAN TUNG *rushes in from right with the* IMPERIAL WATCHMAKER.)

CHAN TUNG (*Breathlessly*): The Imperial Watchmaker, Your Majesty. (WATCHMAKER *tries to push the spring back into place without success.*)

WATCHMAKER (*Turning to* EMPEROR *with an apologetic bow*): It is no use, Your Majesty. This bird will never sing again. (WATCHMAKER, DOCTOR *and* NURSE *stand the* TOY NIGHTINGALE *in a corner.* LADIES *sigh.* CHAN TUNG *wails, and the* EMPEROR *sits dejectedly on the throne.*)

EMPEROR: Leave me, all of you. I want to be alone. (*As they exit slowly,* PROPERTY MAN *plays a funeral march on a comb covered with tissue paper.* EMPEROR *leans back and closes his eyes.*) There will be no more happy music now. The real Nightingale has flown away. I shall die of a broken heart. (*At this moment, the* NIGHTINGALE *flutters onstage from right, trilling a long note which drowns out the funeral march.* PROPERTY MAN *stops playing.*)

NIGHTINGALE: No, my Emperor! You shall not die! I will sing and make you happy again! (NIGHTINGALE *sings and* EMPEROR *opens his eyes and raises his head.*)

EMPEROR: You heavenly little bird, you have come back to me! I drove you out of my kingdom, and yet you have returned to drive the sadness out of my heart. How can I ever repay you? (*He rises and stretches out his hands.*)

NIGHTINGALE: But you *have* repaid me. I brought tears to your eyes the first time I sang to you, and I shall never forget it. Those are the jewels that gladden the heart of a singer.

EMPEROR: Stay with me always and I will break this other bird into a thousand pieces. (*He makes a move to smash the* TOY NIGHTINGALE, *but* NIGHTINGALE *stops him.*)

NIGHTINGALE: Please don't do that! It is not to blame for what happened. It did the best it could.

EMPEROR: But will you stay?

NIGHTINGALE (*Gently*): I can't live indoors in the palace, but let me come here to this garden whenever I like, and I will sing to you. I will sing of the joy and sorrow in your kingdom—the good and evil that you do not see. A bird can fly to many places a long way off from you and your court—to the fisherman's hut and the farmer's fields. Yes, I will sing to you. But you must promise me one thing.

EMPEROR: With all my heart.

NIGHTINGALE: You must not let anyone know that you have a little bird who tells you everything. It will be better that way.

EMPEROR: I promise you that. (NIGHTINGALE *bursts into song, and the* EMPEROR *joins in. All enter, and are amazed when they see the* NIGHTINGALE.)

NIGHTINGALE (*Bowing*): Good evening!

ALL (*Bowing low*): Good evening, O most welcome Nightingale!

STAGE MANAGER (*Stepping forward and speaking to the
audience*): Honorable and patient audience, our play
is over. For your kind attention we bow, and bow, and
bow. (*All bow three times to the audience. Curtain*)

THE END

The Pied Piper of Hamelin

by Robert Browning

Characters

KURT, *a lame boy*
JAN, *his friend*
WIDOW WERNER, *Kurt's mother*
MAYOR
PIED PIPER
CHILDREN
TOWNSPEOPLE
THREE ALDERMEN

TIME: *A summer day, in the late thirteenth century.*
SETTING: *The Public Square of Hamelin Town. Running across the back of the Square is a parapet which borders the river bank.*
AT RISE: KURT *is seated on a bench right stage, playing jacks with his friend* JAN. *Excited voices are heard off right, and presently several* CHILDREN *enter, carrying picnic baskets. They form two circles, one inside the other, and skip around, in clockwise direction, as they sing to the tune of "Hippity Hop to the Barber Shop."*

CHILDREN (*Singing*):
Hippity Hop to the river bank,
We're going to have a picnic.

(CHILDREN *stop circling and face their partners.*)

A cake for you—

(*Each child holds up a cupcake.*)

A cake for me—

(*They exchange cupcakes.*)

And cookies for the others.

(CHILDREN *pass cookies to each other around the circles, then resume skipping as before.* CHILDREN *in inside circle move in one direction, while those in outside circle move in the opposite direction to meet a new partner.*)

Hippity Hop to the river bank,

We're going to have a picnic.

A plum for you, a plum for me,

(*Each child holds up plum or apple.*)

And apples for the others.

(*They exchange fruit.*)

Hippity Hop to the river bank,

We're going to have a picnic.

I'll eat with you, you'll eat with me,

We'll have our lunch together.

(*They skip off up left, still singing, followed by* JAN, *who has been dancing about circles, trying to snatch the goodies.* KURT *rises and limps upstage, watching* CHILDREN *go out of sight. His mother,* WIDOW WERNER, *enters from right with a market basket on her arm.*)

WIDOW WERNER: Kurt, what are you looking at?

KURT (*Turning to her*): Oh, Mother, they're going to have a picnic down on the river bank.

WIDOW WERNER (*Gently*): Are they, dear?

KURT: They have cookies and cakes and plums and apples, and I don't know what else. (*Pleading*) Mother, may I go with them, just this once?

WIDOW WERNER (*Shaking her head sadly*): I wish you

could, Kurt, but what if the rats should come? You know you can't run as fast as the other children.

KURT: But there's not a sign of a rat around anywhere, and it's only down the path a little way. *Please!*

WIDOW WERNER (*Admonishing him*): Remember what happened last time.

KURT: That was because I didn't keep a sharp lookout. If I'd kept my eyes open, I'd have seen the rats before they bit me. I promise I'll watch out today, Mother.

WIDOW WERNER (*Weakening*): I do hate to have you miss all the fun.

KURT (*Hopefully*): I'll be *ever* so careful.

WIDOW WERNER: All right, Kurt, but you must be home in half an hour.

KURT (*Whooping joyously*): Oh, thank you, Mother! (*He gives her a hug and starts away.*)

WIDOW WERNER: Now *do* be careful!

KURT: I will. (*Suddenly from off left the frightened screams of children are heard.*)

WIDOW WERNER: Good heavens, what is that?

KURT (*Crying out*): It's the rats, Mother! They've broken up the picnic! They're carrying away the food—hundreds of them, bigger than ever!

WIDOW WERNER: Come away, Kurt! (*She helps him to a bench as* CHILDREN *run in up left, shrieking.* TOWNSPEOPLE *hurry into Square.*)

TOWNSPEOPLE (*Ad lib*): What's the matter? . . . What has happened? . . . Jan, are you all right? . . . You're not hurt, Gretel? . . . Anna, don't cry, Mother is here . . . (*Etc.*)

CHILDREN AND TOWNSPEOPLE (*Ad lib*): Rats, Mama, rats! . . . Big rats, little rats! . . . Old rats, young rats! . . . Brown rats, gray rats! . . . Hungry rats! They ate all the food and spoiled our picnic! (*Etc.*) (NOTE: *The following lines should be said in chanting rhythm.*)

ALL: Rats!

FIRST MAN:
They fight the dogs, and kill the cats!

FIRST WOMAN:
And bite the babies in the cradles!

SECOND MAN:
And eat the cheeses out of the vats!

SECOND WOMAN:
And lick the soup from the cook's own ladles!

THIRD MAN:
Split open the kegs of salted sprats!

MEN:
Make nests inside men's Sunday hats!

WOMEN:
And even spoil the women's chats,
By drowning their speaking
With shrieking and squeaking
In fifty different sharps and flats.

ALL: Rats! Rats! Rats!

FIRST WOMAN: What will become of us? Why can't something be done?

FIRST MAN: It's all the Mayor's fault! If he were half a Mayor, he'd find some way to get rid of the rats.

SECOND MAN: That's right! What's the use of having a Mayor if he doesn't look after our town?

SECOND WOMAN:
To think we buy gowns lined with ermine
For dolts that can't or won't determine
What's best to rid us of our vermin!

THIRD WOMAN: Let's throw him out and get a new Mayor!

FIRST MAN: Yes, yes! We'll throw him out! We'll send him packing! (TOWNSPEOPLE *start moving toward Town Hall.*) The Mayor! . . . We want to see the Mayor! . . . Come out, Mayor! We know you're in there! . . . Come out! The Mayor! The Mayor!

(Mayor *and* Aldermen *appear in entrance to the Town Hall.*)

Third Woman: Here he comes! See how fat he is!

Third Man: Like a fat *rat!* (Townspeople *jeer.*)

Mayor: Silence! What is the meaning of this uproar?

First Man: Mr. Mayor, we are here to tell you once and for all to get rid of the rats. We've had enough of your shilly-shallying. You've done absolutely nothing about these rats—

Mayor (*Interrupting*): Oh, but I have! (*He turns to* Aldermen *for agreement.*) Haven't I, gentlemen? (*They nod.*)

First Woman: What have you done?

Mayor: I've had hundreds of traps made—

Second Man (*Snorting derisively*): Traps! Not one of them is big enough to hold the rats.

Mayor (*Whining*): But what more can I do?

First Man: Well, you'd better figure out something.

Second Man: If you don't, we'll get ourselves a new Mayor.

Mayor (*Stunned*): *What!* A new Mayor?

First Man: That's what I said. If this town isn't rid of rats by tomorrow, you—*and* your Aldermen—will be out of office. That's final, Mr. Mayor.

Third Man:
   Rouse up, sirs! Give your brains a racking
   To find the remedy we're lacking,
   Or, sure as fate, we'll send you packing!

Aldermen (*Conferring together, ad lib*): Dear me, dear me! This is a quandary! . . . I haven't the slightest idea. . . . What in the world shall we do? (*Etc.*)

Mayor (*In desperation, addressing* Townspeople *as they start to move away*): Just a moment, my good people! I will offer a large reward to anyone who will clear the rats out of Hamelin Town.

FIRST ALDERMAN: Fifty guilders!

SECOND ALDERMAN: One hundred guilders!

MAYOR: No, my friends—one *thousand* guilders!

THIRD ALDERMAN (*Protesting*): That's a lot of money!

MAYOR (*To* THIRD ALDERMAN *in a whisper*): Don't be a fool! What are a thousand guilders compared to losing our jobs? (*He speaks to the* TOWNSPEOPLE *again.*) I repeat—I will offer one thousand guilders to the person who can rid Hamelin of the rats! (*The sound of distant piping is heard from off left.*)

KURT: Listen! I hear someone playing a pipe.

THIRD WOMAN: It's probably a rat! (*General laughter*)

WIDOW WERNER: It seems to be coming from the mountain. (*All turn and look off left toward mountain.*)

SECOND MAN: It sounds nearer.

JAN: Can you see anyone?

SECOND MAN: Not yet. (*Pause*)

SECOND WOMAN: There he is!

THIRD WOMAN: Where?

SECOND WOMAN (*Pointing*): There! Why, it's a queer fellow in a suit of two colors—half yellow and half red.

JAN: Look at him! Isn't he tall and strange-looking?

KURT: But he makes beautiful music!

MAYOR: Stand back, stand back there, and let him through! (PIED PIPER *enters, playing his pipe, which is hanging from a ribbon around his neck. He comes down center and bows.*)

PIPER: Good day to you all.

MAYOR (*Pompously*): Who are you to come piping into my presence like this?

PIPER (*Smiling*): I pipe for a living, your Honor.

MAYOR: What is your name?

PIPER: I am called the Pied Piper, and with this pipe of mine I can draw all living creatures after me. I can lead them where I wish.

MAYOR (*Startled*): What's that?

PIPER: Any thing that creeps, or swims, or flies, or runs will follow me. Moles—toads—snakes—

MAYOR (*Eagerly*): And rats, too? What about rats?

PIPER: I have only to play the right notes and all the rats in Hamelin Town will leave the kitchens and cupboards and cellars and stables, and follow, follow, follow me! (*He pirouettes, and* TOWNSPEOPLE *cheer.*)

TOWNSPEOPLE (*Ad lib*): Hurrah! He can free us of the rats! (*Etc.*)

MAYOR: It is possible? Will you do it?

PIPER: What reward will you give me?

MAYOR: Anything you like, only save us.

PIPER: Be careful what you promise, your Honor. I shall keep you to your bargain. Will you give me one thousand guilders?

MAYOR: One thousand? Why, Piper, if you can free Hamelin of rats, I'll give you *fifty* thousand guilders!

FIRST WOMAN: Yes, yes! . . . Why, a thousand is dirt cheap!

SECOND MAN: It's worth fifty thousand at least!

PIPER (*Holding up his hand in protest*): No! One thousand guilders is my price—no more, no less. Is it a bargain, your Honor?

MAYOR (*Impatiently*): Of course, of course! Now get to work, man, get to work! (PIPER *steps into the middle of the square and lifts his pipe to his lips. Everybody is breathless with expectation.*)

WIDOW WERNER (*In a tense whisper to* KURT): Oh, I hope he can do it!

KURT: I *know* he can, Mother. (PIPER *starts to play a strange tune, then with a rhythmical, swinging walk he goes off up left toward river. A low rumbling sound is heard which grows in volume.*)

FIRST WOMAN: What's that rumbling noise? Thunder?

FIRST MAN: It's the rats coming out of the houses.

WIDOW WERNER: They're tumbling out of everywhere!

KURT: Look at them dance and skip along! (TOWNSPEOPLE *crowd against parapet at rear and look over it in terror.*)

ALL:
Great rats, small rats, lean rats, brawny rats,
Brown rats, black rats, gray rats, tawny rats!

BOYS: Grave old plodders—

GIRLS: Gay young friskers—

BOYS *and* GIRLS:
Fathers, mothers, uncles, cousins,
Cocking tails and pricking whiskers!

MEN *and* WOMEN:
Families by tens and dozens,
Brothers, sisters, husbands, wives—
Following the Piper for their lives!

FIRST WOMAN: Where is he taking them?

THIRD MAN: To the river. He is piping the rats into the river!

SECOND MAN: Good, they'll drown! (*Pause*) See how they hurry to get into the water.

FIRST MAN: They are sinking out of sight! (*Pause*) There goes the last one! (*Pause*) Hurrah! The rats are drowned! (*There is general rejoicing.*)

MAYOR (*Coming downstage*): Not a rat left in the whole town of Hamelin! I proclaim a holiday! Tonight we'll have a banquet with dancing and songs!

CHILDREN (*Ad lib*): Hurrah for the Mayor! Hurrah for the Pied Piper! (*Etc.*)

KURT (*Still at the parapet, searching river bank anxiously*): Where *is* the Piper? I don't see him anywhere. Mother, you don't suppose the Piper is drowned too?

MAYOR: What if he is drowned? The rats are gone, and if

the Piper is gone too, why, there is nothing to pay. (*To* ALDERMEN.) Isn't that right, gentlemen? (ALDERMEN *nod in agreement, and* MAYOR *turns to* KURT.) So you see, boy, it makes no difference *where* the Piper is as long as he isn't *here!* (*He laughs uproariously, and* ALDER-MEN *join in. Suddenly* PIPER *leaps over parapet.*)

PIPER: Oh, but I *am* here, your Honor! I am here to claim my reward.

MAYOR (*Taken aback for a moment, then bluffing*): Reward? What reward?

PIPER: You promised me a thousand guilders if I got rid of the rats—(*Slyly*) and you yourself admit that the rats are gone.

MAYOR: Quite so, quite so, and I'll see that they stay gone, too. Here, you people! Go and get long poles! Poke out every rat's nest in town, stuff up the holes!

PIPER: Wait! (*He goes to* MAYOR *and holds out his hand.*) First, if you please, my thousand guilders.

MAYOR (*Pretending amazement*): A thousand guilders! You're joking!

ALDERMEN: Yes, yes! He's joking! (*They titter together.*)

PIPER (*Frowning*): It's no joke with me, gentlemen. One thousand guilders, please.

MAYOR: Why, a thousand guilders is a king's ransom. Besides, our business was done at the river's brink. We'll give you fifty guilders and call it square. What d'ye say?

PIPER (*Sternly*): One thousand guilders you agreed to pay, and one thousand guilders I'm going to have.

FIRST ALDERMAN: Give him a hundred guilders and be done with it!

PIPER: *One—thousand—guilders.*

SECOND ALDERMAN (*Sarcastically*): Just for piping?

PIPER: Shall I pipe the rats back again? (*He lifts pipe to his lips.*)

FIRST WOMAN: Merciful heavens, no!

MAYOR (*Sneeringly*): Don't worry, my good people, the rats were drowned. We saw them with our own eyes.

PIPER (*Fingering his pipe impatiently*): Who will bet with me that I cannot pipe them back?

TOWNSPEOPLE (*Ad lib*): Nonsense! . . . Rubbish! . . . Impossible! (*Etc.*)

FIRST WOMAN: Hold on a minute! He may be speaking the truth.

THIRD MAN: What do you mean?

FIRST WOMAN: Just this! Anyone who could toot the rats away as easily as he did, could toot them here again, you mark my word.

SECOND WOMAN: Yes! And how do we know that he didn't send the rats to Hamelin in the first place, so that he could make money by getting rid of them?

THIRD ALDERMAN: Sure, he's a rogue! . . . He's a trickster!

FIRST ALDERMAN: Put him in prison! . . . No, drive him out of town! He might trick us again! (*They turn on* PIPER, *driving him back.*) Away with you! (CHILDREN *run to* PIPER *and form a protective circle around him.*)

CHILDREN (*Ad lib*): Don't hurt him! . . . We like him! . . . Don't go, Pied Piper! . . . Please don't go! Stay here and play for us! (*Etc. They draw him to a bench away from* TOWNSPEOPLE, *who watch with quiet distrust.*)

FIRST GIRL: Piper, how did you charm the rats away?

PIPER (*Tweaking her nose playfully*): They were led by cu-ri-os-ity.

FIRST BOY: Will you play the tune again?

SECOND GIRL (*Timidly*): No, no, the rats might come back!

THIRD GIRL (*Holding up her doll*): Oh, do pipe something for my doll.

JAN: Pipe for me, Piper! I am a mouse! I'll eat you up!

(Squeaking like a rat, he chases the girls and they scream.)

FIRST GIRL: Play and make us dance!

FIRST BOY: Play and make us run away from school.

OTHER BOYS: We're mice, we're mice, we're mice! We'll eat up everything!

WOMEN *(Ad lib)*: Stop it, children! . . . Don't play that dreadful game! . . . You really might be turned into mice! . . . Come away! (CHILDREN *cling to* PIPER, *and he smiles at them.*)

KURT: Where do you come from, Piper?

PIPER: I come from the back of the mountain.

JAN *(Indicating off left)*: Our mountain? (PIPER *nods.*)

KURT: What is it like?

PIPER: It is the fairest place imaginable. There are green fields to run in and clear streams to wade in. Flowers bloom, and trees bear fruit all the year round. It is always spring and summer in my mountain, and the language of those who live there is laughter.

KURT: Oh, I want to see it! How do you get there?

PIPER: This is the way. Listen! *(He plays a few introductory notes on his pipe, then sings to the tune of "The Evening is Coming.")*

You travel the bridge of a rainbow by day,
At night you will take to the white Milky Way;
And it will not matter where else you may fare,
Because you'll be singing until you get there.
You follow the brooklet in whatever way
The brooklet shall flow or the bright sun shall say;
And it will not matter where else you may fare,
Because you'll be dancing until you get there.

CHILDREN *(Excitedly)*: We want to go, we want to go! Please take us there!

MAYOR *(Breaking in)*: Come, come, children! Enough of this foolishness! Would you leave your good homes to

go with this vagabond? Get back to your parents. (CHIL-
DREN *disperse reluctantly.*) Now look here, Piper, the
sooner you clear out of town, the better. We have decided to give you fifteen guilders. Take them and go.
(*He holds out a purse.*)

PIPER: And if I don't take them?

MAYOR: Then you will get nothing.

PIPER (*Addressing* TOWNSPEOPLE): People of Hamelin, do
you consider this a fair price for what I have done?
Think back! Before I came, your children were in constant danger. They could not play out of doors without
being attacked by the rats. Now the rats are gone, and
your children are safe. Is not this worth the price of a
promise made? Speak up! I beg you, for your children's
sake, answer me!

WIDOW WERNER: I say the Piper should be paid in full!

FIRST MAN: No! When was *I* ever paid for the hundreds
of rat traps I made?

SECOND MAN: When was *I* paid for the cheese that was
eaten?

THIRD MAN: When was *I* paid for the loss of my grain?

OTHER MEN (*Ad lib*): When was I paid? . . . Or I? . . .
Or I? (*Etc.*)

MAYOR: Piper, my patience is at an end! Are you going to
take these fifteen guilders?

PIPER (*Decisively*): No, I am not!

MAYOR (*Angrily pocketing the purse*): Then leave this
town at once, you piping tramp, and never set foot in
it again!

PIPER: Watch out, your Honor. Don't trifle with me, or
this piping tramp will play in a way you won't like!

MAYOR (*Angrily*):
  You threaten us, fellow? Do your worst,
  Blow your pipe there till you burst!

PIPER: Very well—but remember, whatever happens, you are to blame.

TOWNSPEOPLE (*Ad lib, excitedly*): What does he mean? . . . Is something going to happen? (PIPER *slowly turns his level gaze from* MAYOR *to* TOWNSPEOPLE, *then he beckons to* CHILDREN *and puts his pipe to his lips. Very softly he begins to pipe a lilting melody.*)

FIRST MAN: He's tuning up again!

FIRST WOMAN: But it's a different tune he's playing this time. (CHILDREN *are fascinated by* PIPER's *tune. They laugh and crowd around him. He pipes louder, moving toward exit, and they move with him.*)

SECOND WOMAN: What's he doing? Where are our children going?

FIRST WOMAN: He's piping our children away, just as he did the rats!

TOWNSPEOPLE: Stop him, stop him! (*As* TOWNSPEOPLE *start to surge forward,* PIPER *faces them and flings up his arm, making a magical gesture.* TOWNSPEOPLE *are rooted to the spot.*)

THIRD WOMAN: I can't move! . . . My feet are stuck to the ground!

FIRST WOMAN: He has cast a spell over us! (CHILDREN *begin to sing, following* PIPER *who plays more gaily and loudly.*)

CHILDREN (*To the tune of "The Evening Is Coming"*):
We'll travel the bridge of a rainbow by day,
At night we will take to the white Milky Way;
And it will not matter where else we may fare,
Because we'll be singing until we get there.
We'll follow the brooklet in whatever way
The brooklet shall flow or the bright sun shall say;
And it will not matter where else we may fare,
Because we'll be dancing until we get there.
(PIPER *and* CHILDREN *dance off left.*)

FIRST MAN: Look! He's leading them towards the river!

FIRST WOMAN: Is he going to drown them like the rats?

SECOND WOMAN: Jan, come back, don't follow that man!

THIRD WOMAN: Child, come here to me!

WIDOW WERNER: There's my Kurt, trying to keep up. Kurt, don't go! Kurt! He doesn't hear me.

THIRD MAN: They can't hear anything but the music.

THIRD WOMAN: Oh, thank heaven, they have turned away from the river!

FIRST MAN: The Piper is leading them up the mountain!

MAYOR (*With contempt*): Huh! The Piper is only fooling. He can't lead them over the mountain. They'll get tired before they reach the top. (PIPER's *music gets louder.*)

WIDOW WERNER: Look there!

SECOND MAN: Why, there's a door opening in the side of the mountain!

FIRST WOMAN: The Piper is taking the children inside!

THIRD MAN: They're going in!

SECOND WOMAN: Jan! Gretel! Anna! (*Suddenly, music stops, and* TOWNSPEOPLE *wail in anguish.*)

THIRD WOMAN: Our children are gone! . . . The mountainside has closed over them! (*Now* TOWNSPEOPLE *move toward* MAYOR, *ominously.*)

FIRST MAN (*With cries of accusation*): The Mayor is to blame! . . . It is all his fault!

MAYOR (*Sputtering*): How is it my fault?

WIDOW WERNER: You would not pay the Piper. But *we* have paid—with our children! You have no children.

MAYOR (*Blustering*): The Piper is a scamp! Follow him, and bring your children back.

FIRST MAN (*Still looking off toward the mountain*): There is one child who is coming back!

FIRST WOMAN: Who is it? Who? . . . Gretel? . . . Anna?

SECOND WOMAN: Jan?

SECOND MAN: It is Kurt.

WIDOW WERNER (*Incredulous*): My boy?

THIRD MAN: He is crying. (*He hurries off to meet* KURT.)

WIDOW WERNER (*Anxiously*): Is he hurt? Why does he cry? (THIRD MAN *returns, with* KURT. *He seats him on a bench, and* WIDOW WERNER *kneels beside him.*) Kurt dearest, what's the matter? Tell Mother.

KURT: I tried so hard to follow, but they walked too fast. The mountain door closed before I could reach it.

FIRST WOMAN: Did all the children go in there? Into that dark place?

KURT: It wasn't dark. A glorious sun was shining in a clear blue sky. I could see sparrows brighter than peacocks, and horses with eagles' wings galloping through the air. Everything was strange and new. And then just as the music was telling me that my lameness would be cured, it stopped—and I found myself outside the mountain— not in that joyful land. Oh, I did so want to go! (*He weeps bitterly, and* WIDOW WERNER *takes him in her arms to console him.*)

WIDOW WERNER: There, there, my child.

FIRST WOMAN: Widow Werner, you are the happiest woman in Hamelin. (TOWNSPEOPLE *separate into family groups and move slowly to the various benches about Square, in utter despair.* WOMEN *weep softly. After a moment, they become conscious of a high-pitched, sustained note being blown on a pipe far away.*)

FIRST MAN: What is that? . . . Someone is whistling. . . . No, it's the Piper! . . . Is he coming back? . . .

FIRST WOMAN: Sh-h-h! Listen!

PIPER (*Offstage*): People of Hamelin! People of Hamelin, do you hear me?

TOWNSPEOPLE: Yes! Yes!

PIPER (*Offstage*): Listen well to what I have to say. People of Hamelin, you have broken your word. You made a promise to me, and you did not keep it. That is dishonorable. You are selfish; you value gold more than your children. You do not deserve to have children, and that is why I have taken them away from you. But I will have pity on you and give you another chance. I will bargain with you once more. If you would have your children back again, let each one of you give up the thing he values most and cast it into the river. When there is no more greed and dishonesty in Hamelin Town, I will pipe your children home. (*A moment of embarrassed silence follows* PIPER'S *pronouncement; then* TOWNSPEOPLE *spring into action.*)

TOWNSPEOPLE (*Ad lib*): Quick! . . . the things we value most! . . . (*They walk toward river, and as each one speaks, he throws valuables over parapet.*)

WOMEN (*Ad lib*): My string of pearls! . . . My ruby ring! . . . My Japanese parasol! . . . My Chinese fan! . . . My shawl from Persia! . . . My gloves from France! (*Etc., etc.*)

MEN (*Following* WOMEN *to parapet and throwing valuables over parapet as they speak ad lib*): My silver stein! . . . My gold-headed cane! . . . My Swiss watch! . . . My Turkish pipe! . . . My hat from England! . . . My coat from Spain! (*When* TOWNSPEOPLE *have thrown their cherished trinkets over the parapet into the river,* ALDERMEN *unhitch money bags from their belts and throw them into river.*)

ALDERMEN: Our bags of gold. (*Everyone turns toward mountain and listens for* PIPER'S *tune, but it does not come.*)

FIRST WOMAN: Where are the children?

SECOND WOMAN: He promised to return them. We have done what he asked.

FIRST MAN: He has cheated us! He has broken *his* word!

SECOND MAN: There is someone who is holding out. (*He looks around and catches sight of* MAYOR *cowering in doorway of Town Hall.*) Look there! The Mayor! What has he given up?

THIRD WOMAN: Nothing! He has no children!

SECOND WOMAN: It's the Mayor who is keeping our children from us!

FIRST MAN: Take off his robe! He prizes that above all things, because when he wears it he can strut about and give orders!

SECOND MAN: And cheat us and fill his coffers with gold!

THIRD WOMAN: And his cellar with the best foods!

THIRD MAN: His robe is the symbol of his power and his office! Take it from him! (TOWNSPEOPLE *surround* MAYOR *and strip off his ermine-lined robe. They throw it over parapet into river, then turn on* MAYOR.)

TOWNSPEOPLE (*Ad lib, angrily*): Traitor! . . . Villain! . . . Thief! . . . Away with you! . . . Go and join the rats in the river! . . . Get out of here, get out, get out! (*Etc., etc.* MAYOR *runs off right in terror, as the sound of* PIPER'S *tune, mingled with merry voices of* CHILDREN, *is heard from off left.*)

WIDOW WERNER: The Piper is bringing the children home!

FIRST ALDERMAN (*To other* ALDERMEN): Quick! We must get the thousand guilders we owe him! (*They run into the Town Hall.* PIPER *enters from left, followed by* CHILDREN, *who are immediately clasped in the arms of their parents. During the jubilation of* TOWNSPEOPLE, THREE ALDERMEN *rush out of Town Hall, each with a bulging money pouch, which they present to the* PIPER.)

FIRST ALDERMAN: Here, Piper, here are your thousand guilders—and two thousand more!

PIPER: No, no, keep the money. It is payment enough for me to know that you have learned your lesson. Always remember it—if you promise anybody anything, you must keep your promise, or you will have to pay the

Piper. Now I must leave you. (CHILDREN *run to him and hold him fast.*)

CHILDREN (*Ad lib*): Don't leave us! . . . Stay with us! . . . Live in Hamelin! (*Etc.*)

PIPER: I cannot. I must be off and pipe.

KURT: Where?

PIPER: Everywhere, the wide world over. There is so much piping left to do, to rid the world of ugliness and make it a more beautiful place to live in. So good morning, good night, goodbye. (*He exits left, playing his pipe.* TOWNSPEOPLE *wave farewell while the* CHILDREN *dance in a circle.*)

CHILDREN (*Singing to the tune of "When I Was a Young Girl," as they dance.*):

Oh, we've learned a lesson,
A very good lesson,
And this is the lesson
That we've learned today.
If you make a promise,
You must keep that promise,
If you break a promise,
The Piper you pay.

(*All continue to dance, as the curtain falls.*)

THE END

Aladdin and His Wonderful Lamp

from The Arabian Nights

Characters

MAGICIAN
MOTHER
ALADDIN
JUSUF, *a boy* ⎫
SHARAH, *a girl* ⎭ *Aladdin's friends*
PRINCESS BEDREL-BADOOR, *the Sultan's daughter*
ABU ABAT, *the Sultan's minister*
SLAVE OF THE RING
GENIE OF THE LAMP
SULTAN
ATTENDANT

SCENE 1

SETTING: *A street in Baghdad. Aladdin's hut is at right. A broom is leaning against doorway, which is covered by curtain. A basket hangs on large hook on wall of hut. There is a cave at left, with large rocks around entrance. A big iron ring is attached to cave door.*

AT RISE: MAGICIAN *enters stealthily down left, glances about cautiously, then goes to cave entrance and tugs on ring in door.*

MOTHER (*Offstage*): Ala-a-ad-din! (MAGICIAN *ducks down behind a rock as the* MOTHER *appears in doorway of hut, right.*) Where *is* that boy? He's never around when I want him. Aladdin! (*Annoyed, she goes back into hut.* MAGICIAN *comes out of hiding and walks to center stage.*)

MAGICIAN (*Thoughtfully*): Aladdin, eh? Hm-m-m-m. He may be just the boy I'm looking for. (*He is interrupted by sound of voices and quickly conceals himself behind a pine tree center.* ALADDIN *enters down left with* JUSUF *and* SHARAH. ALADDIN *is swinging a pole and* SHARAH *is jumping up and down, trying to reach a large paper bag which is tied to the end of pole.*)

SHARAH: Tell me, Aladdin! Please tell me what is in the bag. Is it figs?

ALADDIN: No.

SHARAH: Dates?

ALADDIN: No.

SHARAH: Ginger candy?

ALADDIN: I'm not going to tell you. You will have to find out for yourself.

SHARAH: How can I when you won't let me look in the bag?

JUSUF: I know how you can find out, Sharah.

SHARAH: You do?

JUSUF: Break the bag with a stick. I will blindfold you and Aladdin will get on top of the cave and hold out the bag. You try to hit it, and if you break the bag, you can have whatever is in it.

SHARAH: For keeps?

JUSUF (*Nodding*): For keeps. Isn't that so, Aladdin?

ALADDIN: That's right, Jusuf. (*He crosses to hut and picks up broom.*) Here, you can use my mother's old broom for a stick. (*He gives it to* SHARAH *and climbs to top of cave.* JUSUF *ties his sash over* SHARAH's *eyes, turns her*

around and starts her in the direction of the cave door.
ALADDIN *holds out the pole and dangles the bag above*
SHARAH's *head. The two boys exchange knowing glances*
and snicker as SHARAH *beats air with broom. Finally*
she succeeds in hitting the bag which breaks, showering
confetti down on her head and shoulders. She screams,
pulling off blindfold, while ALADDIN *and* JUSUF *roar*
with laughter. MOTHER *comes out of hut.*)

MOTHER: Aladdin! Shame on you! How could you do such
a thing? (*She goes to* SHARAH *to brush her off.*)

SHARAH (*To* ALADDIN): You mean old thing, you!

MOTHER: Come down from there this minute. Where have
you been? I've been looking everywhere for you.

ALADDIN (*Coming down*): I'm sorry, Mother. I was playing.

MOTHER: There is nothing to eat in the house and you
play! Is that the way to bring home money? It would be
better if you helped me with the work once in a while.
Where is the cotton I need for my weaving?

ALADDIN: I forgot.

MOTHER: You forgot! (*She takes broom from* SHARAH *and*
shakes it at ALADDIN, *driving him toward hut.*) You lazy
good-for-nothing boy!

ALADDIN (*Dodging about*): Don't, Mother! I will get the
cotton for you. (*Suddenly he points out front.*) Look!
Here comes the Princess Bedrel-badoor.

MOTHER: Don't put me off.

ALADDIN: No, really, Mother. The Princess *is* coming.
(PRINCESS BEDREL-BADOOR *comes down aisle walking*
under a parasol held by ABU ABAT. *As they reach the*
stage, everyone bows. ALADDIN *runs to exit down left*
and waits for PRINCESS *to pass. As she draws near, she*
glances at him coyly, hesitates, then lifts her veil and
smiles.)

ABU (*Shocked by* PRINCESS' *behavior*): Your Highness!
Cover your face at once! Dear, dear, *dear!* (PRINCESS

lowers her veil and drops a flower at ALADDIN's *feet. He bows low, and* ABU ABAT *steers* PRINCESS *out left, shielding her face from* ALADDIN *with parasol.* SHARAH *and* JUSUF *skip off after them.* ALADDIN *picks up the flower and gazes at it lovingly.*)

MOTHER (*Staring open-mouthed*): Well! What does all *that* mean?

ALADDIN: Every day I wait for the Princess to pass by here and she always drops a flower for me. Mother, some day I am going to marry the Princess.

MOTHER: You? The son of Mustafa, the tailor? Are you out of your mind?

ALADDIN: Is it so foolish to dream?

MOTHER: No, but your dreams are impossible. Imagining yourself married to the daughter of the Sultan! Well, I suppose I shall have to get that cotton myself.

ALADDIN: No, I'll get it, Mother. (*He tucks flower in his sash.*) You go into the house and count to one hundred, and I will be back with the cotton before you can say one hundred and one. Go along now. (*He gently leads her toward hut.*) Mother, do you really think I am lazy and worthless?

MOTHER (*Lovingly*): I think you are the best boy in all Baghdad, Aladdin. (*She pats his cheek and is about to go into hut when* MAGICIAN *comes out from behind tree.*)

MAGICIAN: Excuse me, madam, but did I hear you call that boy Aladdin?

MOTHER: Yes, that is his name.

MAGICIAN (*Pretending surprise*): Not Aladdin, the son of Mustafa, the tailor?

MOTHER: Yes, but his father is dead.

MAGICIAN: Dead! Then I am too late.

MOTHER: Too late for what?

MAGICIAN: To see my dear brother.

MOTHER: You must mean some other Mustafa. My husband had no brother.

MAGICIAN: Oh, yes, he had, madam. But we quarreled a long time ago, and I went away to live in Egypt. I never let Mustafa know where I was. Now I have come back, hoping to share my wealth with him, only to learn that he is dead. Ah, me!

MOTHER: Alas, my good husband! (*She sits on bench and weeps.*)

MAGICIAN (*Patting her shoulder*): There, there, sister, don't cry. You have a fine son to console you.

MOTHER (*Sniffing*): Aladdin would rather play in the streets than console his poor mother.

ALADDIN (*Hanging his head*): Now, Mother.

MAGICIAN: He needs a father to guide him. With your permission, sister, I shall be glad to give him the benefit of my experience.

MOTHER: If you can make him listen to you.

MAGICIAN (*Effusively*): Oh, we're going to get along famously, aren't we, Aladdin? What do you say we celebrate our meeting with a feast?

MOTHER (*Embarrassed*): I haven't a thing in the house fit to offer you.

MAGICIAN (*Giving her his money pouch*): Here, go down to the market and buy all the food you want.

MOTHER (*Delighted*): I will bargain shrewdly, never fear. (*She gets basket hanging beside the doorway.*)

MAGICIAN: There is no need to bargain when you have a bag full of gold pieces to spend.

MOTHER (*Running up aisle*): I have a bag of gold! (*She clinks coins excitedly.*) We are going to have a feast! Almond cakes soaked in honey! Um-m-m-m. Tiger steaks! Um-m-m-m. (*She exits at back of auditorium.*)

MAGICIAN (*Clapping ALADDIN on his shoulder*): My boy,

you won't regret this day. I mean to show you the greatest treasure the world has ever known.

ALADDIN: Let's go and get it right away. Is it far?

MAGICIAN: No farther than your own yard.

ALADDIN: What do you mean?

MAGICIAN (*Pointing to cave*): There!

ALADDIN (*Incredulously*): That rock pile? You are making fun of me.

MAGICIAN (*Leading him over to cave*): Come here, my boy. Do you see that iron ring in the stone?

ALADDIN (*Disdainfully*): *That?* Why, everyone knows about that! There's not a person in the whole city who hasn't tried to move that stone, and all have failed.

MAGICIAN: Have you tried, Aladdin?

ALADDIN: Of course, many times. (MAGICIAN *removes a ring from his finger and holds it out to* ALADDIN.)

MAGICIAN: Put this ring on your finger and try again.

ALADDIN (*Regarding ring fearfully*): I—I don't think I want to.

MAGICIAN (*Angrily raising his arm as if to strike* ALADDIN): Obey me! (ALADDIN *ducks under the* MAGICIAN's *arm, but* MAGICIAN *is too quick for him. He seizes* ALADDIN *and holds him tightly.*) Listen to me, boy. All I ask is that you obey me—*exactly.* If you do, you will gain much for yourself. (*He releases* ALADDIN.) Behind this stone is hidden a treasure that will make you richer than the Sultan himself. Only you have the power to move that stone and enter the cave.

ALADDIN: Then why wasn't I able to move it before?

MAGICIAN: Because you didn't have this ring. Here, put it on.

ALADDIN (*Putting on ring*): Well, it's on. What next?

MAGICIAN: Rub it.

ALADDIN: Rub it?

MAGICIAN (*His temper rising again*): *Rub it!*

ALADDIN (*Rubbing ring vigorously*): I'm rubbing it. Now what shall I do?

MAGICIAN: Nothing. Just wait.

ALADDIN: Wait for what?

MAGICIAN (*Angrily*): Be still! (*There is a clash of cymbals.* SLAVE OF THE RING *enters left. She stands near door of cave.*)

ALADDIN: Oh! What is it? Who is it?

MAGICIAN: It is the Slave of the Ring. Listen!

SLAVE: I am the Slave of the Ring and of the one who wears the ring—Aladdin, son of Mustafa, the tailor.

MAGICIAN (*Nudging* ALADDIN): Don't stand there gawking! Tell her to open the door.

SLAVE: What will you have me do, master? What will you have me do?

ALADDIN: Please—please open the door. (SLAVE *faces door and gestures with her hands and arms. Finally she opens the door, and then exits left.* ALADDIN *starts eagerly toward open door.*)

MAGICIAN (*Catching hold of him*): Wait! I haven't told you what you must do. Go down into the cave and you will find a large room full of gold and silver. Beyond that is a garden of beautiful trees loaded with jeweled fruit. But don't touch any of it. If you do, you will die instantly! Walk straight ahead until you come to a flight of stairs. At the top of the stairs you will see a lighted lamp. Put out the light and bring the lamp to me. You can take all the treasure you want on your way back. Here, fill this bag. (MAGICIAN *takes a cloth bag from his pocket and gives it to* ALADDIN.) Now go on down and you will be rich for the rest of your life. (ALADDIN *stoops down and backs into cave. He goes down on his hands and knees and seems to be feeling for top rung of a ladder with his foot.* MAGICIAN *stands beside opening, urging him on.*) Go down, boy, go down!

ALADDIN: I *am* going down, Uncle.

MAGICIAN: Are you so slow because you are afraid?

ALADDIN: I am slow because the ladder is old and some of the rungs are gone.

MAGICIAN (*Angrily*): Will you *hurry* and get that lamp?

ALADDIN: I'll get it—but I won't hurry. (*He slowly disappears from sight, as if he were descending a ladder. The* MAGICIAN *crosses to the bench and sits, waiting impatiently. After a moment, he calls to* ALADDIN.)

MAGICIAN: Are you at the bottom?

ALADDIN (*From offstage*): Yes. (*Pauses*) Oh-h-h-h!

MAGICIAN (*Rising*): What is it?

ALADDIN (*From offstage*): Gold and silver!

MAGICIAN (*With irritation*): Don't touch any of it or the walls will roll together and crush you. Touch nothing but the lamp. (*Pauses*) Where are you now? (*Pauses*) Aladdin! Are you in the garden?

ALADDIN (*From offstage*): Yes.

MAGICIAN: Now climb back! Climb the ladder! (*He listens intently.*) Do you have the lamp? (*Pauses*) Aladdin, answer me! *Have you got the lamp?*

ALADDIN (*From offstage*): Ye-e-e-es.

MAGICIAN (*Smiling*): Bring the lamp to me. (*He waits nervously for* ALADDIN *to appear. Finally he can bear it no longer, and he calls through opening.*) What are you doing?

ALADDIN (*From offstage*): Filling the bag.

MAGICIAN: Well, be quick about it! (ALADDIN *bobs head up in opening of cave.*) So! At last you return. Give me the lamp.

ALADDIN: I can't, Uncle. It's at the bottom of the bag.

MAGICIAN: For the last time—*will you give me that lamp?*

ALADDIN (*Vigorously*): *No!* I will *not!*

MAGICIAN: Then stay there in that cave until the earth crumbles to dust!

ALADDIN (*Defiantly*): You can't scare me. I'm not afraid of you.

MAGICIAN: Then I will teach you to be afraid! May red dragons creep through the crannies of the rocks and torment you! (*With a scream of fury,* MAGICIAN *shuts the door of the cave, then turns around and shakes his fists at the sky.*) Curses on him! (*There is a loud clap of thunder.* MAGICIAN *runs off up right. As thunder dies away,* ALADDIN *can be heard from inside cave beating on the door and calling out in a muffled voice.*)

ALADDIN: Uncle, Uncle! Let me out! I will give you the lamp. *Please* let me out! Help, help! Open the door! Slave of the Ring, open the door! (SLAVE OF THE RING *enters from left, and opens door slowly.* ALADDIN *stumbles through opening.*) I'm free! Thank you, good Slave —oh, thank you!

SLAVE: Is there anything else you wish me to do, master?

ALADDIN: Yes, close the door. When I want it opened again, I will summon you.

SLAVE: You have only to rub the ring and I will do your bidding. (*She closes cave door, then exits left.*)

MOTHER (*Calling from back of auditorium*): Aladdin! Aladdin! I'm back! (*She speaks to audience as she comes down aisle, her basket filled with parcels of food.*) Such a feast we shall have! Roasted meats—three different kinds. Turtles on the half shell—swans' eggs—candied rose petals—(*She climbs steps to stage.*) Look, Aladdin, look! (*She stops, confused.*) Why, where is your uncle?

ALADDIN: A fine uncle he turned out to be! He's a magician. He made me go down into that cave to get a lamp.

MOTHER (*Setting basket on the bench*): A lamp? Did you get it?

ALADDIN: Yes, and I took some other things, too. See here. (*He takes a jeweled apple and pear from the bag.*)

MOTHER: What are those things? Toys?

ALADDIN: No, Mother. This—(*Holding up apple*)—is a ruby. And this—(*Holding up pear*)—is a pearl. (*He gives them to her, opens bag and shows it to her.*) And look at these! Sapphire and topaz and amethyst and jade!

MOTHER (*Looking in bag*): How beautiful! But what about the lamp?

ALADDIN: I wouldn't give it to the magician unless he helped me out of the cave. That made him very angry, and he shut me up in there. All he wanted all the time was the lamp.

MOTHER: The wicked, cruel man! How did you escape?

ALADDIN: Do you see this ring? It's magic. I rubbed it and a Slave opened the door and let me out.

MOTHER: Where is the lamp now?

ALADDIN (*Taking it out of bag*): Here it is.

MOTHER (*Taking lamp*): This? This dirty old thing? Why, it's all tarnished and dented and black with smoke! (*She rubs the lamp on her sleeve to polish it. There is a crash of cymbals.* GENIE OF THE LAMP *enters left.* MOTHER *screams and hides behind* ALADDIN.) Wh-where did *that* come from?

GENIE (*Bowing*): I am the Genie of the Lamp.

MOTHER: Oh, the lamp! (*She thrusts it at* ALADDIN.) Here, take it, Aladdin.

ALADDIN: Why, Mother, don't be so frightened.

GENIE: What is your wish?

MOTHER: Go away, go away!

ALADDIN: But, Mother, he is the Genie of the Lamp. He will bring you anything in the world you desire.

MOTHER: I don't believe it.

GENIE: What is your wish? (MOTHER *hesitates, and* ALADDIN *pushes her toward* GENIE.)

ALADDIN: Go on, Mother. Tell him.

MOTHER: Well, I'll tell him a wish, just to prove he can't grant it.

GENIE: Yes, Mistress, what is your desire?

MOTHER: I should like a new tunic—a green one, embroidered with crescent moons and peacocks.

GENIE (*Bowing*): Your wish shall be granted.

ALADDIN: And bring me garments fit for a prince.

GENIE: It shall be done, Master. (*Crash of cymbals. AT-TENDANT enters left and drapes rich clothes across the GENIE's outstretched arms. He exits immediately.*)

ALADDIN: He has done it! (ALADDIN *takes clothing from* GENIE.)

MOTHER: I wish he weren't so noisy. He scares me half to death.

GENIE: It shall be as you command. (*He bows and exits quietly.*)

ALADDIN (*Holding up tunic*): This is yours, Mother. Put it on.

MOTHER (*Shyly*): I can't wear that; it's too grand.

ALADDIN: Of course you can wear it. Isn't today the Royal Audience Day, when the Sultan goes among his people to hear their petitions?

MOTHER: Yes. Why?

ALADDIN: It is said that he will come along this street. Now I want you to dress in your new clothes and present yourself to him.

MOTHER: I? What for?

ALADDIN (*Taking a casket of jewels from bag*): Give him these jewels and ask him for the hand of his daughter in marriage to your son.

MOTHER: Aladdin, are you crazy?

ALADDIN: Tell the Sultan that your son is Prince Aladdin of the Lamp and he has more treasure than any prince in all Arabia. Well, Mother? (*He holds out casket of jewels.*)

MOTHER (*Taking it*): I will do as you say. I will speak to the Sultan.

ALADDIN: Come, come, good Mother, don't look so worried. (*He picks up bag and walks with his* MOTHER *to doorway of hut.*) Everything will go all right, you will see. (*He sets bag inside doorway, holds back the curtain and his* MOTHER *goes into hut.* ALADDIN *removes his old jacket and drops it on bench, then he puts on his new coat and turban. As he is tucking magic lamp into his pocket, sounds of an approaching procession are heard off left.* ALADDIN *listens a moment and then runs off right.* ABU ABAT *enters down left below the cave, carrying a small platform which he places center stage. He faces front and addresses the audience.*)

ABU: Hear, O people of the market place, the words of wisdom of your gracious Sultan, Lord of the Faithful and Protector of the Poor. (*He bows to the left as* SULTAN *enters and mounts platform.*)

SULTAN: What petitions are there in this market place, Abu Abat?

ABU: Is there anyone who has a petition to bring before the Sultan?

MOTHER (*Bursts through curtains of hut, dressed in her new apparel, carrying casket of jewels, and throws herself on her knees before* SULTAN.): I have.

SULTAN: What is your business, good woman?

MOTHER: I bring you a gift from a prince who begs one favor of Your Majesty. If you will grant this favor, O Mighty One, untold riches will be yours till the end of your days.

SULTAN: Who is this prince?

MOTHER: My son, Prince Aladdin of the Lamp.

SULTAN: What does Prince Aladdin want of me that he is willing to give so much?

MOTHER: Exalted Majesty, the gift which is the greatest you can bestow. Prince Aladdin asks for the hand of your daughter in marriage.

SULTAN (*Shocked*): Did you say—*marriage?* (MOTHER *nods.*) And what riches does he promise?

MOTHER (*Holding up casket of jewels*): They are here, Your Majesty. (SULTAN *takes casket and opens it. He and* ABU *stare at jewels in astonishment.*)

SULTAN: Magnificent! Tell me, Abu, is the giver of such a present worthy of the Princess?

ABU (*Looking off left*): Why don't you let Her Highness answer that question herself? (*He bows to* PRINCESS *as she enters from left.*)

PRINCESS: Greetings, honorable Father.

SULTAN (*Scolding her*): Bedrie, why do you persist in taking a walk without your ladies?

PRINCESS: My ladies bore me—and besides, they don't like to walk. (*She notices jewels in casket, and exclaims in delight.*) Oh! How lovely! (*She selects a necklace and tries it on.*)

SULTAN: You are pleased with these jewels, Bedrie?

PRINCESS: They are beautiful!

SULTAN: I am glad you like them. They are a gift from a prince who wishes to marry you.

PRINCESS (*Coldly*): Oh? Who is he?

SULTAN: Prince Aladdin of the Lamp.

PRINCESS (*Dropping necklace back in casket*): I have never heard of him.

SULTAN: He has more treasure than any other prince in all Arabia.

PRINCESS: That makes no difference. I don't want to marry him or anyone else. (*She turns away.*)

SULTAN: Perhaps when you see him . . .

MOTHER: Yes, yes, Your Majesty! When she sees him. He is on his way here now. (*She points to* ALADDIN *who is walking down right aisle with great dignity.*)

ABU (*Speaking out front*): Make way, make way for Prince Aladdin! Back, back there! Out of the way! (ALADDIN *comes up onto the stage, and* ABU *bows low.*) Hail, Prince Aladdin of the Lamp!

ALADDIN (*Kneeling before the* SULTAN): Greetings, O Celestial Sultan!

SULTAN: Greetings, noble Prince! Rise.

ALADDIN: Has my gift found favor in your sight, and may I have the hand of your daughter in marriage?

SULTAN (*Uneasily*): Your gift has found favor in our sight, but—(*He glances at the* PRINCESS *whose back remains turned.*) Look at him, Bedrie! He is really quite handsome.

PRINCESS: No!

ALADDIN (*Pleading gently*): Please look at me, Princess. (*Recognizing his voice, she turns to look at him. She smiles happily.*)

PRINCESS: Oh! It's *you!*

SULTAN (*Surprised*): Do you know him?

PRINCESS: I—I have *seen* him.

ABU: Your Majesty, wouldn't it be wise to make the Prince *prove* his wealth and power? Ask him if he can build a tower or a temple.

ALADDIN: No, Your Majesty—I will build a *palace*. A new palace for the Princess—in the Pond of the Cedar Trees.

SULTAN: What! Build a palace in a pond! Can you do it?

ALADDIN: Certainly. (*To* PRINCESS) What sort of palace do you wish?

PRINCESS (*Delighted*): A wonderful palace of gold and silver and ivory, with gardens full of flowers.

ALADDIN: I shall build it for you right away. Now close your eyes, everybody. Close your eyes, good people of the market place. I, Aladdin of the Lamp, command it! (*Everyone obeys, and* ALADDIN *takes lamp from his pocket and holds it high.*) Let there be built in the Pond of the Cedar Trees a palace such as the Princess desires. (*He rubs lamp, and there is a loud crash of cymbals.* ATTENDANT *brings on a flat indicating turrets of a palace rising against sky in background.*) It is done! Open your eyes, good people. (*They all do so and turn upstage as* ALADDIN *points to the turrets of the palace.*)

ALL: Oh-h-h-h!

SULTAN: Never has such a wonder come to pass in all the history of the Arabian world. Come, let us go and inspect the palace. (SULTAN *leads way off up right, and all follow. When everyone is gone,* MAGICIAN *steps out from behind the rocks.*)

MAGICIAN (*Shaking his fist at the palace*): You won't have that lamp much longer, Aladdin! I will get it from you. I will have revenge!

CURTAIN

*   *   *

SCENE 2

TIME: *Some time later.*

SETTING: *A room in Aladdin's palace. The rear of the room is open and looks out upon a terrace. A lilac tree in full bloom is on terrace.*

AT RISE: PRINCESS BEDREL-BADOOR *is reclining on divan, eating grapes.* ALADDIN *is standing center on terrace, looking off right.*

PRINCESS (*Sitting up*): Oh, Aladdin, do you have to go on that tiger hunt today?

ALADDIN: Yes, I must. The princes I've invited are gathering in the courtyard now. (*Coming down into room, he takes the lamp from his pocket and hands it to her.*) Here, put this lamp away. I am afraid I might lose it while I am hunting.

PRINCESS: Oh, this old tarnished lamp! Why do you always carry it about with you?

ALADDIN: It is a symbol.

MOTHER (*Bustling in up right*): Aladdin! The princes are waiting for you.

ALADDIN: Then I must go. Goodbye, Mother. I will be back in a week, wife. (*He exits right.* MOTHER *sits on hassock and picks up her embroidery.*)

PRINCESS: A week! Seven whole days! Oh, dear! How dirty this lamp is. (*Unconsciously she rubs it.*) I wish he would come back tonight just as the sun goes down. I wish he would be in this room with me. (*Distant crash of cymbals is heard.*)

MOTHER: What was that noise?

PRINCESS: I don't know.

MOTHER: I think I'd better go and investigate. (*She exits up right, leaving her embroidery on hassock.*)

PRINCESS (*Talking to herself*): I wish something different would happen—something new and exciting. (MAGICIAN *is heard calling from rear of the auditorium.*)

MAGICIAN: New lamps for old! New lamps for old!

PRINCESS: What's that? (*She rises from divan and peers down left aisle.*) Someone is coming down the street. He is carrying something on his back.

MAGICIAN (*Walking down aisle with sack on his back*): New lamps for old! New lamps for old!
Old lamps traded for new lamps of gold!

PRINCESS: Oh, peddler! I have a lamp.

MAGICIAN: Is it old?

PRINCESS: Oh, yes, very old.

MAGICIAN: Hold it up so I can see it. (*She does so.*) Hm-m-m-m. It is very old, but I'll take it.

PRINCESS: Oh, *will* you? That's wonderful! Come up here and let me choose a new one. (MAGICIAN *climbs steps onto stage, seizes lamp from* PRINCESS *and leaps up onto terrace. He sets down sack and raises* ALADDIN's *lamp high in the air.* PRINCESS *turns to face* MAGICIAN *in amazement.*) What are you doing? Give me my new lamp.

MAGICIAN (*Triumphantly*): There is no need for a new lamp now. This one will do very well.

PRINCESS (*Turning up center*): Guards! Guards!

MAGICIAN: Your guards are powerless. You are powerless. I am master here now! (*He rubs the lamp.*) O Genie of the Lamp, hear me! Lift up this palace and carry it away and away and away—into the heart of Africa. Do you hear me, O Genie of the Lamp? (*Crash of cymbals.* ATTENDANT *enters and removes lilac tree.*)

PRINCESS (*Calling out*): Aladdin, save me! Aladdin! Aladdin!

MAGICIAN: Aladdin cannot save you. Nobody can save you. (PRINCESS *throws herself on the divan, weeping.*)

MOTHER (*Hurrying in, alarmed*): What has happened? Is it an earthquake?

MAGICIAN: We are flying through the air, sister.

MOTHER (*Recognizing him*): *You!* You wretch, what have you done? (*She joins him on the terrace.*) Where is the lilac tree? Where is the garden?

MAGICIAN: We have left it behind. There are no gardens where we are going. There is nothing but sand—miles and miles of sand. Look down below. Did you ever see so much sand? We are now in the heart of Africa. Enjoy yourselves. (*He exits right, laughing.*)

PRINCESS: It's all my fault. If only I hadn't given the magician that lamp.

MOTHER (*Shocked*): You gave him Aladdin's magic lamp?

PRINCESS: I didn't know it was magic.

MOTHER (*Kindly*): Stop crying, Bedrie. The harm is done. (*She sits on hassock, picking up her piece of embroidery.*)

PRINCESS (*Running up onto terrace*): I wish I could run away across the desert.

MOTHER: And so you could—if you were a camel.

PRINCESS: Do you know, I really think we could cross it. Let's try. I'd rather die in the desert than stay here, a captive of the magician.

MOTHER: Humph! You *would* die, too.

MAGICIAN (*Entering suddenly down left*): Good evening. You, Widow Mustafa! Go to the kitchen and prepare my supper. (MOTHER *scurries out up right, taking her embroidery with her. The* MAGICIAN *joins the* PRINCESS *on the terrace.*) It is nearly sunset. How beautiful the desert is—and how treacherous. One could easily get lost and never be found, trying to cross it.

PRINCESS (*Bravely*): That might be preferred to staying here.

MAGICIAN: You are not afraid, are you?

PRINCESS (*Proudly*): A Princess is never afraid.

MAGICIAN: We shall see. When I return, you shall sing for me. (*He goes out up right with an arrogant swagger.* PRINCESS *comes down from terrace and flings herself weeping on divan.*)

PRINCESS: Oh, Aladdin, Aladdin! Help me! Come to me! Please! (*Crash of cymbals.* ALADDIN *suddenly leaps onto terrace from right.*)

ALADDIN: Bedrie!

PRINCESS (*Rising*): Aladdin!

ALADDIN: Are you all right?

PRINCESS: Yes, yes! But how did you get here?

ALADDIN: I have no idea. I was out hunting tigers one minute ago, and suddenly I am here with you.

PRINCESS (*Clapping her hands*): Oh, I remember! This morning, after you had gone, I wished that you would be with me this evening at sunset, and I rubbed the lamp.

ALADDIN: A lucky wish, Bedrie. Where are we?

PRINCESS: In the middle of Africa. The Genie of the Lamp carried us here.

ALADDIN: Where is the lamp now?

PRINCESS: The magician has it. He keeps it in his sash.

ALADDIN: I must get it back. Let me think. (*He gazes about, studying room.*) I'll hide behind that screen. (*Points to left screen*) When the magician comes back, dance for him, sing for him—do anything to distract him, and when he's not watching, I will grab the lamp from him and wish us all back in Baghdad.

PRINCESS: Shhh! Someone is coming! Hide! (ALADDIN *conceals himself behind left screen. His* MOTHER *enters up right, carrying* MAGICIAN's *supper on a tray.* PRINCESS *pretends to be in a good humor and hums a gay tune.*)

MOTHER (*Reprovingly*): Singing, Bedrie? I expected to find you crying. (*She sets tray on table.*)

PRINCESS: Why should I cry? No, I'd rather dance! Come, look at the sunset. (*She dances* MOTHER *up onto terrace.* MAGICIAN *enters up right, and* PRINCESS *bows deeply.*)

MAGICIAN (*Sitting and placing lamp on table*): Ha! This is better. My words have done some good.

PRINCESS: The words of my lord have brought about a great change in my heart. (*She passes him a bowl of fruit.*) Let me sing for you, my lord. You asked me to sing, you know.

MAGICIAN: Go ahead, then. (PRINCESS *sits on divan and starts to sing.* MAGICIAN *notices that she glances often at screen behind her and becomes suspicious.*) There's something wrong here! (*He jumps up and rushes toward screen.*)

PRINCESS: No, no! (*She pushes him back, as* ALADDIN *jumps out from behind screen.*)

MOTHER: Aladdin! (PRINCESS *quickly grabs lamp from table and hands it to* ALADDIN. *There is a struggle for possession of lamp.* MAGICIAN *wrenches it from* ALADDIN.)

MAGICIAN: I wish Aladdin . . .

ALADDIN (*Snatching lamp back*): I wish this magician locked up in the darkest depths of the mountains. Never let him return! (*Crash of cymbals.* MAGICIAN *exits quickly.*)

PRINCESS: Oh, Aladdin, he's gone, he's gone!

ALADDIN: Yes, but we are still in Africa. Let's go home.

MOTHER: But not so fast as we came, please.

ALADDIN (*Rubbing lamp*): O Genie of the Lamp, carry this palace and all of us in it back to Baghdad—but carry us gently. (*Soft crash of cymbals. Lilting music. They all sway from side to side.*)

PRINCESS: We are moving.

MOTHER: We are floating in the air like clouds.

ALADDIN: We are flying home. (ATTENDANT *enters with lilac tree and places it in its original position. He exits immediately.*)

MOTHER (*Running up onto the terrace*): There is the lilac tree—and the garden! We are home again! (*Shouting is heard offstage, and* SULTAN *and* ABU ABAT *hurry into the room, followed by* JUSUF *and* SHARAH. *There is general rejoicing.*)

ALL (*Clapping hands and forming a circle*): Come, dance and shout and sing! Aladdin and the Princess are home! (*They start to dance, as the curtain falls.*)

THE END

Rumpelstiltskin

from Grimms' Fairy Tales

Characters

RUMPELSTILTSKIN
SHADOW
KING CRISPEN
PRINCESS CORIS ⎤
PRINCESS KIRSTEN ⎥ King's sisters
PRINCESS LISBETH ⎥
PRINCESS MARTHE ⎦
AUNT COCKATOO
MILLER
GRIZEL, *Miller's daughter*
HAPPILY, *the bluebird*

SCENE 1

SETTING: *Rumpelstiltskin's hill and the King's pavilion. The hill is a platform at the back of the stage. The King's pavilion is in the foreground. It is an open space, with arches on three sides. A low wall separates the pavilion from the hill. In the center of the wall, there is a secret door. In the pavilion are a garden bench, a fountain with a circular seat, a stool, and a spinning wheel.*

AT RISE: RUMPELSTILTSKIN *is on his hill, crouched down*

with his back to the audience. His SHADOW *stands
against the back wall, facing him. He leaps to his feet
with a cry, turns to face front, and* SHADOW *jumps up,
too, sharply outlined on the sky behind him.* SHADOW
imitates all of RUMPELSTILTSKIN's *actions.*

RUMPELSTILTSKIN:

Shadow, shadow, on the sky,

You're two times two as big as I!

Two times two both long and wide,

From up to down, and side to side.

Shadow, shadow, in the sun,

Just where you end, I've just begun.

(*Calling to* SHADOW) Shadow, Shadow!

SHADOW: Yes?

RUMPELSTILTSKIN: I have a secret— (*He lowers his voice.*)
a *whispery* secret.

SHADOW (*In a loud whisper*): Is it—your *name?*

RUMPELSTILTSKIN (*Hopping up and down*): Yes! Yes!

Today I wash and iron my clothes,

Tomorrow I shall do the same,

And nobody—never—nowhere—knows

That (*In a loud whisper*) Rumpelstiltskin is my name!

(*He wheels around and faces the* SHADOW.) If you *do*
tell, I'll punch you on the nose! (*He feints a punch, and*
SHADOW *cries out.* RUMPELSTILTSKIN's *mood changes; he
sighs deeply.*) I'm lonely.

SHADOW: How can you be lonely? You have me.

RUMPELSTILTSKIN: But you are only my shadow. You imitate everything I do. Why, you even have my name, and
I want my name all to myself. So—

Today I'll seek, tomorrow I'll find

A playmate of another kind,

Who never any time can claim

That—(*Whispering*) Rumpelstiltskin is *his* name!

(*The* Shadow *begins to cry.*) Now, what's the matter?

Shadow: If you go away and leave me behind, I'll be all alone up here. (*The* Shadow *sobs wildly and* Rumpelstiltskin *holds up his hand for silence.*)

Rumpelstiltskin: Quiet! Listen! (Princesses, *laughing and shouting, are heard off left.* Rumpelstiltskin *sits on the ground. To* Shadow) Get down under me— quick!

Shadow (*Whining*): Why?

Rumpelstiltskin: Do as I say! (*The* Shadow *hides behind hill. The voices come nearer.*) They're coming out to play.

Shadow (*In a muffled voice*): Who?

Rumpelstiltskin: The King's sisters. (*Through the left arch* Princesses Lisbeth, Coris, Kirsten *and* Marthe *enter. They are running a race and* Lisbeth *is in the lead. She dashes to the fountain and touches it.*)

Lisbeth: My goal! I win! It's my turn to choose the game.

Coris: What do you want to play?

Lisbeth: Blindman's buff. Who has a handkerchief?

Kirsten: I have!

Marthe: I want to be "it!"

Coris: No, we'll count out. (*Pointing to each as she recites*)

Hickory, dickory, dockory, down.

Manchester, Winchester, Colchestertown.

Spell pit-a-pat, spell pat-a-pit.

I-T. "It!" (Marthe *is* "it.")

Marthe (*Happily*): I'm "it!" (Kirsten *ties the handkerchief over* Marthe's *eyes, then turns her around three times and runs away.* Marthe *starts groping for the others, who are scattered about the pavilion and nimbly elude her.* Lisbeth, Coris, *and* Kirsten *tiptoe off left and leave* Marthe *pawing the air in every direction.*

Up on his hill, RUMPELSTILTSKIN *jumps to his feet. He calls down to* MARTHE.)

RUMPELSTILTSKIN (*Pointing to the left arch*): They went that way—into the garden. (*Pause*) She doesn't hear me. I'm going down. (*He leaves the hill.*)

MARTHE: Where *are* you? I don't hear you anywhere. (*To herself*) I'll bet they've gone into the garden. I'll just take a little peek. (*She lifts a corner of her blindfold and looks toward the garden.*) I see them. Now I'll catch them! (*She replaces the blindfold and exits left, groping her way. As soon as she is gone,* RUMPELSTILTSKIN *comes through the door in the wall. He snickers with glee as he peers off left, and leaps into the air. The sound of laughter off left sends him scampering down right, where he hides.* PRINCESSES *enter.* MARTHE *is still trying to catch one of them, but they dodge this way and that, finally slipping noiselessly off right, one by one.* MARTHE *stands still, listening.*) How quiet you all are, sisters! (RUMPELSTILTSKIN *leaves his hiding place, stands in front of* MARTHE, *and laughs.*) Oh! Who is it? (*As she reaches out, her hand brushes him.*) Lisbeth!

RUMPELSTILTSKIN (*In a high-pitched voice*): No!

MARTHE: Coris?

RUMPELSTILTSKIN: Guess again.

MARTHE: Well, there's only Kirsten left.

RUMPELSTILTSKIN: Wrong!

MARTHE: Who *are* you? (*She pulls off her blindfold and gives a little scream of surprise.*)

RUMPELSTILTSKIN (*Quickly*): Don't be afraid. I won't hurt you. I just want to play.

MARTHE (*Calling*): Coris! Kirsten! Lisbeth! (PRINCESSES *re-enter, but stop short as they catch sight of* RUMPEL-STILTSKIN.)

LISBETH: Oh! Who's that?

MARTHE: He wants to play with us.

RUMPELSTILTSKIN: Yes! (*He whirls* PRINCESSES *around, one after the other.* AUNT COCKATOO *enters from right with* KING CRISPEN, *a good-looking young man.*)

COCKATOO: What's going on here? (*She crosses to center, clapping her hands.*) Stop this racket instantly! (RUM-PELSTILTSKIN, *who is standing on the fountain seat, titters and jumps up and down.*) Oh! *Who* is that ugly creature?

MARTHE: He came to play with us, Aunt Cockatoo.

COCKATOO: To play, eh? Well, he can play himself right back to where he came from. (*She points to left.*) March, you hideous little man—march! (RUMPELSTILTSKIN *goes to hill, pausing to make a face at* COCKATOO, *who frowns and then sits on the bench.*)

CRISPEN: Sisters, I have been telling Aunt Cockatoo you need new dresses.

COCKATOO: Yes—what's all this?

CORIS: Well, we thought—

COCKATOO (*Interrupting*): You thought! Don't you realize that there are only pennies in the royal treasury?

MARTHE (*Astounded*): Pennies?

COCKATOO: Copper pennies. So there will be *no* new dresses. (*She rises and starts towards exit.*)

RUMPELSTILTSKIN (*From his hill*): Cuckoo! (CRISPEN *and* PRINCESSES *giggle.* COCKATOO *swings around and faces them.*)

COCKATOO: Which one of you did that?

KIRSTEN (*Innocently*): Did what, Aunty?

COCKATOO: Made a noise like a—a—

RUMPELSTILTSKIN: Cuckoo!

COCKATOO (*Glaring at them*): Which one?

CRISPEN (*Trying to keep a straight face*): No one, Aunty.

COCKATOO: Humph! (*She turns to start out again.*)

RUMPELSTILTSKIN: Cuckoo! Cuckoo! (CRISPEN *and* PRIN-CESSES *burst out laughing.* MILLER *and his daughter,* GRIZEL, *enter through the right arch and come into the pavilion.* MILLER *carries a sack of flour.*)

MILLER: Duchess, begging your pardon—

COCKATOO: Well, Miller, what is it?

MILLER: I have brought you a bag of flour. See here! (*He opens the sack and brings out a handful of flour.*)

COCKATOO: It's just flour.

MILLER: But what flour!—smooth as silk and shining like silver. That's what it is—pure silver! And my Grizel milled it—every grain—by the light of the moon.

COCKATOO (*Interested*): Hm-m—wheat into silver. Grizel, you are a *very* clever girl!

MILLER: Indeed she is, Duchess! She can do anything.

COCKATOO: What else can she do?

MILLER: She can spin straw into gold.

GRIZEL: Father!

COCKATOO: She can? Is it magic?

GRIZEL: No, no!

COCKATOO: She shall spin some gold for me.

GRIZEL: But I can't!

COCKATOO (*Scowling at her*): *Can't?*

MILLER (*Hastily*): Can't spin *some,* she means.

COCKATOO: Then she shall spin *much!* Nieces—now you can have your new dresses. Go out to the barn and bring back as much straw as you can carry. (*The* PRINCESSES *run off left.*) Grizel, you shall spin on the royal spinning wheel. (COCKATOO *takes spinning wheel up left and sets it beside bench.*)

GRIZEL (*To* CRISPEN): Please, Your Highness, help me.

MILLER: His Highness can't help you to spin, daughter.

GRIZEL: I want him to help me *not* to spin!

COCKATOO (*Sharply*): What do you mean by that?

MILLER (*Rattled*): She means she can't spin if anyone watches her. She always spins alone.

COCKATOO: Oh, she'll be left alone, never fear. But let me tell you this, Miller—either she spins all the straw into gold by tomorrow morning, or you will hang from your own mill! (GRIZEL *cries out in dismay.*)

MILLER (*Shaking with fear*): H-h-hang, Duchess?

COCKATOO: That's what I said. (*The* PRINCESSES *return with two large bales of straw.* NOTE: *These are square boxes constructed of fine wire overlaid with a layer of flameproofed raffia. The boxes are placed against the back wall in front of concealed openings through which a strong yellow light will shine when the straw "turns to gold."*) Put the straw back there. (PRINCESSES *set the bales of straw against the rear wall, one at left, the other at right, and then exit.*) Now, Grizel, my girl, get to work.

MILLER: Oh, my poor Grizel! What have I done, what have I *done*? (*He exits.*)

COCKATOO (*To* CRISPEN, *who is comforting* GRIZEL): Crispen, are you coming?

CRISPEN (*Facing her resolutely*): Aunt Cockatoo, I intend to make Grizel my queen tomorrow.

COCKATOO: What!

CRISPEN: And I will not have her sitting out here spinning straw the night before her wedding day.

COCKATOO: Hoity-toity! She is not your queen yet, Crispen, and she won't be until she has spun all this straw into gold. So, my girl, make your choice—spin the straw or lose your father and the King's hand. Which shall it be?

GRIZEL (*Wearily*): I will spin.

CRISPEN (*Pressing her hand*): Keep up your courage,

Grizel. I shall see to it that no harm comes to you or your father. (*He exits right.*)

COCKATOO (*To* GRIZEL): All the straw, or your father will be hanged. (*She turns to go.*)

RUMPELSTILTSKIN: Cuckoo!

COCKATOO (*Shaking her fist at the sky overhead*): Cuckoo yourself! (*She exits right.* GRIZEL *puts her head on the spinning wheel and weeps.*)

RUMPELSTILTSKIN (*Appears dancing about on his hill*): Cuckoo! Cuckoo! That bumbling Miller and his boasting! His daughter can't spin straw into gold—but *I* can, *I* can! I'll make a bargain with the Miller's daughter. I'll bargain for a playmate—a human playmate!
Tonight Grizel shall once be told
That I will spin the straw to gold,
But ere the straw is two times spun,
I'll bargain for her first-born one!
(*He laughs jubilantly and leaves the hill.*)

GRIZEL (*Raising her head*): What shall I do? Oh, what shall I do? (*There is a cheerful chirp off left, and* HAPPILY, *the bluebird, "flies" in.*)

HAPPILY (*Twittering*): Cheer up! Cheer up! Happily, the bluebird, at your service, Grizel.

GRIZEL: Oh, I know you! You sing outside my window every day.

HAPPILY (*Chirping*): That's me! That's me!

GRIZEL (*Hopefully*): Do you know how to spin straw into gold?

HAPPILY: Could be! Could be!

GRIZEL: Tell me how.

HAPPILY (*Hopping to the door in wall*):
Fool a fellow, follow me.
Here the how-to-spin will be.

GRIZEL: There? In the wall? I don't understand.

HAPPILY: Wait a little! You'll see. (*She hops off left. Suddenly* RUMPELSTILTSKIN *flings open door and leaps forward.*)

RUMPELSTILTSKIN: Good evening, Grizel!

GRIZEL (*Startled*): Oh! Who are you?

RUMPELSTILTSKIN: Never mind. I've come to help you.

GRIZEL: Can you spin straw into gold?

RUMPELSTILTSKIN: Pooh! That's easy. (*Cunningly*) What will you give me if I spin for you?

GRIZEL: What do you want?

RUMPELSTILTSKIN (*In a sudden fury*): I'm—asking—you! (*He jumps up and down and shakes his fists.* GRIZEL *is alarmed and tries to calm him.*)

GRIZEL: Don't, don't! You will fly to pieces.

RUMPELSTILTSKIN (*Stamping his foot*): Of course I'll fly to pieces! I always do! (*He pretends that his foot sticks to floor, and he tugs at it.*) Don't make me stamp so hard. My foot sticks. (*He pulls it free, losing his balance.* GRIZEL *helps him up.*) Now, what will you give me?

GRIZEL: I haven't anything of real value. Will you take my beads? (*Offering her necklace*)

RUMPELSTILTSKIN: It's a bargain. (*He puts necklace around his neck and dances over to bale of straw. He pulls from bale a long strand of straw, which he attaches to the spindle of spinning wheel.*)

GRIZEL: You are going to spin *all* the straw, aren't you?

RUMPELSTILTSKIN: All? I bargained to spin only that bale. (*He points to bale.*)

GRIZEL: But the Duchess said all the straw had to be spun.

RUMPELSTILTSKIN (*Craftily*): Ah! In that case, we must bargain again. What will you give me *this* time if I spin for you?

GRIZEL: I have nothing left to give.

RUMPELSTILTSKIN: Nothing? It's impossible to make a bargain with nothing.

GRIZEL: Won't you spin for me, anyway? I can pay you later—after I'm married to the King.

RUMPELSTILTSKIN: Oho! So you are going to marry the King, are you?

GRIZEL: Yes, and then I will be able to pay you well.

RUMPELSTILTSKIN: *Very* well, Grizel!
In the seed is the leaf and the bud and the rose,
But what's in the future, why, nobody knows.

GRIZEL: What does that mean?

RUMPELSTILTSKIN: See here, Grizel. Promise me your first-born child when you are Queen, and I will spin, spin, spin! (*He gives the wheel three turns.*)

GRIZEL (*Shocked*): Oh, I couldn't do that!

RUMPELSTILTSKIN (*Folding his arms and walking away*): Your child—one year from today—or I won't spin.

GRIZEL (*Aside*): Who knows what may happen in a year? (*She glances at* RUMPELSTILTSKIN.) He may never come back. (*To* RUMPELSTILTSKIN) All right, I promise.

RUMPELSTILTSKIN (*Turning to her*): Your first-born, boy or girl?

GRIZEL (*Nodding*): Yes.

RUMPELSTILTSKIN: A promise is a promise. Now let me get to work. (GRIZEL *sits on the stool down left.* RUMPELSTILTSKIN *goes to other bale of straw and pulls out a long strand which he winds on the spindle of the spinning wheel. Music is heard. The lights dim as* RUMPELSTILTSKIN *starts chanting spinning song, and a color wheel flashes different-colored lights all around him. He dances about and makes spinning motions.*)
Wheel, whirl! Spindle, spin!
Straw go out and gold come in!
What will be has not yet been.
Wheel, whirl! Spindle, spin!
(*A bright yellow light begins to glow inside the bales of straw.*)

Wheel, stop! Spindle, unspin!
Straw is out and gold is in!
What is now has never been.
Wheel, stop! Spindle, unspin!
(*The color wheel stops. The lights in the pavilion come up gradually.* RUMPELSTILTSKIN *detaches the two lengths of straw from the spindle. Music fades.*) There you are, Queen Grizel!

GRIZEL (*Running to look at the bales*): It's gold—real gold! You've done it! You've spun it, Whatever-your-name-is!

RUMPELSTILTSKIN: He, he, he! Whatever-my-name-is! You don't know my name, do you?

GRIZEL: You haven't told me yet.

RUMPELSTILTSKIN (*Taunting her*): Not yet—and won't, either! (*Sound of voices is heard off right.*) Here they come! I must be off. (*He bows low.*) Goodbye, Grizel. Remember your promise! (*He exits left.*)

GRIZEL (*Looking after him and sighing*): My promise! It frightens me to think about it. (COCKATOO *enters, followed by* CRISPEN, PRINCESSES, *and the* MILLER. *They all exclaim in amazement, as they see the gold.*)

COCKATOO: Sakes alive, she has really done it!

MILLER (*Rejoicing*): That means I can keep my neck—and head! After all, what good is one without the other, eh, daughter?

GRIZEL (*Laughing as she hugs him*): No good, Father.

CRISPEN: Grizel, we have more gold than we can ever spend. Not many queens have brought their husbands such a rich dowry. Marthe! Coris! Kirsten! Lisbeth! Run to the palace and call the heralds! Let them announce my wedding day! (*The* PRINCESSES *run out right, chattering with excitement.*)

MILLER: Oh, Duchess! To think that I'm to be father of a queen! I'm—flabbergasted! (COCKATOO *and the* MILLER

exit right, arm in arm, followed by GRIZEL *and* CRISPEN.
When they are gone, RUMPELSTILTSKIN *peeks through
the left arch, runs across to right and looks off joyously.*)

RUMPELSTILTSKIN:

Tonight Grizel has promised me
Tomorrow's child upon my knee,
And when I come the child to claim,
She'll never, never guess my name!

(RUMPELSTILTSKIN *pantomimes his name, speaking
each syllable aloud beforehand. He rumples his hair for
the syllables, "Rumpel"; he walks stiff-legged with his
arms straight down at his sides for the syllable, "stilt";
he strokes the skin on the back of his hand for the syllable, "skin."*) Rumpel—stilt—skin! (*He laughs and
exits through the door in the wall.* HAPPILY *enters from
left in time to see* RUMPELSTILTSKIN *exit. She faces front
and puts her wing to her beak.*)

HAPPILY:

Fool a fellow, follow after,
Grizel's tears shall change to laughter.
Sh-h-h! (HAPPILY *hops through the door as curtain falls.*)

*   *   *

SCENE 2

TIME: *A year later.*

SETTING: *Same as Scene 1. The spinning wheel and straw
have been removed. An elaborate cradle is at center.*

AT RISE: RUMPELSTILTSKIN *is crouched on his hill watching* GRIZEL, MILLER, COCKATOO *and* CRISPEN, *who are
grouped around the cradle.*

GRIZEL: He's fast asleep, bless him!
MILLER: My grandson!

COCKATOO: My grandnephew!

MILLER: He looks just like his mother—don't you, punky-wunky? (*He pretends to tickle the baby's nose.*)

COCKATOO: I think he favors his father—'itty bitty lamb-kins. (*She tickles the baby's chin.*)

GRIZEL: Don't wake him. Set the cradle over here. (COCKATOO *and* MILLER *set the cradle down left.*) Now let him have his nap in peace. Shoo, everybody, shoo! (*She waves others off right.* MILLER *and* COCKATOO *exit.*) Crispen, I left my embroidery in the summer house. Please get it for me. (CRISPEN *exits left and* GRIZEL *sits on the stool beside the cradle. Up on his hill,* RUMPELSTILTSKIN *leaps to his feet.*)

RUMPELSTILTSKIN:

Today I seek, today I find,
A playmate of a human kind,
Promised me a year ago
By one who'll never, never know
My name is Rumpelstiltskin! (*He leaves the hill.* GRIZEL *rocks the cradle and sings softly. Presently* RUMPELSTILTSKIN *enters through the wall door and tiptoes to center. He bows with a great flourish.*) Good day, Queen Grizel, who was once a miller's daughter.

GRIZEL: Good day. (*She rises with a start as she recognizes* RUMPELSTILTSKIN.) Oh! It's you!

RUMPELSTILTSKIN: Yes, it's me! He, he, he!

GRIZEL (*Fearfully*): Have you come for—?

RUMPELSTILTSKIN: Yes, I've come for! (*He points to the cradle.*)

GRIZEL (*Quickly shielding it*): No!

RUMPELSTILTSKIN: The year is up today, Grizel. Remember your promise—the child is mine. (*He tries to push by her.*)

GRIZEL (*Barring his way*): No! Give me back my promise.

Here—you can have all the jewels in my crown. (*She starts to lift the crown from her head.*)

RUMPELSTILTSKIN: There is no jewel like your first-born. I'll take him! (*He bounds past her, but she catches his arm and holds it fast.*)

GRIZEL: You shan't have him! I'll give you my kingdom!

RUMPELSTILTSKIN (*Angrily, wrenching his arm free*): A hundred kingdoms cannot buy a promise!
A bargain's a bargain, a vow is a vow
To the very last word of it! Settle up now!

GRIZEL (*Throwing herself on her knees*): Have mercy, little man! Don't take my child away from me. (*She breaks into a fit of weeping.*)

RUMPELSTILTSKIN: Stop it! Stop crying! I can't *stand* it!

GRIZEL: Pity—have pity, little man!

RUMPELSTILTSKIN (*Stamping his foot*): Will you stop crying? It makes me feel sorry for you. (*He turns away.*)

GRIZEL: Please leave me my little son.

RUMPELSTILTSKIN (*Running around the fountain and shaking his fists*): No, no, no, no, *no!*

GRIZEL (*Standing*): Yes, yes, *yes!* Whatever-your-name-is, yes!

RUMPELSTILTSKIN (*Stopping suddenly, a sly expression coming into his face*): Hah! Whatever-my-name-is, eh? All right, Grizel, I'll bargain with you once more, for the last time. I have the strangest name in the whole wide world. No one has ever guessed it. I'll give you nine guesses. If you can tell me what my name is, you may keep your child. But if you fail, then, whisk!—the child is mine and there's an end to it.

GRIZEL: Nine guesses?

RUMPELSTILTSKIN (*Nodding*): He, he, he! Come now, what's my name?

GRIZEL: Is it Redbeard?

RUMPELSTILTSKIN: No, it's not! That's one.

GRIZEL: Is it Bandylegs?

RUMPELSTILTSKIN: It's not that, either! That's two.

GRIZEL: Is it—Wheatstraw?

RUMPELSTILTSKIN: Of course not! That makes three. Guess
six more.

GRIZEL (*Making up names in desperation*): Could it be—
Dicker-rubble-gerber?

RUMPELSTILTSKIN: That's not a name—it's a turkey!
Gobble-gobble!

GRIZEL: Is it—Archius-lurchius?

RUMPELSTILTSKIN: I wouldn't be caught dead with a name
like that!

GRIZEL (*Beginning to cry*): Heilen-hollen-zollen?

RUMPELSTILTSKIN: There you go, crying again! *Do* stop it!

GRIZEL: But I have only three guesses left. (*She sits beside
cradle, weeping violently.*)

RUMPELSTILTSKIN: Don't, *don't!* I'll give you more time.
I'll give you until tomorrow. I'll go back on my hill and
wait until tomorrow morning.

GRIZEL (*Suddenly quiet*): Where is your hill?

RUMPELSTILTSKIN (*Backing away*): A long way off.

GRIZEL (*Moving to him*): Which way? North? East? South?
West? Which way?

RUMPELSTILTSKIN: Every way. (*He bows.*) Until tomorrow,
Grizel. (GRIZEL *covers her face with her hands and sinks
onto fountain seat, sobbing.* RUMPELSTILTSKIN *exits
through wall door.* CRISPEN *enters from left with* GRIZ-
EL's *embroidery.*)

CRISPEN (*Going to her*): Grizel, dear! What's the matter?

GRIZEL: Oh, Crispen! Do you remember the little man I
told you about, who spun all the straw into gold? (CRIS-
PEN *nods.*) He came back today to claim our baby.

CRISPEN: What!

GRIZEL: And if I don't guess his name by tomorrow, he'll take our little son away from us.

CRISPEN: I will find out his name. Where has he gone?

GRIZEL: I don't know. He said he lives on a hill, but he wouldn't tell me where it is. (HAPPILY *"flies" in from left, twittering.*)

HAPPILY: I know! I know!

GRIZEL (*Rising*): Oh, do you?

HAPPILY: I followed him!

GRIZEL: When?

HAPPILY: Last year! Last year!

GRIZEL: Do you know his name?

HAPPILY: Not yet! Not yet!

CRISPEN: Can you take me to his hill?

HAPPILY (*Nodding*): Chirrup! Chirrup!

CRISPEN: Then fly, bluebird, fly! I'll follow you.

HAPPILY: Follow me! Follow me! Fool a fellow, follow me! (*She exits through the wall door and* CRISPEN *goes through after her.* GRIZEL *sits beside the cradle.*)

GRIZEL: Hope, little son, hope! Your father has gone to save you, and I shall keep watch over you until he returns. (*The lights in the pavilion fade out. Pause. Then the lights on the hill come up. After a moment* HAPPILY *hops up the hill, followed by* CRISPEN.)

HAPPILY: This is it! This is it!

CRISPEN (*Looking about*): There's nobody here.

HAPPILY: He'll be here! He'll be here! (*Off right* RUMPELSTILTSKIN *can be heard singing as he approaches.*) He's coming! He's coming! (HAPPILY *and* CRISPEN *hide behind the hill.*)

RUMPELSTILTSKIN (*Enters, runs up the hill and leaps into the air, clicking his heels together*):
Tomorrow will become today,
As yesterday today became,

But nobody—nowhere—hears me say
That—(*He pantomimes his name, speaking each sylla-ble aloud as he did in the previous scene.*) Rumpel—stilt—skin is my name! (*He bursts out laughing and prances off left.* HAPPILY *and* CRISPEN *come up from behind the hill.*)

CRISPEN (*Looking after* RUMPELSTILTSKIN): Now we know! His name is Rumpelstiltskin.

HAPPILY (*Agreeing*): Chirrup!

CRISPEN: Come back to the palace to tell Grizel. (*They exit down the hill. The lights fade out. Pause. The lights in the pavilion come up. It is the next morning.* GRIZEL *is still beside the cradle, but she is seated on the ground with her arm thrown over the stool, fast asleep.* HAPPILY *enters through the secret door, followed by* CRISPEN.)

HAPPILY: We know it! We know it!

CRISPEN (*Crossing to* GRIZEL): We know his name, Grizel!

GRIZEL (*Waking up*): You do? What is it?

CRISPEN: It's Rumpel—(*He breaks off.*) Rumpel—Good heavens, I've forgotten it!

GRIZEL: No, no!

CRISPEN (*To* HAPPILY): What *is* it?

HAPPILY (*Plaintively*): Forgot it! Forgot it!

GRIZEL: Oh, try to remember!

CRISPEN (*Pacing about*): Rumpel—Rumpel—Rumpel-stimpski?

HAPPILY: Not right! Not right!

CRISPEN: Rumpel-stitchkin?

HAPPILY: Not quite! Not quite!

CRISPEN: Rumpel-what, then?

GRIZEL (*Sinking onto the bench*): Oh, dear!

CRISPEN: There was something he did in pantomime. If only I could remember! (RUMPELSTILTSKIN *enters through the wall door.*)

RUMPELSTILTSKIN: Good, good, good, good morning! (*He glances around.*) Or is it bad, bad, bad, bad morning? Well, let's get it over with. What is my name?

GRIZEL: I don't believe you *have* a name!

RUMPELSTILTSKIN: Oh, I have a name, all right. Come on, guess it in three. What is your first guess?

GRIZEL: Are you called—Maximilian?

RUMPELSTILTSKIN (*Dancing about*):
No, I'm not. There goes one!
Two to come, and then you're done!

GRIZEL: Is it—Ulric?

RUMPELSTILTSKIN:
No, it's not! There goes two!
One to come, and then you're through!
He, he, he! Do you give up?

CRISPEN (*Putting his arm around* GRIZEL): Of course we don't give up.

RUMPELSTILTSKIN:
Cudgel your brain as much as you may,
Not you nor any who play this game
Can guess by night or guess by day
That—(*He pantomimes his name silently*) is my name!

CRISPEN (*Excitedly*): I know what it is!

CRISPEN and HAPPILY: Rumpelstiltskin! (RUMPELSTILTSKIN *howls with rage. He jumps up and down, shaking his fists, and stamps hard on the ground. His foot sticks, and* GRIZEL *and* CRISPEN *help him to free it. They help* RUMPELSTILTSKIN *to bench. He sits down dejectedly.*)

RUMPELSTILTSKIN (*Piteously*): Now I'll never get what I want.

GRIZEL: What do you want?

RUMPELSTILTSKIN: A human playmate.

GRIZEL: You mean, you just want a playmate?

RUMPELSTILTSKIN: Yes, I'm lonely. I live by myself with only my shadow to play with.

GRIZEL: Then come and live with us, here in the palace, and you can play with my baby every day.

RUMPELSTILTSKIN: I can? (*He leaps to his feet and faces upstage with his arms outstretched.*) Did you hear that, Shadow, Shadow? (*Pause*) Shadow!

SHADOW (*Behind hill*): Yes?

RUMPELSTILTSKIN: Show yourself! (SHADOW *stands on hill with outstretched arms.*) I have a playmate, and I'm going to live down here with him always.

SHADOW: What's to become of me?

RUMPELSTILTSKIN: Do you want to live down here, too?

SHADOW: Oh, yes!

RUMPELSTILTSKIN: All right, come along down. (RUMPELSTILTSKIN *and* SHADOW *lower their arms.* SHADOW *leaves the hill and the spotlight fades.*) After all, I couldn't very well go about in the sun without my shadow, now, could I?

GRIZEL: I should say not. (PRINCESSES *run on from right, followed by* COCKATOO *and* MILLER.)

MARTHE (*As they enter*): Let's play a game! (*She sees* RUMPELSTILTSKIN.) Oh, there's that nice little man! Do you want to play the game of Names?

RUMPELSTILTSKIN: Yes!

CORIS: Then choose a name!

RUMPELSTILTSKIN: Rumpelstiltskin! (SHADOW *steals through the door and stands behind him.* PRINCESSES *form a ring and dance around them.*)

PRINCESSES (*Singing*):
Play the game! Play the game!
Rumpelstiltskin is his name!
Play the game! Play the game!
Rumpelstiltskin is his name!
(*Curtain*)

THE END

Tom Sawyer, Pirate

by Mark Twain

Characters

AUNT POLLY
SID SAWYER
TOM SAWYER
BECKY THATCHER
ALFRED TEMPLE
JOE HARPER

HUCK FINN
MRS. HARPER
BEN ROGERS
AMY LAWRENCE
GRACIE MILLER
WIDOW DOUGLAS

SCENE 1

TIME: *An afternoon in September, 1847.*
SETTING: *Aunt Polly's back yard.*
AT RISE: AUNT POLLY *is seated on a stool paring potatoes.*
SID SAWYER *enters up left from the street, carrying his schoolbooks in a leather strap.*

SID: Hello, Aunty.
AUNT POLLY (*Looking up*): Why, Siddy! Is school out already?
SID: It's after four o'clock.
AUNT POLLY (*Rising and shaking out her apron*): Land sakes! I'd better get these potatoes on to boil right away.
SID (*Swelling with pride*): I got one hundred in arithmetic today, Aunty!

77

AUNT POLLY (*Suitably impressed*): My! You don't say! (*Changing her tone*) What did Tom get?

SID: He wasn't there.

AUNT POLLY: He wasn't there? (SID *shakes his head.*) Why, where was he?

SID: I don't know, Aunty. He wasn't in school all afternoon.

AUNT POLLY: Humph! Playin' hooky, like as not. Oh, that child! Well, you just wait till I lay my hands on *him!* (TOM *is heard whistling a merry tune offstage.*)

SID (*Gleefully*): Here he comes now! (TOM *enters jauntily. He is barefoot and wears his jacket buttoned.*)

TOM: Hello, Aunt Polly. (*She looks at him severely, and he stops whistling, casting a suspicious glance at* SID. *Suddenly he reaches for the pan of potato peelings.*) I'll throw away the peelings for you, Aunty.

AUNT POLLY (*Checking him*): Just a minute, Tom Sawyer. It was powerful warm in school, wasn't it?

TOM (*Warily*): Yes'm.

AUNT POLLY: Didn't you want to go swimmin'?

TOM (*Uneasily*): No'm—well, not very much.

AUNT POLLY (*Feeling the front of* TOM's *coat*): But you're not too warm now, though.

TOM: Some of us pumped water on our heads. Mine's damp yet. (*Leaning towards* AUNT POLLY) See?

AUNT POLLY: Tom, you didn't have to undo your shirt collar where I sewed it, to pump water on your head, did you? Unbutton your jacket. (TOM *calmly opens his jacket. His shirt collar is securely sewn.*) Bother! I was sure you'd played hooky and been a-swimmin'.

SID (*With feigned innocence*): Well, now, Aunty, I thought you sewed his collar with *white* thread this mornin'. That thread is black.

AUNT POLLY: Why, I *did* sew it with white! Tom! (TOM *runs off.* AUNT POLLY *calls after him.*) Tom Sawyer! I never did see the like of that boy! Well, I'll just have to put him to work sawin' wood to punish him. He hates work more'n anythin' else. (*She gathers up the pans of potatoes and peelings.*) Come on, Siddy. You can get the fire started for me. (*They exit through gate, into house.* TOM *comes back and crouches by the barrel, looking after them.*)

TOM (*Muttering*): She'd never have noticed if it hadn't been for Sid. (*He examines two large needles thrust into the lining of his jacket. One needle carries white thread and the other, black.*) Confound it! Sometimes she sews it with white and sometimes with black. I wish she'd stick to one or the other. I can't keep track of 'em. (*He goes to gate and shakes his fist at house.*) But I'll bet you I'll beat Sid up! I'll learn him! (BECKY THATCHER *enters from the street with* ALFRED TEMPLE. ALFRED *is dressed very properly. He is carrying* BECKY's *books, and she smiles up at him coyly as they stop near her gate.*)

BECKY: Thank you for carrying my books, Alfred.

ALFRED (*Giving books to her*): That's all right, Becky. I'll tell you some more about St. Louis tomorrow and show you the pictures. We can look at them during recess.

BECKY: Oh, that will be nice. (TOM *thrusts out his chin and chest and approaches* ALFRED.)

TOM: I can lick you!

BECKY: For shame, Tom Sawyer!

ALFRED (*Calmly*): I'd like to see you try it.

TOM: Well, I can do it. (BECKY *gives a little scream, hurries out of the way, as the boys approach each other.*)

ALFRED: No, you can't.

TOM: Yes, I can.

ALFRED: You can't.

TOM: Can!

ALFRED: Can't! (*The boys watch each other carefully.*

When one moves, the other moves, but only sideways, in a circle.)

TOM (*Looking* ALFRED *up and down*): You think you're *somebody* now, *don't* you? I could lick you with one hand tied behind me.

ALFRED: Why don't you *do* it, then? Are you afraid?

TOM: I'm *not* afraid.

ALFRED: You are!

TOM: I am not!

ALFRED: You are! (*They are now shoulder to shoulder, glowering, and shoving each other.*)

TOM: Get away from here!

ALFRED: Go away yourself!

TOM: I won't!

ALFRED: I won't, either!

TOM (*Laughing*): Where did you get that hat?

ALFRED: I dare you to knock it off.

TOM: For two cents I *will!* (ALFRED *takes two pennies from his pocket and holds them out.* TOM *knocks them to the ground, and knocks* ALFRED's *cap off. The two boys grapple.* BECKY *tries to separate them.*)

BECKY: Stop it, Tom! Don't, Alfred! Shame on you both! Please, *please* stop! (ALFRED *breaks* TOM's *hold and withdraws from the tussle.*)

ALFRED: All right, Becky. I won't fight—for *your* sake. (*He picks up his cap and brushes it off.*)

BECKY (*Angrily to* TOM): You're a bad boy, Thomas Sawyer! Bad, bad, bad! Don't you ever speak to me again. I *hate* you! (*She tosses her head and goes off up right, arm in arm with* ALFRED.)

TOM (*Looking after them furiously*): Any other boy! Any boy in the whole town but that St. Louis smarty who thinks he's so great. You just wait, mister, till I catch you! I'll just take you and . . . (*He goes through the motions of thrashing an imaginary* ALFRED.) Oh, you do, do you? You holler enough now, do you? Let that be a lesson to you, then! (*He continues the imaginary fighting, as* HUCK FINN *and* JOE HARPER *enter left.* JOE *walks to the left of* TOM, HUCK *to the right.*)

JOE: Say, Tom, whatcha doin'?

TOM (*Finishing off with a vicious punch*): Uh! (*Turns to boys*) Hullo, Joe. Hullo, Huck. (*He sits on the barrel dejectedly.*)

HUCK: Who was that you were trouncin', Tom?

TOM (*Shaking his head*): Nobody. (*Mournfully*) Joe. . . .

JOE: Huh?

TOM: Huck.

HUCK: Huh?

TOM: Don't you forget me. I'm goin' away. *She* will be sorry, then.

HUCK: What?

TOM: I'm goin' into the unknown countries beyond the seas—and never comin' back again. (*He sighs heavily.*) Nobody loves me.

JOE (*Putting his arm around* TOM'S *shoulder*): Me, too, Tom! My mother just scolded me for drinkin' cream I never even tasted and don't know anythin' about.

TOM: I try to do the right thing and get along, but they won't let me. They won't be happy until I'm gone. All right, I'll go. When they find out what they've done to me, maybe they'll wish they'd treated me better.

JOE: It's plain my mother is tired of me. If she feels that way, I might just as well go along with you, Tom.

HUCK: Where you goin'? (TOM *thinks, then jumps off the barrel excitedly.*)

TOM: I'm goin' to be a pirate, that's what!

HUCK: What do pirates do?

TOM: Oh, they just have a great time! They take ships and burn 'em and get heaps of money and bury it on an island.

HUCK: Do pirates always have an island?

TOM: Of course!

HUCK: Can I go along?

TOM: Sure. You just have to take the oath.

HUCK: How do I do that? (TOM *steps between* JOE *and* HUCK *and puts his hand on top of the barrel.*)

TOM: Put your hand on mine. Joe, you, too. Now. (*In a serious tone*) We swear to stand by each other, and never separate from each other, till death ends this oath.

HUCK: That's perfect.

JOE: We have to have a countersign.

TOM: I know a good one—blood!

ALL (*In low, grim tones*): Blood!

HUCK: We have to have an island.

TOM: Jackson's Island is right handy. It isn't more than two miles down the river.

JOE: How will we get there?

TOM: We'll have to build a raft.

HUCK: I know where there's an old one that would do.

TOM: Could we capture it and be off by midnight?

HUCK: I reckon so.

JOE: We'll each bring hooks and lines and somethin' to eat.

TOM: This is the life!

HUCK: It's a whack!

JOE: It's the nuts!

TOM: Hucky, you're Huck Finn, the Red-Handed, and Joe, you're Joe Harper, the Terror of the Seas. (*He stands on barrel, draws an imaginary cutlass from his belt and raises it over his head.*) And I am Tom Sawyer, the Avenger of the Spanish Main. Shove off, mates. (*He jumps down, and they all start to walk stealthily upstage toward the street.* TOM *suddenly stops and holds up his hands.*) Hssst! (*The others halt.*) At midnight!

JOE: On the dot!

HUCK: At the raft!

ALL: B-L-O-O-D!

CURTAIN

* * *

SCENE 2

TIME: *Early morning, two days later.*

SETTING: *The island. A campfire is at center, in front of the curtain.*

AT RISE: HUCK *enters from left with a string of small fish, followed by* JOE *who is carrying a handmade pirate flag.*

HUCK (*Looking about as he crosses to center*): Tom hasn't turned up yet.

JOE: Nope. (*He puts flag in a knothole of log near campfire.*)

HUCK: You don't reckon he's given us the slip?

JOE: No, Tom's true blue, Huck. He won't desert. He's up to somethin' or other.

HUCK: I wonder what.

JOE: Fix the fish. (HUCK *moves near fire and puts the fish in the hot ashes.*) We'll go ahead and eat if Tom isn't here before they're done.

TOM (*Entering from left, with a swagger*): Which he is!

JOE: What have you been up to, Tom?

TOM: Let me near the fire to dry my clothes and I'll tell you. (*He sits on the log.*) Well, after you boys were asleep last night, I swam across to the other shore.

HUCK (*Alarmed*): What made you do that, Tom?

TOM: I got to wishin' Aunt Polly knew we hadn't drowned. So I wrote on this piece of bark here (*He takes piece of bark out of his pocket.*) and thought I'd sneak into the house and put it where she'd find it.

JOE: What's it say? (*He takes it from* TOM *and tries to read it.*)

TOM: It got pretty wet, but you can read it.

JOE: "We haven't drowned. We're only off bein' pirates." Why didn't you leave it?

TOM: I got another idea. (*He grins.*) You just wait till you hear my idea! It's a whiz! (*He slaps* JOE *on the back enthusiastically.*)

JOE: Well, tell it!

TOM: I'm not ready yet.

JOE: Aw, come on!

HUCK: Did you see anythin' over in town?

TOM: Well, when I got there, there was nobody on the streets. All the houses were dark. But when I turned up my street, I saw a light in my house. I looked in the window, and who do you think I saw?

JOE: Your aunt?

TOM: Yes, and someone else.

JOE: My mother?

TOM (*Nodding*): Yes. They were sittin' close together and talkin' and cryin'. I heard 'em sayin' what noble boys we were and what comforts to them we were. I could hardly keep from rushin' right in and surprisin' them. And then I got my idea. Oh, will it be a winner! (*He rises, slapping his thighs in exaggerated laughter.*)

HUCK (*Grabbing* TOM's *arm*): Well, come on, tell us!

JOE (*Shaking* TOM): What is it?

TOM: I haven't got it all thought out yet. When I have, I'll tell you. Got anything to eat? I'm starved.

HUCK: There's fish. I don't know if it's done though.

TOM: Pirates eat things any sort of way. (*Each takes a fish from fire and eats it.* HUCK *and* JOE *squat by fire.* TOM *stands with one foot on log, at* JOE's *left.*)

JOE: Cracky! No fish ever tasted as good as this before.

TOM: This is the life for me! You don't have to get up mornings, and you don't have to go to school, and wash, and all that foolishness.

HUCK: What will we do when we're through eatin'?

TOM: We'll explore the island again. I'll bet there's been pirates here before. And then tomorrow, we'll have to go back, on account of my idea.

JOE (*Rising*): Go back!

HUCK (*Rising*): What *is* this idea, Tom? I wish you'd stop talking about it, or else tell us.

TOM: All right, I'll tell you. Well, when I was listenin' to Aunt Polly last night, I found somethin' out.

JOE *and* HUCK: What?

TOM: They're goin' to have a funeral for us tomorrow.

JOE: A funeral?

HUCK: For us?

TOM: Preachin' and everythin'! And when I heard 'em plannin' it, I got the idea to go back, all three of us, and listen to Reverend Kellerman preach our funeral sermon.

JOE: Whoopee!

TOM: And in the middle of it, we'll march in among 'em!

HUCK: Hey! That's great! (TOM *starts to sing the chorus of "The Sweet Bye and Bye."*)

TOM: "In the swee-eet—"

JOE *and* HUCK (*Joining in*): "—bye and bye, We shall meet on that be-oo-ti-ful shore—" (*With* TOM *leading the way, the boys march off, continuing to sing. When they are off,* JOE *runs back for the pirate flag and exits waving it in time to the rhythm of the hymn.*)

CURTAIN

*　　*　　*

SCENE 3

TIME: *The next afternoon.*

SETTING: *Same as Scene 1. The barrel and stool have been removed from the center lawn.*

AT RISE: *The stage is empty.* TOM, HUCK *and* JOE *enter stealthily left.* HUCK *stubs his toe, and* TOM *frantically shushes him.* TOM *goes to vine-covered arbor down right and beckons to other boys. They all hide behind arbor as voices are heard offstage.* BEN ROGERS, AMY LAWRENCE, ALFRED TEMPLE *and* GRACIE MILLER *enter and group themselves self-consciously near* AUNT POLLY'S *gate.*

BEN: I reckon just about everybody in town will be here for the funeral.

AMY: My goodness, yes! Do you remember, Ben, the last time we saw Tom? He wanted to trade his white marble for your mouth-organ and you wouldn't do it. I'll bet you wish you had now.

ALFRED (*Boasting*): I guess I was the last one to see Tom alive. It was the afternoon before he went away. He licked me.

BEN: Aw, that's nothin'. Tom's licked every boy in town.

GRACIE (*Looking toward the Thatcher garden*): Here come Becky and Mrs. Harper. My, I reckon Mrs. Harper feels badly about Joe.

AMY: I reckon Becky feels worse about Tom.

GRACIE: Yes, I heard they were engaged.

AMY (*Proudly*): Tom and *I* were engaged once. (*As* BECKY *and* MRS. HARPER *appear at the Thatcher gate,* WIDOW DOUGLAS *comes out of* AUNT POLLY'S *house and speaks to the children.*)

WIDOW DOUGLAS: Come along in, children. Don't stand there gawking. We'll just have time to practice singing the hymn before the service begins. (*Children go into house, followed by* WIDOW DOUGLAS. BECKY *and* MRS. HARPER *come out onto lawn.* BECKY *is crying, and* MRS. HARPER *is trying to comfort her, sniffing into a handkerchief herself.*)

MRS. HARPER: Shhh, Becky, dear.

BECKY: I can't help it, Mrs. Harper.

MRS. HARPER: Control yourself, child. There, there. (BECKY *is standing close to the arbor.*)

BECKY: Oh, Mrs. Harper, if I only hadn't said it.

MRS. HARPER: Said what, dear?

BECKY: What I said to Tom the last time I saw him. It was right out here, and that nasty Alfred Temple— (*She sobs again, and* TOM *beams with pleasure.*) If I could have another chance, I wouldn't say it for the whole world. But he's gone now, and I'll never, never see him again.

MRS. HARPER (*Sympathetically*): I reckon Tom knows you are sorry, Becky.

BECKY: I'll never know if he does. He'll never come and ask me to make up again, never, never, never. (TOM, *deeply moved, starts to go to her, but* JOE *and* HUCK *hold him back. He wipes his eyes on his shirt sleeve. Inside the house, a choir of young voices starts singing "In the Sweet Bye and Bye." The boys choke with laughter and beat time to the music.* AUNT POLLY *and* SID *enter through gate. She greets* MRS. HARPER.)

AUNT POLLY (*Embracing* MRS. HARPER *tearfully*): Oh, Mrs. Harper, I don't know how to give Tom up. He was such a comfort to me. He was full of mischief, but he never meant any harm, and he was the best hearted boy that ever was.

MRS. HARPER: It was just so with my Joe. He was as unselfish and kind as he could be. And to think I whipped him for takin' that cream, never once recollectin' that I threw it out myself because it was sour—poor, poor abused boy. (JOE *grins happily.*)

SID: I hope Tom's better off where he is, but if he'd been better in some ways—

AUNT POLLY (*Glaring at him*): Sid! Not a word against my

Tom! God will take care of *him*, never you trouble *yourself*, sir! (TOM *looks delighted. The hymn singing stops, and* WIDOW DOUGLAS *steps out of house, followed by children.*)

WIDOW DOUGLAS: Miss Sawyer, Mrs. Harper, Reverend Kellerman has just arrived. We're ready to begin the service.

AUNT POLLY (*Emotionally*): Oh, I wish Tom were alive again! (MRS. HARPER *and* BECKY *join* AUNT POLLY *in a chorus of anguished sobs.* TOM *signals to other boys, and they all come out from hiding.* AUNT POLLY *is the first to see them*) Tom Sawyer!

TOM: Ma'am?

MRS. HARPER: Joe Harper!

JOE: Yes'm. (*The two women hug and kiss the boys.*)

AUNT POLLY: Tom! Is it really you? You're not dead and playin' tricks on me?

TOM: No, Aunt Polly. We were just off bein' pirates on Jackson's Island. (BEN, AMY, ALFRED *and* GRACIE *come out of house.*)

ALL: Pirates! (HUCK *starts to slink away, but* TOM *seizes him and drags him back.*)

TOM: It's not fair. Somebody's got to be glad to see Huck.

WIDOW DOUGLAS: And so they shall. *I* am glad to see him, poor motherless thing, and I am going to take him straight home with me.

AUNT POLLY (*Teasing* TOM): So you were off bein' pirates, were you?

TOM: Yes'm.

AUNT POLLY: I suppose you did a powerful lot of swimmin'.

TOM: Yes'm. Pirates always swim when they capture boats —with knives between their teeth.

AUNT POLLY: You don't say! Did pirates ever chop up kindling wood for the kitchen stove?

TOM: I reckon not, Aunt Polly. They mostly had camp-fires. (*He starts to back off.*)

AUNT POLLY (*Taking* TOM *by the ear*): Well, young man, here's one pirate who's goin' to chop kindling—right now.

TOM: But Aunt Polly!

AUNT POLLY: No arguing! (*She points off left.*) There's the woodshed. March!

TOM: Aw, shucks! (*He goes slowly in direction of wood-shed, but when he reaches exit he turns and dashes up center for street. As he passes,* AUNT POLLY *grabs him by collar of his jacket. He slips his arms out of sleeves, leaving her holding an empty jacket.*)

AUNT POLLY (*Watching* TOM *disappear*): Drat that boy! (*Everyone bursts out laughing and, in spite of her exasperation,* AUNT POLLY *joins in good-naturedly, as the curtain falls.*)

THE END

The Elves and the Shoemaker

from Grimms' Fairy Tales

Characters

JOHANN, *the shoemaker*
FRIEDA, *his wife*
SIX VILLAGE CHILDREN
TUMBLE ⎫
TICKLE ⎬ *the elves*
TWIRL ⎭
DUKE OF ANSBACH
DUCHESS OF ANSBACH
ELSA, *their daughter*
FREDERICK, *their son*
LADY MARIA

SCENE 1

TIME: *Three days before Christmas.*

SETTING: *The shoemaker's shop. Upstage center there is a counter with empty shelves behind it. There is a cobbler's bench near the counter.*

AT RISE: JOHANN *is standing in the open doorway at left. His wife,* FRIEDA, *enters from right.*

FRIEDA: Are you waiting for someone, Johann? (JOHANN *turns.*)

JOHANN: Yes, Frieda, I am waiting for a customer.

FRIEDA (*Sighing*): There will be no customers today. It is late.

JOHANN (*Coming inside and closing the door*): There will be no customers any day, I'm afraid, late or early. For a month now, not a single customer has come in to buy a pair of shoes.

FRIEDA (*Patting his arm sympathetically*): I know, I know.

JOHANN: Why is that, Frieda? I make *good* shoes, don't I?

FRIEDA: You make very good shoes, Johann.

JOHANN: I can't understand it. Other years at Christmastime, the villagers have wanted shoes—for themselves, or to give away. But this Christmas—(*He shakes his head sadly.*) nothing.

FRIEDA: It's that new shoemaker in Sycamore Lane. He has taken away all your trade. He is young and quick.

JOHANN: But his shoes are not made as well as mine. They wear out in six months. Mine last for years. You know that, Frieda.

FRIEDA: Of course I do! Haven't I always said you are the best shoemaker in the kingdom?

JOHANN: Then why aren't the villagers still coming to *me* for shoes? Doesn't quality count for anything any more?

FRIEDA (*Explaining patiently*): Times are changing, Johann. The world moves faster nowadays. Everybody wants things done in a hurry. You should hire a young apprentice to help you.

JOHANN: How can I afford an apprentice if there's no work? And what are we going to do about Christmas gifts for the village children? There's not a penny in the house and we've always given the children *some*-thing.

FRIEDA: There, there, don't fret, Johann. The children will understand. (*There is the sound of children singing off left as they approach the shop. They are singing the*

*familiar round, "Christmas Is Coming." Then they en-
ter, carrying among them an evergreen wreath, garland,
doll, and gaily decorated cut-out cardboard shoe. They
march around shop, singing, and then encircle* JOHANN
and FRIEDA. *When the song is over, they ad-lib greetings.)*

1ST BOY: We have some things for you, Johann and
Frieda.

1ST GIRL: We made them ourselves. (*They hold up the
cardboard shoe between them.*)

JOHANN: What is that?

1ST BOY: It's a Christmas shoe!

1ST GIRL: See, it's trimmed with tinsel.

1ST BOY: We're going to hang it on the door.

2ND GIRL: My brother and I made this wreath.

FRIEDA: It's lovely! Where shall we put it?

2ND BOY: Over there is a good place. (*He points to the
window.*)

JOHANN (*To* 3RD GIRL *and* 3RD BOY): And what do *you*
have for old Johann, eh?

3RD GIRL: A garland for the counter.

3RD BOY: Could we have a hammer and nails?

JOHANN: Help yourselves. (*The children set to work deco-
rating the shop.* FRIEDA *supervises.* JOHANN *chuckles as
he watches* 1ST BOY *nail the shoe to the outside panel
of the street door.*) So, my young friend, at last you
bring a shoe to the shoemaker—but to hang on the
door, not to be repaired. Wouldn't you like to have a
new pair of shoes for Christmas?

1ST BOY: Oh, no. These you made for me a year ago are
still like new.

1ST GIRL (*Holding out her doll*): My dolly needs a new
pair of shoes.

JOHANN: Does she now!

1ST GIRL (*Thrusting the doll into* JOHANN's *hands*): Will you make them for her—please?

JOHANN: Let me see, what size does she wear? (*He measures the doll's foot with a ruler.*) Hmmm—fairy size, one and a half. (*Searching the shelves at back*) There's a piece of leather about somewhere. It's the last piece I have. (*He spies it under the counter*) Ah, here it is!

1ST GIRL: Oh, how pretty! It's red! (JOHANN *pretends to cut and sew the shoes—which are already made.*)

3RD BOY: When I grow up, Johann, I'm going to be a shoemaker like you.

JOHANN: Like me, eh?

3RD BOY: Yes, you make wonderful shoes. Will you show me how?

JOHANN: How old are you, Peter?

3RD BOY: I'm twelve. I could help you after school and Saturdays.

JOHANN: Alas, Peter, I have no work for you. The new shoemaker has taken away all my customers. I'm afraid, dear children, there will be no gifts for you this Christmas.

2ND GIRL: That's all right, Johann. You have given us enough already.

3RD GIRL: It's our turn to do something for you.

2ND BOY: That's why we're here.

JOHANN (*Deeply touched*): Bless you, children. (*He slips the finished shoes on the doll's feet.*) There you are, little one. Shoes for your doll. A perfect fit!

1ST GIRL: Thank you, thank you, Johann!

1ST BOY (*Calling from the door*): I'm finished. How about the rest of you?

OTHER CHILDREN (*Ad lib*): We're through. So am I. Half a minute—one more nail. There! (*Etc.*) (*The children return hammer and nails to the cobbler's bench.*)

FRIEDA: Thank you, children. The shop looks very cheerful.

CHILDREN: Goodbye, Frieda. Goodbye, Johann. (JOHANN
and FRIEDA *smile and wave, as the children exit singing.*
Then FRIEDA *turns back sadly, looking at the empty*
shelves.)

FRIEDA: Oh, Johann, what will become of us? We have
only a little dry bread left in the cupboard.

JOHANN: I don't have any leather left, except this scrap.
(*He holds up remnant of red leather.*)

FRIEDA: It is enough for a small pair of shoes, isn't it?

JOHANN: Perhaps, if I cut it carefully. But nobody will buy
the shoes.

FRIEDA: Why not make them anyway? It will at least give
you something to do.

JOHANN: Very well, I will do it to please you.

FRIEDA: I'll put the kettle on to boil, and we'll have a cup
of tea and the last of the dry bread. (*She exits into back*
room. JOHANN *puts leather on the counter and begins*
to cut it with a pair of scissors.)

JOHANN: Frieda is right. It is good to have busy hands, and
who knows? Perhaps I will sell the shoes after all. (*He*
sings to himself as he works, to the tune of "This Old
Man.")
Snip and slice, heel and toe,
Trim it here and shape it so,
This way, that way, cutting to and fro,
That's the way my scissors go!
(*The lights dim slowly, and after a while* JOHANN *puts*
down his scissors.) It has grown too dark to work, and
there is no oil for the lamp. Well, I'll just leave the
pieces here on the counter, ready to stitch together in
the morning. (*He goes out right. Music is heard and*
shop becomes flooded with "moonlight." A clock strikes

twelve. Street door opens and TUMBLE, TICKLE *and*
TWIRL, *the elves, skip into the room. They are barefoot
and dressed in ragged suits.*)

ELVES: Here we are!

TUMBLE: I'm Tumble! (*Tumbles on floor.*)

TICKLE: I'm Tickle! (*Tickles himself and giggles.*)

TWIRL: I'm Twirl! (*He whirls in a circle. Elves sing, as
they pantomime making a pair of shoes.* TUMBLE *measures off a length of thread, threads a needle and stitches
the pieces of leather together.* TWIRL *sits on cobbler's
bench and taps shoe last with a hammer.* TICKLE *picks
up glue pot and pretends to glue the heels to the soles
and the soles to the uppers.*)

ELVES (*Singing to the chorus of "Jingle Bells"*):

Hurry up! Hurry up!
    We know what to use.
We three merry elves are here
    To make a pair of shoes.
Stitch and tap, just like that,
    There's no time to lose.
Hurry, hurry, hurry and
    We'll make a pair of shoes.

(*Elves "finish up" the shoes, and place them on counter.*
NOTE: *Finished shoes are actually underneath counter.
Then they polish the shoes.* TUMBLE *grips one end of
the cloth,* TWIRL *and* TICKLE, *the other, and they pull
back and forth as they sing.*)

Faster now, faster now,
    Sew and tack and glue.
If we stop to dance and play,
    We never will get through.
Pull to left, pull to right—
    Listen to our news!

Goody, goody, goody for
  We've made a pair of shoes!
(*Elves put everything back in place, and skip out the door. A cock crows as the curtain falls.*)

CURTAIN

*   *   *

SCENE 2

TIME: *The next morning.*

SETTING: *Same as Scene 1.*

AT RISE: JOHANN *comes into shop from back room, yawning and stretching. He goes to counter, and then calls out in surprise as he sees the shoes.*

JOHANN (*Calling*): Frieda! Frieda, come quickly! (FRIEDA *hurries in.*) Look at what I have here! (*He shows her the shoes.*)

FRIEDA (*Astonished*): Why, where did they come from?

JOHANN: Could someone have done this for me? No, it's my own work. This is the way I make my stitches.

FRIEDA: How beautiful they are—the most beautiful shoes you have ever made!

JOHANN: I know. It is very strange that I don't remember sewing them. Perhaps I did it in my sleep.

FRIEDA: Well, it doesn't matter. Put them in the window. Someone is bound to buy them.

JOHANN (*Putting the shoes in the display window*): I can't understand it. I never worked in my sleep before. And if I spent half the night finishing these, why am I not tired?

FRIEDA (*Looking out window*): There is a fine carriage coming down the street. Two ladies and a gentleman are in it—and a little girl and boy.

JOHANN: I wonder who they are. They're not from this village.

FRIEDA: Oh, look! The carriage is stopping here. What did I tell you? They have seen the shoes in the window.

JOHANN: They're coming in!

FRIEDA: My, my, what fine people! (*She smooths down her hair and apron. The street door opens, and* DUKE *and* DUCHESS OF ANSBACH *enter, followed by their children* ELSA *and* FREDERICK, *and* LADY MARIA.)

DUKE: Good morning. Are you the shoemaker?

JOHANN: Yes, your lordship, I am Johann, the shoemaker.

DUKE: I am the Duke of Ansbach, and this is the Duchess. (FRIEDA *curtsies,* JOHANN *bows.*) We were driving by and noticed the shoes in your window. May we see them, please?

JOHANN: Certainly, your graces. (*He hands shoes to the* DUKE *who shows them to* DUCHESS.)

DUCHESS: Are they for a girl or a boy?

JOHANN: Either one, milady.

ELSA: I want them!

FREDERICK: I want them!

ELSA: They won't fit you!

FREDERICK: They will, too!

ELSA: I saw them first, didn't I, Mama?

FREDERICK: I saw them first, didn't I, Papa?

DUKE: Hush, children! Stop your bickering! (*To* JOHANN) Do you have another pair of shoes like these?

JOHANN: No, your grace, but I could make them by to-morrow.

ELSA: I don't want them tomorrow, I want them now. Let me try these on. (*She sits on bench and, at a nod from* DUKE, JOHANN *removes her slippers and puts the shoes on her feet.*) They are exactly the right size. (*She struts about.*)

FREDERICK (*Making a face*): Show-off!

DUCHESS: They really are lovely. I think I will order a pair of slippers for myself, to wear to the King's Christmas ball. (*To* JOHANN) Could you have them ready by tomorrow?

JOHANN: Yes, indeed, milady. May I measure your foot, please? (DUCHESS *sits on the bench and* JOHANN *takes the necessary measurements.*) Hm-m, very dainty.

DUKE: Well, my dear, if you are going to have a new pair of slippers for the ball, then so shall I—and Lady Maria, too. (JOHANN *measures the feet of* DUKE *and of* LADY MARIA.) That's three pairs of dancing slippers, Johann, and one pair of shoes for my son. Here are five gold pieces. My footman will call for the shoes tomorrow afternoon.

JOHANN: Oh, thank you, your grace.

DUCHESS: There is no shoemaker like you in our town. Your shoes will be the talk of the King's ball. Everyone in the kingdom will want your shoes, you wait and see! (*All start to leave.*)

JOHANN (*Noticing* ELSA's *old shoes on floor near bench*): Just a moment, your grace. I'll wrap these for you.

DUKE: I doubt if Elsa will put them on again. She will want to wear her new shoes everywhere—even to bed! (*He laughs and takes the shoes.*) Good day, Johann. You will see us soon again. (*He follows others out street door.* JOHANN *cups gold coins in his hands and jingles them in* FRIEDA's *ear.*)

JOHANN: Listen to that, Frieda! Five pieces of gold! Now I can buy all the leather I need.

FRIEDA: And we can have fresh bread and meat and vegetables for dinner.

JOHANN: Did you hear what the Duchess said? People will be coming from all over the kingdom to order shoes.

FRIEDA: It's such a large kingdom! You will never run out of customers.

JOHANN: I shall be able to take Peter on as an apprentice.

FRIEDA: And best of all, we can buy gifts for the children! (*They bustle about, humming a Christmas carol.*)

CURTAIN

* * *

SCENE 3

TIME: *Late that night.*

SETTING: *The same. The lamp is burning brightly on the counter which is strewn with shaped pieces of leather.*

AT RISE: JOHANN *finishes cutting a piece of leather and puts down his scissors.*

JOHANN: There! All the shoes are cut out, ready to be stitched. (*He yawns and stretches.*) My, but I'm tired—and the night is only half over. What shall I be like in the morning? (FRIEDA *appears in the doorway at right.*)

FRIEDA: Johann?

JOHANN: Frieda! Haven't you gone to bed yet?

FRIEDA: How can I go to bed when you haven't eaten your supper? I've warmed it over three times already.

JOHANN (*Surprised*): My supper? Didn't I eat it? *That's* why I'm so tired—and hungry! Well, I'll go eat now, Frieda, and then I'll come back and work right through till breakfast time. (*He exits into back room with* FRIEDA. *A pause, and then clock strikes twelve. Music of "Jingle Bells" is heard. Presently the street door opens and the three elves bound into the shop.* TUMBLE *turns a somersault,* TICKLE *tickles himself and giggles, and* TWIRL *whirls in a circle.*)

TUMBLE (*Spying pieces of leather on the counter*): Ah! Our work is cut out for us!

TWIRL: It's my turn to wax the thread and sew tonight!

TICKLE: It's mine to hammer the heels! (*They repeat song and pantomime of previous night, but change the num-*

ber of shoes to be made to "four pairs" in place of "a pair." JOHANN *and* FRIEDA *peek around the curtain in doorway at left. They are astounded by what they see, and, partially hidden by curtains, they watch entire proceedings. When the first verse is sung,* TICKLE *sits astride cobbler's bench, instructing* TUMBLE *who holds the glue pot.*) Put a little daub of glue here—no, there —no, here.

TUMBLE: Well, make up your mind! Where do you want it?

TICKLE (*Pointing*): There! (*He giggles.*)

TWIRL (*Stitching the leather*): This leather is like velvet. (*The elves take four pairs of finished shoes from under the counter, line them up on top.* TUMBLE *and* TWIRL *fetch polishing cloth, and* TICKLE *takes this opportunity to tickle himself and giggle.*)

TUMBLE: Come on, Tickle, you're not through yet. Lend a hand here.

TWIRL: Yes, stop fooling! It will soon be dawn. (TICKLE *joins* TWIRL *at his end of the cloth, and they begin polishing motion.*)

TWIRL (*To* TUMBLE): Pull a little harder, will you?

TUMBLE: But there are two on your end. It's not fair! (*Elves sing second verse, then quickly fold polishing cloth and scamper about, putting tools away.*)

TWIRL: Hurry, hurry! We have only a minute more!

TICKLE: Not even that. Listen—the cock is crowing. (*A cock crows.*)

TUMBLE: Thank goodness! I'm all worn out.

TICKLE: We barely finished in time.

TWIRL: But finish we did.

TUMBLE: And now—we're off! (*Elves make hasty exit.* JOHANN *and* FRIEDA *come out from behind curtain.*)

JOHANN (*Incredulously*): Elves! Three elves! Frieda, did you see them, too?

FRIEDA (*Nodding*): Were they real?

JOHANN: They must have been. Both of us couldn't be dreaming. (*They go to counter and gaze admiringly at the shoes.*)

FRIEDA: Isn't it wonderful, Johann? The shoes are all finished exactly as you would have done them yourself.

JOHANN: No, not exactly. The elves have made them more beautiful than I ever could.

FRIEDA: We should do something for them to show them how grateful we are.

JOHANN: Yes, but what?

FRIEDA (*Thoughtfully*): The dear little things were dressed in rags, and their feet were bare. Did you notice?

JOHANN: Why, I could make shoes for them!

FRIEDA: And I will make some warm suits and socks and knitted caps.

JOHANN: Let's start right away. (*He selects a piece of leather from counter.*) This leather will be perfect for their tiny feet, it's so soft.

FRIEDA: I'll get my best velvet skirt. It will make such pretty red jackets.

JOHANN (*Enthusiastically*): Frieda, tonight is Christmas Eve! We'll have a Christmas tree and hang the clothes on it.

FRIEDA: Oh, I can hardly wait to see what will happen! (*She exits at right to get her sewing materials, while* JOHANN *sets finished shoes out of the way on shelves on back wall.*)

CURTAIN

*   *   *

SCENE 4

TIME: *Twelve o'clock, Christmas Eve.*

SETTING: *The same. A lighted Christmas tree stands in the center of the shop. Hanging from its branches are three*

sets of clothes for the elves: jackets, trousers, shirts, socks
and stocking caps. There are three pairs of shoes under
the tree. The shoes the DUKE *ordered have been re-*
moved.

AT RISE: FRIEDA *is fussing with garments on tree, trying*
them in different places. JOHANN *hovers nervously at*
her side. Clock begins to strike midnight.

JOHANN: Stop fussing, Frieda, it's time for the elves to
come!

FRIEDA: Just a moment. I want to arrange everything
nicely.

JOHANN (*Impatiently*): Everything *is* arranged nicely! Now
come away. (*He steers her toward the right doorway.*)

FRIEDA: I do hope they will be pleased.

JOHANN: Shhhh! (*He pushes her behind curtain, as the*
music of "Jingle Bells" is heard. Street door opens, and
elves enter, going through their individual routines of
tumbling, giggling, and whirling about.)

TUMBLE: It's my turn to hammer the heels tonight!

TICKLE: It's mine to stitch the soles!

TWIRL: It's my turn to—to—(*They all stare at the Christ-*
mas tree in amazement.)

TUMBLE: Oh, *my!*

TWIRL: Oh, my *goodness!*

TICKLE: Oh, my goodness *gracious!*

ALL: It's a Christmas tree!

TWIRL (*Pointing to clothes*): What are those things?

TUMBLE: They must be presents—for *us!*

TWIRL: But what are they for?

TICKLE: They're to put on, silly! (*He giggles and puts*
a stocking cap on his head. With shouts of laughter, the
elves dress themselves in their new clothes and shoes.)

ELVES (*Singing to the tune of "Jingle Bells"*):

Here's a coat! Here's a cap!
   Trousers one, two, three!
Woolen socks and shirts to match,
   And shoes beneath the tree!
Put them on, put them on,
   Button, hook and tie;
Oh, what handsome elves we'll be,
   You and you and I!

Look at us, look at us
   In our Christmas clothes,
We are spruce and dandy
   From our heads down to our toes!
All dressed up, all dressed up,
   Now we're gentlemen;
We will never stitch a sole
   Or tap a heel again!
(*The cock crows.*)

TUMBLE: Listen!

TWIRL: The cock is crowing!

TICKLE: Our night is over!

ALL (*Singing*):
   Hip hooray! Hip hooray!
     We'll be on our way,
   But before we go we have
     A few last words to say:
   Bless this shop, the cobbler, too,
     And the cobbler's wife.
   Merry, merry Christmas
     And good fortune all your life!

(*They pause at the door and shout in unison.*) Merry Christmas to all and a happy New Year! (*They exit.* JOHANN *and* FRIEDA *hurry across the room to look out window.*)

FRIEDA: There they go, the little dears! They do look nice, don't they?

JOHANN: The shoes fit perfectly.

FRIEDA: And so do the suits. (*Wistfully, turning away.*) I suppose we shall never see them again.

JOHANN: No matter, my dear. They have blessed this shop with prosperity and happiness. We could wish for no greater gift than that. (*They turn back to the window as the bells of Christmas ring out and the curtain falls.*)

THE END

Dummling and the Golden Goose

from Grimms' Fairy Tales

Characters

MOTHER	GROOM
KARL	BRIDESMAIDS
HUMBERT } her sons	BAKER'S BOY
DUMMLING	FLOWER WOMAN
INNKEEPER	MAYOR
BELLA	FOUR CHILDREN
NELLA } his daughters	HERALD
STELLA	TWO PAGES
GRAY MAN	GUARD
SEXTON	KING MODRED
PARSON	PRINCESS DOLORA
BRIDE	TWO LADIES-IN-WAITING

SETTING: *A country road. At the right there is the door of an inn. Over the door hangs a sign:* GANDER INN.

AT RISE: MOTHER *enters from left with* KARL *and* HUMBERT. *Each boy carries an ax over his shoulder.* MOTHER *carries a cloth bundle and an earthen jug.*

KARL: Well, Mother, I hope you have a good dinner there for Humbert and me. Chopping wood makes us as hungry as bears.

MOTHER (*Giving him the cloth bundle*): There's plenty of bread and cheese—and here's a jug of goat's milk.

(HUMBERT *takes the jug.*) If you should see your brother Dummling anywhere, send him home. He hasn't done a lick of work this morning. (*As she crosses toward inn door, whistling is heard from back of audience.*)

HUMBERT: Wait, Mother. (*He points out front.*) Here comes the simpleton now, with his fishing pole. (DUMMLING *comes down aisle whistling and carrying a home-made fishing pole over his shoulder. A tiny fish dangles from end of fishline.*)

KARL (*Peering toward front*): Did he catch anything?

HUMBERT: Him? Oh, maybe an old boot or two. (*The brothers laugh in derision.* DUMMLING *comes up on stage, and they see the tiny fish.*) Well, did you ever! He's caught a minnow!

KARL: *That* will fill our empty stomachs! (*They laugh again.*)

MOTHER (*To* DUMMLING, *exasperated*): Where have you been, you stupid boy? This is washday, have you forgotten? And not only that, but it is rumored the King and Princess are touring the land, and who knows? They might stop here at this inn. Would you have them eat on a dirty tablecloth and sleep on grimy sheets? Now go along home and fill the tubs with water from the well, then come back here to the inn and help me carry the bed and table linen that has to be washed. Get a move on! (DUMMLING *exits slowly at left.* MOTHER *gazes after him and shakes her head hopelessly.*) I don't know what's to become of him, I'm sure. Oh, why can't he be smart like his brothers? (*She turns and enters the inn.*)

KARL (*Setting down his ax*): It's a long time since breakfast, Humbert.

HUMBERT (*Nodding as he sets down the ax*): Yes—and a longer time to dinner.

KARL: Exactly. So let's sit down here and eat before we go

into the forest. Woodcutting is hard work. (*They sit at a table at right.* KARL *opens cloth bag of food and* HUMBERT *drinks from jug. As they start to eat,* GRAY MAN *comes out of the forest at left and hobbles over to the table.*)

GRAY MAN: Good day, young sirs. (*They pay no attention to the greeting but cram bread and cheese into their mouths.*) Would you show a little kindness to a poor old man?

KARL (*With a hostile glance*): What do you want?

GRAY MAN: Only a piece of bread, sir. I'm so hungry I think I shall die if I don't get a scrap of food.

KARL: Then go and eat chokecherries with the birds.

GRAY MAN (*To* HUMBERT): A drink of milk, please? Only a sip.

HUMBERT: Go and drink water from the rain barrel over there. We have hardly enough milk for ourselves.

KARL: Why don't you earn your food as we do? Be off with you, lazy beggar. (GRAY MAN *walks away toward forest, stopping to shake his fist angrily at the brothers, unobserved, before he exits.* KARL *wipes his mouth with his sleeve and stands up and stretches.*) All right, Humbert. We'd better get to work.

HUMBERT: I suppose so. (*He takes a last gulp from the jug.*)

KARL (*Picking up his ax and pointing to a gnarled tree that stands a little apart from the other trees*): Why don't we start with this old oak tree? It's about ready to topple over, anyway.

HUMBERT: Good idea. We won't have to wear ourselves out chopping it down. (*While* HUMBERT *is getting his ax,* KARL *takes a swing at the tree trunk. The ax slips from his hands, and falls on his foot. He hops around on one foot, howling in pain.* HUMBERT *goes to him.*) What happened?

KARL: What does it look like, you fool? The ax slipped and hurt my foot. Oh, oh! (*He hops over to table and sits, holding injured foot with both hands.*)

HUMBERT: How could you be so careless? Now I have to do all the chopping by myself. (*He raises his ax but suddenly drops it behind him with a yell. He grabs his elbow, bending over in pain.*)

KARL: What's the matter?

HUMBERT: Matter? Matter? I twisted my elbow, that's what's the matter! (*He runs in circles, rubbing his elbow.* GRAY MAN, *laughing and nodding his head with satisfaction, peeks out from behind tree. He jumps up and down in vicious glee, then disappears into forest, as door of inn opens and* MOTHER *hurries out, carrying a clothes basket filled with sheets. She is followed by* INNKEEPER *and his three daughters.*)

MOTHER (*Crossing to the brothers*): Sakes alive, whatever is the trouble?

KARL: I've hurt my foot. I can't walk.

HUMBERT: I've twisted my elbow. I can't chop.

MOTHER (*Setting the basket on the table*): Well, here is a pretty kettle of fish! How am I to heat the water for washing if there's no wood to put on the fire? Answer me that!

KARL: Let Dummling do it.

MOTHER: Do what?

KARL: Chop the wood. (*The* INNKEEPER *and his daughters hoot with laughter.*)

INNKEEPER: Dummling! That nitwit! Chop wood?

BELLA: Aye, and chop off his wooden head in the bargain!

NELLA: He wouldn't miss it!

STELLA: He wouldn't know the difference!

MOTHER: At least he can do no worse than his brothers. (*She calls off left.*) Dummling! Dummling!

DUMMLING (*Calling from off left*): Yes, Mother.

MOTHER: Come here. (*After a pause*, DUMMLING *enters and his* MOTHER *hands him* HUMBERT's *ax.*) Go into the forest and chop some wood for the fire—and don't dawdle! (KARL *and* HUMBERT *start to go left*, KARL *limping and using his ax as a cane*, HUMBERT *groaning and rubbing his elbow.* INNKEEPER *goes into the inn, but his daughters linger behind.*)

DUMMLING (*Watching his brothers exit*): What happened to Karl and Humbert?

MOTHER: Never you mind, get on with your work. (*She indicates the leftover food on the table.*) There's your brothers' dinner. You can eat that when you're hungry.

DUMMLING: They didn't leave much.

MOTHER: It's enough for a simpleton like you.

DUMMLING (*Innocently*): Maybe I'm not as simple as you think, Mother. Maybe I shall find a fortune in gold buried under one of those trees. (*He points to the forest.*)

MOTHER: Gold, indeed! If you ever have as much as a dozen copper pennies in your pocket, it will be a miracle. (*She picks up the basket.*)

DUMMLING: I may surprise you yet, Mother.

MOTHER: Bring home an armful of wood and that will be surprise enough for me. (*She exits left. The three girls go into the inn, snickering together.* DUMMLING *gathers the crusts of bread and cheese into the cloth and is about to tie it up when the* GRAY MAN *comes out of the forest.*)

GRAY MAN: Good day to you, lad. Before you tie up that food, would you give a poor old man a mouthful? I haven't eaten in days.

DUMMLING: It's not much, I'm afraid, but what there is, I will gladly share with you. (*He hands bundle of food to* GRAY MAN *who sits and gobbles it down in a twinkling.*) Hey there! Not so fast. You'll choke!

GRAY MAN (*Smacking his lips*): Ah, that tasted good! Now

could I have a sip from your jug, please? I'm very thirsty.

DUMMLING: Of course. (*He gives the jug to the* GRAY MAN *who drinks without stopping.*) Hold on! Slowly, slowly!

GRAY MAN (*Returning the jug to* DUMMLING): You have done an old man a good turn, and you will not lose by it. If you do as I say, you shall always have plenty to eat and drink after this.

DUMMLING: Eh? How's that?

GRAY MAN: You have shared what you had with me, now I will share what I have with you. Listen to me carefully, and do as you're told:

Take one step left,
    Then two and three,
Twist around right
    And face that tree.
(*He points to the oak tree.*)
Follow your nose
    And you will find
Your just reward
    For being kind. (*He doffs his cap and starts away.*)

DUMMLING: Wait a minute! What is it I'll find?

GRAY MAN: See for yourself. Do as you're told.

DUMMLING: Give me a hint?

GRAY MAN: It rhymes with "told." (*He disappears into the forest.*)

DUMMLING (*Thoughtfully*): Hm-m-m. It rhymes with "told," does it? Now what were those directions? One step to the right—no, *left!* Then two and three. (*He takes the steps clumsily.*) Twist around right—and face this tree. (*He faces the oak tree.*) Follow your nose—(*He draws an imaginary line from end of his nose to back of tree trunk.*) Why, the tree is hollow and—*yes!* Here is something that rhymes with "told"! (*He reaches behind the trunk and brings forth a golden goose.*) A goose of *gold!* Oh, wait until I show this to Mother and the others! They laughed at me when I said I'd find my fortune under a tree. (*He strokes the goose, then tucks it under his arm.*) Now I will go to court and see the King. But first I'll get some dinner, the finest dinner that money can buy. (*He goes to the inn door and raps loudly on it.*) Ho, innkeeper! Innkeeper, I say!

INNKEEPER (*Opening the door*): What do you want, you silly?

DUMMLING: Bring out the best you have to eat and drink.

INNKEEPER (*Mockingly*): Oho! Is Master Dummling a rich man now?

DUMMLING: Indeed I am. Look here. (*He sets the golden goose on the table, plucks out a feather and gives it to* INNKEEPER.)

INNKEEPER: What's this? A feather of pure gold? I can't believe it. (*He stares at the goose, then shouts into the inn.*) Bella! Nella! Stella! Bring food and drink! Bring the best we have in the house! (*His three daughters hurry out carrying dishes which they place on the table before* DUMMLING. *They stare in admiration at the golden goose.*)

BELLA: A solid gold goose!

NELLA: Did you ever see the like?

STELLA: Never heard of such a thing!

BELLA: What a lucky boy you are, Dummling!

NELLA: Does the meat suit you?

STELLA: Is everything to your taste?

DUMMLING (*Grandly*): Why, it's all good enough, I suppose. But I shall have better at the King's court.

INNKEEPER: Are you going to court?

DUMMLING: Yes, indeed!

INNKEEPER (*Bowing*): Let me put up a lunch for you to take along. Stella, the bread is ready to come out of the oven. (INNKEEPER *and* STELLA *exit into the inn.* DUMMLING *yawns and stretches.*)

DUMMLING: Dinner has made me sleepy. I think I'll have a little nap before I start out. (*He places his arm on the table and rests his head on it. With his other hand, he holds the goose firmly.*)

BELLA (*Drawing* NELLA *aside, softly*): I wish I had a feather from that wonderful goose.

NELLA: So do I.

BELLA: He'd never miss one feather.

NELLA: Of course not. (DUMMLING *snores.*)

BELLA: He's fast asleep. Now is our chance.

NELLA: You do it first. (*They tiptoe to the table, and* BELLA *starts to pull a feather from goose's tail. She jerks her hand but is unable to take her hand away.*)

BELLA (*In a frantic whisper*): Nella, my hand is stuck to the goose. I can't let go. Pull me away. (NELLA *takes hold of her sister and pulls, then discovers that she is fastened as securely to* BELLA. *She yanks on* BELLA'S *arm.*) Stop, Nella, you're hurting my arm. Let go!

NELLA: I can't! I can't get my hand loose! (STELLA *comes out of inn, wrapping a loaf of bread in a napkin.*)

STELLA (*Crossing to her sisters*): What are you up to? Oh, I see. You are pulling feathers from the golden goose. Well, if you can have a feather, so can I. (*She sets the loaf on the table.*)

BELLA: No, no, don't touch the goose!

NELLA: Don't touch us! Keep away! (STELLA *grabs* NELLA *to push her out of the way and finds herself held fast to* NELLA. *The three girls twist and tug, and their cries awaken* DUMMLING, *who leaps to his feet.*)

DUMMLING: What's going on here? (*The girls straighten up and try to appear innocent. They curtsy all together.* DUMMLING *notices* BELLA's *hand holding goose's tail.*) What are you doing to my goose?

BELLA: You mean, what is your goose doing to us?

NELLA: We are all stuck fast to him and to each other.

STELLA: You must tell the goose to let us go.

DUMMLING: Ha! Trying to steal feathers, were you? Well, it serves you right. (*He picks up goose and tucks it under his arm. The girls are still held fast.*)

BELLA: Oh, please let us go!

NELLA: *Please!!*

STELLA: PLEASE!!!!

DUMMLING: Shan't, girls. Can't, girls. Where I go, goose goes, and I'm off to see the King. (*He walks downstage, and girls stumble after him.* INNKEEPER *comes out of inn.*)

INNKEEPER: What's this? Bella, Nella, Stella, have you gone mad? Come back here! There's work to be done.

GIRLS: We can't let go!

INNKEEPER: I'll soon make you let go! (*He cuffs* STELLA, *and his hand sticks to her ear.*) What sort of trick is this? I can't let go either. Help, help!

DUMMLING: It seems to me I'm going to have lots of company.

BELLA: Oh, Dummling, good Dummling, the kitchen floor isn't swept and the beds aren't made. Please let me go!

NELLA: The meat is on the spit, it will burn to a cinder. Please let me go!

STELLA: Six pies are in the oven. Please let me go!

INNKEEPER: There's so much work to be done. I beg you, let us go!

DUMMLING: Shan't, sir. Can't, sir. Where I go, goose goes, and I'm off to see the King. (*The procession moves across the stage as* DUMMLING *whistles a jolly march tune.* NOTE: *Recorded music may be played.* SEXTON *enters from right and goes to inn door. He sees procession and calls out.*)

SEXTON: Innkeeper! Innkeeper! Where are you going? Have you forgotten that you are to serve a wedding feast?

INNKEEPER: No, Sexton, but I can't get away!

SEXTON: Tut, tut, man, all the arrangements have been made. You can't go off like this. (*He runs and grabs* INNKEEPER'S *arm.*) Why, what's the matter? I can't get loose. (*He shouts down line to* DUMMLING.) Young man, if this is your doing, I order you to stop at once!

DUMMLING: Shan't, sir. Can't, sir. Where I go, goose goes, and I'm off to see the King. (PARSON *enters from right and throws up his hands in consternation at the sight of the procession.*)

PARSON (*Shocked*): What is this? The Sexton playing some silly game? Fie, fie! (*He catches up with* SEXTON.) This is not at all proper! Think of your position.

SEXTON: Don't touch me, Parson. (*The* PARSON *clamps his hand on* SEXTON'S *shoulder.*)

PARSON: Help! I'm stuck fast! It's the devil's work! (*A wedding party arrives at the inn. It consists of* BRIDE, GROOM *and* BRIDESMAIDS.)

BRIDE (*Pointing*): There he is. There's the Parson! (*She takes* GROOM'S *arm, and they trot beside* PARSON, *as* DUMMLING *leads the procession past.*)

GROOM: Are you going to the church? We're ready to be married. (*He grabs* PARSON *by his coattails, and the entire wedding party joins the procession.* BAKER'S BOY *runs on from right, a wedding cake balanced on his head. He stops in amazement as the procession approaches.*)

BAKER'S BOY (*Calling to* BRIDE): What shall I do with this wedding cake?

BRIDE (*Nodding toward the end of the line*): Give it to a bridesmaid. (*He presents cake to bridesmaid who is last in line. As she grips one side of the plate, he finds he can't let go of the other side.*) Come on, take it, will you? (*They are tugging cake back and forth, when* FLOWER WOMAN *enters from right with a basket of flowers. She waves a bouquet of roses toward* BRIDE.)

FLOWER WOMAN: Here you are, dearie, here's your bouquet! (*She tries to reach* BRIDE, *but being old and lame, she falls back to end of line where she becomes attached to* BAKER'S BOY. *Next,* MAYOR *enters. He scowls at the sight of the procession and confronts* DUMMLING, *who continues to walk forward, forcing* MAYOR *to walk backward as he speaks to* DUMMLING.)

MAYOR (*Wagging his finger in* DUMMLING'S *face*): Young man, do you have a permit for this parade? Show it to me or stop at once.

DUMMLING: Shan't, sir. Can't, sir. Where I go, goose goes, and I'm off to see the King.

MAYOR: You wretched rogue, I forbid you to take another step! How dare you treat me like this? I am the Mayor. I shall have you put in jail! I shall have the whole lot of you put in jail! (*He tries to halt procession, but it goes steadily on. Exasperated, he starts shaking* FLOWER WOMAN *and discovers, to his horror, he can't free himself.* FOUR CHILDREN *skip out of the forest. They are carrying bunches of wild flowers and baskets of berries.*)

1ST CHILD: Look at all the people!

2ND CHILD: What are they doing?

3RD CHILD: I think they are playing a game.

4TH CHILD: Let's play with them! (CHILDREN *fall in behind* MAYOR, *hanging on to him and to each other.*)

CHILDREN: Hey, this is *fun!*

DUMMLING: All right, everybody, step along lively! Now then, all together: left foot, right foot, left foot, right foot. (*Procession marches off stage and up aisle, then down again. There is a flourish of trumpets offstage. Procession comes to a standstill, facing stage, as* HERALD

enters from right and raises his hand. At the same time,
KARL *and* HUMBERT *enter from left with their* MOTHER.)

HERALD: Hear ye, hear ye! His Majesty, King Modred, and
the Princess Dolora are traveling through the land in
search of a cure for the Princess.

MOTHER: What ails Her Highness?

HERALD: She does nothing but moan and sigh and sigh and
moan from morning till night.

MOTHER: Does she never laugh at all?

HERALD: Laugh! Her Highness has never been known
even to smile since the day she was born. Therefore—
(*He unrolls a proclamation and reads*) "The King pro-
claims that whoever makes the Princess laugh shall be
rewarded by her hand in marriage and one half of the
kingdom. But whoever tries and fails shall have a good
drubbing." (HERALD *rolls up scroll. There is a second
flourish of trumpets.*) Make way, make way for His
Majesty, King Modred, and Her Royal Highness, the
Princess Dolora. (Two PAGES *enter, each carrying a gilt
chair which they place center stage and then stand behind. They are followed by* GUARD *who takes up his
position left of the chairs.* PRINCESS DOLORA *enters on
the arm of her father,* KING MODRED. *She is weeping
audibly into a large handkerchief. Behind her walk* TWO
LADIES-IN-WAITING, *one with a fancy box marked "Dry
Handkerchiefs," the other with a similar box marked
"Wet Handkerchiefs."* KING *and* PRINCESS *seat themselves, and* TWO LADIES *stand beside the* PRINCESS'
chair.)

PRINCESS: Oh, boo-hoo-hoo! I'm so unhappy. Boo-hoo-hoo!
Give me another handkerchief, this one is all w-w-wet.
(1ST LADY *supplies her with a dry handkerchief, giving
the wet one to* 2ND LADY *who disposes of it in her box.*)

KING (*To* HERALD): Have you read the proclamation?

HERALD: I have, Your Majesty.

KING: Is there no one here who wishes to try his luck at making the Princess laugh?

HUMBERT (*Stepping forward and bowing*): Your Majesty, I'd like to try.

KING: Very well, proceed.

HUMBERT (*To* PRINCESS): I am sure I can make you laugh, Your Highness. Just listen while I tell you a funny story. Once upon a time there was a mouse who wanted to be an elephant—

PRINCESS (*With a sniff*): I know that one.

HUMBERT: Then let me tell you the tale of the soldier·who lived in a drum.

PRINCESS: I've heard it a hundred times.

HUMBERT: Well, there's the story of the three robbers who sat on a hornet's nest.

PRINCESS: I know it by heart and it's *not* funny. Oh, boo-hoo-hoo! Take him away-ay-ay! He makes me cry!

KING: Young man, you are wasting your breath. (*To* GUARD) Take him away and give him a good drubbing. (GUARD *leads* HUMBERT *out.*)

PRINCESS: Oh, boo-hoo-hoo! Life is s-s-so s-s-sad! Give me another handkerchief. (KARL *limps to center and bows to* KING.)

KARL: Your Majesty, I will make the Princess laugh if I die doing it.

KING: Oh, you needn't go *that* far.

KARL (*To the* PRINCESS): Look at me, Your Highness. Did you ever see a funny face like this? (*He makes a funny face.*)

PRINCESS: Oh, the poor man!

KARL: Or like this? (*He makes a worse face.*)

PRINCESS: Oh, oh! I think he must be in great pain! (GUARD *re-enters.*)

KARL: Or one like this? (*He makes another weird face.*)

PRINCESS: Oh, boo-hoo-hoo! I can't bear it! Take him away! Where is my handkerchief?

KING (*To* GUARD): Take him away and give him a good drubbing. (GUARD *exits left with* KARL.)

PRINCESS: Oh, how miserable I am!

KING: It is useless to stay here. We had better go on to the next village. (*He rises and offers his arm to* PRINCESS.)

DUMMLING (*Calling out*): Your Majesty!

KING (*Turning and looking toward* DUMMLING): Yes, what is it, lad?

DUMMLING: I have brought you a goose—and a whole flock of geese that follow after. (*He speaks to long line of people behind him.*) Come now, all together! Left foot, right foot. Step right up and bow to the King and Princess. (*He leads procession up onto stage before* KING.)

INNKEEPER: Help ho!

STELLA, BELLA *and* NELLA: Oh, we're so tired!

SEXTON: Let me go!

PARSON: Somebody stop him!

MAYOR: Put the rascal in jail!

ALL: Your Majesty, we appeal to you!

PRINCESS (*Bursting into peals of laughter*): Oh, ha, ha, ha! Hee, hee, hee! Just look at them! Did you ever see such a sight? Oh, what a joke! Ha, ha! Hee, hee!

LADIES-IN-WAITING: She laughed! The Princess laughed!

KING: She laughed! She's cured!

PRINCESS: Ha, ha! Life is so funny! (GRAY MAN *suddenly appears from forest and goes to* DUMMLING.)

GRAY MAN: Now I will break the magic spell. (*He waves his stick over the procession.*)
Take one step right,
    Then two and three—
(*They all do so together.*)

Twirl around left
   And you will be free!
(*They let go of each other and twirl around left individ-
ually. There is a general shout of joy as they all scatter
about the stage.* DUMMLING *kneels before* KING *and
gives him golden goose.* PRINCESS *is quite breathless
from laughing.*)

KING: Rise, my lad. You have made the Princess laugh.
   Your reward is her hand in marriage and one half of
   the kingdom. (*He puts* PRINCESS' *hand in* DUMMLING'S.
   KARL *and* HUMBERT *enter from left.*)

KARL (*Limping twice as much as he did before*): Oh, what
   a drubbing! I'm sore all over.

HUMBERT (*Bent over double, holding on to his back*): I
   can't stand up straight. We won't be able to chop wood
   for a month.

DUMMLING: Brothers, you won't ever have to chop wood
   again. I'm going to marry the Princess!

ALL (*Ad lib*): Three cheers for Prince Dummling and the
   golden goose! Hip, hip, hooray! Three cheers for
   laughter! (*Etc. There is a general outburst of laughter
   which increases in volume as the curtain falls.*)

THE END

The Three Wishes

An English folk tale

Characters

ADAM ROODE, *a woodcutter*
MOLLY, *his wife*
TREE FAIRY
FIVE BOYS AND GIRLS

BEFORE RISE: *There is a log center, in front of curtain. ADAM ROODE enters left, whistling. He carries a wooden ax in one hand and a paper bag in the other. He goes right, stops, turns and sits on log. He puts down his ax and paper bag, yawns and stretches and starts to lie down when suddenly a voice is heard.*

MOLLY (*Calling from off left, impatiently*): Adam! Adam Roode! (ADAM *picks up ax and paper bag and rises, but not before* MOLLY *enters. She plants herself firmly beside him with arms akimbo.*) And just what do you think you're doing, Adam Roode?

ADAM: Why, I—I was going to take a little rest, Molly.

MOLLY: Oh, you were, were you! And I suppose you were going to have a little nap and dream that your ax was cutting wood for you without your having to lift a finger.

ADAM (*Foolishly*): Heh, heh! That would be quite a funny dream, wouldn't it, wife?

MOLLY: It would indeed! And about as likely to come true as the dreams I have of being a fine lady, living in a mansion, with servants to wait on me hand and foot. (*Sighing*) It was a sad day when I took you for my man. You're a lazy, good-for-nothing loafer, that's what you are.

ADAM: Yes, I know, Molly, you told me that yesterday.

MOLLY: Well, you still are. You'd rather starve for a penny than work for a pound. How do you expect we're going to live when you do nothing? Now take your ax and get to work! (ADAM *shoulders his ax and exits right.* MOLLY *calls after him.*) And if you want any supper tonight, you'd better split some wood for the fire! (*As she goes toward left, she notices that* ADAM *has left behind the paper bag. She picks it up.*) There, now, he has gone off without his lunch. What a muddlehead! (*Shrugs*) Oh, well, I'll ask one of the village children to take it to him. (*She exits.*)

* * *

SCENE 1

SETTING: *The forest.*

AT RISE: ADAM *is sound asleep and snoring under a tree. His ax lies on the ground beside him.* BOYS AND GIRLS *enter, singing a gay folk song.* 1ST GIRL *carries* ADAM's *lunch in the paper bag.* 1ST BOY *points to* ADAM, *and gestures for others to follow.* BOYS AND GIRLS *surround* ADAM.

1ST BOY (*Shaking him*): Wake up, Mr. Roode, wake up!

ADAM (*Opening his eyes and getting to his feet*): Eh? Oh. I must have dozed off.

1ST GIRL (*Holding out paper bag*): Here is your lunch.

Your wife asked us to bring it to you. You went off this morning without it.

ADAM: Well, what do you know! I don't often do that, you may be sure. (*Taking bag*) Thank you, my dear.

2ND GIRL: Aren't you awfully hungry, Mr. Roode? It's long past noon.

ADAM: Is it now? Dear, dear, and I haven't chopped a stick of wood yet. I'll just have to get busy and chop, chop, chop, won't I? (*Looking around at* BOYS AND GIRLS) Where are you young people off to?

1ST GIRL: We're going to pick wild flowers for the old folks in the village.

ADAM: That's very thoughtful of you.

3RD GIRL: I don't think we should do it.

ADAM (*Surprised*): Not take flowers to the old folks?

3RD GIRL: Not *wild* flowers.

2ND BOY (*Scoffing*): Oh, she says wild flowers should stay in the ground where they belong.

3RD GIRL: So they should. They droop and die when they are picked, even before you can put them into water.

ADAM: May I make a suggestion? (*The children nod eagerly.*) There is a bank of primroses growing back there. (*He points off left.*) If you dig up the flowers, roots and all, you could plant them in flower pots when you get home and then take them to the old folks.

BOYS AND GIRLS (*Excitedly; ad lib*): That's a wonderful idea! Why didn't we think of it ourselves? Let's go! (*Etc.*)

1ST BOY: Thank you, Mr. Roode.

1ST GIRL: We'll bring you some flowers when we come back! (BOYS AND GIRLS *go off left, singing.*)

ADAM: Now let me see. (*He picks up his ax and then looks at his lunch bag.*) Shall I eat first and chop afterwards, or chop now and eat later? Hm-m-m. Why can't I do both things at the same time? I can! (*He bites into a sandwich as he studies the trees.*) Which of these trees shall I cut down? (*He points to tree.*) There's a good one, I'll start on that. (*He walks over to tree and lifts his ax for the first blow.*)

TREE FAIRY (*From inside the tree*): Adam! (ADAM *stops, his ax suspended in mid air.*) Adam!

ADAM (*Lowering his ax and peering about*): Is that my wife calling? Molly? Is that you, Molly? Humph! I must be hearing things. (*He raises his ax again.*)

FAIRY (*From inside tree*): Don't, Adam! Please don't!

ADAM (*Setting down his ax*): Who's there? Where are you?

FAIRY (*From inside tree*): I'm in the tree.

ADAM (*Looking up*): Where? I don't see you. Come down! (*To himself*) It must be one of those children.

FAIRY (*From inside tree*): I'm *inside* the tree.

ADAM: *Inside* the tree? How did you get in *there*?

FAIRY (*From inside tree*): Let me out and I'll tell you.

ADAM: Let you out? How?

FAIRY (*From inside tree*): Cut a hole in the bark. The tree is hollow. (ADAM *pretends to chop at the trunk.*) Don't cut too deep, now. (ADAM *pretends to give a final blow, the bark falls away, and* FAIRY *steps out.*) Thank you, Adam. I have been shut up in this tree for a hundred years.

ADAM: A hundred years! Then you must be very old.

FAIRY: Not really. You see, I am the spirit of the wood.

ADAM: The spirit of the wood!

FAIRY: Yes, and I want to reward you for setting me free. It's terrible to be shut up inside a tree for a hundred years. It's like being in a dark prison cell, and I longed to see the light of day once more. I used to call out whenever a woodcutter passed by, but he always became frightened and ran away. You are the first one to listen to my pleas, and you deserve to be rewarded for your good deed. (*Going to* ADAM) Tell me, what would you like?

ADAM: Why, I guess I'd like a great big load of wood to take home with me. I'll never hear the end of it if I come home empty-handed.

FAIRY: There's something better than wood for you to take home.

ADAM: What is that?

FAIRY: I can give you three wishes—three wishes that will come true as soon as you wish them.

ADAM: That would be fine. It's much easier to wish than to chop wood. But my wife would want some part in this, too.

FAIRY: Very well, you can share the wishes between you. But remember, you have only *three* wishes, so be careful that you don't waste them.

ADAM: Oh, we won't. We shall think carefully before we use a single wish.

FAIRY: Goodbye, Adam. Choose wisely—wisely!

ADAM: Thank you, good fairy, and goodbye. (FAIRY *exits right into the forest.* ADAM *dances to left, reciting.*)
As I was chopping in the wood,
I met a fairy, kind and good.
Three wishes she did give to me,
I'll choose the wishes carefully.
(*He exits.*)

CURTAIN

*   *   *

SCENE 2

SETTING: *The kitchen of Adam's cottage. There is a fire-place at left with an iron pot hanging on a crane over fire.*

AT RISE: MOLLY *is at the fireplace, left, stirring soup in the pot.* ADAM *can be heard from off right.*

ADAM (*In a singsong, off right*):
Three wishes she did give to me,
I'll choose the wishes carefully.
(ADAM *enters, right, carrying his ax.*) Good day, Molly!
(*He stands his ax in a corner and skips over to* MOLLY, *who is watching him with a puzzled expression. Taking the ladle from her, he taps it on the side of the pot.*)
Rub-a-dub-dub! Roast mutton for me—fat fowls—a side of beef! Rub-a-dub-dub! Pasties! Puddings! Pies! (*He whirls about, waving the ladle over his head.*) Heigho, heigho, heigho!
MOLLY: What ails the man?
ADAM: When luck comes into a house, it tumbles in! (*He turns a somersault, then stands up and makes a deep bow to* MOLLY.) Wife, give me a curtsy. I'm as grand a man as the King, or I will be.
MOLLY: Have you lost what little wit you had?
ADAM: Maybe yes and maybe no. Strange things have happened today. I'm likely to jump out of my skin! (*He springs into the air and clicks his heels together.*)
MOLLY: Then jump back into a handsomer one.
ADAM: We're done with poverty! We're done with turnip soup! Throw it to the pigs! (*He tosses the ladle into the pot and starts to lift the pot off the crane.*)
MOLLY (*Taking hold of pot*): I'll throw *you* to the pigs! Let go of that pot. (*She puts pot back on crane.*)
ADAM: Be quiet, woman, and listen. (*He sits her down on a stool and seats himself on the table.*) Today while I was chopping wood, I found a fairy inside a tree.
MOLLY: Now I *know* you're daffy.
ADAM: But it's true! I set her free.

MOLLY (*Sarcastically*): Aye, and as a reward she gave you three wishes, I suppose.

ADAM (*Slyly*): No—she gave *us* three wishes.

MOLLY (*Interested*): Us? You mean me, too?

ADAM: We are to share the wishes between us.

MOLLY (*Looking at him shrewdly*): You mean, there really *was* a fairy?

ADAM: Cross my heart. (*He does so.*)

MOLLY: Three wishes, eh? Do you believe it, Adam? Let's try it now. (*Thoughtfully*) I wish that—

ADAM (*Clapping his hand over her mouth*): Hush, Molly! Don't pop a wish out like that. The fairy said we must choose carefully, because if we waste the wishes, we'll be sorry.

MOLLY (*Rising excitedly*): Oh, Adam, how shall we ever know what to ask? Think of it! Three wishes! Think of all that we shall own.

ADAM (*Swaggering about the room*): We'll have a coach to ride in, and six white horses!

MOLLY: I'll have a gown of silk and a necklace of diamonds!

ADAM: A suit of velvet for me. Knee breeches with silver buckles.

MOLLY: A great house! Servants! Rose gardens! Picture it, Adam!

ADAM: We shall live like a king and queen.

MOLLY: Our pockets filled with gold!

ADAM (*At the fireplace*): No more turnip soup, but fried pheasant and chicken and sizzling brown sausage! Oh, how I wish there were a string of sausages in the pot right this minute! (*Looking into pot*) Why, look, there it is! There's a real string of sausages in the pot!

MOLLY: You fool! You glutton! You have wasted a wish on a string of sausages when we might have been rich, or young, or a thousand other things!

ADAM (*Sheepishly*): Well, I've had my wish, and you can have the other two. (*With his back to the audience, he peers into the pot, his hands shielding his eyes.*) At least we have a fine string of sausages.

MOLLY: Sausages—*sausages!* Plague take you and your string of sausages! I wish it were stuck to the end of your nose! (ADAM *cries out and raises his head. The string of sausages is firmly attached to his nose.* MOLLY *screams.*) Oh! The sausages really *are* stuck to your nose!

ADAM (*Horror-struck*): Cut them! Cut them off! (MOLLY *takes knife from the table and pretends to saw away at the sausages.*)

MOLLY: The knife won't go through! It won't cut!

ADAM: Pull them, pull them! (*She pulls with both hands.*)

MOLLY: They don't budge! (*She tries again to pull the sausages from* ADAM'S *nose.*) It's no use. They seem to have turned to stone. (*Sinking onto a stool in despair*) I can do nothing, nothing. What will the neighbors say when they see you? Oh, we shall be the laughingstock of the village!

ADAM (*Imploringly*): *Wish* it off, Molly. We still have another wish.

MOLLY: Do you think I will waste the last wish of all?

ADAM: It was you who wished the sausages on.

MOLLY: It was you who wished for them in the first place. No, I shall use the last wish to make us rich and happy.

ADAM: Happy! How can we be happy if I have to go through life with a string of sausages stuck to my nose?

MOLLY (*Obstinately*): But we'll be rich—that's something.

ADAM: What good are riches if I can never face any people? (*There is a knock at the door.*) Listen! What's that? I thought I heard someone knocking. (*Another knock is heard.*) There it is again.

BOYS AND GIRLS (*Calling from off right*): Mr. Roode! Mr. Roode!

ADAM: It's the children back from the woods!

MOLLY: If they see you with those sausages on your nose, the whole village will hear of it. Hide, hide!

ADAM (*Sadly*): I can't hide forever, Molly. I'll have to show my face sooner or later. I may as well do it now. (*He starts for the door, but* MOLLY *runs to him and holds him back.*)

MOLLY: No, no, Adam! Not for all the riches on earth would I have the neighbors laugh at you. I wish the sausages off your nose! (*The string of sausages drops off into* ADAM's *hands, and he places it on table. Knocking is heard again, and* MOLLY *hurries to open the door.* BOYS AND GIRLS *troop in, carrying clumps of primroses.*)

1ST GIRL: See all the primroses we've brought for the old folks!

2ND GIRL: Thank you for telling us where to find them, Mr. Roode.

3RD GIRL: We picked the biggest bunch for you. (*She gives it to him.*)

ADAM: Thank you, children.

1ST BOY (*Noticing sausages on table*): Look! What delicious-looking sausages!

MOLLY: Would you like to have some? You children must be hungry after your long walk in the woods.

2ND BOY: Oh, we are, ma'am.

MOLLY: Then go and wash your hands at the well. I'll put the sausages on to fry, and we'll all have a feast. (*Children exit, chattering excitedly.* MOLLY *sets large skillet on fire, and* ADAM *drops sausages into it. Then he puts his arm around* MOLLY's *waist, and they dance a polka.*)

ADAM *and* MOLLY (*Singing, to the tune of "There Was A Jolly Miller Once"*):
We'll not complain about our lot,
   Heigho, heigho, heigho!

We're satisfied with what we've got,
   Heigho, heigho, heigho!
We don't need fairies' help a bit,
   Heigho, heigho, heigho!
We'll wish and then we'll work for it,
   Heigho, heigho, heigho!
(*Children return in time to join in singing the last verse, skipping about kitchen.*)
ALL (*Singing together*):
   We don't need fairies' help a bit,
      Heigho, heigho, heigho!
   We'll wish and then we'll work for it,
      Heigho, heigho, heigho!
   (*Curtain*)

THE END

The Saucy Scarecrow

An original fairy tale

Characters

FARMER BARLEY

MAGGIE, *his daughter*

LORD FOPPINGTON SCARECROW

RAG

TAG $\Big\}$ *three witches*

BOBTAIL

WITCH-BOY

SLEEPY WITCH

COOK-WITCH

WITCH WANT-ALL

OTHER WITCHES

CROW

MAGPIE

JAY

OTHER BIRDS

BESS, *the milkmaid*

TIME: *Halloween.*

SETTING: *Farmer Barley's barley field. A fence, with a wide center gate, runs across the stage and separates the field, which is upstage, from road, which is downstage. Outside the gate is a rustic bench. There is a wooden support in field for the Scarecrow.*

AT RISE: FARMER BARLEY *and* MAGGIE *are putting finishing touches on* SCARECROW, *who stands with outstretched arms resting on his support.* FARMER BARLEY *brushes* SCARECROW's *coat with a whisk broom, and* MAGGIE *fluffs out the bows of a Windsor tie.*

FARMER BARLEY (*Standing back to admire his handiwork*):

Maggie, I do believe this is the handsomest scarecrow I've ever made!

MAGGIE (*Enthusiastically*): Oh, he is, Pa, he is! You couldn't tell him from a real man.

FARMER BARLEY: And why not? He's wearing Great-grand-father's Sunday coat and a pair of my breeches. Your Ma starched his shirt. Why wouldn't he look like a real man?

MAGGIE: He'd be as proper as a minister, if he had a hat.

FARMER BARLEY: Yes, he should have a hat, but I couldn't find a spare one anywhere.

MAGGIE: How about mine? (*She takes off her sailor hat.*) He can have this. I'm sick and tired of it.

FARMER BARLEY (*Putting it on* SCARECROW): Well, it's not exactly a man's hat, but it will have to do. There! Now, give him a name, Maggie. He's your scarecrow, you know.

MAGGIE (*Delighted*): *Is* he, Pa?

FARMER BARLEY: He's standing in your very own barley field, isn't he? That makes him yours.

MAGGIE (*Hugging her father*): Oh, thank you, Pa! He's such a dandy, I think I'll call him Lord Foppington— Lord Foppington Scarecrow. (*She curtsies to him.*)

FARMER BARLEY (*Teasing her*): I hope that grand name won't put ideas into his head.

MAGGIE: Ideas? Like what?

FARMER BARLEY: Like feeling too uppity to drive away the crows and jays and magpies.

MAGGIE: Oh, I've made sure he'll do that.

FARMER BARLEY: You have? How?

MAGGIE: Look here! (*She takes a wooden clacker out of her pocket and gives it a twirl.*) I'll bet every bad bird in Christendom will fly away when they hear this!

FARMER BARLEY: Why, Maggie, it's just the thing! Give it here, and I'll put it in his hand. (*He closes* SCARECROW's *fingers around the handle of the clacker and rotates his wrist.*) Now he knows how to use it. (*He looks up at sky.*) We'd better be getting home, Maggie. It will be dark before long, and tonight's Halloween. (*In a whisper, with pretended fright*) There'll be witches about, and we don't want to be carried off on a broomstick.

MAGGIE (*Giggling*): Oh, Pa, how you talk! I'd *love* to have a ride on a broomstick behind a howling witch. (*She follows her father through the gate and closes it.*) Good night, Lord Foppington. Don't let the witches get you!

FARMER BARLEY: I've no doubt they'll fall head over heels in love with him. (FARMER BARLEY *and* MAGGIE *exit left on the road, laughing together. The music of the Birds' Dance is heard, and* CROW, MAGPIE, JAY, *and* OTHER BIRDS *hop onstage right and left. They perform a dance-pantomime in which they tease and rail at* SCARECROW, *who makes no movement or sound. As dance goes on, the lights gradually change from daylight to dusk to moonlight. Suddenly,* CROW *holds up his wings for silence.*)

CROW: Caw! Stop! Listen! (*In the distance, there is a sound of weird laughter and outcries, and* BIRDS *huddle together.*)

BIRDS: Witches! Witches! Witches all around! Witches everywhere! (*They glance fearfully overhead and right and left, then out front as if witches were flying over the audience. They chant the following verses in an eerie, ominous whisper.*)
Witches on pickets,
    And Witches on posts,
Witches alive,
    And dead Witches' ghosts!
Fly away, fly away,
    Fly away fast!
If we stay here,

We shall soon breathe our last! (*The* BIRDS *swoop off-stage except* CROW, JAY, *and* MAGPIE.)

JAY (*Rooted to the spot in terror*): Oh, dear! (*He looks back over his shoulder.*)

CROW: Never look back, Jaybird, if you're afraid. Always look straight in front of you.

JAY (*Facing front and staring out over audience*): They're coming, I can see them! All the witches in the world are coming, riding on broomsticks and whizzing through the air! Oh, dear, what shall I do? (*His legs begin to wobble.*)

MAGPIE: Only a silver bullet can catch a witch, they say.

JAY: Help me, Magpie. I'm awfully scared. I couldn't move, even if I tried. (*His legs collapse under him.*)

MAGPIE (*Raising him to his feet with the help of* CROW): There's only one way to deal with witches, and that's to *scare* 'em.

JAY: S-s-scare *them?*

MAGPIE: Yep, face 'em and scare 'em good.

JAY: Oh, I c-c-couldn't d-d-do that! Here they come! (*The screeching of* WITCHES *is very close now.* CROW *and* MAGPIE *drag* JAY *offstage in a hurry.* WITCHES *enter down aisles of the auditorium, each one mounted on a broomstick, a caldron hanging from each. They are screaming and galloping at top speed.* RAG, TAG *and* BOBTAIL *are in the lead.* RAG, *as her name implies, is dressed in rags.* TAG's *costume is covered with tags, and* BOBTAIL *has a long pony tail hanging from the peak of her hat. When all the* WITCHES *have reached the stage,* RAG, TAG *and* BOBTAIL *give a signal, and the* WITCHES *jump off their broomsticks.*)

ALL (*Singing to tune of "Ki-yi-yi-yi"*):
Ki-yi-yi-yi, Ki-yi-yi-yi!
Work, work! Evil do!
Ki-yi-yi-yi, Ki-yi-yi-yi!
Work, work! Mischief brew! (WITCHES *lift their cal-*

drons from their broomsticks and, setting them down in various places about the stage, they begin to stir with large ladles. WITCH-BOY *has a wire carrier filled with bottles. He sits on bench and assumes "thinking" pose, with a mean expression on his face.* RAG *discovers* SCARECROW.)

RAG (*Beckoning to* TAG *and* BOBTAIL): Come here, sisters! Lookee, a scarecrow! A bloomin' scarecrow!

TAG (*Mockingly to* BOBTAIL): Ho, sister Bobtail, is this the *man* you said was spying on us? We needn't waste our spells on punishing *him!*

BOBTAIL: Well, what if I did take him for a man? He's elegant enough to *be* one.

RAG: Bah! He's like all scarecrows, stiff and stupid-looking.

BOBTAIL: He is *not!* He's very handsome, and I'm going to kiss him! (*She puts her arms around* SCARECROW *and gives him a loud smack on his cheek.*)

TAG (*Tauntingly*): Aha! Now we know all about it, don't we, sister Rag?

RAG: Indeed we do, sister Tag! Bobtail's in love with a scarecrow!

BOBTAIL (*Crossly*): Oh, be quiet!

TAG: Why don't you carry him off on your broomstick?

RAG: Let him be your partner in the dance! (*She makes a magical sign with her hands.*) I will give him life!

TAG (*Making another sign*): I will give him breath!

BOBTAIL (*Making the most elaborate sign of all*): And I will give him a heart as long as it is mine!

RAG: I will give him sight!

TAG: I will give him speech!

BOBTAIL: And I will give him thought as long as he thinks of me!

RAG: Take care! You go too far.

BOBTAIL: Oh, pooh! (*In the meantime, a change has been*

taking place in SCARECROW *as each* WITCH *intones her charm. First,* SCARECROW *shudders violently; then he begins to breathe hard and move his limbs and blink his eyes. He opens his mouth several times and finally speaks.*)

SCARECROW: What are you going to do with me?

RAG (*Jeering at him*): Eat you!

SCARECROW (*Boldly*): If you eat me, Farmer Barley will come after you with a big stick.

RAG (*Licking her lips*): Farmer Barley will never know.

BOBTAIL: Oh, leave him alone! (*She seizes his hands.*) Come with me, Scarecrow. I want to show you off to the others. (*She leads him through the gate into the road.*)

SCARECROW (*Looking about at the* WITCHES *bent over their caldrons*): What are they making?

BOBTAIL (*Slyly*): Different things.

SCARECROW (*Stopping beside* SLEEPY WITCH *who is stirring slowly with half-shut eyes*): What are *you* making?

SLEEPY WITCH (*Yawning*): I make bad dreams in this pot. I stir all day and all night, but I still can't turn them out fast enough. (*She drowses off and wakes up immediately from a bad dream.*) Oh, oh, oh! (SCARECROW's *attention is attracted by the strange behavior of the* WITCH-BOY. *Every few seconds,* WITCH-BOY *breaks out of his "thinking" pose as if to pluck something out of the air and put it inside a bottle, carefully corking it up again.* SCARECROW *leans over bottles to examine them and puts out his hand as if to lift one up.* WITCH-BOY *raps him sharply on the knuckles.*)

SCARECROW: Ow!

WITCH-BOY: Don't touch!

SCARECROW (*Sucking his knuckles*): I just wanted to see what you're putting inside the bottles.

WITCH-BOY (*Scowling*): Nobody's allowed to touch these bottles but me. Now, go away!

SCARECROW: But what *is* inside?

WITCH-BOY: None of your business!

BOBTAIL (*Ominously*): Tell him, Witch-Boy.

WITCH-BOY: I think up naughty things to do, and each time I have a naughty idea, I put it in a bottle.

SCARECROW (*Puzzled*): Don't you put in *good* ideas as well?

WITCH-BOY: Don't have any good ideas. If I had, I wouldn't be a Witch-Boy. Now, *will* you stop pestering me and let me *think?*

BOBTAIL: Come along, Scarecrow, he's in a vile temper tonight.

SCARECROW: May I see what that Witch over there is doing? (*He goes to* COOK-WITCH *who is stirring her caldron.*) Mm-m-m, it smells good. I'm awfully hungry.

COOK-WITCH (*Lifting up her ladle*): Have a bite of stew.

SCARECROW: Oh, thank you. (*He takes ladle, then nibbles stew.*)

COOK-WITCH: Bigger bites! You can't taste it properly like that.

BOBTAIL (*With a crafty smile*): I shouldn't if I were you. (SCARECROW *takes a big mouthful and chokes.*) I told you so. She makes all the nasty tastes, and she's always trying out a new recipe on someone. (*Suddenly* RAG *and* TAG *stop stirring their caldrons and jump into the air.*)

RAG *and* TAG (*Singing to the tune of "Ki-yi-yi-yi" as before*):

Ki-yi-yi-yi, Ki-yi-yi-yi!
Dance, dance! Work is done!
Ki-yi-yi-yi, Ki-yi-yi-yi!
Dance, dance! Let's have fun! (*All* WITCHES *join in the song, leaping about with screams of joy.*)

BOBTAIL (*Seizing* SCARECROW *and seating him behind her on her broomstick*): Hold on tight and don't let go! (*Before he realizes what is happening,* SCARECROW *is off on a mad ride astride her broomstick.* SCARECROW *clutches stick.*)

SCARECROW (*Frightened, as* WITCHES *dash around*): Oh, please slow down! Not so fast! Let me off! (*They stop suddenly, and* BOBTAIL *tips up her end of broomstick like a seesaw.* SCARECROW *slips off his end and lands in the road with a bump. As he manages to get to his feet,* BOBTAIL *catches him around the waist and whirls him about in a wild dance. Sometimes she brushes him from behind with her broom to make him step livelier.* SCARECROW *giggles.*) Oh, stop it, you're tickling me! (*He really is enjoying himself by now.*) Oh, I *like* this! This is fun! Please, *please* may I stay?

BOBTAIL: Stay? Why, of course, stay as long as you wish. (*Other* WITCHES *gradually quiet down and listen attentively.*)

SCARECROW: No, I mean may I stay as I *am*, and not go back to what I was.

BOBTAIL: Oh! (*Evasively.*) Well, you just be a good scarecrow and amuse me, and then maybe we'll see about it.

SCARECROW (*Pleading*): But couldn't you tell me now? I want to know *now!*

WITCH WANT-ALL (*Coming forward and speaking to* SCARECROW): What's the matter, lovey? Won't she make you a promise? (*She clicks her tongue disapprovingly.*) And after all the fine dancing she has had with you! Tsk, tsk, what a shame! Well, you just come along with me, ducky, and I'll not haggle over a promise.

BOBTAIL (*Giving her a hard push*): Get away, Witch Want-All! I know you! The scarecrow is mine! I made him, and he's no concern of yours!

WITCH WANT-ALL: And what if you did make him? If you gave him any wits, he'll come with me. (*She grabs* SCARECROW's *arm and pulls him toward her.*)

BOBTAIL (*Pulling back on* SCARECROW's *other arm*): Don't

go with her! You'll get nothing from that old bag of bones!

WITCH WANT-ALL: He will! I'll give him his wish.

BOBTAIL: And so shall I!

WITCH WANT-ALL: But *I* will give him *more!* I will give him—a *conscience!* (*All* WITCHES *howl with glee.*)

SCARECROW: What's a conscience?

BOBTAIL (*Angrily*): It's a terrible thing! Don't have anything to do with it!

SCARECROW (*Persisting*): But I want to know! What *is* a conscience?

WITCH WANT-ALL (*Maliciously*): I'll give you one, lovey, and then you'll find out.

BOBTAIL: No, no! (WITCHES *cringe as* WITCH WANT-ALL *points to* SCARECROW *and taps him on forehead.*)

WITCH WANT-ALL (*Chanting*):
Prick of conscience,
    Stick in there,
Quickly drive out
    Devil-May-Care! (*She turns in triumph to* BOBTAIL.)
Now he is lost to you forever! (*With a diabolical laugh, she mounts her broomstick and rides away.*)

WITCHES (*Singing to the tune of "Api-kai-i"*):
Hie, hie, hie away!
    Broomstick, fly to Hellstone Quarry!
Hark, hark, the cock crows once,
    Giddy-up, broomstick, do not tarry! (*All, except* BOBTAIL, *mount their broomsticks and gallop offstage, down through the audience.*)

BOBTAIL: Goodbye, Scarecrow!

SCARECROW: Where are you going?

BOBTAIL (*Singing to the same tune*):
Broomstick, hie away!
    Fly to Devil's Peak away!

Hark, hark, the cock crows twice,
Giddy-up, broomstick, do not stay!

SCARECROW: You're not going to leave me behind, are you?

BOBTAIL: Of course I am. You're no use to me now. You have a conscience.

SCARECROW (*Forlorn*): But what shall I do?

BOBTAIL: Suit yourself. It was you who wanted it this way. (*She hops around on her broomstick and sings.*)
Hie, hie, hie away!
Broomstick, fly to Witches' Cave!
If three times the cock crows,
I'll be lying in my grave! (*Kicking her heels and beating the broomstick with her hands, she swoops down the aisle and exits at back of auditorium. When she is gone, lights dim to indicate passage of time, then come up again.* SCARECROW *sits disconsolately on the bench.*)

SCARECROW: I'm hungry and cold and lonely. (*He hears someone whistling a merry tune and sees* BESS, *the milkmaid, entering the barley field at the extreme end. She clumps across field in her heavy boots, whistling and swinging her pails. When she reaches the place where* SCARECROW *ordinarily would be standing, she notices the empty support.*)

BESS (*Surprised*): That's funny! I thought Farmer Barley put up a scarecrow here yesterday. (*She shrugs her shoulders and walks through gate, into road.* SCARECROW *confronts her angrily.*)

SCARECROW: Here, what are you doing, walking where you shouldn't?

BESS (*Startled*): Wh-what?

SCARECROW: You're trampling down the barley with your big boots.

BESS: Who—who are you? (*She stares at him, then over*

her shoulder at the empty support in the field and back again at SCARECROW.) Why, you're Farmer Barley's scarecrow! (*Terrified*)

SCARECROW: That's right!

BESS: I didn't know scarecrows were ever *alive!*

SCARECROW: Well, you know now, and the sooner you get out of that field, the better. Be off with you!

BESS (*Dropping her milk pails in fright*): Oh, oh! (*She runs along the road to left, screaming.*) Farmer Barley! Maggie! Help, help! (*She exits.*)

SCARECROW (*To himself*): She has gone off without her milk pails! Such a muddlehead! Just look at that barley where she stomped through it, all bent over and broken. (*Sadly*) And the witches' dance last night didn't help it, either. I'll get my clacker and drive away anything that dares to come here again. (*He goes through gate into field, walking carefully as he searches for clacker.* BESS *returns with* FARMER BARLEY *and* MAGGIE.)

MAGGIE: There's nobody here but Lord Foppington.

BESS: Lord Foppington?

MAGGIE: My scarecrow there.

BESS: Yes, but he's *alive!*

MAGGIE: Well, what if he is? (*She speaks as if it were the most natural thing in the world for a scarecrow to be alive.*) Come here, Lord Foppington. (*He comes to gate.*) I thought maybe the witches got you last night.

SCARECROW: They did, Maggie, they did!

MAGGIE: Poor Lord Foppington! Were you scared?

SCARECROW: A little at first, but then we danced, and that was fun! (*Ashamed*) Only we danced on the barley and squashed it. It won't happen again, though, because now I have a conscience.

MAGGIE: A conscience? However did you get it?

SCARECROW: One of the witches gave it to me.

FARMER BARLEY (*Chuckling*): Well, well, if that isn't the

strangest thing! A scarecrow with a conscience! That means I'll have to pay you wages. What'll it be?

SCARECROW: A cup of buttermilk, if you please. I am thirsty, and there's nothing to drink.

FARMER BARLEY: Buttermilk, eh? You shall have a gallon of it, and some bread and cheese besides. Bess, see to it!

BESS (*Snatching up her pails*): Yes, master! Right away, master! (*She runs down the road.*)

SCARECROW (*Calling after her*): Mind you stay out of the barley and keep to the road!

FARMER BARLEY (*With a hearty laugh*): You really mean business, don't you?

SCARECROW (*Earnestly*): I tell you, Farmer Barley, I'll guard Maggie's field with my life! There won't be a single grain of barley missing, you'll see. Now, I'd better get back to my post. Those thieving birds will be here any minute, and I want to be ready for them. (*He takes his place in front of the support and twirls clacker.*)

MAGGIE (*Admiringly*): My, you look just like a king standing before his throne!

SCARECROW: A king, am I? (*He straightens his shoulders and swings clacker again.*) Well, I shall be a king who works for a living and be of some use in the world. It's a fine thing to have a conscience. Stand back! Here they come! (FARMER BARLEY *and* MAGGIE *step behind* SCARECROW, *as* CROW, MAGPIE, JAY *and* OTHER BIRDS *enter right and left cawing and chirping excitedly. When they reach gate,* SCARECROW *raises his arm, holds clacker aloft, and speaks in a commanding tone.*) Halt! (BIRDS *stop in astonishment.* SCARECROW *sings lustily to the tune of "April"*)

Fly away, you naughty birds,
  Shoo, shoo!
  Fly away, do,
Or Scarecrow will frighten

The wits out of you! (*He twirls clacker, and* BIRDS *flutter about in alarm.*)

CROW: That Scarecrow is more alive than he was yesterday. He's squeaking and squawking something terrible, and his eyes are looking all about him.

SCARECROW (*Continuing to sing and twirl clacker*):
Clicky-clack-clack, clicky-clack-clack, shoo!
    Fly away, crows!
This is not your barley,
    As everyone knows.
Clicky-clack-clack, clicky-clack-clack, shoo!
    Fly away, jays!
This barley is Maggie's,
    And right here it stays.
Clicky-clack-clack, fly away, magpies,
    You must not steal.
If you peck at this barley,
    'Twill be your last meal.

CROW: We can't settle for a minute, but that Scarecrow shouts at us. Let's go somewhere else. (BIRDS *take flight as* SCARECROW *sings last verse.*)

SCARECROW:
Clicky-clack-clack, clicky-clack-clack, shoo! Click-click-click-clack!
Fly away, you thieves and robbers,
    And never come back! (*As last* BIRD *disappears,* FARMER BARLEY *and* MAGGIE *congratulate* SCARECROW.)

MAGGIE: You are wonderful!

FARMER BARLEY (*Happily*): You're the best scarecrow I've ever seen.
(*Curtain*)

THE END

King Alfred and the Cakes

An old English folk tale

Characters

WILFRID, *a farmer*
INA, *his wife*
EDWIN, *13*
ETHELDRA, *12*
CUTHBERT, *10* } *their children*
ROWENA, *9*
KING ALFRED
CEDRIC
ULFSTAN } *Saxon noblemen*

TIME: *The ninth century.*
SETTING: *The kitchen of a Saxon farmhouse in Somerset, England. A fireplace is at right, and there is a cradle in front of it.*
AT RISE: INA *is sweeping coals from hearthstone back into fire.*

INA (*Calling off left*): Etheldra!
ETHELDRA (*From off left*): Yes, Mother?
INA (*Calling*): The hearthstone is hot. Bring the cakes. (*She stands broom in the chimney corner.* ETHELDRA *stumbles as she enters carrying the cakes on a board.*) Careful! Don't drop them! It's the last bit of flour in

the house. Heaven knows when we'll get any more. The Danes burned down the mill last month. Those heathen vandals! (*She takes board from* ETHELDRA *and slides cakes off of it onto hearthstone.*)

ETHELDRA: Why can't they stay in their own land and leave us in peace?

INA: Aye. Have you finished churning the butter?

ETHELDRA: Another few minutes should do it. (*As* ETHELDRA *exits left,* WILFRID *enters from upstage door, carrying a rake and a hoe, which he leans against back wall.*)

WILFRID: Good even, wife. Are the young ones home yet?

INA: No, Wilfrid. They are still out rounding up the pigs.

WILFRID (*Closing door*): There's a fog rolling up from the marshes.

INA (*Dismayed*): Fog! The children will lose their way.

WILFRID: Don't worry, Ina. Cuthbert and Rowena could find their way home blindfolded.

INA: But what if the pigs take a wrong path in the forest or wander into the marshes? We shall never get them back. (*She opens upstage door and looks out.*) I can't see beyond the barn, the fog is so thick. You had better go and meet them. (*Lifting torch from bracket beside door*) Here, take this torch. I will light it for you.

WILFRID: I don't need a torch, wife. (*He replaces it in bracket.*) There is still enough daylight to see by.

INA: They have never been as late as this. They are lost, I'm sure.

WILFRID: Nonsense! Cuthbert has a good sense of direction. So has Rowena. They'll get home safely, never fear, and all the pigs, too.

INA (*Clutching his arm*): Oh, Wilfrid, do you think the Danes—?

WILFRID: Calm yourself, Ina. There are no Danes within fifty miles of here.

INA: Sh-h-h! I hear someone running.

WILFRID: It's Rowena, I expect. She always runs on ahead. (*Standing at door*) Yes, here she comes. (ROWENA *runs in.*) You are late, my child. Is everything all right?

ROWENA: Yes, Father, but the pigs gave us some trouble on the forest path.

INA: There, I knew it! Did you lose any of them? (*She helps* ROWENA *remove her cloak.*)

ROWENA: No, Mother, not one, thanks to our new friend.

INA: Your new friend?

ROWENA (*Hanging up her cloak*): He is helping Cuthbert put the pigs in the pen.

WILFRID: But who is he, my dear?

ROWENA: I don't really know. We met him in the forest, and he stopped the pigs from running away. We should never have caught them if he had not been there.

INA: He is a stranger, then?

ROWENA: Yes. I have never seen him before.

INA (*Suspiciously*): He's not a Dane, is he? (CUTHBERT *enters with* KING ALFRED, *who wears a hooded cape over a minstrel's costume. He has a small harp strapped on his back, and he carries a sack.*)

CUTHBERT: Father, here is our new friend. (ETHELDRA *enters left and watches from side.*)

WILFRID: Welcome to my house, minstrel.

ALFRED: Thank you, good sir.

WILFRID: Rowena has been telling us how you saved our pigs.

ALFRED: I am very glad that I was able to help. (*He goes over to hang up his cloak beside* ROWENA'S, *as* INA *talks aside with* CUTHBERT *and* ROWENA. ALFRED *stands with his back to others so they cannot see him. He takes off crown, which has been hidden beneath his hood, and puts it into his sack. He hangs up cloak, places sack beneath it, and then turns to others.*)

ROWENA: Mother thinks you might be one of the wicked Danes. You are not, are you?

ALFRED: No, I am a true Englishman.

CUTHBERT (*Boasting*): *I* knew he was an Englishman right away.

ALFRED (*Smiling*): You did? How?

CUTHBERT: By the way you speak. You talk the same way we do.

ALFRED: That is so, lad, but your mother has every reason to be suspicious of strangers these days. (*He turns to* INA.) If you wish me to be on my way, madam, I shall leave.

WILFRID: Certainly not. You will stay and share our supper and spend the night here. Let me introduce my family. My good wife, Ina—my elder daughter, Etheldra. (*He gestures to them, and they nod and smile.*) Rowena and Cuthbert you already know, and my eldest son, Edwin, is driving the cows down from pasture and will be in shortly. And over here (*Going to cradle*)—here is the best-natured member of the family—he sleeps all the time. Baby Alfred, named for our brave and beloved king. God grant that when he is our age, minstrel, England will be free of all her enemies and united in peace.

ALFRED: Our age? It will be sooner than that, sir, much sooner than that.

INA: Come, Rowena, Etheldra—we must get supper ready. Cuthbert, sit by the hearth and keep an eye on those cakes. Don't let them burn. (*She exits left with girls.*)

WILFRID: Come, minstrel, sit down by the fire and warm yourself. (ALFRED *sits on bench, and* CUTHBERT *sits on a low stool nearby.*)

CUTHBERT (*To* ALFRED): Have you ever seen the Danes?

ALFRED: Yes, my boy, I have seen them many times.

CUTHBERT: Is it true that their warships look like dragons?

ALFRED: Yes, it's true, and the whole army of the Danes is like one mighty dragon, spreading fire and destruction over the land. Yet I know that with God's help, King Alfred will slay this dragon.

WILFRID (*Doubtfully*): Does the King have men enough to do this?

ALFRED: He will have enough when the time comes. England will rise again, you'll see.

CUTHBERT: Have you ever been in a battle?

ALFRED: I have been in every battle of the last eight years, and even though the Danes drove us from the field time after time, still we were not defeated.

CUTHBERT: Not defeated?

ALFRED: Listen to me, Cuthbert. To be defeated means not to return. We have always returned. And we will return again and again, until the enemy is conquered.

CUTHBERT (*Admiringly*): That takes courage!

ALFRED: The King's men *have* courage, but they have something more, too. They have hope. (INA *and* ROWENA *enter, carrying plates. They start to set table.*)

WILFRID: It cheers me to hear you so confident, minstrel. Stay with us as long as you will, and rest from your long journeys and fighting.

INA: And what, pray, can he do to pay for all this?

ALFRED (*Rising*): Why, I can do odd jobs about the house, madam, and I can play on my harp in the evenings.

INA: Hm, if you had said you could plow and plant, it would have been better. (*Outside door is flung open, and* EDWIN *rushes in.*)

EDWIN: Father, the bull calf is mired down in the bog. I need help to pull him out.

WILFRID: Right away, Edwin. (EDWIN *exits.*) Cuthbert, get the heavy rope in the barn and come with us. Rowena, bring a torch. (ROWENA *gets torch and pretends to light it at fire.* NOTE: *A flashlight may be concealed inside torch.* ROWENA *hurries out after* WILFRID *and* CUTHBERT *as* ETHELDRA *enters left.*)

ALFRED (*Starting toward the door*): Perhaps I could help them.

INA: You can help me. Do you know how to milk a cow?

ALFRED: No, I—I've never tried.

INA: Humph! Well, Etheldra, we shall have to do it ourselves. There's no telling how long your father and the boys will be. (ETHELDRA *exits.*)

ALFRED: Surely there is *something* I can do.

INA: You can mind the baby and tend to the cakes. The baby will be no trouble at all—he's asleep. But the cakes need constant watching. They are already done on one side. Here (*Thrusting a spatula into his hand*)— turn them! (*He does so awkwardly, dropping a cake on the floor.*) No, no, not like that! Don't you know how to do *anything*? (*She snatches the spatula from him and turns over the cakes.*) Now see to it they don't burn.

ALFRED (*Humbly*): Yes, madam. (ETHELDRA *enters, carrying two milking pails. She gives one to her mother.*)

ETHELDRA: Here's your milking pail, Mother. (*Exits*)

INA: Now, mind! *Don't burn the cakes!* (*She goes out, closing the door behind her.* ALFRED *sits and stares fixedly at cakes for a while, then he goes to cradle and peeks at baby, smiling tenderly. He begins to pace back and forth, deep in thought. Baby makes a sound, and* ALFRED *stops beside the cradle.*)

ALFRED: So, Alfred, my namesake, you have decided to wake up and say hello to your king. (*The baby coos.*) Shall I sing you wide-awake? (*He unstraps harp from his back, puts one foot up on a bench, rests the harp on his knee, and starts to play and sing an old English folksong. At the end of the song,* ALFRED *looks into the cradle.*) Bless him, he has gone back to sleep again. Well, sleep on, baby Alfred. The night, which brings darkness to our land, will bring no darkness to your life, I promise you. I will give you years of peace. I want to build schools and fine towns instead of warships and fortresses. I want to teach my people to read, not to fight and kill. I look forward to the day when all free-born Englishmen will be able to read and write. Do you hear that, farmer's son? You shall read and write. I, King Alfred, will see to it that you do. (*He strums on his harp and speaks, in rhythm to the music.*)

> Read and write,
> Read and write,
> Farmers' sons
> Shall read and write.
> Millers' daughters,
> Butchers' wives,
> Learning lessons
> All their lives.

> Write and read,
> Write and read,
> All my court
> Shall write and read.
> Even I, the King,
> Has need
> To go to school
> And write and read.

(*Suddenly, outside door opens, and* INA *stands there, sniffing.*)

INA: I thought so! The cakes are burning! I could smell them way out in the barn! Have you no nose at all that *you* could not smell them? Idiot! (*She boxes* AL-FRED'S *ears, then turns to cakes on hearth.*) Burnt to a cinder, every one! And no more flour to make new cakes! Oh, what a dolt! (WILFRID *enters, followed by* ROWENA, CUTHBERT *and* EDWIN.)

WILFRID: What is the matter now, wife?

INA: Matter enough! This lout has burned the cakes. Of all the stupid fellows who ever came to this farm, he is the worst.

CUTHBERT (*Springing to* ALFRED's *defense*): He can manage the pigs well.

ROWENA: Better than anyone—you ought to see him.

ALFRED (*Apologizing to* INA): I'm sorry about the cakes, madam. I never learned how to cook. It was all done for me.

INA: Yes, and everything else was done for you, too, I'll warrant. You are no use in the world for lending a hand to poor working folk.

WILFRID (*Trying to calm her*): Now, now, Ina. (ETHELDRA *runs in, out of breath.*)

ETHELDRA: Father, there is a band of soldiers riding up the hill.

WILFRID: Soldiers? Are they coming here? (*He looks out the door.*)

ROWENA: Are they Danes?

WILFRID: I pray not. Stay here, all of you. I will go out to meet them.

EDWIN: I will go with you, Father. (EDWIN *and* WILFRID *exit.*)

INA (*Hurrying to the door*): Edwin, come back!

ETHELDRA (*Putting her arm around* INA): Don't worry, Mother. Edwin is safe with Father.

INA: Why should soldiers bother us? We have done no wrong.

ETHELDRA: They may have lost their way.

CUTHBERT: Here come Father and Edwin, and two of the men are with them.

EDWIN (*Running in*): It's all right, they are Saxon soldiers, looking for someone. (WILFRID *enters, followed by* CEDRIC *and* ULFSTAN.)

WILFRID (*Pointing to* ALFRED): There is the man. (*The two noblemen drop down on one knee before* ALFRED.)

ALFRED: No, no, my good Cedric and Ulfstan, do not kneel. You kneel to God, not to me. If you would serve me, serve me on your feet. (*The noblemen rise.*)

CEDRIC: My lord, we have found you at last!

ALFRED: Do you bring good news? Come over here and tell me. (ALFRED *and* CEDRIC *sit on the bench and talk in low tones.* ULFSTAN *stands apart.*)

INA (*In a stage whisper, to* ULFSTAN): Who is he?

ULFSTAN: Who *is* he? Do you mean to say you don't know who he is?

CUTHBERT: He helped us bring home the pigs.

ULFSTAN: The pigs! He? The *King?*

INA (*Gasping*): The King!

ULFSTAN: Yes, woman, King Alfred of Wessex.

INA: Mercy on me! Oh, dear! Oh, dear! I have scolded him up hill and down dale, because he let the cakes burn. What *shall* I do?

EDWIN: Sh-h-h! He's looking at us. (ALFRED *rises from the bench.*)

INA (*To others*): Kneel to him.

ALFRED: No, my friends. While I am in your home, I am still Alfred the minstrel, not Alfred the King.

INA: Will you ever forgive me for being so hasty?

ALFRED: There is nothing to forgive, my good woman. I deserved to have my ears boxed for letting the cakes burn. (*Turning to* WILFRID) Wilfrid, these lands you farm—you make payment each year to the lord who owns them, do you not?

WILFRID: Aye, Your Majesty. That I do.

ALFRED: Then you shall do so no more. I hereby give you these lands, and they shall belong to you and your heirs forever.

WILFRID: My gracious lord, that is the dream of my life.

ALFRED: Now I must leave you. We have a chance to strike against the Danes and we must not delay.

WILFRID: Let me come with you, my lord. Edwin will take care of the farm. (*To* INA) You can manage, can't you, wife?

INA (*Bringing* WILFRID *his spear*): Go, with my blessing. (WILFRID *exits, followed by* INA, EDWIN *and* ETHELDRA.)

CEDRIC (*To* ULFSTAN): Get the horses ready, Ulfstan. (ULFSTAN *exits.*)

CUTHBERT: May I ride on a horse to the bottom of the hill?

CEDRIC: You may ride with me, lad. Come along. (*They exit.* ALFRED *takes his cloak and picks up sack holding his crown. He puts crown on, goes to cradle and smiles down at the sleeping baby.*)

ALFRED: Goodbye, Alfred, my namesake. I shall keep my promise to you.

ROWENA: What promise?

ALFRED: Your brother will tell you himself when he is older.

ROWENA: I wish I were a man! Then I could go with you to fight the Danes.

ALFRED: You have a much harder job to do, Rowena. You have to stay at home and carry on with all the ordinary, everyday work about the farm. That is harder than fighting. And I know you will do it better than I could.

ROWENA: Better than you, my lord?

ALFRED: Yes, my dear. *You* won't burn the cakes! (*They laugh. He takes her hand, and they walk out the door together, as the curtain falls.*)

THE END

The Apple of Contentment

by Howard Pyle

Characters

MANIKIN REDCAP	TREE OF CONTENTMENT
DAME TINNEY	KING
CHRISTINE ⎤	PAGE
WILLA ⎬ her daughters	HERALD
NILLA ⎦	

TIME: *Early autumn.*

SETTING: *A meadow near the home of Dame Tinney.*

AT RISE: MANIKIN REDCAP *stands beside large rock at right, fishing. He is singing merrily to the tune of "Skip to My Lou."* TREE OF CONTENTMENT *is crouched left of rock, covered with brown hooded cloak and facing upstage.*

MANIKIN:
Fish for a minnow, fish for a whale;
Fish for a trout and fish for a snail;
Catch little fishes by the tail—
    Fishing is fun on Friday.
(*Suddenly his pole starts jiggling.*) Whee! I have a bite!
(*He braces himself against rock.*) It must be an awfully big fish. It's pulling hard. (*He tugs on the pole and lifts up an old boot, which is hooked to the end of his*

153

line.) An old boot! Dearie me, what a pity it's not a fish. (*He unhooks the boot and then sits down again and resumes fishing. His pole begins to jiggle*.) It must be a fish, this time—but I will just make sure. (*As he bends over the water to get a closer look, his cap tumbles into the water*.) Oh, there goes my cap! I need my cap! (*He reaches down into the water for his cap, and finally hooks it with his fishing pole. He stands and continues singing, acting out the words*.)

Pull up the cap and wring it out;
Squeeze it hard and twirl it about;
(*He skips to a bush where he hangs cap*.)
Hang it on a bush to dry it out.
    Dry out the cap on Friday.
Back to my fishing, one, two, three!
(*He skips back to the rock*.)
Haven't caught a fish yet, dearie me!
(*He picks up his pole*.)
Should have a fish to eat for tea.
    Fishing is fun on Friday.

(*He is about to cast his line into the water, when he sees* CHRISTINE, *who has entered right, carrying a basket containing bird feed*.) Who's that? I'd better hide. (*He puts down his pole and hides behind the rock*.)

CHRISTINE (*Singing*):
Goosey, goosey, gander,
Whither shall I wander?
Upstairs and downstairs
And in my lady's chamber—

WILLA (*From offstage, crossly*): Christine!
NILLA (*From offstage, crossly*): Christine! (WILLA *and* NILLA *enter*.)
WILLA (*Running to* CHRISTINE): Come back!
NILLA (*Following* WILLA): Why did you come here?
WILLA: You lazy good-for-nothing!

NILLA: What do you mean by going off and leaving us to wait on ourselves?

CHRISTINE: I am sorry, sisters. I have to feed the geese.

WILLA (*Angrily*): Feed the *geese!* You neglect *us* to wait on the *geese?* Buckle my shoes!

NILLA (*Turning her back to* CHRISTINE): Hook up my dress!

WILLA (*Waving a comb*): Comb my hair!

NILLA (*Waving a hair ribbon*): Tie my ribbon! (DAME TINNEY *enters.*)

DAME TINNEY (*Scolding*): Willa! Nilla! Don't yell! You must *not* yell! You will ruin your voices. Speak sweetly —as I do. (*With affected sweetness.*) You must try to be like me, my dears. (*Holds hands together and smiles sweetly.*)

WILLA *and* NILLA: But we *are* like you, Mama. (*They imitate* DAME TINNEY)

DAME TINNEY: Yes, yes, I know. Now come back to the house and finish dressing. Someone might see you.

NILLA (*Pouting*): We can't dress by ourselves, Mama.

DAME TINNEY: I will help you. (*She turns to* CHRISTINE *and speaks harshly to her.*) Christine, go and feed the geese. After you have done that, you will make the beds and wash the linen, scrub the floors and scour the pots and pans. Do you have that straight?

CHRISTINE: Yes, Mother.

DAME TINNEY: Come, girls. (DAME TINNEY, WILLA *and* NILLA *exit.* CHRISTINE *scatters a handful of seed behind bushes.*)

CHRISTINE: Here, darlings, here is pay for your pretty songs. Now, greedy, greedy, let the little ones have their breakfast. (*Puts down basket, reaches between shrubs and gently picks up gosling.* Little ones, eat all you want. (*Cradles the gosling in her arm and strokes its head.*) You mustn't eat too much, dear. (MANIKIN's *red stocking cap catches her eye.*) Oh, what a pretty red cap! (*She shakes its bell.*) I wonder where it came from. (*Puts down gosling, lifts the cap off the bush.*) Why, it's all wet! How strange! Well, I will just take it along with me and dry it out. (*Turns to leave.*)

MANIKIN (*Calling softly*): Christine! (*She glances about, trying to locate the voice.*) Over here, Christine. (*He steps out from behind the rock.*)

CHRISTINE (*Staring at* MANIKIN): Oh! What do you want?

MANIKIN (*Going to her*): I only want what is mine. (*He points to the cap.*)

CHRISTINE: Is this your cap?

MANIKIN: It is—and I can't go back home to the hills without it.

CHRISTINE: How did it come to be hanging on this bush?

MANIKIN: I was fishing in the brook, and it fell into the water, so I hung it up to dry—that's all. Now, young lady, will you please give me my cap? (*He holds out his hand for it.*)

CHRISTINE (*Quickly putting the cap behind her back to tease him*): Perhaps I will and perhaps I won't. Maybe I will keep it. It's a very pretty cap. (*She turns sideways and plays with the bell*)

MANIKIN: It won't fit you. It will probably shrink.

CHRISTINE: It won't shrink if I put it on my head and wear it until it is dry. (*She puts it on.*) It will be just my size.

MANIKIN: No, no, take it off! You will stretch it all out of shape. (*Chasing her about the stage.*) Give it to me! I will chase you until you give it back.

CHRISTINE: Oh, all right, you can have it back. But you must give me something in exchange.

MANIKIN: I will give you five silver coins. (*He starts to untie his money pouch.*)

CHRISTINE: It's not money I want. I don't care much for money. What else do you have?

MANIKIN: What else? (*He pauses, then reaches into pouch again.*) This! (*Holds up a large black seed*)

CHRISTINE: What's that? A lump of *coal*?

MANIKIN: This is no lump of coal, Christine. This is a seed.

CHRISTINE: A seed? What kind of seed?

MANIKIN: A seed from the apple of contentment. Plant this seed on top of a rock and a tree will grow, and on the tree, an apple. Everybody who sees that apple will want it, but nobody can pick it except you, Christine. When you have picked it, another one will grow in its place. The tree will always feed you when you are hungry, and warm you when you are cold. You will be the happiest girl in the world because no one can have more than contentment, and that is what the apple will bring you. (*Puts the seed in* CHRISTINE's *hand.*) Now will you give me my cap?

CHRISTINE (*Contritely*): Oh, yes, here it is. I really wasn't going to keep it, you know. I was only teasing you.

MANIKIN (*Cheerfully*): I know it! I'm a great one myself for teasing. Goodbye! (*He puts on his cap and goes to the rock for his fishing pole, then turns and waves to* CHRISTINE.) Be sure you plant that seed on top of a rock. It will grow like lightning. (*He waves again and exits.* CHRISTINE *looks after him for a second and then looks at the seed.*)

CHRISTINE: He said to plant it on top of a rock. Here's a good one. (*She goes to the "rock" and pretends to plant the seed.*) There! Now I will go and feed the geese, and when I come back, maybe the tree will be growing. The little man said it would grow fast. (*She picks up her basket and exits left singing, "Goosey, Goosey, Gander."*

As her voice dies away, soft music is heard, and the TREE *stands, spreads arms like branches from which a golden apple is hanging. The music fades.* CHRISTINE *enters and stops short, and stares at* TREE.) I can't believe it! It's completely grown. And there is the apple of contentment, shining like pure gold. (*As she reaches up for apple,* TREE *lowers her branch.* CHRISTINE *picks the fruit and then watches as* TREE *takes another apple from her pocket, hangs it on the branch and raises branch above* CHRISTINE's *head*) It's just as the little Manikin said! Another apple grows as soon as one is picked. (*She bites into her apple.*) Mm-m-m. It tastes like pancakes with honey and milk. (DAME TINNEY, WILLA *and* NILLA *enter in single file, calling.*)

DAME TINNEY (*In low-pitched voice*): Christine!

WILLA (*In medium-pitched voice*): Christine!

NILLA (*In high-pitched voice*): Christine! (CHRISTINE *quickly hides behind a bush.* DAME TINNEY, WILLA *and* NILLA *stop at center stage.*)

DAME TINNEY: She's not here.

WILLA (*Looking offstage left*): She's not with the geese, either.

NILLA (*Pointing to* TREE): Mama, what's this tree? It wasn't here before, was it?

DAME TINNEY (*Going to the* TREE): I don't remember it.

NILLA (*Pointing*): There's an apple up there. (WILLA *and* DAME TINNEY *look at apple.*)

WILLA (*Reaching for it*): I want it!

NILLA (*Reaching for it*): I want it!

DAME TINNEY (*Reaching for it*): I want it!

NILLA: I saw it first!

WILLA: No, I did!

DAME TINNEY: No, I did!

NILLA: I am the youngest. It's mine!

WILLA: I am the eldest. It's mine!

DAME TINNEY: I am your mother. It's mine! (*Each one shakes* TREE *in turn, pushing one another out of the way.*) Boost me up!

WILLA: You are too heavy. Boost *me* up!

NILLA: I am the lightest. Boost *me* up! (*They push each other trying to reach the apple and fall in a heap on the ground.* CHRISTINE *comes out from behind the bush, laughing.*)

CHRISTINE: Mother, sisters! It's no use. You might as well reach for the moon. (*She takes a bite of her apple.*)

NILLA (*Getting to her feet*): Look! She's eating an apple! (DAME TINNEY *and* WILLA *jump up and look.*)

DAME TINNEY: So she is!

WILLA: How did you get it?

CHRISTINE: I picked it, of course.

DAME TINNEY: Humph! Did you stand on a ladder?

CHRISTINE: No, I stood on the ground, and the tree bent down to me.

WILLA: Do you expect us to believe that?

NILLA: Show us.

DAME TINNEY: Yes, pick that apple. (*She points to the apple on the branch.*)

CHRISTINE: I am not hungry now, thank you. (*Puts her apple in basket*)

DAME TINNEY: Well, I *am* hungry, and I want that apple.

CHRISTINE: You are not the first one to want the apple of contentment when it is hanging right over your head.

DAME TINNEY: What do you mean by that?

NILLA: She's stalling, Mama. *Make* her pick the apple.

DAME TINNEY (*Harshly*): Oh, I will, I will! (*Gripping* CHRISTINE *by the shoulders and shaking her*) Christine, you—pick—that—apple! (*Faint sound of offstage trumpet is heard.*)

WILLA: Listen! What's that? (*She runs to the edge of the brook and looks offstage*) It's the King! He's coming this way!

CHRISTINE: The King? Oh, let me see him! (*She wrenches herself free and joins* WILLA.)

WILLA (*Grabbing her*): Come away from there! (*She drags* CHRISTINE *from the brook with the help of* NILLA *and* DAME TINNEY)

NILLA: The idea! Showing yourself to the King, in your patches!

DAME TINNEY: Go to the house immediately!

CHRISTINE: Oh, please may I stay—just for a minute?

DAME TINNEY: No, you have work to do. Go home and do it. If it is not done when we get back, you will go without your dinner.

WILLA: And if you spy on us, you will go without your breakfast as well.

CHRISTINE: But I have never seen the King. *Please* let me have one look. Then I will go, I promise.

DAME TINNEY: No! Out of sight, *at once!*

NILLA: Get along now. (*All push* CHRISTINE *toward right.*)

CHRISTINE (*Resisting*): No, no, no! (*Sound of offstage trumpet is heard, louder this time.*)

WILLA: Oh, hurry, hurry! (*They exit right, pushing* CHRISTINE *before them.* PAGE *and* HERALD *enter left, followed by* KING. PAGE *and* HERALD *stop and gaze at* TREE *while* KING *pauses a short distance behind.*)

PAGE: Is this the tree, Your Majesty?

KING (*Studying it*): I think it's the one I saw from the road. Yes, there is the golden apple. I simply *must* have it! (*He looks about.*) I wonder who owns this land.

HERALD: There is a house over there beyond that wall. Shall I go and ask, Your Majesty?

PAGE: That won't be necessary. Three women are coming out of the house now. (*Excited voices are heard from offstage.* DAME TINNEY, WILLA *and* NILLA *enter and curtsy to the* KING.)

DAME TINNEY: Dame Tinney, Your Majesty—and my daughters, Willa and Nilla. (KING *bows slightly.*) We heard your trumpet and came as fast as we could.

KING: Is this tree on your property, madam?

DAME TINNEY: Yes, indeed.

KING: I should like to buy that apple. I will give you a bag of gold for it. (*He unloosens a pouch from his belt.*)

DAME TINNEY: A *whole* bag of gold for one apple?

KING (*Weighing pouch on his palm*): Here it is. (WILLA *and* NILLA *squeal with delight.*)

WILLA: We can have dozens of silk dresses, Mama!

NILLA: And hats with plumes, Mama!

DAME TINNEY: Hush, girls! (*To* KING) The apple is yours, Your Majesty. (KING *gives the pouch to* PAGE, *who gives it to* DAME TINNEY.) Thank you, Your Majesty.

WILLA (*Gushing*): Yes, thank you *ever* so much.

NILLA (*With a wave*): Goodbye, Your Majesty. (DAME TINNEY, WILLA *and* NILLA *bow themselves out tittering.*)

PAGE (*To the* KING): Shall I pick the apple, Your Majesty?

KING (*As he goes to the bench and sits*): Yes. I don't know when I have been so hungry for an apple. (*When* PAGE *reaches up to pick apple,* TREE *raises it just beyond his fingertips.* PAGE *starts jumping to try to reach apple, and the branch is raised higher.*)

PAGE: That's funny. I can't reach it. It's higher than I thought.

HERALD (*Coming over to* PAGE): Why don't you shake it off? (*The* PAGE *shakes the* TREE, *and the* HERALD *tries to knock off the apple with his trumpet.*)

KING (*Impatiently*): Here, let me try. I am taller than you. (KING *walks to* TREE *and tries to pick apple, but the branch is too high.*) It's a stubborn thing, isn't it?

Bring over the bench. (PAGE *and* HERALD *get the bench and set it under* TREE. *They help* KING *onto the bench.* KING *stands on tiptoe and strikes at the branch with the* HERALD's *trumpet.*) Bah! (*He steps off the bench.*) I can no more get that apple than I can get the sun in the sky!

PAGE: The thing is bewitched!

KING: Fire and brimstone! Am I to die of hunger? Chop down the tree! Pull it up by the roots!

TREE (*Crying out*): No, no, don't do that! (PAGE, HERALD *and* KING *look about bewildered.*)

KING: Where are you? Who spoke?

TREE: It was I, Your Majesty—the apple tree. There is only one way you can get this apple.

KING: How?

TREE: Ask the one to whom I belong, and she will pick it for you.

KING: You mean Dame Tinney?

TREE: No, I am not *her* tree. I belong to her daughter.

KING: Which daughter?

TREE: You must find that out for yourself.

KING: Herald, blow your trumpet! Call the Dame here at once! (HERALD *hurries downstage right and sounds his trumpet.* PAGE *returns the bench to its original position.* KING *sits.*) I can't understand *why* I have such a hankering for that apple. Apples are not my favorite fruit. I much prefer oranges. But I feel as if I will *die* if I don't get a taste of that apple.

PAGE: It's very strange, Your Majesty.

HERALD: Here they come, Your Majesty. (DAME TINNEY, WILLA *and* NILLA *enter.*)

DAME TINNEY (*Nervously*): Is anything wrong, Your Majesty?

KING (*Rising*): Everything is wrong, madam. I paid you a bag of gold for that apple, and there it hangs—and there it *will* hang until it is picked by one of your daughters.

DAME TINNEY (*Frightened*): Who—who told you that?

KING: Never mind. Is it true?

DAME TINNEY (*Stammering*): Yes, Your Majesty.

KING: Then have her pick it for me right away. I will take her home and marry her and make her a queen.

WILLA *and* NILLA (*Squealing*): A *queen!*

KING: Yes, a queen. Now which one of you will it be?

WILLA (*Running to* KING): Me, Your Majesty!

NILLA (*Following* WILLA): No, me!

WILLA: Me, me!

NILLA: Me, me!

KING (*Turning away impatiently*): Madam, control your daughters. I am losing patience. *Which one?*

DAME TINNEY (*Firmly pulling* NILLA *aside*): It is Willa, Your Majesty. (*Whispering to* NILLA) Get Christine and bring her here—quickly! (NILLA *exits right hurriedly.*)

KING (*To* WILLA): Well, what are you waiting for? Pick the apple.

DAME TINNEY (*Wagging her finger at him playfully*): Tut, tut, Your Majesty! You wouldn't have your future bride climb the apple tree before the members of your court, would you? (*She indicates the* PAGE *and* HERALD.) It would be most improper. They must turn their backs. (KING *gives an embarrassed little cough, glancing at* PAGE *and* HERALD, *who turn away.*) You, too, Your Majesty. (*Smiling sweetly*) Willa is not your queen yet, you know. (*The* KING *scowls and turns his back.*) No peeking, now!

KING (*Swinging around indignantly*): Madam!

DAME TINNEY (*Shaking her finger*): Ah, ah! (*The* KING, *looking vexed, turns and steps into line with the* PAGE *and* HERALD.)

WILLA (*Whispering*): Mama, what shall I *do?*

DAME TINNEY (*Whispering*): Pretend to climb the tree. I have sent for Christine. (*She looks anxiously offstage right.*) What can be keeping her?

KING: Willa, are you climbing the tree? I don't hear anything.

WILLA: Yes, oh, yes, I'm climbing the tree. Hear me? (*She shakes a branch frantically, then whispers to* DAME TINNEY.) I wish Christine would hurry!

KING: What are you whispering about?

DAME TINNEY (*Turning to* KING): Ah, ah! Secrets, Your Majesty. You mustn't eavesdrop. (*She returns to watching for* CHRISTINE.) Where *is* that girl? Oh, here she comes! (*To* KING) We will have the apple for you in a minute.

KING: Humph! I should hope so! (NILLA *enters with* CHRISTINE.)

DAME TINNEY (*Coaxingly, in an undertone*): Listen, Christine, dear. The King wants an apple more than anything in the world. You must pick it for him.

CHRISTINE (*Loudly*): Oh, I will be *glad* to—

DAME TINNEY: Sh-h-h! Not so loud!

CHRISTINE (*Lowering her voice*): Why all the secrecy?

DAME TINNEY: It's a—a kind of game. We're going to surprise His Majesty. (*She pushes* CHRISTINE *toward the* TREE.)

KING (*Starting to turn around*): What's going on?

DAME TINNEY (*Screaming*): Don't look, Your Majesty! Not yet.

KING: Please hurry, madam. I can't wait much longer. (CHRISTINE *stands under* TREE. *The branch is lowered, and she picks the apple.* WILLA *snatches it away from her.*)

CHRISTINE (*To* DAME TINNEY): You said it was for the King!

WILLA (*Wrapping it in her handkerchief*): It is—and *I* am going to give it to him.

CHRISTINE: Then I will give him *this* one. (TREE *has hung another apple on the bough, and* CHRISTINE *picks it.*)

NILLA (*Seizing it*): Oh, no, you won't. *I* will! (*She wraps apple in her handkerchief.* TREE *hangs another apple on the branch.*)

KING (*Becoming restless*): Madam, I warn you—I shall count to three, and then I am going to turn around. *One!* (CHRISTINE *is about to call out when* DAME TIN-NEY *claps a hand over her mouth and with the help of* WILLA *and* NILLA *forces her down behind the rock.*) *Two!*

DAME TINNEY (*In a fierce whisper to* CHRISTINE): Get down there and keep quiet! (*She stands guard over the rock.*)

KING: *Three!* (*He turns around.* PAGE *and* HERALD *turn also.* WILLA *runs to* KING, *waving her knotted handkerchief at him.* NOTE: WILLA *and* NILLA *have exchanged the handkerchiefs for others in their pockets.*)

WILLA: Here is the apple, Your Majesty!

KING: At last! (*He takes the handkerchief from her and unties it. Inside is a round stone the size of an apple.* KING *stares at it angrily.*) What is the meaning of this?

WILLA: The meaning of what, Your Majesty?

KING: Where is the apple?

WILLA (*Stammering*): Isn't it there?

KING: Do you call *this* an apple? (*He holds up the stone as* WILLA *stares.*)

WILLA: Why, it's a stone! But—but—

KING: *Where is the apple?*

NILLA (*Running to his side*): I have it, Your Majesty! *I* am the one who should be queen!

KING: That remains to be seen. Untie your handkerchief.

(NILLA *does so and cries out at what the handkerchief contains.*) What's the matter? (NILLA *hastily tries to cover up the object. The* KING *speaks sternly.*) Let me see what you have there. (*Slowly,* NILLA *folds back the corners of her handkerchief, revealing weeds.*) A bunch of grass! Humph! How dare you play tricks on your king? (*He notices an apple on the* TREE.) Why, look there! You haven't picked the apple at all. It is still on the tree.

WILLA (*Angrily*): It's Christine's fault! *She* did it!

KING: Who is Christine? (CHRISTINE *bobs up from behind the rock, and* DAME TINNEY *shoves her down again.*) Answer me! Who is Christine?

NILLA (*Whimpering*): She's—she's—

DAME TINNEY (*Interrupting quickly*): She's a poor ragged thing, Your Majesty, of no account. She tends the geese.

KING: What has she to do with all this?

DAME TINNEY: Nothing, Your Majesty. She's just a simple goose-girl.

TREE (*Loudly and clearly*): Your Majesty, if you would know the truth about Christine, look behind this rock. (KING *strides to the rock and pushes* DAME TINNEY *aside. He raises* CHRISTINE *to her feet.*)

KING (*Gently*): Are you Christine?

CHRISTINE (*Making a little curtsy*): Yes, Your Majesty.

KING (*To* DAME TINNEY): Is this girl your daughter, madam?

DAME TINNEY (*Grudgingly*): Yes, she is—the good-for-nothing!

KING (*Smiling at* CHRISTINE): Then you must really be the one who can pick the apple from this tree.

CHRISTINE: It is the easiest thing in the world to do when the tree belongs to you. Watch. (*She lifts up her hand, and* TREE *lowers the apple into it. With a curtsy,* CHRIS-

TINE *presents the apple to* KING, *who accepts it with a low bow.*)

KING: Thank you, Christine. (*He bites into the apple and smiles contentedly. He chews slowly with evident relish.*) It is the most delicious fruit I have ever tasted. And you, Christine, are the most beautiful girl I have ever seen. Will you be my queen?

CHRISTINE (*Shyly*): I, a queen, Your Majesty? I, in my patches and heavy boots?

KING: I don't mind them any more than I mind the clouds in the sky or the dew on the grass. I have such a deep feeling of contentment. Why is that?

CHRISTINE: That is because you have eaten the apple of contentment, Your Majesty.

KING (*Taking her hand*): Come, Christine. You shall have the grandest wedding that ever was. Herald, sound your trumpet! I am going to be married! (HERALD *blows on his trumpet and starts toward exit, followed by* KING *and* CHRISTINE, *with* PAGE *bringing up the rear.* PAGE *turns to* DAME TINNEY, WILLA *and* NILLA, *sticks his thumbs in his ears and wiggles his fingers.*)

PAGE: Yah! Yah! (*He exits.* DAME TINNEY, WILLA *and* NILLA *look up at* TREE *and sigh.*)

DAME TINNEY: Never mind, girls. We still have the apple of contentment in our back yard, even if we can't pick it.

TREE: You have nothing of the kind, Dame Tinney. I belong to Christine and to nobody else, and I am going to the palace to be with her. (TREE *pretends to tug at her roots, leaning first to one side and then to the other.*)

WILLA (*Screaming*): Look out! The tree is going to fall! (*They run away from* TREE, *who pulls herself free and moves toward exit.*)

NILLA: The tree is *walking!*

TREE (*Calling*): Goodbye! I will see you at the wedding! (DAME TINNEY, WILLA *and* NILLA *stare after* TREE *in amazement, as curtain falls.*)

THE END

The Swineherd

by Hans Christian Andersen

Characters

PRINCESS AUGUSTINE
EMPEROR, *her father*
EIGHT MAIDS-IN-WAITING
PRINCE OF THE LITTLE KINGDOM (*Swineherd*)
MESSENGER
TWO PAGES

SETTING: *A corner of the Emperor's orchard, next to the imperial pig sty. A stone wall across the back separates the orchard from the sty. A cherry tree bends over the wall at center.*

AT RISE: *The* PRINCESS *and the* EIGHT MAIDS-IN-WAITING *are playing a game, such as "Blind Man's Buff." They dart about and squeal with laughter. The* EMPEROR *enters through a grape arbor which is at left, and claps his hands to get their attention.*

EMPEROR: Ladies! Young ladies! Augustine! (*The* PRINCESS *and the* MAIDS *quiet down. The* MAIDS *curtsy.*) What noisy games you girls do play! (*The sound of pigs grunting is heard from behind the wall.* EMPEROR *points to wall.*) You and the pigs! (*He holds his handkerchief to his nose.*) *Must* you play so close to the pig sty? This is no place for a princess or her maids.

PRINCESS: You can't smell 'em, Papa. The wind is blowing the other way.

EMPEROR (*Sniffing*): Ah, yes, so it is! (*He puts away handkerchief*) Augustine, my dear, I have exciting news for you.

PRINCESS: Oh, what is it?

EMPEROR: A messenger is here with presents from a new suitor.

PRINCESS (*Eagerly*): Presents? Who sent them?

EMPEROR: The Prince of the Little Kingdom.

PRINCESS (*Disappointed*): The Prince of the *Little* Kingdom?

1ST MAID (*Indignantly*): Imagine! The *Little* Kingdom!

PRINCESS: What impudence! Send them back!

EMPEROR (*Sighing*): Very well, my dear. (*He starts left.*)

PRINCESS: Wait, Papa! How many presents?

EMPEROR: Two.

PRINCESS: Only *two?*

2ND MAID: Think of it! *Only* two! (*The* EMPEROR *starts to leave again.*)

PRINCESS: Papa! Do you know what they are?

EMPEROR: No. I didn't look. I thought *you* might like to do that.

PRINCESS: Well, they can't be much—coming from the Prince of the *Little* Kingdom.

3RD MAID: No, not much!

PRINCESS: What could that poor Prince *possibly* have to offer me, the daughter of the Emperor?

EMPEROR (*Slyly*): It might be interesting, my dear, to find out.

PRINCESS (*Thoughtfully*): Hm-m, it might be at that. All right, Papa, I'll look at the presents—but only to satisfy *your* curiosity. (*She sits on bench beside apple tree at right.* MAIDS *group about her. The* EMPEROR *steps left to the arbor.*)

EMPEROR (*Calling offstage*): Send in the Messenger from the Little Kingdom. (MESSENGER *enters, followed by* TWO PAGES *who carry the gifts. The* 1ST PAGE *carries a small ornamental box; the* 2ND PAGE *carries a bird cage covered with a silk scarf. The* MESSENGER *bows before the* PRINCESS.)

PRINCESS (*Disdainfully*): Do you come from the Prince of the Little Kingdom?

MESSENGER: Yes, Your Highness.

PRINCESS: Let me see what you have brought. (*The* MESSENGER *beckons to the* 1ST PAGE *who steps forward and hands box to* MESSENGER.)

MESSENGER: This is the first gift, Your Highness.

PRINCESS: It's very little—like his kingdom. Oh, I do hope it's a pussy cat! (*The* MESSENGER *opens the box and takes out a beautiful red rose which he gives to the* PRINCESS.)

MESSENGER: A perfect rose, Your Highness.

1ST MAID: How pretty!

2ND MAID: So big!

3RD MAID: So red!

4TH MAID: And so very well made!

PRINCESS (*Wailing*): But it's *real!*

MAIDS (*Wailing*): *Real?* Oh, fie!

PRINCESS: What an insult! A *real* rose!

MESSENGER: Your Highness, this rose came from a tree that blooms only once in every five years, and then it bears only one rose. But what a rose! Anyone who smells it forgets all care and sorrow.

PRINCESS (*Peevishly*): I have no care or sorrow. I do not like the rose. (*She returns it to the* 1ST PAGE.)

EMPEROR: Well, let us see the other gift before we lose our tempers. (*The* 2ND PAGE *comes forward. The* MES-

SENGER *takes cage, removes the scarf, and holds the cage, which holds a bird, before the* PRINCESS. *She peers between the bars. The sound of a bird singing is heard.*)

5TH MAID: Delightful!

6TH MAID: A singing bird!

7TH MAID: Listen to it trill!

8TH MAID: Right on pitch!

EMPEROR: It sings as though all the sweet songs in the world were in its throat.

PRINCESS: I wonder what the bird is made of.

EMPEROR: My dear, look more closely.

PRINCESS: Such a dull color! It must be tarnished.

MESSENGER: It's a nightingale, Your Highness.

PRINCESS: A nightingale! Do you mean to say it's—*real?*

MESSENGER: Yes, a real live bird, Your Highness.

PRINCESS (*Angrily*): Then let it fly away and be gone! I will have none of it. (*She pushes cage from her with displeasure, and* MESSENGER *hands it back to* 2ND PAGE.)

MESSENGER: What shall I tell the Prince, Your Highness?

PRINCESS (*Rudely*): Tell him to stay in his little kingdom and mind his own little business.

MESSENGER: But he has already left his little kingdom and he's on his way here. For all we know, he may be ringing the front doorbell right now.

PRINCESS: Then tell him to *stop* ringing and go back home! I won't see him. Go away, fellow, go away. (*She stamps her foot at the* MESSENGER *and he exits left, followed by* PAGES.)

EMPEROR (*Wistfully*): They were very nice gifts, Augustine.

PRINCESS: A common rose! A common nightingale! Fie! (*She rises*) Come along, ladies. Let's go wading in the brook. (*She goes off right with her nose in the air.* MAIDS *follow, also with noses in the air.* EMPEROR *gazes after them, sighing and shaking his head. After a moment,* MESSENGER *re-enters left.*)

MESSENGER (*Bowing*): Your Majesty! May I have a word with you?

EMPEROR: Certainly, sir. I apologize for my daughter's behavior.

MESSENGER: You couldn't persuade her to change her mind, could you? I mean about seeing the Prince.

EMPEROR (*Pointing overhead*): You might as well try to persuade the sun to change its course, as to get Augustine to change her mind.

MESSENGER: But the Prince really is a very charming young man and his kingdom isn't *that* small, you know. It's big enough to marry on, and his Highness has set his heart on marrying—your daughter, no less.

EMPERER: Isn't it rather bold of him to say "Marry me!" to the Emperor's own daughter?

MESSENGER: Not at all, Your Majesty. You see, his name is known far and wide, and there are dozens of princesses who would be glad to answer "Yes!" and "Thank you!" too, if he asked one of them to be his wife.

EMPEROR (*Impressed*): You don't say! He must be a very popular prince.

MESSENGER: Indeed he is, Your Majesty.

EMPEROR: Well, I'll see what I can do. But don't get your hopes up. Augustine has turned down the offers of every eligible prince in the country—not to mention a few kings, too. I'm afraid there's no pleasing her. Well, good day, sir. (EMPEROR *exits left. Laughter is heard from off right.* MESSENGER *takes a step in that direction, hesitates, considers, then shakes his head and crosses to left, then stops.* PRINCE, *disguised as a swineherd, suddenly pops up from behind the wall of the pig sty.*)

PRINCE: Pssst! Charles! Wait!

MESSENGER: Your Highness! What are you doing in the pig sty?

PRINCE: Where else would a swineherd be but in the pig

sty? (*He climbs nimbly over the wall. He carries a small cooking pot hung around with tiny bells.*)

MESSENGER: A swineherd!

PRINCE (*Laughing*): Don't look so shocked, Charles. Sometimes pigs have better manners than princesses. So Augustine won't have me, eh?

MESSENGER (*Sadly*): Neither you nor your gifts.

PRINCE: I expected as much—that's why I disguised myself.

MESSENGER: But if you couldn't win her as a prince, how will you ever win her as a swineherd?

PRINCE: Easily. (*Indicating pot*) With this cooking pot— and this rattle. (*From his pocket he produces a gaily painted rattle which is also hung around with bells.*)

MESSENGER: It can't be done!

PRINCE: Stay around, Charles, and you shall see if it can be done or not. (*Sound of voices is heard off right*) Here they come! Get out of sight—and watch. (MESSENGER *hurries off left while* PRINCE *hangs cooking pot on a limb of the cherry tree, then hides behind the wall.* PRINCESS *and her* MAIDS *enter right. They are barefoot and carry their slippers in their hands.*)

PRINCESS (*Stopping at center and holding her nose*): Phew!

MAIDS (*Holding their noses*): Phew.

PRINCESS: Smell the pigs! The wind must have changed. Let us go elsewhere. (*As they walk left, the music of the song, "Ach, du lieber Augustin" is heard. The music is accompanied by bells so as to seem to be coming from the cooking pot.* PRINCESS *comes to a halt.*) Stop! Listen! (MAIDS *stop and listen.*) Why, that is the same tune I play—with one finger. (*She pantomimes playing the tune on a keyboard with her index finger, singing the traditional words as she does so. The* MAIDS *sway in time to the music and applaud at the conclusion of the song.*)

1ST MAID: Her Highness is a musician!

PRINCESS (*Looking all about as the music continues*): I wonder who can be playing *my* tune?

2ND MAID (*Going to the cherry tree*): Your Highness, I think it is the cooking pot.

PRINCESS: Who?

2ND MAID: This cooking pot hanging on the cherry tree.

PRINCESS (*Going to the cherry tree*): Oh, what a darling little pot! (*She reaches up to lift it off the branch.*)

PRINCE (*Jumping up from behind the wall*): Don't touch!

PRINCESS (*Startled*): Oh! (*Drawing herself up haughtily*) And why shouldn't I touch? *I* am the Emperor's daughter. (*She reaches for the pot again.* PRINCE *climbs over wall and goes to* PRINCESS.)

PRINCE (*Wagging his finger at her*): Ah-ah! You'll burn your royal fingers! The pot is hot. I've been cooking my dinner in it.

PRINCESS (*Coldly*): I've never seen you before. Who are you?

PRINCE (*With a sweeping bow*): I am the new swineherd, Your Highness, the Imperial Pig Tender.

PRINCESS: Oh, we're always needing extra help with the pigs. We have so many of them. (*Turning up her nose and pinching it*) Phew!

MAIDS (*Turning up their noses and pinching them*): Phew!

PRINCESS: Where did you get that pot, swineherd?

PRINCE: I made it.

PRINCESS: Does it always play that tune?

PRINCE: Always.

PRINCESS (*Arrogantly*): It's *my* tune, therefore the pot belongs to me.

PRINCE: You shall have it when you give me what I want.

PRINCESS: And what is that?

PRINCE: One kiss from you, Your Highness. And I won't take less. (MAIDS *giggle*.)

1ST MAID: Oh, isn't he naughty!

2ND MAID: But so handsome!

PRINCESS (*Outraged*): Rude fellow! You most certainly will take less! You will take nothing. And so shall I. (*She starts to exit left.*)

PRINCE (*Undaunted*): Just a moment, Your Highness! The pot can do more than play. (*He takes off the lid and sniffs.*)

PRINCESS: Why do you sniff the pot? Is your dinner so delicious?

PRINCE: Oh, it's not my dinner I smell. It's all the dinners that are being cooked in the town.

2ND MAID: What fun!

PRINCESS: How do you know whose dinner it is you smell?

PRINCE: Just say someone's name and you will smell exactly what that person is cooking. (*All gather around the pot.*)

PRINCESS: The Imperial Chef. What is he cooking for our dinner? (*She sniffs several times.*) Saffron asparagus. Topsy-turvy rice. Roast wild duck with prune-orange stuffing. Oh, not again! We had that on Tuesday.

3RD MAID: The baker. (*She sniffs.*) The baker's bread is burning!

4TH MAID: The fishmonger. (*Sniffing*) He's having fried chicken.

5TH MAID: The butcher. (*Sniffing*) The butcher is having fried trout.

6TH MAID: They are making sausages from yesterday's dinner at the inn.

PRINCESS: Really, I must have this pot!

PRINCE: One kiss is my price.

PRINCESS: Oh, how tiresome! Well, stand around me, all of you, so that no one can see. (*MAIDS form a circle around PRINCESS and PRINCE, spreading out their skirts, for a moment, then stand aside.*)

PRINCE: That is fair play. The cooking pot is yours, Princess.

PRINCESS (*To* MAIDS): Don't you tell how I got it.

7TH MAID: Good gracious, no! (MAIDS *shake their heads.*)

PRINCESS: After all, I *am* the Emperor's daughter.

PRINCE: Your Highness, I have something else here that might take your fancy.

PRINCESS: Oh? What is it?

PRINCE (*Taking rattle from his pocket*): A rattle.

PRINCESS: A rattle! Pooh! Give it to the washerwoman's baby.

PRINCE: Not this! It's rather special.

PRINCESS: What's so special about it?

PRINCE: If you hold it to your ear and shake it, you can hear all the dance tunes in the world.

PRINCESS: I don't believe you!

PRINCE: It's the truth. Try it. (PRINCESS *shakes the rattle in her ear and smiles with delight. She waltzes about, then, still shaking the rattle in her ear, changes to a jig.*)

PRINCESS: Oh, I like it! I'll keep it and pay you for it. (*Firmly*) But no more kisses, swineherd!

PRINCE (*Just as firmly*): Five kisses is the price of the rattle, Princess.

PRINCESS: You must be out of your mind if you expect me to—to—(*Hesitating*) Oh, well, I suppose a princess should pay the asking price of an article without quibbling. You can have one kiss as you did before, but the other four you will take from my maids-in-waiting.

MAIDS (*In unison*): Oh, we'd rather not!

PRINCESS: Nonsense! If *I* can kiss him, surely you can. Remember, I pay your wages.

PRINCE: Five kisses from the Princess or I keep the rattle.

PRINCESS: Very well. Gather around us, ladies. (MAIDS *surround the pair and spread their skirts.* EMPEROR *enters left from the arbor.*)

EMPEROR (*Speaking to himself*): What's going on? What mischief are those girls up to now? (*He walks around the group, trying to peek between* MAIDS *as they count in unison.*)

MAIDS: One. Two. Three. Four. *Five!*

EMPEROR: Stop it! Stop it, I say! (MAIDS *turn and gasp.*)

MAIDS: Your Majesty! (*They hastily back away, tripping over each other as they curtsy.*)

EMPEROR (*Shocked*): Augustine, what are you doing?

PRINCESS: I am buying a rattle, Papa.

EMPEROR: You're *what?* Do you mean to say you are kissing a swineherd for a rattle?

PRINCESS: It's a most unusual rattle and the swineherd doesn't smell piggy at all.

EMPEROR (*Exasperated*): Augustine, have you no sense at all? You are willing to kiss a swineherd for a tinkling toy, but when an honorable prince offers you his crown and throne, you send him packing because his kingdom isn't large enough to suit you. You spurn his gifts because you can not appreciate their real worth. I have never seen such poor judgment! (*He turns his back on her.*)

MAIDS (*Turning their backs in unison*): Fie! (PRINCESS *sits on the bench.*)

PRINCESS (*Weeping*): Oh, miserable me! What a fool I have been! (PRINCE *approaches her.*) Aren't you going to turn your back on me, swineherd?

PRINCE (*Gently*): No, Princess.

PRINCESS: You don't despise me?

PRINCE: Quite the contrary.

PRINCESS: Oh, I do like you! I'm sorry I was so snippy. (*Sighing*) And I wish I had been kinder to the Prince, too.

PRINCE (*Interested*): The Prince of the Little Kingdom?

PRINCESS: It's not his fault that his kingdom is little. I wish I hadn't sent him away.

PRINCE: Oh, but you didn't!

PRINCESS: Do you mean he's still here?

PRINCE: Absolutely here. (*He takes a crown from his pocket and sets it on his head.*) Behold! The Prince of the Little Kingdom!

EMPEROR *and* MAIDS (*Turning in unison*): *What?*

PRINCESS: I don't believe you!

PRINCE (*Calling toward the arbor*): Charles! (MESSENGER *enters and bows.*) Tell them, Charles.

MESSENGER: This is truly the Prince of the Little Kingdom.

EMPEROR (*Amazed*): But—but, Your Highness, why did you disguise yourself as a swineherd?

PRINCE: It was the only way I could get to see the Princess.

PRINCESS (*Bowing her head in shame*): Oh, what must you think of me, Your Highness?

PRINCE: I think you are very beautiful and—(*Glancing at* EMPEROR) very spoiled, and ought to be spanked at least once a week. I beg you to give me that privilege. Will you be my wife?

PRINCESS (*Mischievously*): Yes, if you will give me something—free of your customary charge of kisses.

PRINCE (*Smiling*): Name it and it is yours.

PRINCESS: The rose and the nightingale. (PRINCE *beckons to* PAGES *who enter from left with gifts and kneel before* PRINCESS. *She gives* PRINCE *her hand, and others dance around them in a circle, singing.*)

ALL (*Singing*):
Ah! my dearest Augustine, Augustine, Augustine,
Ah! my dearest Augustine,
You have my heart. (*Curtain*)

THE END

Rapunzel

from Grimms' Fairy Tales

Characters

WITCH
FRANZ, *a dollmaker*
EMMA, *his wife*
RAPUNZEL, *their daughter*
PRINCE FREDERICK
BOY ⎱ *village children*
FOUR GIRLS ⎰

SCENE 1

TIME: *A day in summer.*

SETTING: *The Witch's garden and the front yard of Franz's cottage. The garden, at left, is separated from the yard at right by a stone wall which extends a short way from the back down center, ending in a high iron gate. The wall continues along the back of the garden, in the center of which is a bed of lettuce. Oddly shaped rocks are scattered about. In Franz's yard are a bench and a work table, strewn with material and tools for making dolls. Down right is a sign:* FRANZ—DOLLMAKER.

AT RISE: FRANZ *is seated on the bench, humming to himself as he puts the finishing touches on a doll, painting its lips and cheeks.* WITCH *enters her garden from left*

with a watering can and trowel. She goes to the bed
of lettuce and sprinkles it.

WITCH (*Chanting*):
Rapunzel, sweet lettuce,
So tender and rare,
Spread out your green leaves
And perfume the air.
(*She sets down the watering can and begins to weed the*
bed. The WITCH *continues to work quietly in the gar-*
den, pulling weeds and digging with a trowel. Children's
voices are heard off right and FRANZ *looks up from his*
work, smiling. FOUR GIRLS and a BOY enter down right
and gather around FRANZ.)
CHILDREN (*Ad lib*): Hello, Franz! We've come to watch
you make dolls. You said we could. Is that doll finished?
(*Etc.*)
BOY (*In a superior tone*): Of course it's not finished! Can't
you see? It hasn't any hair yet.
FRANZ (*To* BOY): Well, well! And who is this fine fellow?
1ST GIRL: He's my cousin from Hamburg.
BOY: I didn't want to come. She made me. (*Snorting in*
derision.) Dolls! They're for girls. Don't you make anything for boys?
FRANZ: What did you have in mind?
BOY: Oh, tin soldiers and tigers and jack-in-the-boxes. Do
you make them?
FRANZ: No, I'm afraid not. Only dolls. (BOY *turns away to*
explore the yard.)
2ND GIRL (*Indicating the doll*): Franz, what color is her
hair going to be?
FRANZ: Brown, to match her eyes. I have a nice brown wig
here somewhere. (*He searches for it on the table.*)
3RD GIRL (*Holding up wig*): Is this it?
FRANZ: Yes, thank you. (*He fits brown wig on the doll's*

head.) What do you think, children? (*The children express their approval. Suddenly the wig falls off the doll's head.*)

4TH GIRL: Good gracious! The doll's wig fell off!

FRANZ: Probably I didn't have it on straight. (*He replaces the wig.*) There! It's on straight now. (*The wig falls off again.* FRANZ *shakes his head, puzzled.*) Whatever is the matter? I never knew a wig to do that before.

3RD GIRL: Maybe she doesn't like brown hair.

2ND GIRL: Why wouldn't she like brown hair? It's thick and curly and looks well with her dress.

FRANZ: I'll glue the hair on, then it can't come off.

1ST GIRL: Here's the glue. (*She holds the pot while* FRANZ *glues the wig to the doll's head, pressing it on firmly with both hands.*)

FRANZ: Now, my little lady, budge that if you can! (*No sooner has he taken his hands away than the wig topples off.*) Well, I never!

3RD GIRL: I *told* you she doesn't like brown hair! I think she wants yellow hair.

FRANZ: All right, let's try this wig of long golden braids. (*He sets blonde wig on the doll's head and they all hold their breath, but nothing happens. They sigh with relief, and* FRANZ *proceeds with the business of gluing the wig onto the doll's head. The* BOY *is now looking through the gate into the* WITCH'S *garden.*)

BOY: What a funny garden!

1ST GIRL: Come away from there! (*She pulls him by the arm.*)

BOY (*Resisting*): What for?

1ST GIRL: That garden belongs to a witch!

BOY (*Shaking her off*): Huh! I'm not afraid of witches! (*Pointing to* WITCH, *who is watering the lettuce.*) Is that her?

GIRLS (*Crowding behind him excitedly*): Where? Where?

BOY: That old woman with the watering can.

2ND GIRL: My word! Did you ever *see* such big lettuce!

3RD GIRL: She's singing to herself. Listen!

WITCH (*Chanting*):

Rapunzel, sweet lettuce,

So tender and rare,

Spread out your green leaves

And perfume the air.

4TH GIRL: What a frightful old hag!

3RD GIRL: Shh-h! Don't speak so loud—she'll hear you.

2ND GIRL: She might put some kind of a spell on us!

BOY (*Swaggering*): I'd like to see her do it! What's her name?

1ST GIRL: She's called Dame Gothel.

BOY (*Shouting through the gate*): Hey! Old woman! What's your name? Witch Gothel, that's your name! You don't scare me!

1ST GIRL: Stop it! (*The* WITCH *turns to them, shaking her trowel menacingly.*) Now see what you've done! You've made her angry. *Run!* (*The children scream and run off down right. The* BOY *stops to make a face at the* WITCH, *then laughs and dashes off after the* GIRLS. WITCH *comes to gate.*)

FRANZ (*Nervously, to* WITCH): Don't mind them, Dame Gothel. You know children, they don't mean anything.

WITCH (*Sarcastically*): Oho! Don't they! (*Pointing to doll he is holding*) That's a pretty doll you have there. I like golden hair. There's magic in golden hair.

FRANZ: Is that so? Well, well! (WITCH *walks away abruptly and exits left.* EMMA *enters up right, carrying a sewing basket from which she takes a doll's pinafore.*)

EMMA: Franz, here is the doll's apron. May I put it on her now?

FRANZ (*Handing her the doll*): Yes, Emma, I'm finished with her.

EMMA: Why, she has golden hair! I thought you decided on brown.

FRANZ: I did, but she would have none of it. (*Chuckling*) She's a very independent young lady.

EMMA (*At the table, tying on the pinafore*): She's beautiful. How I wish we could have a real little girl just like her.

FRANZ (*Gently patting her shoulder*): Maybe some day we will, Emma.

EMMA: There, she's all dressed. She *is* a darling! I shall hate to part with her. Franz, couldn't we keep her for our own little girl when she comes?

FRANZ: Of course, my dear. To tell the truth, I've become quite fond of her myself.

EMMA (*Sniffing the air*): Mmm-m, what's that perfume I smell?

FRANZ: It's rapunzel—a kind of sweet lettuce that grows in Dame Gothel's garden.

EMMA (*Eagerly*): Let me see! (*She peeks through the gate.*) Oh, how good it looks! I must have some for dinner.

FRANZ: But that's impossible! You know Dame Gothel wouldn't give us a single leaf.

EMMA: Then we'll buy it from her. She might be willing to sell it. (*The* WITCH *re-enters left and goes to the bed of rapunzel.*) There she is now. Call to her and ask her if we can buy some of her lettuce. (*As he hesitates*) Please, Franz!

FRANZ (*Calling*): Dame Gothel!

WITCH: Yes, what is it?

FRANZ: Would you sell us some of that fine lettuce?

WITCH: Sell this lettuce? Indeed I won't.

EMMA: Oh, I wish you would. You've no idea how much I want some of it.

FRANZ: I'll be happy to pay you, and pay you well.

WITCH (*Holding up a head of lettuce she has picked*): You

haven't enough money to buy this. It's priceless. From this lettuce I make my magic potions. Do you think I'd sell it? Now go about your business and don't bother me again. (*She exits left with the head of lettuce.*)

EMMA (*Sitting at the table*): Oh, the mean old thing! (*She bursts into tears.*)

FRANZ: Now, now, Emma, don't cry. It's not that important.

EMMA: Well, maybe it isn't to you but it is to me. Oh, Franz, I've never wanted anything so much in my life as that lettuce. If I don't get it, I'll die.

FRANZ (*Trying to calm her*): Nonsense, my dear.

EMMA: You don't care!

FRANZ: Of course I care, but what can I do?

EMMA: *Get me some of that lettuce!*

FRANZ: Very well, you shall have the lettuce. I'll get it for you tonight.

EMMA (*Stamping her foot*): No! I want it now—*now*, do you hear? (*She runs off up right, sobbing.*)

FRANZ (*Looking after her, shaking his head*): What ails her? I've never seen her in such a state—and all over a bit of lettuce. Well, I'd better get it or she'll never forgive me. (*He tries gate.*) It's locked. I'll just have to take my chances and climb over the wall. I hope Dame Gothel doesn't see me. Then I *would* be in a pickle. (*He disappears behind back wall of garden and a few moments later reappears over the top of the wall. He looks about cautiously.*) So far, so good. (*He jumps down into the garden and goes to the bed of rapunzel.*) Two heads of lettuce should be enough to satisfy Emma. (*As he kneels to pull up lettuce,* WITCH *enters stealthily from left.* FRANZ *has his back to her and is not aware of her presence until she speaks.*)

WITCH: Not so fast, my friend! (FRANZ *cries out and leaps to his feet.*) Stealing my lettuce, are you?

FRANZ: But you wouldn't sell it to me, and if my wife doesn't have some of it to eat, I don't know what she'll do.

WITCH: Very well. I will make a bargain with you. You may have all the lettuce you want—on one condition.

FRANZ: Name it.

WITCH: When your first child is born, you must give it to me.

FRANZ: *What!* Oh, no!

WITCH: Oh, *yes!*

FRANZ: No, I couldn't agree to do that. And neither would Emma. You can keep your lettuce. (*He throws it down and turns to leave.*)

WITCH: Stop! You're not going to get out of it as easily as that. You came into my garden uninvited. You tried to steal my precious rapunzel and you have refused to bargain with me. Do you know what it means to defy a witch? It means you shall be put under a spell!

FRANZ (*Trembling*): What kind of spell?

WITCH: Do you see these stones here in my garden? Once they were real people. But they came into my garden to steal my rapunzel and I changed them into stones. And that is what you will be—a stone!

FRANZ: No!

WITCH: And I shall put a curse on your wife. She will hunger for my lettuce until she dies!

FRANZ: Oh, don't hurt Emma, I beg of you!

WITCH: Do you promise to give me your first-born child?

FRANZ: I'd promise anything to save Emma.

WITCH: Good! I have your word and I'll hold you to it. Now take the lettuce to your wife. I hope she enjoys it! (*WITCH laughs and goes to unlock the gate. FRANZ slowly picks up the heads of lettuce and exits into his own yard. As WITCH locks the gate, she jeers at him.*)

Don't forget to tell your wife the good news! (*She cackles as she exits left.*)

FRANZ (*To himself*): I won't tell Emma. I can't. It would break her heart. (EMMA *enters up right.*)

EMMA: Oh, Franz, you have the lettuce! Give it to me! (*She grabs it from him and sits at the table, eating it hungrily.*) How delicious it is! Did you have to steal it?

FRANZ (*Quietly*): No.

EMMA: Don't tell me Dame Gothel *gave* it to you, after all the fuss?

FRANZ: No, I paid for it—dearly.

EMMA: Don't look so glum, Franz. Whatever you paid, it's worth it. (*She smacks her lips with relish.*)

FRANZ: Is it, my dear? I wonder. (*He gazes fearfully at garden.* EMMA *is too busy devouring the lettuce to notice.*)

CURTAIN

*   *   *

SCENE 2

TIME: *A year later.*

SETTING: *Same as Scene 1.*

AT RISE: FRANZ *enters from up right, carrying a bassinet, followed by* EMMA, *who carries the doll.*

FRANZ (*Singing boisterously as he waltzes about the yard*): Rock-a-bye, baby, on the treetop,
When the wind blows, the cradle will rock—

EMMA: Careful now! Don't drop her.

FRANZ (*Indignantly*): What! Drop my little girl? What do you take me for? (*Singing*)
When the bough breaks, the cradle will fall—

EMMA (*Clearing a space on work table*): Here, set her down. (FRANZ *swings the bassinet in a wide arc as he lowers it to the table.*) Gently, gently!

FRANZ (*Singing*):
Down will come baby, cradle and all! (*He sets the bassinet on the table with a slight bump.*)

EMMA (*Exasperated*): Oh, men are so rambunctious!

FRANZ (*Strutting about*): And why shouldn't we be rambunctious? We men are the fathers of the world.

EMMA: Indeed? And what about the mothers? What about the mothers? What about us, eh?

FRANZ (*Patting her cheek affectionately*): Ah, mothers! They are the *angels* of the world.

EMMA: No, Franz, the children are the angels. (*She gazes adoringly into bassinet.*) Just look at her! If she isn't the image of an angel, I don't know what is.

FRANZ: I've never seen a more beautiful baby. Her hair is like spun gold.

EMMA (*Placing the doll in the bassinet*): What shall we call her, Franz? It should be something that goes with her hair, don't you think? Like Glorianna, or Oribel— that means "golden beauty."

FRANZ: A flower-name would be nice. There's Marigold and Mignonette and Primrose—(*While they are choosing a name,* WITCH *enters her garden from left and swiftly crosses to gate, where she stands listening.*)

EMMA: Arelia? Dorlisa? What shall it be?

WITCH (*Speaking suddenly*): Why not name her Rapunzel?

FRANZ (*Whirling to face her and crying out in alarm*): Dame Gothel!

EMMA: Why, how do you do, Dame Gothel? Have you been away? I haven't seen you since my husband bought the lettuce from you last summer.

WITCH: That's right, dearie. Would you like some more?

EMMA: Oh, no, thank you. I haven't been hungry for it since that day.

WITCH: Is that your baby? I want to see her. (*She unlocks the gate and comes out of garden.*)

FRANZ (*Quickly stepping in front of bassinet*): No!

EMMA: Why, Franz, where are your manners? Let Dame Gothel see the baby.

FRANZ (*Vehemently*): No, no!

EMMA: What's the matter with you, Franz?

WITCH: I'll tell you what's the matter. He made a bargain with me and he hasn't kept it.

EMMA: What bargain?

WITCH: In exchange for the rapunzel you wanted, he promised me your first-born child.

EMMA (*Horrified*): Franz, is this true?

FRANZ: Yes, Emma. It was the only way I could get the rapunzel for you. And she threatened to harm you if I refused.

EMMA: Oh, Franz, how could you do such a thing?

WITCH: Come now, give me the child.

EMMA: Please, Dame Gothel, don't take my baby!

WITCH: Why shouldn't I take what belongs to me? You had your lettuce—now I will have the child. A bargain is a bargain.

EMMA: *I* made no bargain with you. You shall not have her.

WITCH: Very well. If you won't give her to me, then I shall have to get her in another way.

EMMA: Never! I will die first!

WITCH: No, not die, but be changed into stone—both of you! (*She raises her arms and chants.* EMMA *and* FRANZ *freeze.*)

Change to stone, change to stone!

Flesh and hair, skin and bone.

Statues be and statues stay,

Do not move when I'm away.
(*She picks up bassinet and goes to gate, where she turns to face rigid forms of* EMMA *and* FRANZ.)
My curse forever on you lies
Unless for love Rapunzel cries.
And she will never cry for love, I'll see to that! I will shut her up in a tower and teach her how to become a witch. She will learn the fun of mixing potions and making spells. And then she will laugh! She will laugh for *hate!* But never cry for love—never, never, never! (*With a weird cry,* WITCH *passes into the garden, closes and locks the gate and runs off left.*)

CURTAIN

*　　*　　*

SCENE 3

TIME: *Fifteen years later.*
SETTING: *A tower room. A casement window is at right, and near it are a table and a stool. The bassinet and the doll are on a cot at left.*
AT RISE: RAPUNZEL *is seated on stool, gazing out of window. Her golden hair is plaited in one long braid, which is wound about her waist like a sash, the end hanging down to the floor. As she looks out window, she sings an appropriate folk song such as "Greensleeves." At end of song, she sighs, then leans forward out window to look at something below.*

RAPUNZEL: Here comes Dame Gothel with my food for today. I hope she's brought something special.
WITCH (*Calling, from offstage*): Rapunzel! Rapunzel! Let down your hair! (RAPUNZEL *unwinds the braid from around her waist and lowers it out window.*)

RAPUNZEL (*Calling down*): Here you are, godmother. (*She grips the braid with both hands and braces herself.*) Ow! Please don't yank so hard! It hurts!

WITCH (*Louder, from offstage*): Stand still, will you! (*Presently she appears outside window with a knapsack strapped to her back.* RAPUNZEL *helps her over the sill.*) How do you expect me to get a good foothold if you jerk the braid like that?

RAPUNZEL: I'm sorry, godmother, but it does pull, you know. I shall never get used to it.

WITCH (*Swinging the knapsack onto the table*): Here is your food—and a surprise.

RAPUNZEL: Oh, I was hoping there would be a surprise. What is it? Indian pudding? Gingerbread?

WITCH: It's a book. (*She takes book from knapsack.*)

RAPUNZEL (*Disappointed*): A book! It's awfully big. (*The* WITCH *hands it to her and she reads the title.*) *The Black Arts.* What does that mean?

WITCH: Enchantment! Sorcery! Witchcraft! This is my book of spells, Rapunzel.

RAPUNZEL: But what has it to do with me?

WITCH: It has everything to do with you, my little salad. (*Tapping the book with her finger.*) This book will teach you how to become—a *witch!*

RAPUNZEL (*Dropping book on table*): But I don't want to become a witch!

WITCH: Bah! You are fifteen years old now and it's time you made something of yourself.

RAPUNZEL: Then let me go out into the world and live like a human being.

WITCH: When you go out into the world it will not be as a human being but as a witch, a powerful witch! Now open that book and start studying. Learn the first lesson by heart. I shall test you when I return. (*She goes to the window.*) Goodbye, my little lettuce leaf. Mind you study your lesson well. (*She steps over the window sill, and disappears, as if climbing down* RAPUNZEL's *braid.* RAPUNZEL *draws up her hair, goes to table, opens book, and reads.*) "Lesson Number One. Make a brew of the following ingredients: the eyes of a lizard; the tail of a mouse; the legs of a spider; the wings of a bat; the skin of a toad." Ugh! (*She shivers.*) "Let stand for three days, then drink a thimbleful by the light of the waning moon." Oh, it's horrible! I won't do it, I won't, I won't! (*Sound of birds twittering is heard.* RAPUNZEL *turns to window.*) Hello, little birds! You sound very happy. How I envy your freedom! You can go wherever you like, but I can't. I'm locked in a cage.

PRINCE (*Calling from offstage*): Rapunzel! Rapunzel! Let down your hair!

RAPUNZEL (*Starting up in dismay*): Oh, good heavens, it's Dame Gothel! She's back already, and I haven't studied the lesson. She will be furious with me! (RAPUNZEL *hastily places book open on stool by window and starts memorizing text, at the same time lowering her braid out the window. She keeps her eyes on the page, mumbling to herself as she studies. Soon* PRINCE FREDERICK *appears outside window and jumps into room.*)

PRINCE: Good morning!

RAPUNZEL (*Looking up from book in alarm*): Oh! Where is Dame Gothel?

PRINCE: You mean that old woman who just left? Far away, I hope. Don't be afraid. I won't harm you.

RAPUNZEL: Who are you?

PRINCE: My name is Prince Frederick. I was riding through the forest and heard you singing. Your song was so sad, it touched my heart, and I stopped to listen. As I stood at the foot of this tower, I saw the old woman come, so

I hid in the trees, and heard her call to you—"Rapunzel! Rapunzel! Let down your hair!" Then, when she left, I called to you myself, and here I am.

RAPUNZEL: You must go away at once. If Dame Gothel finds you here, I don't know what she'll do.

PRINCE: I'm not afraid of her. But why are you shut up in this tower—a beautiful young girl like you?

RAPUNZEL: Dame Gothel keeps me here. She's a witch—and she's going to make me a witch, too!

PRINCE (*Horrified*): Then you must come away with me at once!

RAPUNZEL: How can I? There is no way of getting down from this tower except by my hair.

PRINCE: I have a strong rope in my saddlebag. I'm sure it is long enough to reach down to the ground. I'll get it. (*He climbs out the window and disappears.*)

RAPUNZEL (*Calling after him*): Hurry! Dame Gothel may be back any minute. (*Looking off into distance*) Oh, here she comes! Slide down quickly! There, he's safe. (*Calling to the* WITCH) Godmother! I saw you coming and let down my hair. (*Presently* WITCH *appears outside the window.*)

WITCH: Help me up, will you?

RAPUNZEL (*Helping her into the room*): Oh, you're so much heavier than the Prince! (*She exclaims in horror as she realizes what she has said.*)

WITCH: Prince? What prince?

RAPUNZEL: N-n-nobody, godmother.

WITCH: So! A prince has been here, has he? And is coming back, no doubt! Well, he'll get a warm welcome from me. Come here! I'll teach you to deceive me. (*She picks up a pair of huge scissors from table.*)

RAPUNZEL (*Backing away*): What are you going to do?

WITCH: This won't hurt. (*She grabs* RAPUNZEL'*s braid and cuts it off.*) Snip! Snap!

RAPUNZEL: Oh! You've cut off my hair! How can the Prince climb up to me now? (*She starts to weep.*)

WITCH: I'll show you how. (*She fastens the braid to a hook by window.*) Wait until he comes, my pretty. Wait until he sees who is holding this golden braid. (*A whistle is heard.*)

RAPUNZEL: There he is! (*She rushes to window but* WITCH *seizes her and pushes her back.*)

WITCH: Keep still! Now stand over there out of the way. (*She points to the other side of the room.*)

PRINCE (*Calling from offstage*): Rapunzel! Rapunzel! Let down your hair! (WITCH *lowers the braid out window, then crouches at one side so that* PRINCE *does not see her until he has jumped into room. A length of rope is coiled over his shoulder.*) Rapunzel, here is the rope.

WITCH: Aha! You have come to fetch your lady love, have you? Well, look on her for the last time because you will never see her again. When your sight returns, she and I will be far, far away. (WITCH *raises her arms and chants.*)

Demons of darkness,
    Black cats of night!
Scratch out his eyes,
    Take away his sight!

(PRINCE *cries out and falls to his knees, covering his eyes with his hands.*)

RAPUNZEL (*Running to him*): Frederick! What has she done?

PRINCE: She has cast a spell over my eyes! I cannot see!

RAPUNZEL (*Turning on* WITCH *in a fury*): You wicked old hag!

WITCH (*Picking up her book of spells*): Come with me! I'm taking you far away from here. (*She grips* RAPUNZEL *by the arm.*)

RAPUNZEL (*Pulling back*): I won't go!

WITCH: Oh yes, you will. Come along now. (*She drags* RAPUNZEL *to window and climbs onto sill.*)

RAPUNZEL: Let go of me! Let *go!* (*With a mighty effort, she jerks her arm free.* WITCH *loses her balance and falls from sight.*)

PRINCE (*Anxiously*): Rapunzel! What happened? Are you all right?

RAPUNZEL (*Leading him to a chair*): Yes, I am all right. But the witch has fallen from the tower and is gone forever.

PRINCE (*Sitting*): Thank heaven, you are saved.

RAPUNZEL (*Pityingly*): But you, my prince, you are not saved. The witch is not here to remove the spell. (*She weeps.*) Oh, whatever will we do?

PRINCE (*Putting his hands to her eyes*): What do I feel? Tears?

RAPUNZEL: Yes, dear Frederick, tears of love. I shall never leave you. I will take care of you always.

PRINCE (*Looking at her in amazement*): Why, what is this? I can *see* you, Rapunzel!

RAPUNZEL: You can *see?*

PRINCE: Oh, Rapunzel, your tears of love have broken the witch's spell! (*Suddenly there is a loud thunderclap, and lights flicker.*) Quickly, we must leave this tower! Is there anything you want to take with you?

RAPUNZEL (*Getting doll from cot*): Yes, this doll. My true parents gave it to me when I was a baby. (PRINCE *helps her out the window, then climbs down after her as the stage is in darkness, and thunder is heard. The curtains close. After a moment, the lights come up, and* RAPUNZEL *and* PRINCE *hurry in right, in front of curtain.*)

PRINCE: We escaped the tower just in time.

RAPUNZEL (*Pointing off right*): Look, Frederick! The tower is gone! It has disappeared. Was it a spell that did it?

PRINCE: Yes, Rapunzel, the spell of love, the greatest magic of all. (*Voices are heard off left and* EMMA *and* FRANZ *enter, looking about them, dazed.*)

EMMA: Where are we, Franz? How did we get here?

FRANZ: I haven't the slightest idea, Emma. (*He crosses to* PRINCE.) Your pardon, sir. Could you tell us, please, where we are?

PRINCE: You are at the edge of the enchanted forest.

FRANZ: The enchanted forest! Well, well! That probably accounts for it.

PRINCE: Accounts for what, my man?

FRANZ: Why, the way it happened. It was very strange. There was a loud thunderclap and suddenly we were here. (EMMA *has been staring at* RAPUNZEL *all this time and now she takes* FRANZ *aside.*)

EMMA (*Speaking with subdued excitement*): Franz, that doll—in the girl's arms. Isn't that the doll you made for our baby?

FRANZ (*Peering at the doll*): Why, I believe it is!

EMMA (*Hopefully*): Do you think—? Could it possibly be—?

FRANZ (*Going to* RAPUNZEL): Young lady, may I ask where you got that doll?

RAPUNZEL: Why, I've had it ever since I was a baby. My parents gave it to me.

EMMA: Who were your parents, my dear?

RAPUNZEL: I don't know. I was brought up by a witch called Dame Gothel.

FRANZ *and* EMMA: Dame Gothel!

EMMA: Oh, Franz, it *is* our child! Rapunzel!

RAPUNZEL: Mother! Father! (*They rush into each other's arms.*)

EMMA: My little girl!

FRANZ: My dearest daughter!

RAPUNZEL (*Introducing* PRINCE): Father, Mother—this is Prince Frederick, who rescued me from the witch. Oh, I have so much to tell you!

PRINCE: But not here, Rapunzel. Come, let us go to my kingdom where we can all talk to our heart's content, happily ever after. (*He leads the way off left.*)

THE END

The Magic Nutmeg-Grater

An original fairy tale

Characters

KARL
ELSA
FRAU STROPKEN, *their mother*
TINKER HANS
FRAU WELZEL, *the Mayor's wife*
LENA, *her daughter*
HEINRICH, *an artist*
HEIDI, *a milkmaid*
BEGGAR
PLAYMATES *of Karl and Elsa*

TIME: *A morning in May.*
SETTING: *A town square in old Germany. A low wall runs across the back of the stage, with a gateway center.*
AT RISE: KARL, ELSA *and* PLAYMATES *are in a circle, singing and dancing a folk game. (See "Swedish Song Games," by Kastman and Kohler [Ginn and Company]).*

ALL:
  And so we say good day, good day,
  All in the merry month of May.
  We shan't forget you; this is why:
  Because we are playmates, you and I.

And now I say, "Oh, go away!
I will not play with you today."
(*They stop singing as the voice of* TINKER HANS *is heard off, calling faintly.*)

TINKER HANS (*Off*): Kettles to mend! Kettles to mend!

KARL (*Holding up his hand for silence*): Listen!

ELSA: What is it, Karl?

KARL: It's Tinker Hans. Don't you hear him?

ELSA (*Listening*): No, I don't hear anything.

FIRST PLAYMATE: Neither do I.

KARL (*Going to the wall*): He's away down the street around the corner. You'll see him soon. (*All crowd around him and look off left.*)

TINKER HANS (*Sounding nearer*):
Tinker Hans, Tinker Hans,
Here he comes to mend your pans.

KARL: There! Hear him now?

FIRST PLAYMATE (*Whimpering*): Oh, Karl, I'm afraid!

SECOND PLAYMATE: So am I.

THIRD PLAYMATE: Me, too.

KARL: Afraid? Of what?

PLAYMATES (*In a chorus*): Tinker Hans!

ELSA: For mercy's sake, *why?*

SECOND PLAYMATE: I don't like him. He looks crazy, with all those pans and things dangling around him and banging together.

FIRST PLAYMATE: They say he's a wicked sorcerer.

THIRD PLAYMATE: And a mind reader.

FOURTH PLAYMATE: You mean, Tinker Hans can tell what you're thinking about without your saying a word?

THIRD PLAYMATE: That's right. All he has to do is look at you and he knows what's passing through your mind.

FIRST PLAYMATE: Mother says he bewitches the things he mends, so that the cakes all fall and the porridge burns.

THIRD PLAYMATE: That's because he uses *magic* metals

to mend them with. (*She cocks her ear.*) He says so him-self—listen!

TINKER HANS (*Close by*):

Tinker Hans will mend old kettles

With all sorts of magic metals.

THIRD PLAYMATE: See? What did I tell you. *Magic* metals.

FOURTH PLAYMATE (*Squealing*): He's coming! I'm going to run!

FIRST PLAYMATE: Come on! Let's go! (*All the* PLAYMATES *exit through the gateway.*)

ELSA (*Looking after them in disgust*): What ninnies they are—to be afraid of a poor old man!

KARL: That's because they don't understand him, Elsa. People are always afraid of what they don't understand.

ELSA (*Musing*): But if he really *can* read our thoughts—

KARL: Humph! I'd like to see him do it.

ELSA: Then you don't believe he can?

KARL: No-sir-ee!

TINKER HANS (*Still offstage, but distinctly, to tune of "This Old Man"*):

Here I come, Tinker Hans!

Will you let me mend your pans?

Many a pleasant tale they will surely tell

When they come back whole and well.

KARL: There's a big hole in Mother's tea kettle. I wonder how much he'd charge to mend it.

TINKER HANS (*To tune of "Reuben, Reuben, I've Been Thinking"*):

I will mend it for a penny.

If you're poor and haven't any,

I will mend it if you say:

"Please," and "Thank you," and "Good day." (TINKER HANS *appears behind the wall. Pots and kettles are slung over his arms. Saucepans and frying pans, cake*

*tins and trays hang from his neck and waist on lengths
of twine. Ladles are stuck through the band of his
broad-brimmed hat. He carries a brazier for heating
metals, and a bag of tools.)*

ELSA (*In a whisper of awe*): Oh, my goodness, Karl! He
answered you. And he couldn't possibly have heard
what you said. He wasn't even here!

KARL: Nonsense, Elsa! He just happened to say that. It's
one of his regular trade rhymes, I'll bet. (TINKER HANS
stops at the gate.)

TINKER HANS: Good morning, children.

KARL *and* ELSA: Good morning.

TINKER HANS (*To* KARL): Now, laddie, you run and fetch
your mother's tea kettle, and by the time you're back
with it, I'll be back, too, and I'll mend it for you. (*He
exits.*)

ELSA: Well, *that* certainly wasn't one of his trade rhymes!
He said it right out—*your mother's tea kettle.* If that
isn't reading people's minds, I'd like to know what is.

KARL (*Convinced*): You go and get the kettle, Elsa, and
I'll wait here. (ELSA *starts out left and meets* FRAU
STROPKEN, *who is entering.*)

ELSA: Oh, Mother, Tinker Hans wants to mend your tea
kettle.

FRAU STROPKEN: No, dear. We can't afford it.

ELSA: But, Mother, he isn't charging us much—only a
penny.

KARL: Or maybe nothing at all—if we say "thank you."

FRAU STROPKEN: Very well. (ELSA *exits left.* FRAU STROPKEN
crosses to KARL, *taking a penny from her pocket.*) Here,
Karl. Give this penny to Tinker Hans, and tell him
I wish it were more.

KARL: All right, Mother. (*He takes the penny and turns
it over in his palm, studying it thoughtfully.*) Mother

—what's the matter? Why are we so poor all of a sudden? (FRAU STROPKEN *puts her arm around* KARL'*s shoulder, and leads him to the bench, where they sit.*)

FRAU STROPKEN: It's not sudden, Karl. It's been coming ever since your father died. He was ill such a long time, and his entire savings were spent on medical care. We still owe Dr. Moritz a lot of money, and now he's asking me to settle up.

KARL: The whole amount?

FRAU STROPKEN: Yes. He's been quite disagreeable about it, too. He says he must have the money by next Thursday, and not a day later.

KARL: The old skinflint! What will you do?

FRAU STROPKEN: I'm going now to plead with him again for more time (*Sighing*) though I doubt if he will give it to me.

KARL: What will happen if he doesn't?

FRAU STROPKEN (*Faltering*): Then—then I'm afraid we shall have to sell our home to raise the money.

KARL (*Rising in consternation*): Sell our home! But, Mother, we can't do that! We'll have no place to live.

FRAU STROPKEN: I know, dear. (*She rises and takes his hand.*) Perhaps Dr. Moritz will have a change of heart. I'll be back as soon as I can. (*She exits.* ELSA *skips on left, carrying a tea kettle.*)

ELSA: Where's Mother?

KARL: She has gone to see Dr. Moritz about some money she owes him.

ELSA: Is it very much?

KARL: More than she can pay now—or maybe ever. Oh, Elsa! We may have to sell our home!

ELSA: Oh, no, Karl! Isn't there anyone who can help us?

TINKER HANS (*Off right, to tune of "Reuben, Reuben"*): When you're in a peck of trouble,

And expect that it will double,
Tinker Hans, if he's about,
Will be glad to help you out.

ELSA (*Excitedly*): Karl, did you hear that? Do you suppose—?

KARL: Tinker Hans? How could *he* help?

ELSA: I don't know, but he just said he could, and it will do no harm to ask him. (TINKER HANS *enters and comes downstage.*)

TINKER HANS (*To* ELSA): Hand over the tea kettle, my dear, and I'll have it mended in next to no time. (*He places his brazier of glowing coals on the ground, and opens his tool bag. Sings*)
I will teach it how to sing,
And to boil like anything. (*Sets to work*)

KARL: Tinker Hans, we—we thought perhaps—

TINKER HANS (*Humorously*): Is that so? Well, well!

ELSA (*Fidgeting*): You see, Tinker Hans—you—(TINKER HANS *looks up from his work and gazes steadily, first at one and then the other.*)

TINKER HANS: Is it something about your mother?

ELSA: How did you know?

TINKER HANS:
Wherever Hans the Tinker goes,
Every secret he soon knows. (*Pauses*)
Well? *Is* it your mother?

KARL: Yes, it is. She's in trouble.

TINKER HANS: Money matters, laddie?

KARL (*Nodding*): Yes. We always had enough until Father was sick. Now it's all gone, and Mother is deep in debt.

ELSA (*With an anguished cry*): We may lose our home!

TINKER HANS: Dear, dear! We can't let that happen.

KARL: It's so important to do something for Mother.

ELSA: And you're the only one we could think of who might be able to help.

TINKER HANS (*Looks at them sharply*): You know what folks call me, don't you?

KARL (*Meeting his gaze squarely*): Yes.

TINKER HANS: A wicked sorcerer—that's what they call me.

ELSA (*Hotly*): We don't!

KARL: They're a pack of fools!

TINKER HANS (*Continues working*): You're not afraid of me?

ELSA: I should say not!

KARL: We like you a lot. Oh, I do hope you'll be able to help us.

TINKER HANS: Hmmm. We shall see. (*Holds kettle out to* ELSA) Here you are, my dear. As good as new. And singing already. Listen! (*He whistles like a tea kettle and sings*)

Since Tinker Hans has mended me,

I feel as gay as gay can be.

ELSA *and* KARL (*Laughing*): Oh, thank you, Tinker Hans.

KARL: Here's your penny. I wish it were a gold piece.

TINKER HANS: But you've already paid me—when you said "Thank you."

KARL: No, no, please take it. Mother insists.

TINKER HANS (*Taking the penny*): Very well. Now I am in debt to your mother, and that means only one thing —I must help her. (*He feels in his pockets and brings out a nutmeg-grater.*) Do you know what this is?

ELSA (*Examining it*): It's a nutmeg-grater, isn't it?

KARL: But what are these strings for, stretched across the back here?

TINKER HANS: Ah, this is no ordinary nutmeg-grater, children. These four strings are tuned to the four winds. Each string has its wind, and each wind its song. And whatever the song, you will hear it when the wind blows. Hold it to your ear now, and listen. (KARL *and*

ELSA *share the nutmeg-grater between them, each with an ear to it.*) Do you hear anything? (*Sound of harp music is heard.*)

KARL: Oh my, yes! I hear music like a great wind wailing through the trees and the rigging of ships.

ELSA: Now it comes moaning. Oh, my gracious! (*She and* KARL *scream and drop the nutmeg-grater.*)

KARL: It shook so hard it nearly took my fingers off!

TINKER HANS: Don't be afraid of it. Pick it up. It will never vibrate enough to hurt you. Just hang on to it, no matter what. (*He gathers together his tools and brazier.*) I must go now. (*He starts to leave, and* KARL *grips his arm anxiously.*)

KARL: But Tinker Hans! You've forgotten about Mother.

TINKER HANS: Oh, no, I haven't. (*Smiles*) I never forget anything. Now listen to me carefully, and remember every word I say. (*He raises his hand to hold their attention, and speaks slowly, with great emphasis.*) *Whoever gives the nutmeg-grater to the one who needs it most shall have good fortune.* That is all. Goodbye, children. (*Sings to tune of "This Old Man" as he exits*)
Tinker Hans, Tinker Hans,
He has mended all your pans.
He must now be on his merry way,
He'll come back another day. (*Exits*)

KARL (*Studies nutmeg-grater and repeats*): "Whoever gives the nutmeg-grater to the one who needs it most shall have good fortune." What do you make of it, Elsa?

ELSA: I've no idea. It's such a worthless-looking thing. Not pretty at all. (*She sniffs it.*) Smells spicy, though. Let me listen to it again. (*She takes the grater and holds it to her ear.*)

KARL: Do you hear the wind? (*Sound of harp music is heard.*)

ELSA: It's a different song this time—sweet and swaying.

KARL: That must be the West wind.

ELSA: Oh! It's beginning to vibrate! (*Her hand shakes violently.*)

KARL: Hang on to it! Don't drop it! Remember Tinker Hans said it wouldn't hurt you. (ELSA *steadies the grater against her ear and looks astonished.*) What is it?

ELSA (*Breathlessly*): I hear people talking. They're talking about me.

KARL: What do you mean?

ELSA: Someone is saying that I do the worst embroidery in town. That's not true!

KARL (*Reaching for the nutmeg-grater*): Do you hear *voices* in that thing?

ELSA: Shhhhh!

KARL: You're dreaming. Give it here. (*He tugs the grater from her and holds it to his ear. After a moment*) Nothing. Nothing but the wind.

ELSA: But wait! Wait till it vibrates again. That's when *I* heard the voices.

KARL (*Scoffing*): Look here, Elsa. You don't think this nutmeg-grater can *talk*, do you?

ELSA: No, but I think it lets you hear what other people say.

KARL: Balderdash! *Ow!* (*His hand begins to tremble with the vibration of the grater.*)

ELSA: Quick! Listen before it stops shaking. (*Pauses*) Well? Is anyone speaking?

KARL (*Frowning*): Yes—Dr. Moritz.

ELSA: What's he saying?

KARL: He says, "It's time that good-for-nothing boy of yours went to work, instead of loafing around like a rich man's son."

ELSA: He must be talking to Mother. Anything else?

KARL: Nothing. It's all quiet. (*He lowers the grater and*

regards it thoughtfully.) You know, Elsa, I believe I've
guessed the secret of this thing.

ELSA: Oh, tell me!

KARL: Have you noticed that when *you* hold it, the voices
say things only about *you?* And when *I* hold it, they say
things only about *me?*

ELSA: That's right.

KARL: Then what we have to work out is whom to give it
to—who is the one who needs it most?

ELSA: How shall we find the right person?

KARL: We'll have to try it out on different people and
see what happens.

ELSA: You mean, just anyone?

KARL: No—people of importance, who can pay us well
for it.

ELSA (*At the gate, looking off right*): Well, here comes the
Mayor's wife with her daughter. They're pretty important people. Shall we begin with them?

KARL: A good idea. (FRAU WELZEL, *the Mayor's wife, and*
LENA, *her daughter, enter up right, heads held high.*
KARL *bows.*) Good morning, Frau Welzel.

ELSA: Good morning, Lena. (FRAU WELZEL *and* LENA
barely nod.)

KARL: Frau Welzel, I have something here that's very unusual. I think it might interest you.

FRAU WELZEL (*Haughtily*): What is it?

KARL: A nutmeg-grater, ma'am. (*He shows it to her.*)

LENA (*Tittering affectedly*): Oh, Mama, how droll!

FRAU WELZEL: And why, pray, would I be interested in
that rusty old thing?

KARL: There's not another one like it in the whole world.
It is a *magic* nutmeg-grater.

FRAU WELZEL: What's magic about it?

LENA (*Sarcastically*): Perhaps, Mama, it will grate nutmeg
all by itself.

ELSA: It will do better than that.

LENA: Indeed?

ELSA: It will tell you what people are saying about you. (LENA *laughs and* FRAU WELZEL *snorts in derision.*)

FRAU WELZEL: Do you take me for a numbskull, girl?

KARL: Elsa is right, ma'am. Please try it. Hold it to your ear, and when it begins to vibrate, that means someone has mentioned your name.

FRAU WELZEL: Well, I suppose it won't do any harm to try it. (*She takes the grater and raises it to her ear.*)

LENA: I want to hear, too, Mama.

FRAU WELZEL: After me, dear. (*The grater starts to vibrate almost immediately.*)

KARL: Don't let go of it, ma'am, or the voices will not speak. (FRAU WELZEL *grips grater firmly. After a moment, her face lights up with pleasure.*)

LENA: Who is it, Mama?

FRAU WELZEL: It's my dressmaker, dear. She's telling your Papa about my new gowns. She calls me "that most gracious, bountiful, beautiful and noble lady." Now she's asking your Papa to pay her for the dresses.

LENA: How much?

FRAU WELZEL: Two thousand guilders. (FRAU WELZEL'S *expression changes from delight to rage.*) Why, the wretch! The heartless wretch!

LENA: Who, Mama?

FRAU WELZEL: Your Papa! He says I'm *not* gracious or bountiful or beautiful or noble! I'm bad-tempered, and greedy, and ugly, and vain, and—and—*Oh!* (*She thrusts the grater into* KARL'S *hand and grabs* LENA'S *arm.*) We're going home, Lena! Wait till I see your Papa!

LENA (*Pulling back*): But, Mama, I didn't have *my* turn! *I* want to listen!

FRAU WELZEL: And hear your Papa say disgraceful things

about *you?* I wouldn't put it past him, the viper! Come
along, now. (*They exit.*)

KARL: Whew! I wouldn't want to be the Mayor when she
gets hold of *him!*

ELSA: Serves her right, the pompous old High-and-Mighty!
And that stuck-up Lena, too! Well, what shall we do
now? Wait for the next person?

KARL (*Nodding*): It's the only way we'll find the right one.
(*He looks up and down the street.*) Say, there's Heinrich, the artist! Let's try him. (*He calls off*) Heinrich!
Heinrich! Come here! (*Presently* HEINRICH *enters, carrying an easel, a small canvas and his paint-box. He comes
through gate.*)

HEINRICH: Hello, there! I'm on my way to the river to
paint the fishermen. Would you two like to come along
and watch?

KARL: Not today, thank you. Uh—Heinrich?

HEINRICH: Yes?

KARL: Do you believe in magic?

HEINRICH (*Coming downstage*): Well, I've seen a few
strange things in my travels.

KARL: Would you be surprised if I showed you something
magic?

HEINRICH (*Smiling*): What is it?

KARL: This nutmeg-grater.

HEINRICH: Let's see it. (*He sets down his equipment, and
scrutinizes grater.*) Hmmm. It looks about as magical
as—well, as a nutmeg-grater.

KARL (*Laughing*): That's just it! But these strings are
tuned to the four winds. And if anyone is speaking
about you, no matter where—north, east, south or west
—the strings will vibrate, and then you can hear what
is being said by holding the grater to your ear.

HEINRICH: Amazing!

KARL: Try it. (HEINRICH *sits on bench and holds grater to his ear. Harp music is heard.*)

HEINRICH: What lovely music!

KARL: That's the song of the wind. You can hear that any time. But it's only when the nutmeg-grater vibrates all over that voices can be heard. There! It's beginning to shake now. (HEINRICH's *hand shakes.*)

HEINRICH (*Listening eagerly*): There's quite a babble of voices. It sounds like a gathering of some kind. Yes— it's a group of artists. They're talking about my paintings. (*Pauses*) What's that? All *bad!—my* paintings? (*He takes grater away from his ear.*) Bah! I'm a fool to listen. (*He rises and extends the grater to* KARL.) Here! Take the wretched thing back.

KARL (*Anxiously*): I hope it hasn't upset you.

HEINRICH (*Bitterly*): Upset me! It has ruined my peace of mind, that's all! It has shaken my belief in myself.

KARL: I'm sorry, Heinrich, truly I am.

HEINRICH: There, there! You're not to blame. It's my own fault.

ELSA: How is it your fault?

HEINRICH: I should have more sense than to let a pack of tuppenny artists provoke me like this. Forgive me, children. (*He gathers up his things.*) Now I'm off to regain my self-confidence by painting the finest picture of my life. You wait and see! Goodbye, Karl. Goodbye, Elsa. (*He exits through gateway with a jaunty air.*)

KARL (*Sitting on bench*): Well, we don't seem to have gotten very far toward helping Mother. This thing isn't so wonderful, after all. Nobody wants it.

ELSA (*Sitting beside him*): I wish we could see Tinker Hans again. Perhaps he would tell us more about it.

KARL: I doubt it. Folks who deal in magic never tell you much. They just say, "Take this magic ring, or hat, or stick, or whatever it is, and see what you shall see." (*Dur-*

ing this speech, HEIDI, *a milkmaid, enters unnoticed. She stands listening for a moment, then speaks.)*

HEIDI: Hello. (KARL *and* ELSA *jump to their feet in surprise.)*

ELSA (*Crossing to her*): Oh, hello, Heidi.

HEIDI: That's a curious thing you have, Karl. What is it?

KARL: This? It's a magic nutmeg-grater.

HEIDI: Magic, did you say?

ELSA: You sound as if you didn't believe in magic.

HEIDI: That depends. What can your nutmeg-grater do?

KARL: It can make music when the wind blows. And it lets you hear what people say about you, too.

HEIDI: You mean, gossip and such?

KARL: I suppose you'd call it that. Would you like to try it?

HEIDI: What for? Just to hear myself talked about? No, thank you. Folks have to talk, I know, and if they want to talk about *me,* I don't mind. But *listen* to them? (*She shakes her head.*) I'd rather spend my time lying in the meadow, watching the clouds sail by. I don't have time to listen to gossip. That's not my idea of magic.

ELSA (*Earnestly*): Tell me, Heidi—what is?

HEIDI: It would be magic if I could hear the footsteps of a ladybug, walking on a blade of grass—or the splash a star makes when it shines in the river. I'd say that was *true* magic. (*Smiles*) Goodbye. I must be on my way. (HEIDI *leaves as quietly as she came.* KARL *and* ELSA *look after her.*)

ELSA (*Wistfully*): Karl, wouldn't it be wonderful if we *could* hear things like that in the nutmeg-grater?

KARL: Yes. Then, perhaps, we'd have some luck with it. As it is now, nobody will have anything to do with it.

ELSA: There *must* be someone who needs it, or Tinker Hans wouldn't have said so.

KARL (*Grumpily*): Oh, bother Tinker Hans!

ELSA (*Suddenly*): Karl! I know! I know someone who needs it!

KARL (*With indifference*): You do?

ELSA: Someone who really would be helped by hearing himself talked about.

KARL: Who?

ELSA: The King!

KARL (*Startled*): The *King?*

ELSA: Yes. Aren't people always talking about him, day and night? And isn't it important for him to know what they say, so that he can rule his kingdom well?

KARL (*Awe-struck*): Yes, but—take *this* to the *King?* I wouldn't dare.

ELSA: Not even for Mother's sake?

KARL: But how could I reach him?—I mean, get into the palace to see him?

ELSA: You'd stand a better chance than a grown person, because he's not much more than a boy himself, and very friendly, I've heard. Why, I'll bet he'd be *glad* to try the nutmeg-grater.

KARL: At least he'd be rich enough to pay us for it.

ELSA: Rich enough! Why, he could pay Mother's debts ten times over and never know he had opened his purse.

KARL (*Warming to the plan*): We could walk to the palace in two hours and be back by nightfall. Mother needn't know.

ELSA: Let's start now! (*They go through gateway and collide with a* BEGGAR *who has entered up right.*)

KARL: Oh, we're sorry!

ELSA: Are you all right?

BEGGAR: I think so. Where are you off to in such a hurry?

KARL: To see the King.

BEGGAR: Oho, that's glibly said. But will the King see you? The King is closely guarded, and few people get to see him.

ELSA: How do *you* know about the King?

BEGGAR (*Evasively*): Oh, I hang around the palace. Tell me, why do you want to see the King?

KARL: We want to sell him this nutmeg-grater.

BEGGAR (*With an amused smile*): What would the King do with a nutmeg-grater? He probably has a pantry full of them already.

KARL: Well, you know the King has many enemies—I mean, traitors who want to take his crown away and whatnot—and so we figured this would help him find them out.

BEGGAR: How would it?

KARL: It's magic, and when anyone speaks about you— anyone, anywhere in the world—you can hear what's being said right inside this nutmeg-grater. (*The* BEGGAR *stares hard at* KARL *for a moment, then he holds out his hand.*)

BEGGAR: Give it to me.

KARL (*Putting the grater behind his back*): No, it's for the King.

ELSA: Oh, let the poor man see it, Karl. (KARL *gives grater to* BEGGAR, *who studies it curiously.*)

BEGGAR: So you want to sell this thing. Why?

KARL: To help Mother. You see, our Father was sick a long time before he died, and now Mother has nothing. She's about to sell our home to pay her debts.

BEGGAR: What is your name, boy?

KARL: Karl Stropken. And this is my sister, Elsa. (*The grater begins to tremble violently.*) Don't be afraid of the trembling. It's a warning that someone is talking about you.

BEGGAR (*Putting it to his ear*): Oh! There are so many voices—like a crowd chattering. It's so confused and mixed-up, I can hardly make out anything.

KARL: It will clear up soon, and then you'll be able to understand.

BEGGAR: It's still quite noisy. Everybody is talking at once —"The King this and the King that."

KARL: But why is the King's name mentioned? You must be mistaken. You should hear only your own name, and what is being said about *you*.

BEGGAR (*Horrified by what he hears*): It *is* being said about me!

ELSA (*In a whisper*): Karl, you don't think—? Can he be—?

KARL: Are *you* the *King*?

BEGGAR (*Nodding solemnly*): Yes, I am the King. And sometimes I wish I'd never heard the word. I wish I'd been born poor, like this beggar I pretend to be.

ELSA: Why do you pretend to be a beggar, Your Majesty?

BEGGAR: So that I can go among my people, unrecognized, and get to know them better. It's not the people who betray me. It's my own flesh and blood. Just now I heard my cousin plotting to overthrow me and take my throne. Luckily, I have found out in time, thanks to this magic nutmeg-grater.

KARL: At last, Elsa—here is "the one who needs it most."

BEGGAR: What did you say, Karl?

KARL: When Tinker Hans gave us the nutmeg-grater, he told us that if we gave it to the one who needs it most, we should have good fortune.

BEGGAR: And so you shall, children. I'll settle your mother's debts, and give her five hundred gold pieces besides. As for you, Karl—how would you like to live in the palace and be my page?

KARL: Oh, Your Majesty! I'd like nothing better.

ELSA: It's just the way things happen in a fairy tale, Karl

—good fortune comes from the last place you expect to find it! (*They gaze happily at nutmeg-grater. Harp music is heard, swelling to a crescendo, as curtain falls.*)

THE END

Christmas Every Day

by William Dean Howells

Characters

KINDHEART, *the Christmas Fairy*
TINSEL ⎱
TASSEL ⎰ *two Christmas Elves*
MRS. PHILLIPS
MR. PHILLIPS
ABIGAIL ⎱
ROBIN ⎰ *their children*
JENNY
JIM

SCENE 1

TIME: *Christmas Eve.*

SETTING: *The living room of Abigail's home, decorated for Christmas and flooded with "winter moonlight." There is a fireplace, center in the rear wall, with four stockings hanging from the mantelpiece.*

AT RISE: *After a moment, the French windows at left open, and* KINDHEART *and her helpers,* TINSEL *and* TASSEL, *tiptoe into room. The Elves dance about, giggling as they turn on the lamps.*

216

KINDHEART: Sh-h-h!

TINSEL: Is this where she lives?

KINDHEART: Yes, Tinsel. Now be quiet, both of you, or you'll wake her up.

TASSEL: Wake up *who*, Kindheart?

KINDHEART: The little girl who wants it to be Christmas every day.

TASSEL: Every day in the year?

KINDHEART: Yes, Tassel. She began sending me post cards right after Thanksgiving asking if she might have it that way.

TASSEL: What's her name?

KINDHEART: Abigail.

TINSEL: Did you answer her?

KINDHEART: You know how fussy I am about my mail. I never answer post cards—only letters.

TASSEL (*Relieved*): So you haven't written her.

KINDHEART: Oh, yes, I have. About a week ago, she sent me a real letter.

TINSEL: I guess you couldn't ignore *that*.

KINDHEART: I should say not. (*Taking letter from pocket of cape*) I have the answer right here.

TASSEL: Christmas every day! What a horrible idea!

TINSEL: You couldn't just—*lose* your answer, and forget the letter, could you?

KINDHEART: No, my conscience would bother me. I really think I should grant her wish.

TASSEL: Not for always, Kindheart. Please, *please*—not for always!

KINDHEART: No, not for always. Just for one year. She'll want it stopped long before then.

TASSEL: How greedy she is!

KINDHEART: I think we'll change that. (*Holds up letter and looks around*) Now, where shall I put this so she'll be sure to find it first thing tomorrow morning?

TINSEL: Read it to us first!

KINDHEART: All right. (*She removes the letter from the envelope and reads.*) "Dear Abigail. After careful consideration, I have decided to grant your request for Christmas every day. Beginning December 25th, every one of the next three hundred and sixty-five days shall be Christmas. With sincere holiday greetings, Signed, Kindheart, the Christmas Fairy." (*She returns letter to envelope.*)

TASSEL (*Going to the fireplace*): Why don't you put the letter in her stocking? She's bound to find it there.

KINDHEART: Good idea! (*She tucks letter in top of ABI-GAIL's stocking.*) There! Now, turn out the lights, my dears, and we'll be off. (*The Elves skip about, snapping off lamps, and then they follow KINDHEART through French windows, closing them without a sound.*)

CURTAIN

*   *   *

SCENE 2

TIME: *Christmas morning.*

SETTING: *Same as Scene 1.*

AT RISE: ABIGAIL *runs through the archway in her night-gown, and goes to the fireplace. She is followed immediately by* ROBIN *in his pajamas.*

ROBIN: Merry Christmas, Abigail!

ABIGAIL (*Turning to him*): Oh, Robin, I wanted to say it first!

ROBIN: You can say it now.

ABIGAIL (*Hugging him*): Merry Christmas! (*She turns back to the stockings.*) Everything's here.

ROBIN: I told you it would be. Which is mine? This is yours.

ABIGAIL: Here's yours. (*In the excitement of exchanging stockings,* KINDHEART'S *letter falls unnoticed to hearth of the fireplace.* ABIGAIL *and* ROBIN *sit on floor and start emptying their stockings.*)

ROBIN: Hurray! A jackknife!

ABIGAIL: I want a jackknife, too.

ROBIN: You're a girl. You can't whittle.

ABIGAIL (*Reaching for knife*): I'll show you!

ROBIN (*Pushing her hand away good-naturedly*): No you don't! Look in your own stocking. (ABIGAIL *unwraps a fruitcake, baked in the shape of Santa Claus.*)

ABIGAIL: A Santa fruitcake!

ROBIN (*Snatching at it*): Give me a piece!

ABIGAIL: Wait! I'll break it in half. (*She divides cake and hands* ROBIN *his portion.* MR. *and* MRS. PHILLIPS *enter right, in dressing gowns.* MR. PHILLIPS *yawns and stretches.*)

MRS. PHILLIPS: Merry Christmas, children! (ABIGAIL *and* ROBIN *leap to their feet.*)

BOTH: Merry Christmas, Mamma!

ABIGAIL (*Crossing to* MR. PHILLIPS *and shaking him*): Wake up, Papa! It's Christmas morning!

MR. PHILLIPS: It can't be morning. I just went to bed.

ABIGAIL: Yes, it is! Look in your stocking. (*She pushes him toward fireplace, and together they take down his stocking.* MRS. PHILLIPS *digs down into hers, with* ROBIN *helping.*)

ROBIN (*As* MRS. PHILLIPS *takes out a small parcel wrapped in tissue paper*): I know what it is!

MRS. PHILLIPS (*Unwrapping it and laughing*): A potato!

MR. PHILLIPS (*Pulling a lumpy parcel from his stocking and unwrapping it*): Lumps of coal!

ABIGAIL (*Laughing*): You always get coal for Christmas, don't you, Papa?

ROBIN: And Mamma always gets a potato.

MRS. PHILLIPS: Now, run along to the playroom, my darlings, and look at the Christmas tree. But remember, we don't open our presents till after we're dressed.

ABIGAIL: I know what they'll be! Books, and games, and parasols, and dolls' houses—

MRS. PHILLIPS:—and boxes of handkerchiefs—

ROBIN:—and skates, and sleds, and sets of water colors—

MR. PHILLIPS:—and little easels and raincoats—

ABIGAIL and ROBIN (*Together*):—and *dozens* of ties for Papa! (*General laughter as* ABIGAIL *and* ROBIN *run off right.*)

CURTAIN

*   *   *

SCENE 3

TIME: *The day after Christmas.*

SETTING: *Same as Scene 1.*

AT RISE: ROBIN *is leading* ABIGAIL *through archway right. She is wearing a blindfold over her eyes. Both are wearing their nightclothes. The four stockings are filled and hanging from the fireplace mantel as in Scene 1.*

ABIGAIL: What is it? What's the matter?

ROBIN: Nothing's the matter. It's Christmas Day!

ABIGAIL: You can't fool me, smarty.

ROBIN: Who's a smarty? You just take off this blindfold and look. (*He helps her undo the blindfold, and she stares in amazement at bulging stockings.*) You see, it really *is* Christmas.

ABIGAIL (*Crossing to the fireplace*): But how can it be? Yesterday was Christmas. Don't you remember? (*She feels stockings.*) You got a jackknife, and I got a Santa fruitcake.

ROBIN: I can't help that. I have a jackknife and you have

a Santa fruitcake again—today. See? (*He shows her jackknife he has taken out of his stocking.*)

ABIGAIL (*Unwrapping fruitcake*): Oh, dear! Do you think I'll get a stomach ache again, too?

ROBIN: That depends. If you eat too much of it, you will.

ABIGAIL (*Nibbling fruitcake*): I won't. (MR. *and* MRS. PHILLIPS, *looking baffled, enter in their dressing gowns. They are carrying neatly wrapped presents.*)

MR. PHILLIPS: What's the meaning of this? The Christmas tree is blazing away in the playroom—with presents piled up a mile high!

MRS. PHILLIPS: Not a single one of them is unwrapped, either.

MR. PHILLIPS: It seems to me we had something like this yesterday—or did I dream it?

ABIGAIL (*Laughing*): Oh, Papa!

MRS. PHILLIPS: Where are we going to put everything? The house is crammed to the rafters, as it is.

MR. PHILLIPS (*Exasperated*): And what about the expense? Now I'll have to pay for everything all over again. I'll be bankrupt if this keeps up. (*He starts out right.*)

MRS. PHILLIPS (*Alarmed, following him*): If it keeps up! Are we going to have Christmas every day? (*They exit.*)

ABIGAIL (*Suddenly remembering*): Christmas every day! (ROBIN *catches sight of* KINDHEART'S *letter lying on hearth. He picks it up and looks at the inscription on envelope.*)

ROBIN: Here's a card or something, Abigail, with your name on it. It must have fallen out of your stocking.

ABIGAIL (*Taking it*): I wonder who sent it.

ROBIN: Why don't you open it and find out? I'm going to look at the Christmas tree. (*He exits right.* ABIGAIL *opens letter.*)

ABIGAIL (*Reading*): "Dear Abigail. After careful consideration . . . (*Her eyes skim over letter; she resumes read-*

ing) Beginning December 25th, every one of the next three hundred and sixty-five days shall be Christmas." (*She looks up with shining eyes.*) Oh, my goodness gracious! It's from the Christmas Fairy! I won't tell anyone—not even Mamma. I'll just keep this a secret. I'll have the greatest fun! (*She throws herself on divan, hugging herself in glee.*)

CURTAIN

* * *

SCENE 4

TIME: *The Fourth of July.*

SETTING: *Same as Scene 1. The stockings and Christmas decorations are still up. The French windows are open.*

AT RISE: MRS. PHILLIPS *is seated on the divan, checking her shopping list.* MR. PHILLIPS *is standing center, looking over a sheaf of bills.*

MRS. PHILLIPS: Fred, it's simply terrible! Mr. Giles is charging two thousand dollars apiece for turkeys.

MR. PHILLIPS: Great Scott! I'm sure I saw some at the delicatessen yesterday for *one* thousand.

MRS. PHILLIPS: That was yesterday. Anyway, Mr. Giles says we'd better be careful about buying cheap poultry.

MR. PHILLIPS (*Noticing an item on one of the bills, with a start*): What the dickens! Cranberries—a diamond each? It's highway robbery!

MRS. PHILLIPS: I know, dear. But I bought only one cranberry—for you. You do so love your cranberry sauce.

MR. PHILLIPS: Not at that price, I don't! I'll be satisfied with plain potatoes from now on.

MRS. PHILLIPS: That's another thing, Fred. These past six months, we've used so many potatoes to stuff the toes of our stockings that I can hardly get enough to make salads for Sunday suppers. And it's the same with coal. All the mines are cleaned out.

MR. PHILLIPS (*Exploding*): How are people going to *live*, Dora? On roots? There's no fruit to be had for love or money. All the orchards and woods are cut down for Christmas trees!

MRS. PHILLIPS: That reminds me. (*She goes to French windows and looks off.*) Mrs. Dawson is sending Jenny over with a Christmas-tree pattern.

MR. PHILLIPS: A *pattern?*

MRS. PHILLIPS: Yes. You cut the shape of the tree out of rags and stuff it with sawdust, like an old-fashioned doll.

MR. PHILLIPS: Rags! That's a wonderful idea! There's no scarcity of rags nowadays. What with people buying presents for each other all the time, they can't afford any new clothes, so they just wear their old clothes to tatters. (MRS. PHILLIPS *glances through French windows and waves.*)

MRS. PHILLIPS (*Calling off*): In here, Jenny! (*She turns back into room.*) Here comes Jenny now. I can't wait to start making that Christmas tree. (JENNY *enters through French windows. She crosses to* MRS. PHILLIPS *and gives her a folded newspaper pattern.*)

JENNY: Mom sent over this pattern, Mrs. Phillips. She says if you have any trouble figuring it out, she'll be glad to help you. We have three of them at our house.

MRS. PHILLIPS (*Studying pattern*): I don't think I'll have any trouble, Jenny. It looks simple enough.

JENNY (*Sitting down on divan with a sigh*): My, but it's peaceful here! Over at our house, everybody's getting crosser and crosser, losing their tempers and that sort of thing.

MR. PHILLIPS (*Laughing*): Well, we have our lost tempers here, too, Jenny. And what's more, we've nearly lost our voices saying "Merry Christmas" so much.

MRS. PHILLIPS (*Sighing*): Yes. I simply don't say it any more. Whoever would have thought that we'd be saying "Merry Christmas" every day of the year, even on Valentine's Day, Washington's Birthday, April Fools' Day, and now the Fourth of July?

JENNY: At least all the presents were fake on April Fools' Day. That certainly was a relief. (*A voice is heard off left calling "Jenny." She rises.*) That's Mom. I have to recite the Declaration of Independence at Soldier's Monument this afternoon, and Mom wants me to get ready. (*She walks slowly toward the French windows, reciting as she goes.*) "When in the course of human events it becomes necessary for one people to—" (*Without pausing, she breaks into a carol and sings*) "Deck the halls with boughs of holly, Tra-la-la-la-la, la-la, la, la! 'Tis the season to be jolly, Tra-la-la-la-la, la-la, la, la!" (*She exits left.*)

MRS. PHILLIPS (*Shaking her head sadly*): Isn't it perfectly awful?

MR. PHILLIPS: I have to go and shovel the presents off the sidewalk. If I don't, Constable Duggan says he'll have me hauled into court for obstructing a public way.

MRS. PHILLIPS: But where are we going to put them, Fred? There's not an *inch* of space left in the barn.

MR. PHILLIPS (*Shrugging*): Your guess is as good as mine, Dora.

MRS. PHILLIPS: If only we could find out who's responsible for all this Christmas! (MR. PHILLIPS *starts right and collides with* JIM, *who runs through archway, carrying a paper bag.*)

MR. PHILLIPS: Whoa there, Jim!

JIM: Excuse me, Mr. Phillips. Where's Rob?

MRS. PHILLIPS (*Looking off left*): He was on the porch, getting his fireworks together. There he is.

JIM (*Calling*): Hey, Rob! (*He waves the paper bag.*) I have them!

ROBIN (*Appearing in the French windows*): Have what?

JIM: Torpedoes!

MRS. PHILLIPS: Now, don't burn your fingers off. (*She exits right with* MR. PHILLIPS.)

JIM: No'm. (ROBIN *comes into room with two boxes of fireworks.*)

ROBIN (*Holding them up*): Look, Jim, Roman candles.

JIM (*Rummaging in his paper bag*): You'd better stuff your ears with cotton. I'm going to crash this torpedo right down on these bricks. (*He indicates hearth.* ROBIN *quickly sets his fireworks on divan and covers his ears with his hands.* JIM *hurls torpedo to hearth. There is a dull thud.*)

ROBIN (*Taking his hands away from his ears*): I didn't hear anything. Did you?

JIM (*Puzzled*): No. It must have been a dud.

ROBIN: Let me try one. (JIM *hands him bag.*) All right. Stand back, or you'll be *sorr-eeeee!* (*There is another dull thud as the torpedo hits bricks.* ROBIN *looks into bag*) What's the matter with these things? They make about as much noise as a wad of chewing gum.

JIM (*Snatching bag away*): Let me see them. (*He examines torpedoes.*) For Pete's sake!

ROBIN: Something wrong?

JIM: I'll say. These are no more torpedoes than the man in the moon!

ROBIN: What are they?

JIM: *Big—fat—raisins!*

ROBIN: *Raisins?* (*He takes handful of raisins out of bag.*)

JIM: Yes, raisins! Right out of a Christmas plum pudding, I'll bet! Isn't that something? Raisins instead of fireworks on the Fourth of July!

ROBIN: I wonder if my Roman candles—(*He opens a box.*) Oh, *no!*

JIM (*Nodding grimly*): Oh, *yes!*

ROBIN: They're candy canes! And I paid two dollars for them.

JIM: Doesn't it beat everything? *Another* Christmas Day! (*He sinks onto divan, disgusted, and* ROBIN *collapses beside him with a groan.* ABIGAIL *enters right, dangling a doll in one hand and a toy gun in the other. She throws toy gun at* ROBIN.)

ABIGAIL: Here, take it, you horrid old thing!

ROBIN (*Jumps to his feet, surprised*): What is it?

ABIGAIL (*Sullenly*): Your Christmas present.

ROBIN: Aren't you going to wrap it? (*He picks it up.*)

ABIGAIL (*Furiously*): I'm never going to wrap another Christmas present as long as I live!

JIM (*Rising*): But you just can't go around throwing 'em at people. You have to leave them at the front door, with little cards, saying—

ABIGAIL (*Interrupting; sarcastically*): "For dear Jim" or "Dear Jenny." Well, I *won't!* I'll *slam* them against the front door, or over the fence, or through the window! I hate the *sight* of presents! (*She begins to shake her doll, throwing it on the floor and sitting on it, sobbing hysterically.* MRS. PHILLIPS *hurries in right, and goes to her, worried.*)

MRS. PHILLIPS: Abbie! Abbie! Little sister! There, there. (*She puts her arms around* ABIGAIL *and leads her to divan.*) Run along, boys. Robin, you can help your father clear away the presents in front of the house. (*Boys exit left.* MRS. PHILLIPS *and* ABIGAIL *sit on divan.*)

ABIGAIL (*Bursting into sobs*): Oh, Mamma! It's all my fault!

MRS. PHILLIPS: What's all your fault, dear?

ABIGAIL: That we're having Christmas every day.

Mrs. Phillips (*Aghast*): What are you *saying*, Abbie?

Abigail: *I'm* to blame, Mamma. I wrote to the Christmas Fairy, and begged her to make it happen.

Mrs. Phillips: Whatever made you *do* such a thing, Abbie?

Abigail: I don't know. I was just greedy, I guess. Just a Christmas *pig!*

Mrs. Phillips: Why don't you write again, and ask the Fairy to stop it?

Abigail: I have. I write every day. I've even sent telegrams, but it doesn't do any good.

Mrs. Phillips: You might try calling at her house.

Abigail: I've done that, too, but the Elf who comes to the door always says, "Not at home," or "Engaged," or "At dinner." Oh, Mamma, what am I going to do?

Mrs. Phillips: I wish I knew, Abbie.

Abigail (*Panic-stricken*): What if the Fairy should forget to stop it when the year is up?

Mrs. Phillips: Did she say it would end in a year?

Abigail: Yes—see? Here's her letter. (Abigail *takes letter from her pocket and points to a sentence.*)

Mrs. Phillips (*Reading aloud*): "—three hundred and sixty-five days shall be Christmas." This is July fourth—six months to go. Well, Abbie, all we can do is to get through the rest of the days somehow.

CURTAIN

* * *

Scene 5

Time: *The day after Christmas.*

Setting: *Same as Scene 1.*

At Rise: *No one is in room, but apparently a celebration is taking place outside the house. Bells are ringing, whistles are blowing, people are shouting and cheering. After a moment, Robin gallops through archway right, shaking a noisemaker.*

ROBIN: Yippee! It's over! It's positively over! No more Christmas! Hurray! (*He goes about room, tearing down decorations.*)

ABIGAIL (*Running in right*): Robin, what's happening? Why are the whistles blowing?

ROBIN: It's the end of Christmas, Abbie!

ABIGAIL: Really? You mean I won't have to look at those lumpy old stockings another single solitary minute? Oh, joy! (*She yanks stockings off mantel and throws them into fireplace.*)

ROBIN: Don't throw those there!

ABIGAIL: Why not?

ROBIN: Up on Derry Hill they're making a huge bonfire of all the stockings and presents and decorations that people don't want. Let's take everything up there and burn it.

ABIGAIL: Candy and nuts and raisins, too?

ROBIN: No—the city carts are going around, picking up that junk.

ABIGAIL: What for?

ROBIN: They're going to dump it in the river.

ABIGAIL: But won't it give the fish a stomach ache?

ROBIN: Sure, but they'll survive—just as we did! Take down the rest of the decorations, will you? I'll meet you out front with my express wagon and we'll load it up. (*He exits right. ABIGAIL gets a chair and stands on it to take down wreath over fireplace, when French windows open softly, and TINSEL and TASSEL tiptoe into room, followed by Christmas Fairy, KINDHEART. ABIGAIL turns and sees them.*)

ABIGAIL (*Startled*): Oh! Who are you?

TINSEL: I'm Tinsel.

TASSEL: I'm Tassel.

BOTH: And this is Kindheart, the Christmas Fairy. (*They*

bow to KINDHEART, *who comes forward to center.* ABI-
GAIL *jumps off chair with a delighted cry.*)

KINDHEART: Merry Chr—I mean, good morning, Abigail.

ABIGAIL (*With a quick curtsy*): Good morning, ma'am.

KINDHEART: How did you like it?

ABIGAIL: Christmas every day? It was awful! I'm so glad
you stopped it. I was dreadfully afraid you wouldn't.

KINDHEART: I figured you'd had enough.

ABIGAIL: *More* than enough! It was such a relief to wake
up this morning and find out it wasn't Christmas at last.
I hope it never will be again.

TINSEL (*Plaintively*): No more Christmases?

TASSEL: Not ever?

KINDHEART: Is that what you want, Abbie?

ABIGAIL: Uh-huh. I'm tired of Christmas. I really am.

KINDHEART: Stop and think, Abbie. We can't settle this
matter right off—like *that.* (*She snaps her fingers.*)

ABIGAIL: We can't?

KINDHEART: Of course not. We have to consider it very
carefully.

ABIGAIL: Why?

KINDHEART: Because it's not only you and I who are concerned, Abbie—it's the whole United States—the whole
world. Christmas belongs to everybody.

ABIGAIL (*Deliberating*): Mm-m-m-m, I see. Well, in that
case, maybe we could have Christmas once in a thousand
years.

TASSEL (*To* KINDHEART): She's being selfish again, Kindheart—only the other way around.

ABIGAIL (*With spirit*): I am *not!*

KINDHEART (*Gently*): I'm afraid you are, Abbie.

ABIGAIL (*Ashamed*): Yes, I suppose I am. Well, how about
once every hundred years?

TINSEL (*Shaking her head*): There wouldn't be enough

work to keep Santa Claus busy. He'd be terribly un-happy.

ABIGAIL: Oh, I wouldn't want that! Let's make it once every ten years.

TASSEL: Ten years is a long time to wait for another look at a Christmas tree.

TINSEL: Or to go caroling with your friends or exchange Christmas gifts.

KINDHEART: And most important of all, what if you had to wait ten years to hear the Christmas story again? People might then forget the real meaning of Christmas—the feeling of peace on earth and good will to men.

ABIGAIL: Oh, dear, that mustn't happen!

KINDHEART: Indeed it must *not!* So how about going back to the old-fashioned way?

ABIGAIL: You mean Christmas once a year?

KINDHEART (*Nodding*): Isn't that the *best* way?

ABIGAIL: I *guess* it is—(*Suddenly she makes up her mind.*) I'm *sure* it is!

KINDHEART: Shall we make it a bargain?

ABIGAIL: Yes!

KINDHEART: What are your shoes made of?

ABIGAIL: Leather.

KINDHEART: Bargain's done forever.

ABIGAIL (*Hugging the Fairy*): Forever and ever and ever! (KINDHEART *starts to sing, and is joined by* ABIGAIL *and the Elves.*)

ALL:
Christmas is here, Christmas is here,
All sing with joy, all sing with joy,
It's the merry season, it's the merry season,
Good will to men, good will to men.
(*They sing together loudly and joyously, as the curtain falls.*)

THE END

The Twelve Dancing Princesses

from Grimms' Fairy Tales

Characters

PRINCE OF SERONIA
JOSEPHINA
ROSE
KIRSTEN
VIOLET
BELINDA
ISABELLA
CAROLINE ⎫ *the twelve princesses*
LENORA
DEBORAH
MARGUERITE
KATRINA
IRENE
KING, *their father*
PAGE
FELIX, *a young shoemaker*
CHARWOMAN

SCENE 1

TIME: *Daybreak.*
SETTING: *A room in the King's palace. There is a door at right and a screen in front of up left exit.*

AT RISE: PRINCE OF SERONIA *is asleep on a couch, and is snoring loudly. A cock's crow is heard and, after a brief pause, cock's crow is heard again.* JOSEPHINA, *the eldest princess, peeks into room from doorway, then turns and beckons offstage.*

JOSEPHINA: Hurry up, sisters! The cock has crowed twice already. We are later than usual. (*Other princesses enter from right, leaving door open behind them. They are dressed in ball gowns, carry worn-out slippers in their hands, and are yawning and stretching.*)

ROSE (*Going to couch*): Is the prince still asleep?

JOSEPHINA: Need you ask? Just listen. (PRINCE *gives a deafening snore, and princesses cover their ears.*)

KIRSTEN: Poor fellow! Let him enjoy his sleep while he can. He will be whipped out of bed soon enough.

VIOLET: Hm-m-m. The Prince of Seronia. . . . He's not bad looking, really—but I could never marry a man who snores.

BELINDA: Shall we leave him something to remember us by?

CAROLINE: Yes! But what?

BELINDA (*Holding up her tattered slippers*): Our dancing slippers. (*Stifling their giggles, princesses arrange their slippers on top of the sleeping* PRINCE *until he is completely covered.*)

JOSEPHINA: Now come along to bed before Papa gets here. (*She leads her sisters off left and all but* KATRINA *and* IRENE *exit.*)

KATRINA (*To* IRENE): Don't forget the door. (KATRINA *exits left.*)

IRENE: I won't. (*She faces the open door at right, takes a large, jewel-studded key from her pocket, and raises it as if it were a wand.*)

Key of my godmother,
  Now once more
Work your magic—
  Lock the door!
(*She whirls the key in a circle over her head.*)
Knickety-knack, knickety-knock!
(*She points the key toward the door.*)
Door, close! Bolt, lock!
(*The door swings shut and locks. With a parting glance at the sleeping* PRINCE, IRENE *exits left. Cock crows a third time, and* PRINCE *continues to snore.* KING *unlocks right door and enters, carrying parchment scroll in his pocket. He is followed by* PAGE, *who carries a small switch.*)

KING (*Shaking his head as he sees* PRINCE *fast asleep*): Good grief, not *again!* (*He shakes* PRINCE.) Wake up, Your Highness, wake up!

PRINCE: Huh?

KING: Look here! (*He points at slippers.*) Do you know anything about this?

PRINCE (*Beginning to wake up*): About what?

KING: These slippers—my daughters' slippers.

PRINCE (*Raising his head to look at the slippers*): Slippers, Your Majesty?

KING (*Impatiently*): Yes, yes, twelve pairs of slippers! They have danced them to pieces.

PRINCE (*Sitting up and yawning*): They? Who, Your Majesty?

KING (*Losing his temper*): Who? Why, the princesses, you idiot! They were off dancing again last night. Don't tell me you slept through it all?

PRINCE (*With a sheepish grin*): I guess I did. I'm sorry, Your Majesty.

KING: So am I, Your Highness, so am I. (*Sighing*) Well, it's back to Seronia with you, my prince. Page, earn your breakfast. Whip him out of the palace. (PAGE *slaps his little switch on the floor near* PRINCE's *feet, startling him into action.* PRINCE *snatches up his boots and tries to put them on, hopping first on one foot and then on the other as* PAGE *continues to hit floor with his switch. Squealing comically,* PRINCE *dances over to hatrack, jams his hat on his head, grabs his jacket and scampers off right, followed by* PAGE, *who whips floor as he goes.* KING *bellows off left.*) Girls! Girls! Are you in bed?

PRINCESSES (*From offstage*): Yes, Papa.

KING: Get up at once and come here!

PRINCESSES (*From offstage*): Oh, Papa.

KING: *At once,* I say! (KING *examines the slippers and shakes his head in despair. Princesses straggle in wearing dressing gowns over their ball gowns.*) You naughty girls! You went dancing again last night, didn't you? (*They are silent.*) Didn't you?

PRINCESSES (*Sighing*): Yes, Papa.

KING: Just look at these slippers! They were brand new yesterday, and now they are full of holes. If this keeps up, you will put me in the poorhouse. I will have to sell the crown jewels—mortgage the kingdom!

JOSEPHINA: Oh, Papa, don't exaggerate.

KING: Where do you go when you dance? How can you get out of here when this door is locked all night long? (*Sighing*) I don't know what's the matter with these young noblemen who are supposed to watch you. Why can't they find out what you do?

ROSE (*Mischievously*): They are all such *tired* young noblemen, Papa. (*The others nod, going along with the story.*) They go to sleep with the birds and wake up only when they are whipped out of bed. You should set someone to watch us who has more energy—who keeps late hours. (*The princesses snicker.*)

KING: My sentiments exactly! So I have sent another proclamation throughout the land. (*He takes a parchment from his pocket, and princesses crowd around him.*)

KIRSTEN: What does it say, Papa?

KING (*Unrolling the parchment*): Instead of "Any *nobleman*" it now reads "Any *man, whoever* he may be, who can discover where the twelve princesses dance every night, can have one of them for his bride."

PRINCESSES (*Horrified*): Oh, *no*, Papa!

VIOLET: We wouldn't *think* of marrying anyone but a prince!

KING: Fiddlesticks! Eleven princes have tried already and they have failed. So now the offer is open to anybody.

BELINDA: But he might be a carpenter!

KING: All the better! He can fix the palace roof. It leaks.

CAROLINE: He might be a blacksmith!

KING: Good! He can shoe the horses in the royal stable.

ISABELLA: He might be a cobbler!

KING (*Delighted*): Ah! A cobbler! He would be the best of all! He could shoe my daughters! Let us hope it is a cobbler who wins, because after today you are going to need a cobbler of your very own.

DEBORAH: What do you mean, Papa?

KING: I will have one more pair of slippers made for each of you, and that will be the last pair for a year.

PRINCESSES: Papa!

KING: I am determined to stop this dancing. Now go to your room.

JOSEPHINA (*Leading her sisters in single file left*): You can't stop us from dancing, slippers or no slippers. (*She exits.*)

ROSE *and* KIRSTEN: We will dance tonight—(*They exit.*)

VIOLET *and* BELINDA: And the night after that—(*They exit.*)

LENORA: And the night after that—(*Exits with* CAROLINE *and* ISABELLA)

MARGUERITE: And the night after *that*—(*Exits with* DEBORAH *and* KATRINA)

IRENE: *And* Sunday! (*She makes face at* KING *and skips off after others.* KING *shakes his head disapprovingly and starts to gather up the worn-out slippers.* PAGE *enters from right.*)

PAGE: Your Majesty, there is another fellow here who wants to try his luck.

KING (*Groaning*): Not another prince?

PAGE: No, just a common shoemaker.

KING (*Brightening*): A shoemaker? Oh, happy day! Hooray! (*He jumps into the air and clicks his heels together.*) Show him in, show him in!

PAGE (*Calling offstage*): Come in, young man! The King will see you. (FELIX *enters and bows to the* KING.)

FELIX: Your Majesty, my name is Felix, and I would like to try my luck at finding out where your daughters dance every night.

KING: You are indeed a brave man to ask this of me. You do know the consequences if you fail, do you not? You will be whipped out of the palace, never to return.

FELIX: I understand. Since the hand of one of your beautiful daughters is the reward, I am more than willing to take the risk.

KING: Very well. Have you had your breakfast?

FELIX: No, Your Majesty.

KING: Then go down to the kitchen and eat—third stairway on your left. (*He points toward the hall and* FELIX *starts to exit.*) Wait! First take these slippers to the Royal Cobbler and tell him to make twelve new pairs.

FELIX: Gracious, are these the princesses' slippers?

KING (*Sighing*): Yes. They dance out a pair every night. The Royal Cobbler can scarcely keep up with them.

FELIX: I will help him. (*Proudly*) I am the best shoemaker in my village.

KING (*Interested*): Is that so? Hm-m-m. We shall see what you can do, then. (*He strokes his chin as he thinks, and then turns to* PAGE.) Come, boy, I'll wager you have whipped up quite an appetite this morning. Shall we go to breakfast?

PAGE: Yes, indeed, Your Majesty. (KING *exits, followed by* PAGE. FELIX *begins to collect the slippers as* CHARWOMAN *enters from right. She is bent over with the weight of a bucket she is carrying and appears to be very old. As she enters, she stumbles over the threshold and falls to her knees.* FELIX *quickly drops his armful of slippers onto couch and goes to her.*)

FELIX: Here, let me help you up.

CHARWOMAN: Oh, dear, I think I've sprained my ankle.

FELIX: Sit down, and we'll look at it. (*She limps to the couch, leaning on* FELIX. *He examines her ankle as she sits on couch.*)

CHARWOMAN: Oh, don't, it hurts! What shall I do? I have to scrub this floor before the princesses wake up.

FELIX: I will scrub it for you.

CHARWOMAN: You?

FELIX: Certainly. I'll have it as clean as a whistle in no time. (*He picks up bucket and scrubbing brush and goes to work.*)

CHARWOMAN: Are you a new servant in the palace? I don't remember seeing you before.

FELIX: No, my good woman, I am Felix, a shoemaker, and I have come to find out where the King's daughters dance.

CHARWOMAN: Well, well! That's easy enough to do.

FELIX: Easy! Eleven princes have tried and failed.

CHARWOMAN: Ah, yes—but they wouldn't have failed if they had offered to scrub the floor for me.

FELIX: Scrub the floor—what do you mean? (CHARWOMAN *suddenly rises and walks briskly to left.*) Good woman, your ankle!

CHARWOMAN (*Smiling*): It was a trick to test you. (*She looks off left into princesses' bedroom.*) They are sound asleep. Small wonder, after dancing all night. (*Turning to* FELIX) Now then, Felix. I am the Fairy Fortunetta, and I've been seeking a mortal who is kind and good, so that I can give him the reward he deserves. In return for your kindness to me, I will tell you how to find out where the princesses dance every night.

FELIX: What must I do?

CHARWOMAN: Listen carefully. At bedtime, Princess Josephina will bring you a goblet of milk. Don't drink it—it is a magic sleeping potion. Empty it into this vase (*She points to vase of flowers on table*), then pretend to fall asleep. When the princesses think you are asleep, they will go dancing. Follow them, and you will discover their secret.

FELIX: But won't they see me?

CHARWOMAN (*Taking off her apron*): My apron is a magic cloak. Wear it, and you will be invisible.

FELIX (*Tucking the apron inside his tunic*): Thank you, good fairy.

CHARWOMAN: Now give me my scrubbing brush.

FELIX: Oh, no, I will finish the floor.

CHARWOMAN (*Holding out her hand*): Give it to me! (*He puts brush in her hand, and she holds it over bucket, making a scrubbing movement with it as she chants*)
Rub-a-dub, scrub-a-dub,
    Floor be clean,
The cleanest floor
    That ever was seen!
(*She drops brush into bucket with a plop. If desired, the lights may flicker for a moment.* CHARWOMAN *surveys*

the floor with satisfaction.) There you are, Felix! As clean as a whistle.

FELIX (*Staring in astonishment*): It's a miracle! What my mother wouldn't give for a scrubbing brush like that!

CHARWOMAN (*Laughing*): Run along with you and get your breakfast. (*She gathers up the princesses' slippers and piles them in* FELIX's *arms.*) You have a busy day ahead of you—and a busier night. Good luck! (FELIX *exits right.* CHARWOMAN *picks up bucket and turns toward princesses' bedroom.*)

Rub-a-dub, scrub-a-dub,
 Sleep till noon;
Tonight you'll dance
 To a different tune!

(*She cuts capers about stage and skips off right.*)

CURTAIN

*   *   *

SCENE 2

TIME: *That night.*

SETTING: *Same as Scene 1.*

AT RISE: *Princesses, in their dressing gowns, are lined up one behind the other, listening at right door. Voices are heard from off right.* JOSEPHINA, *who is nearest the door, calls to her sisters.*

JOSEPHINA: Here they come! (*Princesses all run behind the screen at left, as* KING *enters right with* FELIX, *who carries a basket containing twelve new pairs of slippers. Each pair has a name tag attached.*)

KING: Girls! Come and get them! (*Princesses file out from behind screen.*) Remember, this is your last pair for a year.

PRINCESSES (*Unhappily*): Oh, Papa!

KING: It will do you no good to whine. I won't change my mind. Girls, this young man is Felix, a cobbler. He has made these slippers for you and now he is curious to know where you go to wear them out. So he will keep watch here tonight.

KIRSTEN (*Aside, to* VIOLET): How handsome he is! He is the nicest one yet.

KING: Hand me the slippers, Felix. (FELIX *hands* KING *a pair at a time.* JOSEPHINA *and* ROSE *come forward when* KING *calls their names. They accept slippers with a curtsy and exit left.*) Josephina. Rose. Kirsten. (KIRSTEN *stops to flirt with* FELIX. KING *clears his throat warningly.*) Ahem! (KIRSTEN *exits. As* KING *rapidly calls out the names of the other princesses, each one comes up, snatches her slippers and runs out left.*) Violet! Belinda! Caroline! Isabella! Lenora, Deborah, Marguerite, Katrina, Irene! Good night, girls!

PRINCESSES (*From offstage*): Good night, Papa!

KING (*Taking basket from* FELIX): Well, young man, I wish you luck. Watch them carefully, now. I'm sorry I can't offer you more comfortable quarters, but you must think of the reward you will receive if you discover anything. Good night.

FELIX (*Bowing*): Good night, Your Majesty. (KING *exits, locking door.* FELIX *takes magic apron from inside his tunic and hides it under a pillow on the couch; then he sits down and takes off his boots.* JOSEPHINA *enters carrying goblet of milk.* FELIX *rises and bows.*) Your Highness.

JOSEPHINA: I have brought you some fresh milk. I thought you might be thirsty.

FELIX: I am, indeed. Thank you, Your Highness. (KIRSTEN *peeks around screen.*)

KIRSTEN: Pssst! Josephina! Come here. (JOSEPHINA *goes*

left; KIRSTEN *steps out from behind screen and whispers.*) Couldn't we give him a fair chance to stay awake?

JOSEPHINA: No.

KIRSTEN: Please—just this time?

JOSEPHINA: No!

KIRSTEN: But you know what Papa said—no more slippers.

JOSEPHINA: Then we will dance barefoot. (*While princesses are speaking together, their backs to* FELIX, *he pours the milk from goblet into flower vase.*)

KIRSTEN (*Sighing*): Very well—but I *do* like him so much!

JOSEPHINA: Shame on you! He's only a shoemaker. (*She returns to* FELIX *who holds out empty goblet.*) My goodness, you *were* thirsty!

FELIX: The milk was delicious, Your Highness.

JOSEPHINA: Well, good night. Get along, Kirsten. (*She pushes* KIRSTEN *ahead of her and both exit.* FELIX *lies down on the couch, pulls up blanket and pretends to fall asleep. He snores softly. After a moment,* JOSEPHINA, *now wearing ball gown, enters and tiptoes to couch.*) He's fast asleep. (ROSE *enters wearing ball gown and carrying necklace.*)

ROSE: Good! Now we can go dancing. (*The other princesses return one by one, also wearing ball gowns.*)

JOSEPHINA (*To* ROSE): Hook me up, sister.

ROSE (*Doing so, and speaking to* KIRSTEN *as she enters*): Sister, fasten my necklace. (VIOLET *enters.*)

KIRSTEN (*To* VIOLET): Curl my hair, sister.

VIOLET (*To* BELINDA, *who enters carrying hand mirror, and powdering her nose*): Sister, powder my face.

CAROLINE (*Entering and speaking to* BELINDA): My nose is shiny, sister. (BELINDA *turns and powders* CAROLINE'S *nose.* ISABELLA *enters, holding brooch, and speaks to* CAROLINE.)

ISABELLA: Sister, will you fasten this pin for me? (LENORA *and* DEBORAH *enter together.* LENORA *carries hairpins.*)

LENORA: Pinch my cheeks, sister. They're not pink enough.

DEBORAH: Pin up my hair, sister. (MARGUERITE *enters with a brush and hair ribbon followed by* KATRINA, *who also has a hair ribbon.*)

MARGUERITE: I will tie your hair ribbon if you will brush my bangs, Katrina.

KATRINA: I will tie *your* hair ribbon if you will brush *my* bangs.

IRENE (*Lacing her bodice as she enters*): Stop jabbering! You will wake up the shoemaker. (FELIX *snores loudly.*)

JOSEPHINA: *Him?* It would take a cannon to wake him!

ROSE: He is like all the others—a stupid blockhead.

KIRSTEN: He is *not!* He is very nice—even if he does snore. (*Princesses laugh. A clock begins to strike twelve.*)

JOSEPHINA: The clock is striking midnight.

ROSE: It is time for us to dance again.

KIRSTEN: We will dance all night.

VIOLET: Until the cock crows three times.

BELINDA: Until our slippers are worn out.

CAROLINE: We know the way to go.

ISABELLA: Down, down, down a hundred steps.

LENORA: Then up, up, up to the enchanted garden.

DEBORAH: Where the grass is shining with silver.

MARGUERITE: And the flowers are gleaming with gold.

KATRINA: Where every tree is a diamond tree.

IRENE: And the music plays on and on.

JOSEPHINA: We are ready. Irene, the key! (IRENE *faces door at right and holds up the magic key.*)

IRENE:

Key of my godmother,
    Fairy key,
Work your magic,
    Set us free!

(*She whirls the key in a circle over her head.*)

Klippety-klap, klippety-klopen!

(She points key toward door.)

Bolt, unlock! Door, open!

(Door swings open.)

JOSEPHINA: Here we go! *(They all exit, except KIRSTEN, who lingers behind to gaze down at FELIX.)*

KIRSTEN: I'm so sorry, Felix. I wish it could have been you—really I do. *(IRENE returns and stamps her foot.)*

IRENE: Come *on*, Kirsten! You'll be late for the ball. *(She drags KIRSTEN out. As soon as the princesses are gone, FELIX leaps to his feet and puts on magic cloak.)*

FELIX: Now to follow them and find out their secret! *(He runs off.)*

CURTAIN

*   *   *

SCENE 3

TIME: *A few minutes later.*

SETTING: *The enchanted garden.*

AT RISE: *Soft music is playing. The princesses enter from left, swaying to the rhythm of the music.* BELINDA *carries hand mirror, and* LENORA *has handkerchief.* KIRSTEN *is the last to enter followed by* FELIX *in his magic cloak. He catches hold of* KIRSTEN's *skirt and gives it a tug, then moves quietly upstage.*

KIRSTEN: Oh!

IRENE: What's the matter?

KIRSTEN: Someone just pulled my dress!

IRENE: How can that be? There is no one behind you.

KATRINA: You must have caught it on a nail.

KIRSTEN *(Nervously)*: I have the queerest feeling that someone else is here with us.

JOSEPHINA: What a little goose you are! There is nobody

here but the twelve of us. Look around. (*Princesses look about but do not see* FELIX, *who goes from one to the other, mischievously passing his hand in front of their faces and laughing.* LENORA *drops her handkerchief.*)

LENORA: Oh, I've dropped my handkerchief. (FELIX *picks it up and puts it back in her hand.*)

DEBORAH: No, you didn't. It is in your hand.

LENORA: How strange! It flew back by itself. (BELINDA *looks in her hand mirror, and* FELIX *blows on it over her shoulder.*)

BELINDA (*Gasping*): There *is* something here! It breathed on my mirror. See? (*She shows mirror to* JOSEPHINA.)

JOSEPHINA: Don't be ridiculous! You breathed on it yourself. (FELIX *tickles* JOSEPHINA's *nose with a blade of silver grass from garden. She brushes it away, not realizing what it is.*) Shoo! Shoo, fly! Shoo! (*There is a sharp crack as* FELIX *breaks a rose from golden rosebush. He puts rose in his pocket along with blade of grass.*)

ROSE: Listen! What was that strange noise?

KATRINA: It sounded like a twig snapping. (FELIX *breaks a diamond leaf from tree. There is another sharp crack.* FELIX *puts leaf in his pocket.*) There it is again!

JOSEPHINA (*Exasperated*): Really, sisters, you are all being very silly tonight. You are frightening yourselves half to death. Now stop this nonsense and choose your partners for the dance. (*She points out front to the audience.* NOTE: *Partners may be selected from the audience, or twelve "princes" may enter, or, if desired, princesses may dance by themselves.*) There they are, waiting to dance with us. (*Music changes to a lively waltz.* FELIX *capers about as princesses dance. Occasionally, he steps on their toes, and princesses accuse their partners of being clumsy. At the sound of a cock's crow, the music ends, and princesses stop dancing.*)

KIRSTEN: The cock has crowed! (FELIX *runs off left.*)

ROSE: How quickly time flies when we are dancing!

CAROLINE: My slippers are all worn out.

LENORA: So are mine.

JOSEPHINA: Come, girls, we must go. (*The princesses may curtsy and say goodbye to their partners; all exit in haste.*)

CURTAIN

*   *   *

SCENE 4

TIME: *A few minutes later.*

SETTING: *Same as Scene 1.*

AT RISE: FELIX *rushes in from right, yanks off his cloak and stuffs it under pillow. Then he lies down on couch, pulls the blanket up to his chin and begins to snore loudly. Cock crows again. Princesses enter in single file, their slippers flopping as they walk.*

PRINCESSES (*Wearily, in a singsong*):
Here we come home in the morning,
   Flippity-flopping, flippity-flopping,
Dancing all night until dawn, then
   Flippity-flopping home.

JOSEPHINA (*Hustling them along*): Hurry, sisters! He might wake up.

KATRINA: Pooh! He hasn't stirred since we left. (*All exit except for* JOSEPHINA, KIRSTEN, *and* IRENE.)

KIRSTEN (*Gazing down at* FELIX): I wish I might dance with *him* sometime.

JOSEPHINA (*Pushing her off left*): Stop mooning! Papa will catch us. Quickly, Irene—the door! (JOSEPHINA *exits.*)

IRENE (*Facing right door and raising the magic key*):
Key of my godmother,
   Now once more

Work your magic—
  Lock the door!
(*She whirls the key in a circle over her head.*)
Knickety-knack, knickety-knock!
(*She points the key toward the door.*)
Door, close! Bolt, lock!
(*Door closes, and* IRENE *runs off. Cock crows a third time.* FELIX *sits up, then tiptoes to the screen and listens to make sure princesses are all in their room. He then takes from his pocket the blade of silver grass, the golden rose and the diamond leaf that he picked from the enchanted garden.*)

FELIX: I will show these things to the King to prove that I followed his daughters last night. (KING *unlocks right door, and enters with* PAGE.)

KING: Well, young man, I see you are awake. Did you find out anything?

FELIX (*Bowing*): Yes, Your Majesty. (*Princesses enter quietly from left and listen.*)

KING (*Hopefully*): You mean you have discovered where my daughters dance?

FELIX: Yes, Your Majesty. They dance in an enchanted garden underneath the palace. I was there with them last night.

KIRSTEN (*Whispering to the others*): I told you so!

FELIX: This will prove it. (*He hands grass, rose, and leaf to* KING.)

KING: Hm-m-m. Silver grass—a gold rose—and a diamond leaf. (*To princesses.*) Girls, is this true?

PRINCESSES: Yes, Papa.

KING: Then he has earned his reward. Felix, choose your bride.

FELIX (*Kneeling before* KIRSTEN): Your Highness, may I be your dancing partner for the rest of your life?

KIRSTEN: Yes, Felix. (*She gives him her hand and he stands beside her.*)

KING (*To* FELIX *and* KIRSTEN): A good match! A good match, indeed! Now tell me, girls—how did you get out of here? (*To princesses*) I locked that door every night, and there is no other key but this one. (*He holds up his key.*)

IRENE (*Coming forward timidly*): But there is, Papa.

KING: What are you saying?

IRENE: There *is* another key—this one! (*She shows him the magic key.*)

KING (*Taking it*): Where did you get this, Irene?

IRENE: My fairy godmother gave it to me. I thought it would be such fun to fool you—and we all wanted *so* much to go dancing. I'm sorry, Papa. (*She bursts into tears.*)

KING: There, there, I forgive you. After all, you're only—uh—how old are you, Irene?

IRENE (*Sobbing*): S-s-six, Papa.

KING: Six years old! My, my! Now stop crying and listen to me. You must never use this magic key again. Will you promise me that, Irene?

IRENE: Y-y-yes, Papa. (*She takes key from him and, between sniffles, speaks the magic rhyme.*)

> Key of my godmother,
> Nevermore
> Work your magic
> On any door.

KING: Good! Here's my handkerchief. (IRENE *takes handkerchief and curtsies.*)

JOSEPHINA (*Wistfully*): Can't we ever go dancing again?

KING: Oh, I think so. (*He nods to* FELIX.) Now that we will have a cobbler in the family, I think I could let you go dancing once a week. What do you say, Felix?

FELIX: Yes indeed, Your Majesty—and twice a week when birthdays come.

KIRSTEN (*Coyly*): What about wedding days?

FELIX: On wedding days we will dance morning, noon and night.

KING: Then what are we waiting for? You shall be married today! Come, everybody, dance! Dance in honor of Prince Felix and Princess Kirsten! (KING *dances with* JOSEPHINA *to a spirited polka.* FELIX *dances with* KIRSTEN, IRENE *dances with the* PAGE, *and the others join in. They may choose partners from audience, if desired. Curtain falls as dance ends.*)

THE END

Puss in Boots

by Charles Perrault

Characters

PUSS, *the miller's cat*
OLIVER ⎱ *the miller's elder sons*
BERNARD ⎰
PIERRE, *the miller's youngest son*
PRINCESS GABRIELLE
MARIE, *her cousin*
KING
LOUIS, *a courtier*
PAGE
OGRE
LION

SCENE 1

SETTING: *A meadow near an old mill, which may be seen in the background. A stone wall runs across rear of stage with a gate left of center. A rustic table and benches stand right of center, and a tree stump and rock at left.*

AT RISE: *The stage is empty. Presently, a mouse "runs" along top of wall to grain sack, and then goes out of sight, as* PUSS, *meowing loudly, enters on all fours through gate. (*NOTE: *The mouse may be a puppet,*

*manipulated from behind the wall, or a toy mouse on
a string or wire.*)

Puss: Meow! Meow! The miller is dead! What will become of me now! (Puss *sits down near gate, wipes his
eyes with paws, and then settles down for nap. Mouse
cautiously comes out and walks along wall towards grain
sack.* Puss *stirs, and just as mouse reaches sack,* Puss
springs toward mouse.) Meow! A mouse! (*He strikes at
mouse with his paw, and mouse falls back off wall.* Puss
*stretches, lies down again, then looks offstage and jumps
up suddenly.*) Oho! Here come Oliver and Bernard,
the miller's older sons. I'm sure they've been to see the
lawyer about their father's will. I could have told them
what was in it. I was under the table when the will was
drawn up. (Oliver *and* Bernard *enter.* Oliver *is carrying a cloth bag. They stop at gate and look toward mill.*)

Oliver: Well, Bernard, that's some fine property father
has left us—the mill to me and the donkey to you.

Bernard: Shall we go into partnership, Oliver?

Oliver: A good idea! I will grind the grain, and you will
take it to market and sell it.

Bernard (*Noticing* Puss): What about Puss?

Oliver: Well, *what* about Puss?

Bernard (*Sarcastically*): Did the miller leave anything to
his favorite cat?

Oliver: Sh-h-h! We don't want to embarrass him. Puss
gets brother Pierre.

Bernard: Pierre? Just Pierre? And Pierre gets—?

Oliver: Not even his keep.

Bernard: That's hard on poor Puss. Of course he can
forage for himself, but it will hurt his pride. (*To* Puss)
Don't blink your eyes at me! (Puss *arches his back and
snarls at* Bernard, *who kicks* Puss. Pierre *enters.*) Get
out of my way! (Pierre *rushes to protect* Puss.)

PIERRE: Stop it, Bernard! You leave Puss alone!

OLIVER: Well, well, if it isn't brother Pierre! Why weren't you at the reading of the will?

PIERRE: I knew Father wouldn't leave me anything.

OLIVER: Oh, but he did, though! Ha, ha! Father dearly loved a joke.

BERNARD: At someone else's expense. Tell him, Oliver.

OLIVER: Father left you his blessing.

PIERRE: His blessing? Why, that's a priceless legacy!

BERNARD: And that's not all.

OLIVER: No, indeed. He also left you his Sunday boots (*Tossing the cloth bag to* PIERRE)—and the cat.

PIERRE: Puss? (*His brothers nod and grin.*) And you two get the mill and the donkey, I suppose. (*They nod and laugh.*)

OLIVER: We're going into partnership. (PIERRE *sits dejectedly on the bench and places the bag on the table.*)

BERNARD (*Taunting* PIERRE): What will you do with the cat, Pierre? You can't climb on his back and ride away. You can't keep him, either—you can't even keep yourself.

PIERRE: Oliver, if I give you Puss to catch the rats in the mill, will you feed me?

OLIVER: I—feed *you?* (*He bursts into jeering laughter.*)

BERNARD (*Snapping his fingers*): I have it! Pierre could wash the cat with perfumed soap, then tie a ribbon around his neck and sell him. (*He and* OLIVER *laugh loudly. Then* OLIVER *claps* BERNARD *on back.*)

OLIVER: Come on, Bernard, we've got work to do. (*They exit through gate, laughing.* PIERRE *strokes* PUSS, *who is staring at him sadly.*)

PIERRE: Don't pay any attention to them, Puss. I wouldn't sell you. You shall live and share my lot, whatever it may be.

PUSS (*Purring*): Purr-r-r! That's the spirit, Pierre!

PIERRE: I beg your pardon, did you purr?

PUSS: I like you. Scratch my back. (PIERRE *stares at* PUSS *in amazement*.) I dare say we shall get on very well together.

PIERRE (*Startled*): Why, Puss, you can talk! Who and what are you?

PUSS: Your father's old cat, and now yours, master.

PIERRE: And I have thought of you as only a bundle of fur that could say "meow"!

PUSS (*Imitating* PIERRE): Meow!

PIERRE (*Laughing*): You know, I used to imagine I heard voices in Father's room when you were alone with him.

PUSS: Your father was no fool. He knew my real worth— and yours, too, such as it is.

PIERRE: You mean that? Oh, what joy you bring to my heart!

PUSS: The miller once saved my life when I was attacked by a dog. I have always been grateful to him for that, and now I can repay his kindness by helping you. All I ask is that you have confidence in me and do whatever I tell you. Leave me to manage matters in my own way, and the end will be happiness for you and many others. Do you trust me?

PIERRE: Yes, indeed, Puss. I believe that you will make my fortune.

PUSS: I intend to, because on your fortune depends my own. Now—let us begin. What have you to start with?

PIERRE: Nothing. Except yourself, nobody, nothing.

PUSS: Haven't you forgotten the miller's Sunday boots?

PIERRE: By jove, so I have! (*He takes leather boots out of the bag*.) Aren't they splendid! I suppose if worse came to worst, I could sell them. They would bring a good price—but I'd hate to part with the only thing I have that belonged to my father—(*Quickly*) except you, of course.

PUSS: You won't have to sell the boots. Give them to me.

PIERRE: Boots—for a cat?

PUSS: Certainly! If I talk like a man, I must walk like a man.

PIERRE: That's right. Well, here they are. I'll give them to you for luck.

PUSS (*Taking the boots*): And luck they shall bring me, my dear good master. What fine tops they have! Help me put them on. (*Together they pull one boot on* PUSS.) Now the other one. (*They pull on second boot.*)

PIERRE: There you are! Stand up and see if you can walk in them. (PUSS *does so.*) Do they fit?

PUSS: They fit perfectly. (*He struts about.*) Don't you think they give me a rather military appearance?

PIERRE (*Admiringly*): You look like a nobleman's steward at least!

PUSS: And so I am—steward to the Marquis of Carabas. (*He makes a deep bow to* PIERRE.)

PIERRE: Do you mean me?

PUSS (*Making another bow*): Yes, m'lord.

PIERRE: M'lord? *I?*

PUSS: You need a title. (PIERRE *objects.*) Come, Pierre, there are self-made men. Why not self-made marquises?

PIERRE (*Laughing*): What will you think of next?

PUSS: Next, I think I will go hunting in the Ogre's woods.

PIERRE: No, Puss, it's too dangerous. What if the Ogre should catch you?

PUSS: He won't catch me. I've been there dozens of times before. I'm going to bag a couple of rabbits for the King. (PUSS *picks up bag the boots were in.*)

PIERRE: For the King!

PUSS: Roast rabbit is His Majesty's favorite food, and he hasn't had any since the Ogre bewitched all the rabbits in the kingdom and shut them up in his woods.

PIERRE: Why did he do that?

PUSS: To spite the King. He didn't want anyone eating rabbit but himself. Well, I'm off. (*He slings the bag over his shoulder.*) What will you do while I'm gone?

PIERRE: Oh, I will take a swim in the river and wait for you to come back.

PUSS: I won't be long. (*He is about to leave but notices that* PIERRE *is staring at him with an expression of bewilderment.*) Why do you stare at me like that?

PIERRE: I just can't believe it. It's like a fairy tale—a poor lad inherits his father's blessing and a Puss in Boots.

PUSS: And in the end he marries the Princess and they live happily ever after.

PIERRE: What are you talking about? Surely you don't mean—

PUSS (*Interrupting*): But I *do* mean—the Princess Gabrielle.

PIERRE: Take care, Puss! You are climbing too high.

PUSS: Nonsense! If a cat can look at a King, why can't the cat's master look at the King's daughter? Now go along and have your swim and don't ask any questions. (*He steers* PIERRE *down right.*) I'll call you when I get back. (PIERRE *exits, and* PUSS *cuts a caper, meowing in a singsong.*)
Puss in Boots, Puss in Boots, where are you going?
To bag a fat rabbit to take to the King!
La, la, la, la, la, la—
(*As he dances left, toward woods, a trumpet is heard in the distance.* PUSS *stops singing and turns back.*) What's that? (*He peers off and claps his paws together.*) What luck! I won't have to go to the King—the King is coming to *me!* His coach is stopping on the high road, and he is pointing to the mill. What can it mean? Grain for the horses? If that is the case, I will just have time to bag the rabbits and give them to the King. (PUSS *starts toward the woods, then stops abruptly.*) Wait! I have

another idea! I will hide my master's clothes where he can't find them, and then—(Puss *runs off right and returns immediately with* Pierre's *clothing.*) If this plan works, my master is on his way to making his fortune! Meow! (Puss *prances joyfully left, singing.*)

Puss in Boots, Puss in Boots, what are you planning?

To make my young master a noble marquis!

La, la, la, la, la, la—

(*He exits left, as* Princess Gabrielle *runs on chased by her cousin* Marie.)

Marie: Your Highness, you run too fast for me! (*She sinks onto bench, out of breath.*)

Gabrielle: Don't tell me you give up, Marie! It was you who challenged me to the race, remember.

Marie: I know, Gabrielle.

Gabrielle (*Amused*): Did you see the look of horror on Papa's face when we started to run?

Marie (*Giggling*): His Majesty would consider racing most unladylike!

Gabrielle: I'm afraid we are in for a royal lecture. (*Looking about*) This is a pleasant spot. Let's have our picnic here. There is a table with places to sit.

Marie: Shall I go and tell His Majesty?

Gabrielle: Yes, please do, Marie—and *walk!* (Marie *affects a stately gait and starts out, meeting the* King *and* Louis *as they enter.* King *carries a gold-headed cane.* Louis *is foppishly dressed and wears a plumed hat.*)

King (*In a disapproving tone*): My dear Gabrielle and Marie, when I let you out of the coach I had no idea it was for the express purpose of running a race like two peasant girls at a village fair. It was a disgraceful spectacle!

Gabrielle: But, Papa, we had been riding for such a long time. We wanted to stretch our legs.

King: Well, you succeeded most admirably.

GABRIELLE: Don't scold, Papa dear. Could we have our picnic here? It's quite secluded and I'm very hungry.

KING: Yes, I suppose this place is as good as any. Louis, signal the Page to bring the hampers. (LOUIS *walks right and beckons* PAGE, *who is offstage.*)

LOUIS (*Walking back toward* KING): I do hope there are no ants or bees about. I should hate to get stung by a bee or find an ant in my sandwich.

MARIE: Oh, don't be so fussy, Louis! An ant or two won't kill you, and a bee wouldn't know where to light among all those furbelows. (*Gestures at his lace ruffles.* PAGE *enters, carrying two hampers, and begins to unpack the food.* GABRIELLE *and* MARIE *spread a cloth on table.*)

KING (*Sitting on tree stump*): What I wouldn't give for some cold roast rabbit! (PUSS *enters quietly left, and walks to center and bows low to* KING.)

PUSS: Your Majesty. (*He kneels and places bulging bag of game at* KING's *feet.*)

KING: Eh? What have we here?

PUSS: Game for the King's table! (PUSS *stands up, so they can see his face.*)

GABRIELLE (*Delighted*): It's a cat!

KING (*Astounded*): A *cat?*

GABRIELLE: A talking cat!

PUSS: A cat and a man, Your Majesty.

LOUIS (*Nudging* PAGE): A cat in boots—how droll! (*He titters, and* KING *silences him with an impatient gesture.*)

KING: Well, good Puss, what have you in that bag?

PUSS: A gift for Your Majesty.

KING (*Graciously*): A gift for me? Who has sent it?

PUSS: My master, the Marquis of Carabas.

KING: What is it?

PUSS: Two fine fat rabbits.

KING: Rabbits? But how did your master get them? There

hasn't been a rabbit in my kingdom since the Ogre lured them all into his woods and hid them where no human being can find them.

PUSS: Exactly, Your Majesty, no human being can find them—but a *cat* can.

KING: Ah, clever Puss, the Marquis of Carabas is very fortunate to have you for a steward.

PUSS (*Bowing*): You flatter me, Your Majesty.

KING: I don't believe I am acquainted with the Marquis.

GABRIELLE: Neither am I, Papa. (*To* PUSS) Where does he come from?

PUSS: From here. His castle is in that direction. (PUSS *indicates left*) He owns this whole countryside.

KING (*Impressed*): He does? Why hasn't he been presented at court?

PUSS (*Stroking his whiskers*): All in good time, Your Majesty.

GABRIELLE: You must come to court, too, Sir Puss. You bow so beautifully.

PUSS: I bow to you from my heart, Your Highness. (*He bows, holding his paw on his heart.*)

LOUIS (*Sneering*): I have always thought that cats had no heart.

PUSS: If we haven't much heart, sir, we have lots of wit.

LOUIS: Wit?

PUSS: And *cunning*.

KING (*To* LOUIS *pointedly*): I wish I had as witty and cunning a person in my court.

GABRIELLE: I quite agree, Papa. Sir Puss, you should have a hat to match your boots. Louis, give Sir Puss your hat.

LOUIS (*Hanging on to his hat possessively*): But, Your Highness, I paid one hundred gold pieces for this hat.

GABRIELLE: All the better. Give it to Sir Puss—I *command* you! (LOUIS *removes his hat and throws it at* PUSS *like a petulant child.* PUSS *makes no effort to catch it.*) Pick it up and give it to him, Louis. (LOUIS *sullenly complies, and* PUSS *takes hat and, with a flourish, makes an elaborate bow.*) Very elegant.

PUSS: I don't look too stagy, do I? It seems to me a man only puts a hat *on* to take it *off* again.

KING (*Coming forward with the game bag.*): Well, Sir Puss, do thank your master for his generous gift, and tell him I greatly desire to make his acquaintance.

PUSS: In that case, Your Majesty shall make his acquaintance right away. He is close by, swimming in the river. I will fetch him. (PUSS *exits down right, calling out to* PIERRE.) M'lord! Come out now and dress. I have a surprise for you.

GABRIELLE (*Running to* KING, *excitedly*): Papa, you must invite the Marquis to dine with us tonight. It is only fair that you share the roasted rabbits with him.

KING (*Pouting*): But then there will be less for me.

GABRIELLE: Now don't be selfish, Papa. Puss will catch more rabbits for you, I'm sure. (PUSS *re-enters.*)

PUSS: Your Majesty, an unfortunate thing has happened. While my master was in swimming, a thief stole his clothes.

LOUIS (*Amused*): Stole his clothes? How embarrassing! What will the Marquis do without clothes?

PUSS: He will catch a cold, I fear.

KING: We can't allow that! Louis?

LOUIS: Yes, Your Majesty?

KING: You can lend the Marquis your suit for the present.

LOUIS: *My* suit?

KING: Do you think it will fit your master, Sir Puss?

PUSS (*Grinning*): It will fit him perfectly, Your Majesty.

KING: Come, Louis, to the river with you.

LOUIS (*Peevishly*): But what shall *I* wear?

KING (*Snatching up tablecloth*): Here, you can put this on.
    Page, see to it that Louis is properly dressed in this

tablecloth. I shall attend to the Marquis myself. Which
way, Puss?

Puss: Over there, Your Majesty. (*He points right and
stands aside for* King, Page *and* Louis *to pass. He starts
to follow, when* Gabrielle *calls to him.*)

Gabrielle: Sir Puss, Marie and I would like to ask you
some questions.

Puss: Questions, Your Highness?

Gabrielle (*Hesitatingly*): About—about the Marquis. Go
ahead, Marie.

Marie: No, you first, Gabrielle.

Gabrielle: No, *you*—I insist!

Marie: Well—uh—is the Marquis—young?

Puss: Yes, Your Ladyship.

Gabrielle: And is he—is he—?

Puss: Married? Not yet, Your Highness.

Marie: Is he as charming as you, Sir Puss?

Puss: He is the handsomest man in the kingdom.

Gabrielle *and* Marie (*Delighted*): Is he? Oh, how exciting!

Puss: He is a skilled swordsman, a daring soldier—and a
great favorite with the ladies.

Gabrielle *and* Marie (*Sadly*): Oh, is he?

Puss: You can see for yourselves. Here he comes now.
(King *enters right with* Pierre, *who is dressed in* Louis'
costume. Pierre *appears somewhat worried and confused.*) Well, m'lord, how do the clothes fit?

King (*Enthusiastically, answering for* Pierre): As if they
were made for him, Sir Puss! Marquis, may I present my
daughter, the Princess Gabrielle. (Gabrielle *curtsies.*)

Puss (*Prodding* Pierre): Bow and smile!

Pierre (*Bowing and smiling*): I am still a little damp,
Your Highness.

Gabrielle: Oh, don't catch cold! This is my cousin, Lady
Marie. (Marie *curtsies.*)

PIERRE (*Bowing*): Your Ladyship.

GABRIELLE (*Whispering to* MARIE): How graceful he is!

MARIE (*Whispering*): And how respectful!

PUSS: Your Majesty, my master invites you to his castle for a dinner of rabbit pie à la Carabas.

KING (*Eagerly*): When?

PUSS: Now—as soon as Your Majesty's coach can get you there.

KING: Ho, Page!

PAGE (*Entering hastily from right*): Yes, Sire?

KING (*Indicating picnic provisions*): Pack up! We're going to the Marquis' castle for dinner. (*There is a flurry of activity.* GABRIELLE *and* MARIE *help* PAGE *while* KING *supervises.* PIERRE *takes* PUSS *aside.*)

PIERRE: Castle? What castle? I have no castle.

PUSS: Leave that to me. (*He walks over to* KING.) Your Majesty, you will have to take the long way around to the castle in the coach. I will cut through these woods, and prepare for your arrival. (KING *starts off.*)

MARIE: Wait! We've forgotten Louis! Where is he? (KING *pauses.*)

KING (*Calling right*): Louis! Louis, we're leaving! (*After a pause,* LOUIS *enters dejectedly, with the tablecloth draped about him toga-fashion. Everyone laughs at* LOUIS.)

LOUIS (*Angrily*): I do not think it funny in the least. (KING *exits, and others in his party follow, with* LOUIS *trailing out after them.* PIERRE *lingers behind with* PUSS.)

PIERRE: I hope you know what you are doing, Puss. (*There is a shout off left, and* OLIVER *and* BERNARD *enter.*)

OLIVER: Hey! What's going on here?

PIERRE: Nothing is going on, my dear brothers. Everything is going off—extremely well.

BERNARD (*Catching sight of* PUSS): Ho! What's this? A masquerade? (*The two brothers start to snicker.*)

PUSS (*Sweeping off his hat*): Sir Puss in Boots, if you please.

OLIVER (*Dumfounded*): He *talks!*

BERNARD: And *walks!*

PUSS (*Tapping his forehead*): And I *think*, sirs. My master, the Marquis of Carabas, is on his way to his castle, and he wishes you good luck.

OLIVER (*To* PIERRE): The Marquis of Carabas? Does he mean you?

PIERRE: That's what he says—and who knows? (*He wags a finger playfully at* OLIVER.) Who knows?

KING (*Calling from off*): Marquis! We're ready to go!

PIERRE: Excuse me, brothers. The King is waiting for me. Goodbye! (*He exits, waving.* OLIVER *and* BERNARD *stare after him in amazement.*)

PUSS (*Haughtily*): Would you like an invitation to the wedding?

OLIVER: What wedding?

PUSS: The wedding of the Marquis of Carabas.

BERNARD: Whom is he going to marry?

PUSS: Why, the Princess Gabrielle, of course. Well, I must be on my way. (*He sings and capers about.*)
Puss in Boots, Puss in Boots, where are you going?
To visit the Ogre and see how he lives!
Puss in Boots, Puss in Boots, what will you there?
I'll catch a little mouse under the chair!
La, la, la, la, la, la—
(*He dances off left.*)

OLIVER (*Shaking his head glumly*): We should have given Pierre the mill and the donkey, and kept Puss in Boots for ourselves.

CURTAIN

*   *   *

SCENE 2

SETTING: *The entrance hall of the Ogre's castle.*

AT RISE: *The* OGRE *is asleep in his chair, snoring loudly.*

A knock on the door is heard. After a pause, a louder knock is heard. OGRE *continues to snore. A loud bang shakes door open, and* PUSS *enters stealthily. He tiptoes to* OGRE's *chair and peers at him. He tickles* OGRE's *nose with a plume of his hat, and* OGRE *brushes it away in his sleep. This business is repeated until* OGRE *wakes up with a snort.*

OGRE (*Leaping to his feet and staring above* PUSS's *head*): Who's there?

PUSS: Look down and see.

OGRE (*Lowering his gaze*): Oh! How small you are!

PUSS: How big you are!

OGRE (*Puffing out his chest*): Colossal is the word.

PUSS: Couldn't you take a tuck in yourself somewhere?

OGRE: Why should I? (*Suddenly*) How did you get in?

PUSS: The front door was open, so I let myself in.

OGRE (*Chuckling*): It's always open—but whoever comes in never goes out again.

PUSS: Why not?

OGRE: Because first he goes into my pantry, and from there into my stomach. (*He pats stomach.*) Yum, yum! Little boys make the most delicious meals. (*He smacks his lips and bends over to peek under* PUSS's *hat.*) Why, you're not a little boy—you're a little cat in shiny boots. (*He straightens up, disappointed.*)

PUSS (*Bowing*): Puss in Boots, steward to the Marquis of Carabas.

OGRE (*Impressed*): Hmmm, is that so? Well, why are you here? Do you want to shave me? (*Thrusting his bearded chin into* PUSS's *face*)—or black my boots? (*He lifts his huge foot and stomps down heavily.*)

PUSS: Nothing of the sort. I only wanted to see you, sir, because I have heard that you are the richest and most powerful ogre in the land.

OGRE (*Pleased*): Am I so famous that even the cats know about me?

PUSS: Yes, indeed, sir. You are the talk of the alley.

OGRE (*Pleased*): You don't say! Well, Puss, now that you have seen me, what do you think of me?

PUSS: Oh, I think you are wonderful!

OGRE (*Boasting*): You haven't seen anything yet.

PUSS (*Feigning innocence*): What do you mean, Mr. Ogre?

OGRE (*Swaggering about*): I have magic powers. I can change myself into any animal you can name.

PUSS: I'd have to see it before I'd believe it.

OGRE: All right, what shall it be?

PUSS: A lion.

OGRE: Pooh! That's easy enough. Watch me! (OGRE *disappears behind his chair. Then he calls out in a guttural voice.*) Ready?

PUSS (*Apprehensively*): Ready! (*A terrible roaring is heard, and a* LION *springs out from behind the chair.* PUSS *steps on his tail, trips, and falls over backward. The* LION *roars with laughter.* PUSS *scrambles to his feet and runs around the hall chased by the* LION. PUSS *finally climbs up on the table to safety.*)

LION: Had enough?

PUSS: Yes-s-s-s! Meow! (LION *disappears with a bound behind the chair, and* OGRE *steps out on the other side.*)

OGRE: Stop snarling and meowing, and come down off that table. I won't hurt you.

PUSS (*Cautiously obeying*): That was a pretty terrible lion. You frightened me almost out of my boots.

OGRE: Well, do you believe me now?

PUSS: Yes, sir—but can you turn yourself into a *small* animal as well?

OGRE: As small as you wish.

PUSS: How small?

OGRE: A June bug?

PUSS: Oh, you could never get inside a June bug. You'd be very, *very* uncomfortable. How about—a mouse?

OGRE: A mouse it is! Watch me! (*OGRE goes behind chair and after a brief pause calls out.*) Ready?

PUSS: Ready! (*He rubs his paws together gleefully, and dances around in front of chair. A loud squeaking sound is heard from behind chair. PUSS peers behind chair, and addresses "mouse" slyly.*) Oh, you poor, dear little orphan mouse! I think I will adopt you. (*He reaches behind chair, and a loud "eek, eek" is heard. PUSS walks half behind chair and pounces on "mouse" with his paw.*) Meow! There! That's the end of you, Mr. Ogre! (*He holds toy mouse up by tail in full view of audience.*) But it would be foolish to eat you. You'd give me indigestion. I'll take you outside later. (*He drops toy mouse behind chair, comes out in front of chair again, and dusts off his paws.*) And so my master inherits a castle. (*A trumpet blare is heard from off right.*) Just in time, too. Here comes the King. (*He quickly goes to door and flings it open, and bows low.*) Welcome to the castle of the Marquis of Carabas, Your Majesty! (KING *enters, followed by* PIERRE *and* GABRIELLE, MARIE *and* PAGE, *and finally by* LOUIS, *who is clutching his tablecloth-toga about him.*)

KING (*To* PIERRE): It's a fine castle, my lord. You must be a very rich man.

PIERRE: Well, Your Majesty, I don't know how much I really have—do I, Puss?

PUSS (*With a knowing glance to* PIERRE): I haven't had time to take inventory, m'lord. (*To* KING) Now, Your Majesty, if you will excuse me, I will go to the kitchen and see if dinner is ready.

KING: I hope it is. I'm simply ravenous for rabbit! (*On his way out,* PUSS *pauses to speak to* PIERRE.)

Puss: M'lord, why don't you show Her Highness the garden?

Gabrielle: Oh, I'd love to see the garden! (Puss *exits at left.*) May I go, Papa?

King: Run along, my dear.

Pierre: Just a minute, Your Highness. (*He turns to* King.) Sire, I have a confession to make.

King: A confession?

Pierre: I can no longer deceive you. Your Majesty, I have nothing to offer you—nothing.

King: What? No dinner? You don't mean your cook has left?

Pierre: I mean I am not a real marquis. I am only a poor miller's son.

King: Tut, tut, that is all in the past. Now you are a man of property. This castle and estate *do* belong to you, don't they?

Pierre: They do, Your Majesty, thanks to Puss in Boots.

King: Well, Pierre, your honesty in this matter proves to me that you are a true nobleman, and I create you Marquis of Carabas from this hour. Your coat of arms shall be a cat in boots. (Puss *re-enters with a courtier's suit draped over his arm. He looks on happily.*) Kneel. (Pierre *kneels before* King, *who taps him on each shoulder with the royal cane.*) Rise, Lord Pierre, Marquis of Carabas!

Puss (*Stepping forward*): Dinner is served, Your Majesty. And here is a suit of clothes for Louis.

King (*Impatiently*): Oh, I can't wait for Louis to dress for dinner. He will have to come as he is. Puss, is there plenty of rabbit pie à la Carabas?

Puss: The pie is so large that it took six strong men to carry it to the table.

King (*Waving cane excitedly as he cheers*): Three cheers for the rabbit pie! Three cheers for Puss in Boots!

ALL: Hurrah! Hurrah! Hurrah! (*With* KING *leading the way, all march through the doorway at left, as strains of lively music are heard from offstage.* PUSS *brings up the rear, behind* LOUIS. *He lifts* LOUIS' *trailing tablecloth and carries it like a train. Annoyed,* LOUIS *jerks it out of* PUSS's *paws and trips over it as he goes off.* PUSS *doffs plumed hat and bows to audience, as curtain falls.*)

THE END

The Reluctant Dragon

by Kenneth Grahame

Characters

EDWARD, *a shepherd boy*
SELINA, *his sister*
HORACE, *the dragon*
ST. GEORGE
CHILDREN
VILLAGERS

SCENE 1

TIME: *Once upon a time. A summer day.*
SETTING: *A hillside in England. The green rolling country-side can be seen in the distance, with a hint of old gray cities on the horizon. The opening to Horace's cave is left; the path to the village is at right.*
AT RISE: *Inside the cave, but visible to audience, is what appears to be a large green rock. Actually, this is HOR-ACE, the dragon, curled up asleep. EDWARD runs in, stops, and looks around curiously.*

EDWARD (*Shouting and beckoning off right*): Come on, hurry up! This is the place. (SELINA *and* CHILDREN *enter, carrying picnic baskets.*)
SELINA: Oh, Edward, it's a lovely place for a picnic!

1st Girl (*Standing on a rock at back*): Look at the view! I can see the spire of the cathedral a hundred miles away.

1st Boy (*Standing on another rock*): There's the village. I can see my house.

2nd Boy (*Glancing about*): How did you know about this place, Edward?

Edward: I bring the sheep up here.

3rd Boy (*Peering into cave*): What's this cave?

Edward: Oh, just a cave.

3rd Boy: Let's explore it.

2nd Girl: No, let's eat first. I'm starved.

3rd Girl: So am I.

1st Boy (*As he joins* 3rd Boy *in front of cave*): You girls unpack the baskets while we boys explore the cave.

1st Girl (*Coming over*): No, we want to go with you.

2nd Boy (*Catching sight of* Horace *inside cave*): Hey! Look at that rock all covered with emeralds!

Edward: Where?

2nd Boy (*Pointing*): There.

Edward: That's funny. I never saw that rock before.

3rd Boy: I'll bet this cave is full of treasures. Come on! (*As* Children *are about to enter cave,* 2nd Boy, *who is in the lead, suddenly stops short, frightened.*)

2nd Boy: Wait!

3rd Boy: What's the matter?

2nd Boy: That rock just moved!

1st Boy: You're crazy!

2nd Boy: I'm not! It did! (Children *stare at* Horace *in amazement as he slowly gets to his feet, stretches, yawns, then sneezes.* Children *scream and scatter, hiding behind the rocks upstage—all except* Edward, *who stands at center.*)

Edward: Don't be afraid. It's only a dragon.

1st Girl: Only a *dragon!*

3RD GIRL: *Only* a dragon! (HORACE *peeks out of cave.*)

EDWARD: I've always said this cave was a dragon cave and ought to have a dragon in it.

3RD BOY: Well, it has a dragon in it, and I'm going home!

1ST BOY: Let's clear out of here! (CHILDREN *run toward exit, but* EDWARD *bars the way.*)

EDWARD: Why? He's not ramping or carrying on or doing anything wrong, is he?

2ND BOY: Look here, Edward, dragons may be your line, but they're not mine. Let me by! (*He pushes* EDWARD *out of the way.*)

1ST BOY: Come on, everybody, or the dragon will eat you!

3RD BOY: I'll beat you to the village and be the first to tell! (*He runs off, and the other* CHILDREN *race after him.* EDWARD *catches hold of* SELINA's *arm.*)

EDWARD: Selina, you will stay, won't you?

SELINA (*Glancing toward the cave*): I—I'll come back later—maybe. (*She hands* EDWARD *picnic basket and runs off right.* EDWARD *looks after her and sighs, then turns to* HORACE, *who has come out of cave, and is walking upright.*)

EDWARD (*Cheerfully*): Hello, dragon!

HORACE (*Cowering*): Now don't you hit me, or throw stones, or squirt water at me. I won't have it! (*He sneezes.*) Atchoo!

EDWARD: I'm not going to hit you. I just want to ask you how you are, but if I'm in the way, I'll go.

HORACE (*Hastily*): No, no, don't go! I'm sorry I misjudged you. (*He bows apologetically.*) Permit me to introduce myself. My name is Horace. (*He holds out his paw, and* EDWARD *shakes it.*)

EDWARD: Howdy do, Horace. I'm Edward. Are you hungry?

HORACE: Terribly!

EDWARD (*In a matter-of-fact tone*): You don't eat children, do you?

HORACE (*Revolted*): Oh, no! Or grown-ups, either.

EDWARD (*Digging into picnic basket*): That's good, because there are only egg and cheese sandwiches in here. Shall we sit down?

HORACE: By all means. (*He sneezes.*) Atchoo!

EDWARD: Do you have a cold?

HORACE (*Sniffling and wiping his eyes*): No—hay fever. (*They sit on a rock and eat sandwiches as they talk.*)

EDWARD: Are you planning to stay here long?

HORACE: I think I will. It seems a nice enough place— and besides, I'm such a lazy fellow! I'm not much for moving around.

EDWARD (*Politely*): Is that so?

HORACE: All the other dragons I knew were so active and earnest—always rampaging, and chasing knights, and devouring damsels.

EDWARD: And you didn't?

HORACE: No, I liked to get my meals regularly and then snooze a bit. So when it happened, I really got caught!

EDWARD: When what happened, Horace?

HORACE: The earthquake. The bottom dropped right out from under me, and I found myself miles underground, wedged in as tight as tight. After a while, I began to work my way upstairs, and I came out through this cave. (HORACE *rises and looks about with satisfaction.*) Hm-m. This is the place for me, Edward. Nice view— nice country. Quiet, too. And no ragweed. (*He sneezes.*) Atchoo! Well, maybe some.

EDWARD (*Getting up*): What will you do up here all day long?

HORACE (*Looking away bashfully*): Uh—did you ever— just for fun—try to make up—well—poetry?

EDWARD: Of course I have, heaps of it, and some of it is quite good, too.

HORACE: Now you have culture, you have! I hope my other neighbors are as cultured as you are.

EDWARD (*Trying to break it gently*): Horace, I'm afraid there won't be any other neighbors.

HORACE: How's that?

EDWARD: Well, you are a dragon, aren't you?

HORACE (*Throwing out his chest*): Yes, and I'm mighty proud of it!

EDWARD: But being a dragon makes you an enemy of the human race.

HORACE (*Happily*): Don't have an enemy in the world! Too lazy to make them. And what if I do read other fellows my poetry? I'm always ready to listen to theirs!

EDWARD: Oh, dear, don't you understand? When the other people find you out, they'll come after you with shovels and pitchforks and all sorts of things.

HORACE (*Innocently*): Why? I'm not doing anything to them.

EDWARD: That's not the point. The way they see it, you are a scourge and a pest, and they will have to get rid of you.

HORACE (*Shaking his head solemnly*): There's not a word of truth in that. Couldn't I read them my poetry? That ought to convince them I'm harmless. Now, here's a little verse I was working on this morning. (*He removes a piece of bark from under a scale of his costume and reads from it.*) Summer. By Horace Dragon.

Atchoo! Atchoo! The ragweed is in bloom,
Sowing far and wide allergic gloom.
How lavishly it pollinates the breeze,
And, oh! how lavishly it makes me sneeze. *Atchoo!*
(HORACE *pauses to blow his nose.*) Well, Edward, what do you think of it?

EDWARD (*Hesitating*): Well—it's certainly—unusual.

HORACE (*Beaming*): Yes, isn't it! (SELINA *has entered from right during these speeches.* HORACE *sees her and bows elaborately.*) Welcome, fair damsel!

EDWARD (*Pleased*): Selina! You did come back!

SELINA (*Bursting out excitedly*): Oh, Edward, the village is in an uproar!

EDWARD: I thought it would be.

HORACE: What about?

SELINA: About you, sir. They say you are a pest and a scourge and must be destroyed.

EDWARD (*To* HORACE): Didn't I tell you?

HORACE: But I haven't disturbed even a hen roost!

SELINA: That has nothing to do with it. You are a dragon, and they are afraid of you. The funny part of it is, they are proud of you, too.

HORACE: Why, my dear?

SELINA (*Smiling*): It's not every village that has a dragon of its own, you know. You are quite a feather in our cap.

HORACE (*More confused than ever*): Then why do they want to destroy me?

EDWARD (*Breaking in*): Because dragons have been destroyed since the beginning of time. It's the custom.

HORACE: But I don't behave like a dragon.

EDWARD: It doesn't make sense, does it, Horace? But our village is famous for not making sense.

SELINA: That's not all, Edward. They are going to send for St. George!

HORACE: St. George! (*He sneezes.*) Atchoo!

EDWARD (*Shaking* HORACE *by the tail for emphasis*): Now you will have to pull yourself together and do something!

HORACE (*Pulling his tail out of* EDWARD'S *hand*): Don't be so violent, Edward! Sit down and listen to another poem.

EDWARD (*Exasperated*): That's right, take it calmly. I hope you'll be half as calm when St. George gets here. Of course you can lick him—a great big fellow like you!

HORACE: Oh, dearie me, this is too awful! I won't see him, and that's that! When he comes, you must tell him to go away at once. Say he can write if he likes, but I can't give him an interview.

EDWARD: Oh, Horace, don't be so pigheaded! You have to fight him some time or other.

HORACE: I don't see why.

EDWARD: Because he is St. George and you are a dragon.

HORACE (*Gravely*): My dear boy, please understand, once and for all, that I can't fight and I won't fight. I've never fought in my life, and I'm not going to begin now, just to give your village a Roman holiday.

EDWARD (*Miserably*): But if you don't fight, St. George will cut off your head!

HORACE: Oh, I don't think so. You will be able to arrange something, Edward—you are such a good manager. I leave it entirely up to you. And now, if you will excuse me, I should get back to my writing. Thank you for the sandwiches. (*He goes into the cave.*)

EDWARD (*To* SELINA): Arrange something indeed! Horace treats the whole affair as if it were an invitation to play croquet! Come on, let's go home. (*He picks up picnic basket and exits right, followed by* SELINA. *After a moment,* HORACE *appears in entrance to cave, carrying a stool and several pieces of bark. He places stool just outside cave, sits down and begins to scribble on a piece of bark with a lump of charcoal. He ponders over words, rhyming them out loud, and sneezes once or twice. Presently,* SELINA *enters from right and speaks to* HOR- ACE *softly.*)

SELINA: Mr. Horace—

HORACE (*Looking up with a start*): Oh! My dear! (*He rises and bows.*) I didn't expect you back so soon.

SELINA (*Crossing to him*): Mr. Horace, if there's anything I can do for you—like mend things, or set the cave to rights, or cook a little something when you're writing poetry and forget about meals, I—I'd be glad to do it.

HORACE: Thank you, Selina. I'd appreciate that.

SELINA: I'll start tomorrow. Is there anything in particular you'd like?

HORACE: I wonder if you'd bring me a bit of flannel to polish my scales with. (*He sneezes.*) Atchoo!

SELINA: Bless you! I'll bring the flannel and some smelling salts for that hay fever, too. Goodbye!

HORACE: Goodbye, my dear. (SELINA *skips away, singing.*) What a nice child. I'll write a sonnet to her. (*He sits down again, selects a clean piece of bark, and inscribes the title with a flourish.*) To Selina. By Horace Dragon. Now, let me think—how shall I begin it? (*He speaks the lines as he slowly sets them down.*)
Selina in her braids and calico
Is fairer far than any flower I know.
So sweet is she, this dainty shepherd's daughter,
I blush to say she makes my big mouth water. (HORACE *writes on the bark, then holds up his poem and regards it with delight. Suddenly he jumps to his feet with a cry of horror.*) Oh! What am I thinking of? Is it possible that I am a damsel-devouring dragon after all? Oh, dearie, dearie me! (*He reaches behind for his tail and, using it as an eraser, he frantically rubs out what he has written, as curtain falls.*)

*   *   *

SCENE 2

TIME: *Three days later.*

SETTING: *The same as Scene 1.*

AT RISE: ST. GEORGE *is standing on a rock upstage, lean-*

*ing on his sword, lost in contemplation of distant hills.
His red-plumed helmet is resting on the rock beside him.
His spear is stuck upright in a crevice.* HORACE *is nowhere to be seen. After a moment,* EDWARD *enters from
right.*

EDWARD (*Politely*): St. George, sir!

ST. GEORGE (*Turning, startled*): Yes?

EDWARD: I hope I'm not intruding, sir.

ST. GEORGE: Not at all, boy. I'm just getting the lay of the
land. Magnificent view up here. What can I do for you?
(*He comes down from rock.*)

EDWARD: If you please, sir, I'd like to talk to you about the
dragon.

ST. GEORGE (*Sighing*): Alas! Is it another tale of misery
and wrong?

EDWARD: Nothing of the sort! There's a misunderstanding
somewhere, and I want to put it right. The fact is, sir,
this is a *good* dragon.

ST. GEORGE (*Smiling*): Exactly. A good dragon—a worthy
foe of my steel (*He lifts his sword high*), and no feeble
specimen of his noxious tribe.

EDWARD: He's not noxious! I tell you, he's a *good* dragon,
and a friend of mine. Why, he has been so kind to my
sister, she'd do anything for him.

ST. GEORGE (*Clapping* EDWARD *on shoulder*): I like a fellow who sticks up for his friends! What is your name,
boy?

EDWARD: Edward, sir.

ST. GEORGE: Now, Edward, I'm sure the dragon has his
good points, but that's not the question. He has been
stealing and killing—

EDWARD (*Shocked*): Horace? Stealing and killing? (*Impatiently*) Oh, you've been listening to all those yarns the

villagers have been telling. Why, our villagers are the biggest story-tellers in the country.

St. George (*Amazed*): Do you mean that the dragon hasn't molested anybody?

Edward: That's right. Horace is a real gentleman, every inch of him. All the villagers want is to see a fight.

St. George: But what are we to do? (*Pointing to cave.*) In there is the dragon and out here am I, and we're supposed to be thirsting for each other's blood. What do you suggest? Can't you arrange things, somehow?

Edward: That's just what Horace said! Really, the way you two seem to leave everything to me! (*Coaxing*) I suppose, sir, you couldn't be persuaded to go away quietly, could you?

St. George (*Loftily*): Impossible! It's quite against the rules.

Edward: Then would you please see the dragon and talk it over?

St. George: We-e-ell, it's irregular, but I guess it's the most sensible thing to do.

Edward: I'm glad you feel that way, St. George. (*He goes to entrance of cave and calls out loudly.*) Horace! I've brought a friend to see you! (*There is a sneeze inside cave, and* Selina *comes running out, holding a bottle of smelling salts.*)

Selina: He'll be right out.

St. George: What ho! A damsel in distress! (*He draws his sword.*)

Edward: Hold on! That's my sister, Selina. She looks after him.

St. George (*With a sheepish grin*): Oh. (*He puts his sword away.* Horace *appears, rubbing his scales with a square of flannel. He gives the flannel to* Selina *and extends his paw to* St. George.)

Horace: Pleased to make your acquaintance, sir.

EDWARD: This is St. George.

HORACE (*Frightened*): St. George?

ST. GEORGE (*Shaking* HORACE's *paw*): How do you do, Horace.

HORACE: So—so glad to meet you. (SELINA *hovers over* HORACE *during the following scene, polishing his scales and giving him smelling salts whenever he shows signs of sneezing.*)

EDWARD: We've come to talk things over quietly, Horace, so for goodness' sake, do let us have a little straight common sense.

ST. GEORGE (*Pleasantly*): Now, don't you think that the simplest plan would be just to fight it out and let the best man win?

EDWARD: Oh, yes, do, Horace! It will save such a lot of bother.

ST. GEORGE: They are betting on you down in the village, Horace, but I don't mind.

HORACE: Believe me, George, there's nobody in the world I'd sooner oblige than you and Edward, but the whole thing is nonsense. There's absolutely nothing to fight about. Anyhow, I'm not going to fight, so that settles it.

ST. GEORGE (*Slightly angry*): Suppose I make you fight?

HORACE: You can't. I should only go into my cave and stay there. You'd soon get sick of sitting outside and waiting for me to come out and fight.

ST. GEORGE (*As he gazes about*): But Horace, this would be a beautiful place for a fight. What a picture we would make!—I in my golden armor showing up against your big green scaly coils.

HORACE (*Wavering*): Now you're trying to get at me through my poetic sense, but it won't work.

EDWARD: Don't you see, Horace, that there *has* to be a fight of some sort, even if it's only "pretend"?

HORACE: You mean, a mock fight?

St. George (*Eagerly*): Yes! I'm sure we can manage it. (*He studies his sword.*) I would have to touch you somewhere, but I won't hurt you very much. How about here? (*He places the tip of his sword behind* Horace's *knee.*)

Horace (*Giggling*): You're tickling me, George! (*He sneezes.*) That place won't do. I'd only laugh and spoil everything. (*He sniffs the smelling salts that* Selina *holds under his nose.*)

St. George: Well, here, then. (*He flicks his sword at the nape of* Horace's *neck.*) If I nicked you here, you'd never know I'd done it.

Horace (*Anxiously*): Are you sure you can hit the right place?

St. George: Now, don't you fret. Of course you will have to do your share of the fighting, too, Horace. Can you ramp and breathe fire?

Horace (*Confidently*): Oh, I can ramp all right. I'm a little out of practice breathing fire, but I'll do my best.

Edward (*Concerned*): Look here, St. George, if there's to be a fight and Horace is to be licked, what is he going to get out of it?

Horace: That's right, George. What will I get out of it?

St. George: Well, you will be led in triumph down to the market place—

Edward: Exactly—led in triumph by you!

St. George: Then there will be toasts and speeches, and I shall explain that Horace has converted.

Edward: And then?

St. George: Why, then there will be a big banquet, and that is where Horace will come in.

Horace: What do you mean?

St. George: I mean, you will read some of your poetry with the dessert, and everyone will know how clever you are!

HORACE: Splendid! I might even go into society and read my poems at garden parties and teas.

ST. GEORGE (*Picking up his helmet from the rock*): There ought to be a princess chained to this rock. Edward, can't you arrange a princess?

EDWARD (*Firmly*): No, I can't arrange a princess, and anyway, here come the villagers to see the fight. (*Noise of a crowd is heard from off right.*)

ST. GEORGE: Horace, get into your cave and don't come out until I call you. (HORACE *trots into cave.*) Come, Edward, you will be my squire and carry my spear. (*He loosens spear from crevice and gives it to* EDWARD; *then he strides off left of cave.*)

EDWARD (*To* SELINA, *as he follows* ST. GEORGE *off*): Act as if you'd just arrived! (SELINA *hastily tosses flannel cloth into cave and sits on a rock, assuming a casual pose.* VILLAGERS *and* CHILDREN *enter, dressed in their Sunday best, laughing and chattering gaily. They group themselves, sitting and standing, on the rocks,* CHILDREN *in the foreground and* VILLAGERS *behind.*)

1ST BOY: Who do you think will win?

2ND BOY: The dragon.

3RD BOY: St. George.

1ST BOY (*To* 2ND BOY): Hey, don't sit so close to the cave!

2ND BOY: Why not?

1ST BOY: If the dragon wins, he'll bite off your head! (BOYS *cuff at each other. Then* VILLAGERS *on higher portions of the rocks begin to cheer and wave their handkerchiefs as they look off left.*)

VILLAGERS: St. George! Here comes St. George! (ST. GEORGE *enters, followed by* EDWARD, *who carries spear.* ST. GEORGE *takes up a position downstage in front of cave, with* EDWARD *beside him.*)

EDWARD (*In a low tone, to* ST. GEORGE): Do you think Horace can be depended on, sir?

ST. GEORGE: Oh, I think so.

EDWARD: He might consider the whole thing a lot of bosh and change his mind.

ST. GEORGE: Haven't you more faith in your friend than that? (EDWARD *sits cross-legged, with his back to audience.* ST. GEORGE *faces opening of cave, and talks loudly to* HORACE.) Dragon, come forth! (*Inside cave, there is low muttering, mingled with snorts and sneezes, which rises to a bellowing roar. Then a cloud of smoke rolls out of the cave, and* HORACE *prances magnificently forth, lashing his long tail from side to side.*)

VILLAGERS: Ooh! Ooh!

EDWARD (*Applauding wildly*): Bully for you, Horace! I didn't think you had it in you! (ST. GEORGE *draws his sword and charges at* HORACE, *who rears back with a loud roar.*)

VILLAGERS: Missed! (ST. GEORGE *retreats and swings his sword high in the air, then charges again.* HORACE *sits down and roars viciously.*)

EDWARD (*Shouting, as he stands up and waves the spear*): End of Round One! (SELINA *runs to his side and whispers to him uneasily.*)

SELINA: I hope St. George won't get excited and hurt Horace.

EDWARD: I don't think he will. What a regular play-actor that Horace is! (ST. GEORGE *looks toward them as he wipes his brow. He smiles and nods and holds up three fingers.*) That means he will finish off Horace in Round Three. Whatever is that old fool of a dragon up to now? (HORACE *is giving a ramping performance for* VILLAGERS. *He swaggers around and around in a wide circle.* EDWARD *raps on ground with the spear.*) Time! (HORACE *begins to leap from side to side with ungainly bounds, whooping like an Indian.* ST. GEORGE *dances about, thrusting his sword at* HORACE, *but is unable to make contact.* VILLAGERS *cheer.* HORACE *struts to and fro, his tail in the air.* ST. GEORGE *comes toward* EDWARD *and* SELINA, *tightening his armor*) It's a grand fight, St. George. Can't you let it last a bit longer?

ST. GEORGE: No, I'd better not. Horace is getting conceited now that they've started to cheer him. He'll forget all about the agreement and play the fool. There's no telling how far he might go. I'll just finish him off this round.

SELINA: Oh, *do* be careful, sir—of Horace, I mean.

ST. GEORGE (*Kindly*): Now don't you worry. I've marked the exact spot. (ST. GEORGE *turns upstage and cautiously approaches* HORACE, *who crouches, flicking his tail so that it cracks like a whip.* ST. GEORGE *circles warily around him.* HORACE *paces guardedly around the same circle, occasionally feinting with his head. They spar for an opening, while the spectators maintain a breathless silence. Then suddenly there is a lightning movement of* ST. GEORGE's *arm, a whirl and a confusion of scales, claws, tail and flying bits of turf.* VILLAGERS *cheer as* ST. GEORGE *stands astride* HORACE. ST. GEORGE *holds his sword over* HORACE, *menacingly.* EDWARD *and* SELINA *run to* ST. GEORGE.)

EDWARD: Oh, sir, he isn't really hurt, is he? (HORACE *lifts his head slightly, looks at* EDWARD, *then collapses again.*)

1ST VILLAGER (*An old man in the crowd*): Aren't you goin' to cut 'is 'ead off, master?

ST. GEORGE (*Affably*): Not today, grandfather. I'll give him a good talking-to, and you'll find he will be a very different dragon.

VILLAGERS: Three cheers for St. George! Three cheers for the dragon! (*While the crowd is cheering,* ST. GEORGE *pretends to scold* HORACE, *wagging his finger at him with a stern expression.* VILLAGERS *start to form for the march to the village, and* ST. GEORGE *raises his hand to get their attention.*)

ST. GEORGE: Just a moment! I have something to say to all of you. The dragon has been thinking things over, and he says he's not going to rampage any more. He would like to settle down here and write poetry. So you must make friends with him and admit him into society. (VILLAGERS *cheer again.*)

HORACE (*To* ST. GEORGE): I couldn't have done it better myself. Jolly fight, wasn't it? I didn't sneeze once. (*He sneezes, and* SELINA *whips out the smelling salts.*) Thank you, my dear.

ST. GEORGE: Well, shall we start down to the village?

HORACE: Wait! My poems!

SELINA: I'll get them for you! (*She rushes into the cave;* CHILDREN *and* VILLAGERS *joyfully march offstage and down through the audience, singing to the tune of "The Campbells Are Coming."*)

ALL (*Singing*):
  St. George caught a dragon,
    Hooray! Hooray!
  A queer sort of dragon,
    Hooray! Hooray!
  He sits in his cave
    Writing poems all day!
  A queer sort of dragon,
    Hooray! Hooray!

(EDWARD, ST. GEORGE, SELINA, *and* HORACE, *with his poems tucked under his scales, bring up the rear,* HORACE *singing loudest of all, as curtain falls.*)

THE END

The Little Princess

by Frances Hodgson Burnett

Characters

SARA CREWE, *the little princess*
BECKY, *the scullery maid*
MISS MINCHIN, *headmistress of Miss Minchin's Select Seminary for Young Ladies*
ERMENGARDE ⎫
LOTTIE ⎪
LAVINIA ⎪
JESSIE ⎬ *her pupils*
LILLY ⎪
BLANCHE ⎭
MR. CARRISFORD, *the Indian gentleman*
RAM DASS, *his Hindu servant*
CHANDA, *a Hindu boy*

SCENE 1

TIME: *An afternoon in the fall of 1890.*
SETTING: *A dreary attic room at Miss Minchin's Select Seminary for Young Ladies in London. It is furnished as a bedroom, with old, rickety furniture. There are several chairs and a kitchen table at center; a small fireplace is against the left wall.*
AT RISE: *The door slowly opens and* BECKY *tiptoes into*

the room. She looks around, then hurries to the grate and pretends to start a fire. SARA appears in the doorway.

BECKY: You can come in now, Miss Sara. I've started the fire and it'll be warm in a few minutes. But mind the loose boards. Don't trip over them. (SARA *advances cautiously into the room, carrying a large doll in her arms. She is followed by* ERMENGARDE, LOTTIE, LAVINIA, JESSIE, LILLY *and* BLANCHE, *all dressed, like* SARA, *in party clothes.*)

ERMENGARDE: Ooh, it's spooky!

LOTTIE (*Whimpering*): I'm afraid.

LAVINIA (*Nastily*): Fraidy-cat!

LOTTIE (*Running to* SARA): Sa-a-ra!

SARA (*Putting her arm around* LOTTIE): There's nothing to be afraid of, Lottie. Remember—it's all pretend. We're just *pretending* that this attic is the Bastille, and we are prisoners like Dr. Manette in *A Tale of Two Cities.*

JESSIE: But the dark and cold are not pretend. They are *real!* (*She giggles.*)

BECKY (*In a matter-of-fact tone*): It does seem dreary, but you get used to it. And it's not so bad when you get under the blankets. I'm so tired at night, I go right to sleep.

LILLY (*Aghast*): Becky, do you mean you *sleep* up here?

BECKY: My room is next door.

LOTTIE (*Whimpering again*): I want to go back downstairs to your birthday party, Sara.

LAVINIA: Oh, don't be such a crybaby!

LOTTIE: Sa-a-ra!

BLANCHE (*Near the door*): If Lottie doesn't stop, Miss Minchin will hear her. (*She looks anxiously down the attic stairs.*)

SARA (*Soothing* LOTTIE): Now, Lottie, you *promised* Sara.

LOTTIE: She said I was a crybaby.

SARA: If you cry, you *will* be one.

LOTTIE: I haven't any mamma.

SARA (*Cheerfully*): Yes, you have. Don't you know that Sara is your mamma? (LOTTIE *cuddles up to* SARA.)

LAVINIA (*Sneering*): Mamma Sara—huh!

ERMENGARDE: Oh, Lavinia, you're just jealous of Sara, because she's rich, and we all like her.

LAVINIA: I am not jealous!

LOTTIE: Yes, you are!

LAVINIA: Nasty, spoiled little thing! I should like to slap you!

SARA (*With fire*): I should like to slap you, too, Lavinia, but I won't. We are not gutter children. We are both old enough to know better.

LAVINIA (*With a curtsy*): Ah, yes, Your Royal Highness. We are princesses, I believe. At least, *one* of us is. (*She exchanges a glance with* JESSIE, *who giggles.*) The school ought to be very fashionable now that Miss Minchin has a princess for a pupil.

SARA (*Holding her head high*): It's true. Sometimes I do pretend I am a princess, so that I can try to behave like one.

LAVINIA: Dear me! When you ascend the throne, I hope you won't forget us.

SARA (*Staring steadily at* LAVINIA): I won't.

MISS MINCHIN (*Calling from offstage*): Girls! Girls, are you up there?

BLANCHE: I told you so! Miss Minchin is coming. Lottie has spoiled everything with her crying. (MISS MINCHIN *enters, scowling.*)

MISS MINCHIN (*Severely*): Young ladies, what are you doing up here in the attic?

SARA (*Stepping forward*): It was my idea, Miss Minchin. We were waiting for the refreshments to be served and

I started to tell them *A Tale of Two Cities*. Then we began to imagine what it would be like to be prisoners, and when Becky said the attic was something like the Bastille, I—

MISS MINCHIN (*Interrupting as she catches sight of* BECKY *cowering in the background*): Becky, you insolent minx! What business had you to bring the young ladies up here?

SARA (*Coming to* BECKY'S *defense*): Becky didn't bring us up here, Miss Minchin. I did.

MISS MINCHIN: Humph! Well, you can all march straight back downstairs again—*this instant*. You are no credit to Miss Minchin's Select Seminary for Young Ladies. (*The girls file out quickly.*) Not you, Sara. I want to speak to you. (*To* BECKY) I will attend to you later, Becky. Go back to the kitchen where you belong.

BECKY (*Bobbing a curtsy*): Yes, ma'am. (*She scurries through the door, closing it behind her.* MISS MINCHIN *turns to* SARA.)

MISS MINCHIN (*Coldly*): I suppose you are wondering what I have to say to you.

SARA: Yes, Miss Minchin.

MISS MINCHIN: Your father's lawyer has just been to see me. He told me some startling news. Your father is dead. (*There is an outcry from* SARA, *but* MISS MINCHIN *goes right on.*) He lost all his money speculating in a diamond mine that proved a failure. So now you are a little pauper, Sara, instead of a little princess. You haven't a brass farthing to your name. (SARA *stands perfectly still, staring at* MISS MINCHIN *without making a sound.*) What are you staring at? Why don't you say something? Are you so stupid that you cannot understand?

SARA (*In a low tone*): I understand. My papa is dead. He left me no money. I am quite poor.

MISS MINCHIN: You are a beggar. Give me that doll. (*She holds out her hand for* SARA's *doll.*)

SARA (*Firmly*): No. My papa gave her to me. She is all I have.

MISS MINCHIN: You will have no time for dolls in the future. You are like Becky—you will have to work for your living.

SARA (*With relief*): If I can work, it will not matter so much. What shall I do?

MISS MINCHIN: You will do anything you are told. You are a sharp child and pick things up quickly. You speak French very well, and you can teach the younger children.

SARA: Oh, may I? I know I can teach them. I like them, and they like me.

MISS MINCHIN: Don't talk nonsense about people liking you. The time for that sort of thing is past. You will run errands and help in the kitchen as well as in the schoolroom. If you don't please me, you will be sent away. (*There is a pause while* SARA *gazes steadily at* MISS MINCHIN *in silence.*) Well? Don't you intend to thank me?

SARA: What for?

MISS MINCHIN: For my kindness to you in giving you a home.

SARA (*Fiercely*): You are not kind, and this is *not* a home!

MISS MINCHIN: Don't you dare speak to me in that manner! You are not a princess now! You will take off that ridiculous dress and change into something black. (*She crosses to the door and turns angrily.*) And another thing—the room you have occupied on the second floor is no longer yours.

SARA: Where is my room?

MISS MINCHIN: You will sleep here in this attic.

SARA (*Her voice trembling*): Here? In this cold, dark place?

MISS MINCHIN: Cold or not, you will sleep here. (*She exits, shutting the door behind her with a bang.* SARA *hugs the doll to her.*)

SARA: Oh, Emily, if only you could talk! (SARA *sits on the bed and, laying the doll across her knees, she puts her face down upon it and her arms around it, making no sound. After a moment, there is a low tap on the door and it is pushed open.* BECKY *peeps through the crack.*)

BECKY: Miss Sara, might I—would you allow me—just to come in? (SARA *lifts her head and tries to smile.*) I shouldn't have, miss, but I listened outside the door, and I heard.

SARA (*Holding out her hand to* BECKY): Oh, Becky! (*She draws* BECKY *to her side.*)

BECKY (*Anxiously*): Aren't you going to cry out loud, miss?

SARA (*Shaking her head*): No, Becky. You have to bear things. I promised Papa I would. Papa was a soldier and he said soldiers don't complain, so I'm not going to.

BECKY: I just wanted to ask you, miss—you've been such a rich young lady and been waited on hand and foot. What'll you do now, miss, without any maid? Please, would you let me wait on you after I'm done with my pots and kettles?

SARA (*With a sob*): Oh, Becky! Do you remember when I told you that we were just the same? Not a rich girl and a poor girl, but just two girls.

BECKY: Yes, miss. You said it was an accident that I was not you and you were not me.

SARA: Well, you see how true it is, Becky. There's no difference now. I'm not a princess any more. (BECKY *presses* SARA's *hand to her cheek.*)

BECKY: Yes, miss, you are! Whatever happens to you, you'll be a princess just the same—and nothing could make it any different.

CURTAIN

*   *   *

SCENE 2

TIME: *Several weeks later.*

SETTING: *The attic room. An old trunk is under the window. A hat and shawl are hanging on a clothes tree. Emily, the doll, is propped up in a rocking chair.*

AT RISE: SARA *is at the window, looking out and making a low whistling sound.*

SARA (*In a coaxing voice*): Please, little bird, come and sing to me. (*Bird appears on window sill.* NOTE: *The bird is attached to a string and is moved by someone offstage.*) See? I have some crumbs for you. (*She holds her hand out to where bird is perched.*)

MISS MINCHIN (*From offstage*): Sara, are you there?

SARA: Oh, dear! What does she want now? I'm so tired.

MISS MINCHIN (*At doorway*): Come downstairs at once and put some coal on my fire. It's almost out.

SARA (*Wearily*): I'll be right there, Miss Minchin. (MISS MINCHIN *exits.* SARA *turns back to window.*) Goodbye, little bird. (*Bird flies off, and* SARA *closes window and exits. After a moment* RAM DASS *is seen outside of window. He peers in cautiously, then opens window and climbs in. He turns, looks outside, and beckons to* CHANDA, *who then follows* RAM DASS *in through window, climbing over sill.* RAM DASS *walks slowly and quietly around the room, making notes on a pad of paper as he looks carefully at the furnishings. First he walks over to bed and presses his hand on the mattress.)*

RAM DASS: As hard as a stone! *(He lifts the coverlet and examines the pillow.)* What a bed for a child to sleep in! *(He indicates rusty grate in fireplace.)* There has not been a fire in this grate since the child began to sleep here.

CHANDA: You seem to know much about her.

RAM DASS: All her life each day I know. I slip across the roof and look to see if she is safe.

CHANDA: And what are we to do here?

RAM DASS: I told Sahib Carrisford about the child, how kind she is to everyone. She feeds the birds who come to the window, even though she herself has nothing but dried bread to eat many days, and my master wants to make her happy and comfortable.

CHANDA: Can everything be done while she is asleep?

RAM DASS: Yes. Children sleep soundly—even the unhappy ones. We will bring the things across the roof from the Sahib's house tonight. If you will pass them to me through the window, I can do the rest and she will not stir. When she awakens, she will think a magician has been here.

CHANDA: Sh-h-h! I hear footsteps on the stairs.

RAM DASS: Quickly—out through the window! (RAM DASS *and* CHANDA *slip through the window and close it noiselessly. There is a knock on the door and, after a pause,* ERMENGARDE *enters with a pile of books and a large tin box of pastries. She looks about the room and calls out.)*

ERMENGARDE: Sara? Sara? It's Ermie. *(She sets the books on the table and the tin box on the stool.)* I wonder where she is. I thought I heard her come in. Well, I'll just sit down and wait for her. *(She sits on the bed and shivers.)* Brr! She must nearly freeze to death up here.

How can Sara stand it? I wish she'd come. (SARA *opens the door and sees* ERMENGARDE.)

SARA: Ermie! I didn't expect you tonight.

ERMENGARDE (*Jumping off the bed*): Oh, Sara, I'm so glad you've come!

SARA: I'm ready to drop. I've been sent out on errands ten times since breakfast and Cook has done nothing but scold me. (*She notices the pile of books on the table and goes to them eagerly.*) Oh, what are these books, Ermie?

ERMENGARDE (*Sighing*): Papa sent them to me.

SARA (*Looking at the title of the top book*): Oh, joy! Carlyle's *French Revolution*. I've so wanted to read that.

ERMENGARDE: I haven't, and Papa will be very cross if I don't. He'll want me to know all about it when I go home for the holidays. What shall I do?

SARA (*Excited*): Look here, Ermie. If you'll lend me these books, I'll read them and tell you everything that's in them afterwards, and I'll tell it so that you will remember it, too. Then later you can read them yourself when you have time.

ERMENGARDE: Sara, if you'll do that, I'll—I'll give you some of my pocket money.

SARA: I don't want your money, Ermie. I just want your books. (*She gathers them up in her arms and hugs them.*)

ERMENGARDE: Take them, then, and welcome. (*She sits in the rocking chair, holding Emily in her lap.* SARA *piles the books on the foot of the bed.*)

SARA: How are you getting on with your French lessons?

ERMENGARDE: Ever so much better since you began to teach me up here in this attic.

SARA (*Looking around the room*): You know, the attic would be rather nice if it weren't so *very* dreadful. (*She laughs.*) It's a good place to pretend in.

ERMENGARDE: Do you still pretend it's the Bastille?

SARA: Yes—and I am a prisoner who has been here for years and years and everyone has forgotten all about me. Miss Minchin is the jailer and Becky is the prisoner in the next cell. I knock on the wall to talk to her— this way. (SARA *knocks three times on the wall behind the washstand*.) Then Becky knocks back.

ERMENGARDE: It's just like a story!

SARA: It *is* a story. Everything is a story—you are a story, I am a story, all the people who live around us are a story. (*She stands on trunk under window*.) I watch them out of the window here. I can see all up and down the street. That's how I got to know the lascar and the monkey.

ERMENGARDE: What lascar and what monkey?

SARA: The lascar is the Indian gentleman's servant, and the monkey is the Indian gentleman's monkey.

ERMENGARDE: Where do they live?

SARA: Next door. The Indian gentleman's name is Mr. Carrisford, and he's always ill. Last night his monkey ran away and came in through my window. It was so late, I kept him here until this morning, and then I took him back to the lascar. He thanked me with a salaam—like this. (SARA *puts the palms of her hands together and makes a low bow.* ERMENGARDE *giggles and springs to her feet.*)

ERMENGARDE: Let me do it. (SARA *shows her how. Suddenly the door opens and* BECKY *stands there, crying.*)

BECKY: Oh, Miss Sara, Miss Minchin is after me about stealing a pie, but I didn't do it!

MISS MINCHIN (*Off right, calling angrily*): Becky!

ERMENGARDE (*Whispering*): She's coming up here!

SARA (*To* ERMENGARDE): Quick—hide under the bed! (ERMENGARDE *squeezes under the bed just in time to avoid being seen by* MISS MINCHIN.)

MISS MINCHIN (*In the doorway, glaring at* BECKY): You impudent, dishonest child! You should be sent to prison for stealing! Half a meat pie, indeed!

BECKY: I didn't do it, ma'am. I was hungry enough—I could have eaten a *whole* pie—but I never laid a finger on it. Cook gave it to her policeman.

MISS MINCHIN: Don't tell lies! Go to your room! (BECKY *runs out, sobbing.*) Sara, you will stay here in your own room and leave Becky to herself. She is a wicked girl and must be punished. (MISS MINCHIN *goes out, shutting the door. After a pause,* SARA *leans down and whispers to* ERMENGARDE.)

SARA: You can come out now, Ermie. She's gone. (*As* ERMENGARDE *crawls out from under the bed,* SARA *bursts out indignantly.*) It's too cruel! The cook takes things and then says Becky steals them, but she doesn't! Becky's so hungry sometimes, she eats left-over crusts.

ERMENGARDE (*Aghast*): What! Sara, are *you* ever as hungry as that?

SARA (*Passionately*): Yes, I am! I'm so hungry now that I could eat almost anything!

ERMENGARDE (*Sadly*): I didn't know it was as bad as that, or I would have brought it sooner. (*She goes to the stool for the tin box of pastries.*)

SARA: Brought what sooner?

ERMENGARDE: This box of goodies. (*She sets it on the table.*) My aunt sent it to me, and I haven't touched it. There are cakes inside, and buns and jam tarts and chocolates. We'll invite Becky in and have a feast!

SARA: I'll knock on the wall. (*She knocks three times, then two.*) That means, "Come to me through the secret passage." (*There are five quick knocks on the other side of the wall.*) She's coming! (SARA *and* ERMENGARDE *wait impatiently for* BECKY *to appear. She opens the door and comes in, wiping her eyes on her apron and stifling her sobs.)*

BECKY: Oh, Miss Sara, if it weren't for you, and the Bastille, and being the prisoner in the next cell, I should die. Miss Minchin is more like the head jailer every day, and Cook is like the prison guard. Excuse me, Miss Ermengarde, I should have spoken to you.

ERMENGARDE: That's all right, Becky. Come over here. *(She pulls BECKY to the table, points to box.)* Look!

SARA: Ermie has brought us a box of good things!

BECKY: To *eat?*

ERMENGARDE: Take off the cover and see for yourself. *(BECKY opens box and is overwhelmed at the sight of the pastries.)*

BECKY: Oh, miss, miss! How good you are!

ERMENGARDE *(Bustling about)*: Sara, you and Becky unpack the box while I pull the chairs up to the table. *(She places the kitchen chair behind the table, the stool at left and the rocking chair at right. SARA and BECKY put the pastries on table.)*

SARA *(Stepping back to admire table)*: There, I guess we're ready. How does it look, Ermie?

ERMENGARDE: It's like a party!

BECKY: It's like a queen's table!

ERMENGARDE: I'll tell you what, Sara! Pretend that you are a princess giving a banquet.

SARA: But it's your banquet, Ermie—you must be the princess. Becky and I will be your maids of honor.

ERMENGARDE: Oh, I can't! I'm too stupid, and I don't know how. *You* be the princess.

BECKY: Yes, miss, go on—you be the princess.

SARA: Well, if you want me to. . . .

ERMENGARDE *(Removing the lace paper lining of the tin box)*: Here, Princess Sara, here is your crown. *(She sets it on SARA's head.)*

SARA (*Graciously*): Thank you, Lady Ermengarde. (*Indicating chair*) Please be seated at the banquet table. You, too, Lady Becky. (BECKY *sits on stool,* ERMENGARDE *sits in rocker, and* SARA *sits on chair behind table.* SARA *waves her hand.*) What ho, minstrels! Strike up your violins and your bassoons! (ERMENGARDE *and* BECKY *imitate instruments. Suddenly the door is pushed open violently and* MISS MINCHIN *enters.*)

MISS MINCHIN: What does this mean?

ERMENGARDE (*Rising*): If you please, Miss Minchin, my aunt sent me a box of pastries, and we're having a party.

MISS MINCHIN (*Witheringly*): So I see. (*Crossing to* SARA's *chair*) With the Princess Sara at the head of the table. Becky, you audacious creature, you shall leave the house in the morning! Go back to your attic.

BECKY: Yes, ma'am. (*She exits, wiping her eyes on apron*)

MISS MINCHIN: This is your doing, Sara, I know—Ermengarde would never have thought of such a thing. (ERMENGARDE *starts to protest.*)

ERMENGARDE: Oh, but I did, Miss Minchin.

MISS MINCHIN (*Cutting her short*): Put those pastries back in the box at once! (*To* SARA) As for you, I will attend to you tomorrow. You shall have neither breakfast, dinner nor supper.

SARA: I've had neither dinner nor supper today, Miss Minchin.

MISS MINCHIN: Then all the better. You will have something to remember. (*She catches sight of the books on the bed.*) Ermengarde, you have brought your beautiful new books to this dirty attic. Take them to your room. You shall stay there all tomorrow, and I shall write to your papa. What would he say if he knew where you are tonight?

ERMENGARDE: I don't know, Miss Minchin. (*She starts to leave.*)

MISS MINCHIN: Take that box with you.

ERMENGARDE: Yes, Miss Minchin. (*She picks up the box, crosses to the door, and runs out.*)

MISS MINCHIN (*Turning fiercely on* SARA, *who has risen*): Why do you stare at me like that? What are you thinking about?

SARA (*Quietly*): I was wondering what *my* papa would say if he knew where I am tonight.

MISS MINCHIN: You saucy girl! I will leave you to wonder. (*She snatches the paper crown from* SARA's *head and throws it on the table.*) Princess Sara indeed! (MISS MINCHIN *exits, slamming the door.* SARA *stands looking after her for a moment, then speaks emphatically.*)

SARA: I *am* a princess, and you are a poor, stupid, vulgar woman who doesn't know any better. I may be dressed in rags and tatters (*She picks up the paper crown*), but I am a princess, *inside.* (*She sets the crown on her head, then with a sob, falls on her bed and picks up her doll.*) There isn't any princess, Emily. There's nothing left but the prisoner in the Bastille. (*Bravely*) I *won't* cry. I'll go to bed and sleep. I can't pretend any more to-night. (*She takes off her shoes and creeps under the thin blanket with the doll clasped in her arms. There is a brief interval during which music is played to denote the passage of time, then* RAM DASS *and* CHANDA *appear outside the window.* RAM DASS *carries an unlighted lantern. He raises the window without a sound, enters and puts the lantern on the stool.* CHANDA *passes the following things to him through window: wood for the grate; a lamp for the table; a satin quilt which* RAM DASS *gently spreads over* SARA; *a dressing gown and slippers which he places at the foot of the bed; scatter rugs for the floor; several books and a tray of food, which are set on the table.* RAM DASS *then puts wood on grate and pretends to light it.* NOTE: *Flashlights should be hidden in grate and lantern. He lights the lantern, then exits through the window, closing it quietly behind him.* SARA *awakens slowly.*) What a nice dream! I feel quite warm. (*She stretches out her arms and touches the quilt.*) I don't want to wake up. (*She snuggles down again and hugs doll.*) Are you dreaming the same dream, Emily? There's a fire in the grate, and thick rugs on the floor, and a hot supper on the table. (*She opens her eyes, sees everything and is bewildered.*) It doesn't melt away—it stays. I never had such a dream before. See, Emily? It stays even after we've opened our eyes. (*She throws back the quilt and puts her feet on a rug, smiling.*) It *feels* real. (*She sniffs the food on the tray.*) It *smells* real. (*She looks about.*) The room is bewitched—or *I* am bewitched. (*She runs to fireplace.*) There *is* a fire! (*She holds out her hands to the fireplace.*) And it's *hot.* (*She suddenly sees the dressing gown and presses it against her cheek.*) It's soft. (*She puts it on.*) And warm. (*She puts on slippers.*) The slippers are warm, too. It's all real, this food—these books—(*She opens a book and turns to the flyleaf.*) Somebody has written something. What does it say? (*Reading*) "To the little girl in the attic—from a friend." (*She hugs book and speaks with mounting excitement.*) I have a friend, I have a friend! (*Running to wall at right, she knocks, and presently* BECKY *enters, wearing a faded and patched flannel nightgown.*)

BECKY (*Gasping*): Oh! Oh, miss!

SARA: You *do* see it, too, don't you, Becky?

BECKY: Where did it all come from, miss? Who did it?

SARA: I don't know who could have done it, Becky, but whoever it is—wherever he is—someone is my friend.

BECKY (*Looking about her*): Even if it's all gone by morning, miss, at least it's here tonight, and I'll never forget it. (*She stares hard at each thing*) Let me see—the fire is *there* (*Points to it*), and the lamp is on the table, and —(*She pauses to smell the food on the tray.*) and there are sandwiches and soup and muffins! (BECKY *and* SARA *sit down and eagerly begin to eat.*)

SARA (*Happily*): Even if I never know who it is, if I never can even say "thank you," I shall feel happy knowing I have a friend.

CURTAIN

*   *   *

SCENE 3

TIME: *The next morning.*

SETTING: *The attic room. Furniture is back in its usual place; the bed is made; and the empty dishes have been washed and put back on the tray.*

AT RISE: SARA *is standing on the trunk before the open window, feeding the sparrows on the roof outside.*

SARA: No, no, little birds! Don't be so greedy! That crumb was for your mamma.

ERMENGARDE (*Off right, calling*): Sara! Sara! (*She bursts into the room, breathless with excitement.*) Sara, what do you think has happened? The Indian gentleman next door has come to call! Miss Minchin is out, so he's coming up here to see you!

SARA (*Astonished*): To see me? In the attic? (*She shuts the window and runs to* ERMENGARDE.) Oh, he mustn't climb the stairs—he's not well. Stop him.

ERMENGARDE: He's halfway up already. He insisted on coming, Sara. (MR. CARRISFORD *enters, leaning on the arm of* RAM DASS.)

MR. CARRISFORD: How do you do, child. I've come to thank you for taking care of my monkey the other night.

SARA: I was glad to do it, Mr. Carrisford. You shouldn't have climbed all those stairs, you know. Please let the lascar seat you in this rocking chair. (BECKY *peeks through the open door and* ERMENGARDE *beckons her to come in.*)

CARRISFORD (*As* RAM DASS *helps him to the rocker*): How do you know Ram Dass is a lascar?

SARA: Oh, I know lascars. I was born in India.

CARRISFORD (*Interested*): You were? But you are not a pupil here, are you?

SARA: I don't know what I am, sir.

CARRISFORD: Why not?

SARA: Well, at first I was a pupil and a parlor boarder, but now—

CARRISFORD: What do you mean by "at first," child?

SARA: When I was first brought here by my papa.

CARRISFORD: Where is your father?

SARA: He died, sir. He lost his fortune, and there was no money left for me, and so . . . (*She hesitates.*)

CARRISFORD: And so you were sent up into the attic and made a little drudge. That's about it, isn't it?

SARA: There was no one to take care of me. I belong to nobody.

CARRISFORD: How did your father lose his money?

SARA: He didn't lose it himself. It was a friend who lost it. I don't know how.

CARRISFORD (*Agitated*): Ram Dass, the child we've been searching for—is it possible?

RAM DASS: It may be, sahib.

CARRISFORD (*To* SARA, *faintly*): What was your father's name?

SARA: His name was Ralph Crewe, sir—Captain Crewe. Perhaps you knew him. He died in India.

CARRISFORD (*Sadly*): Yes, I knew him. I was your father's friend—the friend he trusted.

SARA: Oh, was it *you* who lost Papa's money?

CARRISFORD: I did not really lose it—I only thought I did. I was ill, and when I recovered, your father was dead, and I didn't know where to find you. I've been searching for you everywhere.

SARA: And to think I was here at Miss Minchin's all the time.

CARRISFORD: I saw you pass by one day, and I was sorry for you, so I told Ram Dass to climb through your window and try to make you comfortable—

SARA: Then it is *you* who are my friend! (*She kneels at his side.*) Oh, I'm so glad it is you! (*Suddenly* MISS MINCHIN *stands in the doorway, livid with rage.*)

MISS MINCHIN: Sara! You have gone too far this time! Your conduct is inexcusable! (SARA *cowers, stands near* CARRISFORD, *who puts a protective arm around her.*) Mr. Carrisford, you were brought up here without my knowledge, I assure you.

CARRISFORD (*Coldly*): You are Miss Minchin?

MISS MINCHIN: I am, sir, and this charity pupil has shamed me for the last time. She shall leave the Seminary at once.

CARRISFORD: Indeed she shall, Miss Minchin. Her home, for the future, will be with me.

MISS MINCHIN: With you? What does this mean?

CARRISFORD: I was an intimate friend of the late Captain Crewe. The fortune which Captain Crewe supposed he had lost is safe in my hands.

MISS MINCHIN: The fortune? Sara's fortune? (*She stares at* SARA, *astounded.*)

CARRISFORD: It will be Sara's fortune.

MISS MINCHIN (*Craftily*): Captain Crewe left Sara in my charge. She must stay at the Seminary until she is of age. The law will decide in my favor.

CARRISFORD: Come, come, Miss Minchin, the law will do nothing of the sort.

MISS MINCHIN (*Sweetly*): Then I appeal to you, Sara. Will you not do your duty to your poor papa and stay here with me?

SARA (*Evenly and politely*): No, I will not. You know why I will not stay with you, Miss Minchin—*you* know.

MISS MINCHIN (*Spitefully*): Then you will never see Ermengarde and Becky again.

CARRISFORD: Oh, yes, she will. She will see anyone she wishes in my home. That is all, Miss Minchin. Your bill will be paid. (MISS MINCHIN *walks haughtily to the door.*)

MISS MINCHIN (*Turning and addressing* SARA *with a sneer*): Well, Sara, I suppose you feel that you are a princess again.

SARA: I tried not to be anything else, Miss Minchin— even when I was coldest and hungriest.

MISS MINCHIN (*Acidly*): Now it will not be necessary to try, will it? (*With a toss of her head, she flounces out.*)

SARA (*Wistfully, to* CARRISFORD): I did not wake up from the other dream last night. Shall I wake up from this one?

CARRISFORD (*Taking her hand lovingly in his*): My dear, you shall wake up only to happiness from now on.

SARA: Oh, Mr. Carrisford, there is another little girl— (*Glancing at* BECKY) she is as lonely and cold and hungry as I have been. Could you save her, too?

CARRISFORD: Yes, of course. Who is she? (SARA *holds out her hand to* BECKY, *who comes forward shyly and bobs a curtsy.*)

SARA: Her name is Becky. She has no one but me, and she will miss me so.

CARRISFORD: You will take care of her.

BECKY: If you please, sir, it's the other way round. *I* shall take care of Miss Sara.

CARRISFORD (*Laughing*): Very well, Becky. Come, Sara, it's time to go home. (RAM DASS *helps* CARRISFORD *stand up, and they walk slowly off right. As* SARA, BECKY *and* ERMENGARDE *start to follow,* SARA *turns to window where bird is perched on sill.*)

SARA: Oh, little birds, I forgot about you. Who will feed your family when I'm gone?

ERMENGARDE: I will bring up crumbs every day, Sara, for your sake. I promise.

SARA (*Hugging* ERMENGARDE): Oh, thank you, Ermie!

CARRISFORD (*Calling from off right*): Sara! Becky!

SARA: We're coming! (ERMENGARDE *exits first. In the doorway,* SARA *and* BECKY *linger for a last look at the attic.*)

BECKY: Oh, Sara, it's just as I said. No matter what happens to you, you'll always be a princess. (SARA *puts her arm around* BECKY *and they go out, closing the door behind them. Curtain.*)

THE END

The Sleeping Beauty

by Charles Perrault

Characters

KING	FAIRY BLUEBELL
QUEEN	FAIRY VIOLET
TWO LADIES-IN-WAITING	FAIRY BANEBERRY
NURSE	PRINCESS AURORA
LORD HIGH CHAMBERLAIN	PRINCE ADRIEN
PAGE	WOODCUTTER
FAIRY ROSE	GRETA⎫ *his grandchildren*
FAIRY LILAC	PETER⎭
FAIRY MARIGOLD	

SCENE 1

TIME: *Princess Aurora's christening day.*

SETTING: *The throne room of the palace. The royal cradle is down left. Up right there is a small table with five gold flowers on it.*

AT RISE: *The* KING, QUEEN, *and* TWO LADIES-IN-WAITING *are gathered around the cradle, admiring the baby princess.*

1ST LADY: She's adorable! She looks like the King.

2ND LADY: She looks like the Queen.

1ST LADY: She has the King's dimples.

2ND LADY: She has the Queen's eyes.

KING (*Proudly*): There never *was* such a baby!

1ST LADY: What are you going to call her, Your Majesties?

QUEEN: Aurora. That means "dawn".

KING: Aurora. It suits her to perfection, don't you think? (NURSE *enters from left with golden rattle.*)

NURSE: Now, now, that's enough admiration for one day! You'll spoil her. (*Shooing them away*) Stand back, stand back! The princess has to breathe, you know. (*She bends over cradle and shakes rattle.*) Listen to that, my lambkin. Pretty bells! Jingle, jingle, jingle! (LORD HIGH CHAMBERLAIN *rushes in.*)

CHAMBERLAIN: Your Majesties, quickly! To your thrones! The fairies have arrived! Where *is* that boy? (*Goes left and calls*) Page! Page, come here at once! We're ready to begin! (*He goes to table, where* KING *is hovering over the fairies' gifts.*)

KING: Are you sure all the fairies' gifts are here? (*Counting*) One, two, three—

CHAMBERLAIN (*Interrupting*): There's no need to count them, Your Majesty. I assure you there are five gold flowers studded with jewels.

KING (*Picking up a flower*): Uh—this is a rose, isn't it? For the rose fairy?

CHAMBERLAIN (*Impatiently*): Yes, yes, a rose! (*Holding up each flower as he identifies it.*) *And* a lilac—a marigold —a bluebell—a violet. You see? They are all here.

KING (*Putting back the rose*): It's very odd, but I have a distinct feeling that there should be *six* flowers.

CHAMBERLAIN: Six! Nonsense, Your Majesty. There are only five fairies in the kingdom.

KING (*Sitting on his throne*): Just the same, I have this feeling—(PAGE *runs in, carrying a velvet cushion.*)

CHAMBERLAIN (*Irritably*): Well, it's about time! Where were you? Do you know what you have to do?

PAGE: Yes, Your Lordship.

CHAMBERLAIN: It's a wonder! (*He sets the jeweled rose on*

the cushion.) The Fairy Rose will be first. She is the eldest. (*Fanfare is heard from off right.*) Here they come! On your toes, everybody! (*He hurries to right and clears his throat in preparation for the introductions.* NURSE *stands by cradle,* QUEEN *sits on throne with* LADIES-IN-WAITING *to her left. Soft background music may be played.*) The Fairy Rose! (FAIRY ROSE *enters.* PAGE *holds rose out to* KING, *who presents it to* FAIRY ROSE, *who curtsies and goes to stand by cradle.* NOTE: *Each* FAIRY *receives gift in same way and goes to stand by cradle.*) The Fairy Lilac! (FAIRY LILAC *enters.*) The Fairy Marigold! (FAIRY MARIGOLD *enters.*) The Fairy Bluebell! (FAIRY BLUEBELL *enters.*) The Fairy Violet! (FAIRY VIOLET *enters. After* VIOLET *has taken position by cradle, all* FAIRIES *may join in dance around the cradle.*)

FAIRY ROSE: And now, sisters, it is time for us to bestow our gifts on the baby princess. Violet, you will begin. (*Each* FAIRY *moves to the cradle in turn, lifts her wand as she places gift in cradle, then steps back to let the next* FAIRY *take her place.*)

VIOLET (*Placing gift in cradle*):
Princess, I give you this violet of gold,
You shall be beautiful, fair to behold.

BLUEBELL (*Placing gift in cradle*):
Kindness is my gift; mercy, too.
A good heart to guide you in all that you do.

MARIGOLD (*Placing gift in cradle*):
I give you wisdom, from scholars and sages.
Knowledge is my gift—the lore of the ages.

LILAC (*Placing gift in cradle*):
Happiness is the gift I bestow,
Laughter and love, wherever you go.
(*Suddenly there is a burst of malicious laughter from right. The music stops. All turn and look in surprise as*

FAIRY BANEBERRY *hobbles into the room.* ROSE *quickly goes to left and conceals herself.*)

FAIRY BANEBERRY: Be merry, everybody! I've been watching your gay celebration. Laugh while you can, because tears will come after.

CHAMBERLAIN (*Going to* BANEBERRY): Old woman, how dare you interrupt the ceremonies? You were not invited here.

BANEBERRY (*Cunningly*): You are right. I was not invited, but I should have been.

CHAMBERLAIN: Who are you?

BANEBERRY: I am the Fairy Baneberry.

KING (*Rising*): That's it! Baneberry! I knew there was another fairy.

BANEBERRY (*Angrily*): If you knew, why didn't you invite me to the christening?

KING: It has been such a long time since I've heard of you. I suppose we simply forgot. . . .

BANEBERRY: I've been hidden away in a cave high up in the mountains for fifty years. Everybody has forgotten about me. (*Cackling*) But you'll soon have something to remember me by. (*She looks at table.*) Where is my gift? Why don't I have a jeweled flower like the other fairies?

CHAMBERLAIN (*Explaining nervously*): Well, you see, I presumed there were only *five* fairies in the kingdom, so I had only five flowers made.

BANEBERRY: So you've cheated me out of my gift!

CHAMBERLAIN: I will have the Court Goldsmith make another flower right away. What would you like? A dandelion? A thistle?

BANEBERRY: No, no, it's too late now! (*She turns to* KING.) Hah! Leave me out, will you? You'll pay for this! Listen to me, all of you! *I* have a gift for the Princess, too! (*She bends over cradle.*) Princess, my sister fairies have said that you will have beauty, kindness, wisdom, and

happiness. And so you shall, my dear, so you shall—
(*Turning to* KING *and* QUEEN)
These gifts shall last, O King and Queen,
Until the Princess turns sixteen.
While spinning in a tower high,
She'll prick her finger, and she'll die!
(*All cry out in horror.* BANEBERRY *laughs triumphantly.*)
Ha! She'll prick her finger on a spindle, and she'll die!
Ha, ha, ha! (*She exits.*)

KING: Stop her, stop her!

CHAMBERLAIN (*As he rushes out after her*): Guards!
Guards! Seize her!

QUEEN (*Sobbing*): My darling child!

KING (*Enraged*): It shall not be! We'll put the Fairy Baneberry in the royal dungeon!

ROSE (*Coming quickly to center*): No, Your Majesty!
That would only make matters worse. No mortal may
harm a fairy and go unpunished.

CHAMBERLAIN (*Re-entering*): She's gone! The wretch has
vanished into thin air! (QUEEN *throws herself on her
knees beside the cradle, weeping.*)

ROSE: Do not despair, Your Majesty. I have not yet made
my gift to the Princess.

QUEEN: Oh, good fairy, save her!

ROSE: I cannot change the wicked fairy's curse entirely.
The Princess will indeed prick her finger on a spindle,
but (*Raising wand over cradle*)—
I'll save the Princess, do not weep,
She shall not die, but fall asleep.
(*Placing rose in cradle*)
And when one hundred years have passed,
A prince shall waken her at last.

KING: The Princess shall fall asleep for a hundred years?

ALL: A hundred years!

QUEEN: Alas! What comfort will that be to us? We shall

never live long enough to see the Princess awaken.

KING (*Nodding sadly*): Yes. There will be no one left alive of all the people the Princess knew before she went to sleep.

ROSE: Wait. I shall add to the spell. When the Princess falls asleep, you shall sleep, too, and wake when she wakes.

QUEEN: Thank you, sweet fairy.

KING (*Calling*): Lord High Chamberlain! (*He comes to* KING's *side.*) I shall issue a proclamation forbidding anyone, on pain of death, to spin with a spindle or to have a spindle in his possession.

PAGE: But what sort of cloth would His Majesty have the spinners spin without spindles?

CHAMBERLAIN: Silence, fool!

KING: All the spinning wheels in the land shall be destroyed! And now, on with the music! That wicked fairy is not going to spoil the christening festivities! (*The music starts again.*)

CURTAIN

*   *   *

SCENE 2

TIME: *Princess Aurora's sixteenth birthday.*

SETTING: *A room in a tower of the royal palace. There is a bed covered with rich velvet up center. A stool and spinning wheel stand left, and an old chest up right.*

AT RISE: *The* FAIRY BANEBERRY *is seated on stool, spinning. Suddenly she stops, hobbles to door, and listens.*

BANEBERRY: Someone is coming up the tower stairs. It's the Princess Aurora! (*Talking to herself, evilly*) Come up, come up, my dear. This is the day I've been waiting for—your sixteenth birthday. Now nothing can save you from the christening gift I gave you. He, he, he!

(*She hurries back to stool and resumes her spinning.* PRINCESS AURORA *pushes open the door and stands hesitantly on the threshold.*) Good afternoon, child. Come in, come in!

AURORA (*Entering*): Good afternoon, dame. Who are you?

BANEBERRY: I'm just an old woman, as you can see.

AURORA: I am the Princess Aurora. (*Excitedly*) Do you know, I'm sixteen years old today!

BANEBERRY (*Pretending surprise*): Are you, my dear?

AURORA: There's going to be a big birthday party tonight. I'm supposed to be resting, but I slipped away to explore the palace. There's so much of it I've never seen. This tower, for instance. I've never been up here before. (*She pauses and watches* BANEBERRY *spin.*) What are you doing?

BANEBERRY: I am spinning, Princess.

AURORA: Spinning? I've never heard of that. And what is that strange wheel you work with?

BANEBERRY: That is a spinning wheel.

AURORA: How fast it turns! And it makes such a pleasant sound.

BANEBERRY: Why, child, you speak as if you had never seen a spinning wheel in your life.

AURORA: I haven't. I don't think there is another one in the whole kingdom. (*Watching*) I wonder if I could do it. Will you let me try?

BANEBERRY (*Rising*): Why, of course. Every young girl should learn how to spin. Here, sit down.

AURORA (*Seating herself at spinning wheel*): How very interesting it is! I must ask Father to have one made for me. (*She works the treadle.*) Oh, this is fun! (*Pointing to the spindle*) What is that pretty thing, made all of ivory and silver?

BANEBERRY: That is a spindle. See how it twirls? (AURORA

rises and goes to examine spindle.) Isn't it pretty? Go on, touch it.

AURORA: May I? (*She bends over and touches spindle, then suddenly jumps back.*) Oh! It pricked my finger! (*She sucks at her finger.*) I didn't know it was so sharp. (*She starts to sway.*) Oh, dear! What has come over me? I feel so sleepy—so-o-o sleepy. I—I—(*Her voice trails off into silence; she sinks down near chest, closing her eyes and resting her head on her arm.*)

BANEBERRY (*Gloating*): Hah! My curse is fulfilled. The Princess Aurora is dead!

FAIRY ROSE (*Entering left with the other* FAIRIES): No, she is *not* dead, you wicked fairy. She is only asleep.

BANEBERRY (*Startled*): How's that?

ROSE: I changed your christening gift so that the Princess would not die, but only fall asleep for one hundred years. When the Princess awakens, her life will go on as if there had been no interruption. You are defeated, Baneberry! Begone! Back to your cave in the mountains! (*The* FAIRIES *drive* BANEBERRY *out, left.*) Come, sisters, let us prepare the Princess Aurora for her long sleep. (*They lift up* AURORA, *place her on the bed, and then stand near the head of the bed. Voices are heard from off right.*)

KING (*Offstage*): Search the palace! Search the grounds!

QUEEN (*Offstage*): Aurora! Aurora! (KING *and* QUEEN *rush into the room, followed by* CHAMBERLAIN *and* NURSE.)

KING: There she is, on the bed!

QUEEN: We're too late!

NURSE: She's dead!

ROSE: No, she is sleeping.

KING (*Sighing*): Ah, yes! One hundred years. (QUEEN *is crying softly, and he comforts her.*) There, there, my dear. It had to be.

ROSE: Now I must complete the spell. (*To* FAIRIES) Are you ready, sisters?

FAIRIES: Yes!

ROSE: Very well, then—to work with your wands! Put everybody in the palace to sleep. The courtiers!

LILAC (*As she exits right*): The courtiers!

ROSE: The ladies-in-waiting!

MARIGOLD: The ladies-in-waiting! (*Exits*)

ROSE: The servants!

BLUEBELL: The servants! (*Exits*)

ROSE: The horses and dogs and cats!

VIOLET: The horses and dogs and cats! (*She exits briefly, then re-enters.*) And the canaries?

ROSE: Naturally the canaries!

VIOLET: Oh, naturally! (*She runs out.*)

ROSE (*Calling off right*): Mind you, don't miss anyone—or anything!

KING: What about us?

ROSE: You will sleep with the Princess up here in the tower. (*She goes from one to the other, touching them with her wand. Soft music is heard.*) Good night, good night, and rest you well. All within these palace walls, sleep peacefully. (*She starts downstage, moving her wand in a slow half circle.*) Enchanted trees, rise up and hide the topmost tower. Keep out the sun, keep out the snow. Stand guard, thorny brier hedge! Let no one through until that day, one hundred years from now, when the true prince shall come. (ROSE *motions with her wand for the curtain to close; then she exits.*)

*   *   *

SCENE 3

TIME: *One hundred years later.*

BEFORE RISE: PRINCE ADRIEN *walks down aisle through audience and up on stage, looking about uncertainly, in front of curtain. He peers off left and right, and finally starts out right, but turns back as* WOODCUTTER *enters left with* PETER *and* GRETA.

ADRIEN: Good evening, old man. I am so glad to find someone at last.

WOODCUTTER: Why, what's the trouble, young sir?

ADRIEN: I am Prince Adrien, and I have become separated from my hunting party.

WOODCUTTER (*Quickly taking off his hat and bowing*): Your Highness!

ADRIEN: I have been walking for hours, trying to find my way out of this forest, but (*Gesturing toward curtain*) these thorn hedges are everywhere. I've never seen anything like them!

WOODCUTTER: Oh, Your Highness, you must not, on any account, attempt to go through those hedges into the woods beyond.

PETER (*Speaking with dread*): That is the place where the witches meet!

GRETA: At night the forest is haunted by ghosts and evil spirits!

PETER: Fierce animals roam about—with *terrible* horns!

GRETA: There's a palace in those woods. You can't see it, but it's there.

ADRIEN: A palace?

GRETA: Yes, and a fierce ogre lives in it. Ooooh! (*She runs to* WOODCUTTER'*s arms.*)

WOODCUTTER: Your Highness, pay no attention to the stories my grandchildren tell you. The truth is that there's a princess in that palace, the most beautiful that ever man saw. She must lie asleep there for a hundred years until one day she will be awakened by a prince. Many have tried to reach the palace, but none have succeeded.

ADRIEN: I must find this palace.

WOODCUTTER: No, Your Highness! Those who have gone beyond this brier hedge never came back. You will die!

ADRIEN: It is strange, old man, but I seem to have been drawn toward this place by some magic power. It may be that today is the last day of the hundred years and *I* am the prince destined to wake the Sleeping Beauty. I will force a way through this hedge of thorns. (*He faces curtains resolutely.*)

WOODCUTTER: I beg you, Your Highness, don't go! (ADRIEN *touches curtain, and it starts to open slowly.*)

GRETA: Look, Grandfather! The hedge is opening for the Prince! (ADRIEN *walks through curtains, and quickly goes off right, behind the curtains.*)

PETER: There is a pathway to the palace! (*Curtains continue to open.*)

WOODCUTTER: Praise be! He must be the prince who was destined to come. There is nothing to be afraid of now. (WOODCUTTER, GRETA, *and* PETER *back away to one side of stage and watch. Curtains open fully, revealing tower room where* AURORA, KING, QUEEN, CHAMBERLAIN, *and* NURSE *are sleeping.* ADRIEN, *who has gone offstage, now enters right.*)

ADRIEN: The whole palace is asleep. They are just as they must have been one hundred years ago. (*He goes to bed and looks down on the sleeping* AURORA.) She is even more beautiful than the old man said. (*He bends down and kisses her.* AURORA *opens her eyes and sits up.*)

AURORA (*Smiling at him*): Is it you, my Prince? I have been dreaming of you for all these years.

ADRIEN: At last, Princess, I have come. (*He takes her hand and she rises from the bed. The others awaken, as* FAIRIES *enter from left.*)

ROSE: We have just awakened the whole palace, everybody and everything. (*Church bells start to ring.*)

AURORA: Listen to the bells!

ROSE: They are ringing to proclaim that your long sleep is ended. Now it is time to finish what was begun one hundred years ago. Let us go down to the banquet hall and celebrate the Princess Aurora's sixteenth birthday! (*All gather about* ADRIEN *and* AURORA.)

ALL (*Singing to tune of "Frère Jacques"*):
Bells are ringing, bells are ringing,
Merry bells, merry bells;
Ringing from the steeple,
Calling all the people!
Ding, ding, dong! Ding, ding, dong!

Bells are singing, bells are singing!
What do they say? What do they say?
"Wake to joy and laughter,
Happy ever after!"
Ding, ding, dong! Ding, ding, dong!
(ADRIEN *and* AURORA *lead others offstage; all may repeat last line of song, as the curtain falls.*)

THE END

Heidi

by Johanna Spyri

Characters

HEIDI
DETE, *her aunt*
ALM UNCLE, *her grandfather*
PETER, *the goatherd*
BARBEL, *a village girl*
CLARA SESEMAN
MR. SESEMAN, *her father*
MADAME SESEMAN, *her grandmother*
FRÄULEIN ROTTENMEIER, *her governess*
TINETTE, *a maid*
TONY, *a street boy*

SCENE 1

TIME: *An afternoon in summer.*
SETTING: *In front of the Alm Uncle's hut, high up on the Alm Mountain in the Swiss Alps.*
AT RISE: *The sound of goat bells and yodelers is heard in the distance from off right, as* BARBEL *and* DETE *enter left.*

BARBEL: Well, Dete, here we are! This is where the Alm Uncle lives.

DETE (*Crossing to hut at right*): I wonder if he's home. (*She knocks on door and calls.*) Uncle! Alm Uncle!

BARBEL (*Pointing off right*): Hold on, Dete! I see him up there in the pasture with Peter and the goats.

DETE (*Going to look where* BARBEL *points*): Oh, I'm too tired to climb way up there. I'll wait for him to come down. (*She sits on rustic bench up center, and fans herself.*) Where's Heidi? I thought she was right behind us.

BARBEL (*Peering off left*): She is just crossing the ledge by the waterfall.

DETE: How slow she is!

BARBEL: It's hard work for the child to climb from Dorfli in all those clothes—two dresses at least, and a heavy coat.

DETE (*Shrugging*): That was the only way she could carry them—to put them on.

BARBEL (*Sitting beside* DETE): Dete, are you sure it is wise to leave Heidi with the Alm Uncle?

DETE: Why not? He's her grandfather, isn't he?

BARBEL: Yes, but you know what he's like. He will have nothing to do with anybody. He lives alone up here on the mountain and everyone is afraid of him.

DETE: Just the same, he *is* Heidi's grandfather and it's time he took care of her. I have had her ever since her mother died, but now I want to go to Frankfurt and work. I can't take Heidi with me, so she must stay with Alm Uncle.

BARBEL: But what on earth will he do with the child?

DETE: He won't have any trouble with her. She's not stupid, you know. She'll be good for the old man. (HEIDI *enters from left, barefoot, wearing a thin summer dress.* DETE *rises with a shriek.*) Heidi! (*Crossing to her*) Where are all your clothes and your new shoes and stockings?

HEIDI (*Pointing off left*): Down there.

DETE (*Shaking her*): You careless child! Why did you take them off?

HEIDI: It's hot. I don't need them.

DETE: Have you no sense at all? Go back down there and get them at once!

HEIDI: Oh, Aunt Dete, I just can't walk any more. (*She sits on stump down left.* PETER *yodels off right and runs on, stopping abruptly as he sees others.*)

PETER: Oh! Hello, Barbel.

BARBEL: Hello, Peter.

PETER (*Pointing to* HEIDI *and* DETE): Who are they?

BARBEL (*Rising*): That is Heidi and her Aunt Dete. Heidi is going to live with the Alm Uncle.

PETER (*Astonished*): She *is?*

HEIDI: Yes, he's my grandfather. (*She goes up to him.*) Who are you?

PETER: I'm Peter. (*Proudly*) I'm the best goatherd in the whole village of Dorfli. (*Looking at her curiously*) So the Alm Uncle is your grandfather! (HEIDI *nods.* BARBEL *starts toward left.*)

BARBEL: Well, goodbye, Dete. I have to see Peter's mother. She does the spinning for me. Good luck with Alm Uncle.

PETER: I'll go along with you, Barbel.

DETE: Wait, Peter! If you will run and get Heidi's things, I'll give you something nice.

PETER: What things?

DETE: Her clothes. She left them on the mountainside.

PETER: What will you give me?

DETE (*Holding up a shiny coin*): This new penny. (*He makes a grab for it but* DETE *quickly slips it into her handbag.*) No! When you come back with the clothes, you can have it. (PETER *dashes out left ahead of* BARBEL, *who follows, laughing. Unnoticed, the* ALM UNCLE *enters right and leans on his long staff, watching* HEIDI *and* DETE *with a frown.* DETE *turns to* HEIDI.) You naughty girl! I don't know what your grandfather will think when he finds out you have scattered your clothes all along the path up Alm Mountain. (*She catches sight of* ALM UNCLE.) Oh, there you are, Uncle. I have brought Heidi to live with you.

ALM UNCLE (*Scowling*): What's that?

DETE: Shake hands with your grandfather, Heidi.

HEIDI (*Going to him*): How do you do, Grandfather. (*She holds out her hand but he pushes her aside, crossing to* DETE.)

ALM UNCLE: She can't stay here with me. I won't have her.

DETE: Oh, yes, you will. I have done my duty by her for eight years, now it is your turn.

ALM UNCLE: Oho, is that so? And when she begins to whine and fret, what shall I do with her then?

DETE: That's your business. No one told me what to do with her when she came to me barely a year old. (*PETER enters with* HEIDI's *clothes tied up in a shawl. He is out of breath from running.*)

PETER (*Throwing down the bundle*): Here are the clothes. Where's my penny?

DETE (*Opening her handbag and handing him coin*): You're in a great hurry for it, aren't you? (*He takes coin, and exits left.* DETE *picks up the bundle of clothes and gives it to* HEIDI.) Here, Heidi, take your clothes into the hut.

HEIDI: Are you leaving, Aunt Dete?

DETE: Yes. You are to stay here with your grandfather.

ALM UNCLE (*Pounding his stick on the ground*): I tell you, I won't have her!

DETE: Very well. If you can't keep her with you, then do whatever you want with her. But it will be your fault if anything bad happens to her.

ALM UNCLE (*Advancing toward her*): Dete, get out of my sight and *don't come back,* do you hear?

DETE (*Backing away hastily*): I hear!—but remember, if any harm comes to that child, you will have to answer for it, not I. (*She exits left.*)

HEIDI (*Running to call after her*): Goodbye, Aunt Dete!

DETE (*From off left*): Goodbye, Heidi! Be a good girl. (HEIDI *waves, then turns to* ALM UNCLE.)

HEIDI (*Hesitantly*): Grandfather—

ALM UNCLE: Well, what is it?

HEIDI: Where shall I put my clothes?

ALM UNCLE: I'll show you. Why did you take them off in the first place?

HEIDI: It was hot. I had on two dresses and a coat and a shawl. Anyway, I'd rather go like the goats. They have such swift little legs.

ALM UNCLE (*Amused*): And so have you, no doubt. (*He takes bundle.*) Are you hungry?

HEIDI: Oh, yes! Climbing up the mountain has made me *very* hungry.

ALM UNCLE: How would you like some toasted bread and cheese and fresh goat's milk?

HEIDI: Mm-m-m, that sounds *good*—and let's eat it out here. Where shall I sleep, Grandfather?

ALM UNCLE: Wherever you want to.

HEIDI (*Pointing to attic window of hut*): What's up there?

ALM UNCLE: That is where I keep the hay.

HEIDI: Oh, I want to sleep up there in the hay and then I can see all the trees and sky through that little window. (*Yodelers are heard in the distance, singing to each other.*) Who is singing, Grandfather?

ALM UNCLE: Shepherds and goatherds, watching their flocks on the high peaks.

HEIDI: Why?

ALM UNCLE: They are calling to each other across the valley so they won't feel lonely.

HEIDI: Oh, Grandfather, I'm going to be happy here.

ALM UNCLE (*Chuckling*): Yes, I think you will be. And I think I'll be happy, too.

HEIDI: Why, I'm happy already. I shall stay here with you and be happy all my life. (*Impulsively she throws her arms around* ALM UNCLE *and he gently strokes her hair. The yodelers continue to call and goat bells tinkle.*)

CURTAIN

*   *   *

SCENE 2

TIME: *Early autumn.*

SETTING: *The same as Scene 1.*

AT RISE: ALM UNCLE *is seated on bench, carving a wooden spoon.* PETER *and* HEIDI *are heard yodeling off right, and presently* HEIDI *enters, carrying small branches of autumn leaves.*

HEIDI (*Running to* ALM UNCLE): Oh, Grandfather, it was so beautiful in the pasture today! The leaves are beginning to turn all red and gold. They shine like jewels in the sun. Here, these are for you. (*She lays branches in his lap.*)

ALM UNCLE: Thank you, my dear, they are lovely. (PETER *enters right.*)

HEIDI: I'm thirsty, and so is Peter.

ALM UNCLE: I'll get a jug of milk. (*He places his carving and branches on bench and goes into hut.* HEIDI *sits and picks up spoon.*)

HEIDI: Grandfather is so clever, Peter. He is carving a

tiny goat on the handle of this spoon. See? (*She holds it out to* PETER, *but he is staring off left down the path.*)

PETER: Look, Heidi! Isn't that your Aunt Dete?

HEIDI (*Going to look*): So it is! Now I wonder what she's coming here for?

PETER (*Giggling*): Look at her hat, will you! It's like a flower pot! (ALM UNCLE *steps out of hut with milk jug.*)

HEIDI (*Running to him*): Grandfather, it's Aunt Dete!

ALM UNCLE (*Setting down jug*): Where? (DETE *flounces on left, wearing a long dress and a hat piled high with artificial flowers and fruit.*)

DETE (*Crossing to center confidently*): How do you do, Uncle. Hello, Heidi. My, you look so well I hardly know you.

HEIDI (*Pleased*): Grandfather takes good care of me.

DETE: That's plain to see. But you must be a great trouble to him.

HEIDI: No, I'm not, am I, Grandfather? (*She turns to* ALM UNCLE, *and he puts his arm about her.*)

ALM UNCLE (*Coldly*): Dete, what have you come for?

DETE: Well, there's a rich man in Frankfurt who has an only daughter. She can't walk, poor thing, and has to spend all her time in a wheel chair. Her father wants a companion for her—someone her own age to play with and share her studies. It's just the place for Heidi. Why, you can't tell—he might even adopt her.

HEIDI: I don't want to be adopted.

DETE (*Crossly*): How do you know what you want?

HEIDI: I know I want to stay here with Grandfather.

DETE: And pass up a wonderful chance like this? You'll have things you never dreamed of—pretty dresses and fine food—

HEIDI: I like the dresses I have, and Grandfather's food is fine enough for me.

DETE (*Losing patience*): Oh, you exasperating child!

ALM UNCLE: Dete, are you through saying what you have to say?

DETE (*Tossing her head angrily*): No, I'm not! Heidi is nine years old and she goes neither to school nor to church. She knows nothing and you won't let her learn anything. She's my sister's child and I have to see to it that she is well brought up.

ALM UNCLE (*Sarcastically*): Brought up like you, I suppose, wearing cheap finery and talking fancy.

DETE: Bah! You can't make me change my mind. I have all the village on my side. There's not a single person there who will not take my part against you.

ALM UNCLE (*Thundering*): *Be silent!* Get out of here and don't ever let me set eyes on you again, or it will be the worse for you! (*He strides into hut and slams door.*)

HEIDI: You have made Grandfather angry.

DETE (*Shrugging*): Oh, he'll get over it. Come along now. (*She takes* HEIDI *by the arm.*)

HEIDI (*Pulling back*): I'm not going!

DETE: Don't be stupid! (*Coaxingly*) You'll have a good time in the city. You can't imagine how exciting it is.

HEIDI: No! Let me go! (*She breaks* DETE's *hold.*)

DETE (*Craftily*): If you don't like it, you can always come back.

HEIDI: Come back? Do you mean I can turn right around and come back tomorrow?

DETE: If you want to.

HEIDI: Oh, that's different. I thought I had to stay. (*With growing enthusiasm*) Can I bring back presents for Peter and Grandfather?

DETE: Yes, of course.

HEIDI (*Going to* PETER): Peter, what would you like?

PETER: A sausage, a whole sausage, as long as this. (*He shows her, spreading his hands apart.*)

DETE: And what for Grandfather?

HEIDI: Some fine tobacco for his pipe. And a bag full of soft white rolls for Peter's grandmother, and a pretty shawl for his mother.

DETE (*Leading* HEIDI *toward path left*): Yes, yes, but we must hurry or we'll miss the train.

HEIDI (*Stopping*): I must say goodbye to Grandfather.

DETE (*Firmly*): No, we'll be late. And anyway, don't you want to surprise him when you come back with the presents?

HEIDI: Oh, let's run! I want to be back tomorrow! (*She runs off, followed by* PETER. DETE *glances at hut and exits.* HEIDI *and* PETER *can be heard yodeling off left.* ALM UNCLE *comes out of hut carrying jug.*)

ALM UNCLE: Heidi? (*He looks about anxiously.*) Heidi! (*He hears the yodeling in the distance and crosses quickly to the left, shouting.*) Heidi! (*After a pause, he turns sadly to bench, picks up the leaves that* HEIDI *gave to him and sits, gazing at them tenderly.*)

CURTAIN

*   *   *

SCENE 3

TIME: *The following spring.*

SETTING: *The drawing room of the Seseman home in Frankfurt.*

AT RISE: TINETTE, *the maid, is dusting the mantel at left with a feather duster. The doorbell rings loudly and insistently.*

TINETTE: Heavens, what a noise! It must be Mr. Seseman. No one rings like that but the master himself. I'm coming, I'm coming! (*She puts duster in armchair beside fireplace, straightens cap and apron and hurries*

out through archway up center then off right. The door-
bell stops, and the sound of a scuffle is heard.)

TINETTE (*Offstage*): Stop! You can't go in there!

TONY (*Offstage*): Yes, I can! (TONY *races in, ragged and
barefoot, with a hand organ on his back and a covered
basket in his hand.*)

TINETTE (*Following him in*): You little ragamuffin, I'll
teach you to ring doorbells! Who are you? What do you
want?

TONY: I want to see Clara.

TINETTE: Miss Clara! What can a dirty street boy like you
want with Miss Clara?

TONY: She owes me five pennies.

TINETTE: What for, pray?

TONY: I showed her the way to the church tower.

TINETTE: When?

TONY: This morning.

TINETTE: That's a lie. Miss Clara hasn't been out of the
house. She can't walk a step. (*She picks up duster and
shakes it at him.* HEIDI *appears in archway from left,
and enters, wheeling* CLARA *in a wheel chair. She comes
to center and stops, and rushes to* TONY.)

HEIDI: Oh, Tony, you've come! Did you bring the kittens?

TONY (*Holding out basket*): Here they are—but I want
my five pennies first.

HEIDI: I will give you *ten* pennies if you will play something for Clara.

TONY: Show me the pennies. (*She takes coins from her
pocket and hands them to* TONY. *He gives her basket
in exchange.*)

HEIDI: Now, play! (TONY *swings the hand organ off his
back and turns the handle. A gay music-box tune is
heard.*) Oh, what a happy tune! It makes me want to
dance! (*She sets basket down and dances about the room.*

CLARA *and* TINETTE *clap to the rhythm of the music.*)

CLARA: Oh, I wish I could dance!

HEIDI (*Stopping beside chair*): Why, Clara, I'm sure you could if you tried. You know the doctor said you could walk if you weren't so afraid. Come on, I'll help you. (*She assists* CLARA *to stand. At that moment* FRÄULEIN ROTTENMEIER *appears in the archway from left, carrying something bulky wrapped in a table napkin.*)

ROTTENMEIER (*Horrified*): Heidi! What are you doing? (*She pushes* HEIDI *aside.*) Do you want Miss Clara to fall? (*She lowers* CLARA *into chair and turns to* TONY.) You little tramp, stop that racket! Clear out of here! (TONY *takes a rolled-up paper snake from his pocket and blows it out in* ROTTENMEIER'S *face. She screams and leaps into the armchair.* TONY *roars with laughter and runs out.* HEIDI *quickly hides basket behind sofa at right.* ROTTENMEIER *steps down off chair.*) Tinette, did you have anything to do with this?

TINETTE: Oh, no, Fräulein Rottenmeier.

CLARA (*Explaining*): Heidi lost her way and Tony brought her home.

ROTTENMEIER: Aha, running away again, were you?

HEIDI: I wasn't running away. I wanted to climb the church tower and look at the mountains.

ROTTENMEIER: Nevertheless, you shall have to be punished. I shall lock you in the cellar.

CLARA: No, no, Fräulein! Wait until Papa comes. He'll be here any minute now with Grandmama, and they will decide what to do with Heidi.

ROTTENMEIER: Very well, Miss Clara, but I shall have something to say to your father myself. Heidi, what do you think is in this napkin? (*She holds it up.*)

HEIDI (*Gasping*): My rolls! Grandmother's rolls!

ROTTENMEIER: Yes, stale musty rolls. I found them in your closet. Tinette, throw them away.

CLARA: No, Fräulein, please! Heidi has been saving them for Peter's grandmother.

ROTTENMEIER: I don't care who she's been saving them for—out they go. Tinette. (*She hands rolls to* TINETTE *and starts out. A loud meow is heard.* ROTTENMEIER *whirls around to glare at* HEIDI.) You saucy girl! How dare you meow at me? (HEIDI *and* CLARA *giggle.*) Heidi, leave the room.

CLARA (*Suppressing her laughter*): Fräulein, it's not Heidi, it's the kittens.

ROTTENMEIER (*Timidly*): What kittens?

HEIDI (*Setting basket on sofa*): Here in this basket. The sexton in the church gave them to me for Clara. (*She raises the lid.*)

ROTTENMEIER (*Retreating across the room in a panic*): Oh, oh! Don't let them out! Put them back, shut them up! I hate cats! I'm allergic to them! (*She whips out her handkerchief and sneezes into it.*) Achoo! Help, Tinette! Achoo! (*As* HEIDI *closes lid, the doorbell rings.* ROTTENMEIER *throws up her hands.*) It's the Sesemans! Oh, heavens, what a time to arrive! Achoo! Hurry, Tinette, get rid of those kittens, I'll answer the door. Heidi, go to your room and stay there until I send for you. (*She exits up center, sneezing and blowing her nose.*)

CLARA: Please, Tinette, keep the kittens somewhere and feed them.

TINETTE: I'll take care of them, Miss Clara, trust me. Come along, Heidi. (*They exit. After a moment,* MR. SESEMAN *enters with* MADAME SESEMAN. *They are both carrying packages wrapped in gift paper.* ROTTENMEIER *follows them in.*)

SESEMAN (*Embracing* CLARA): Clara dear!

CLARA: Papa! I'm so glad you are home. You've been away such a long time in America. Hello, Grandmama.

MADAME SESEMAN (*Kissing her*): Clara, how well and cheerful you look!

CLARA: Oh, I am! Heidi and I have so much fun together. (SESEMAN *sits in armchair, placing his packages on the end table beside it.* MADAME SESEMAN *puts her packages on the coffee table in front of sofa and sits on sofa.*)

SESEMAN: Heidi—that's the little Swiss girl, isn't it? Where is she?

ROTTENMEIER (*Stepping forward*): I sent her to her room, sir. She has been a very naughty child.

MADAME SESEMAN (*Surprised*): Why, what has she done?

ROTTENMEIER: What *hasn't* she done, madame! She goes out without permission and brings home all sorts of horrible riffraff and animals!

SESEMAN: Riffraff? Animals? What do you mean?

CLARA (*Laughing*): Oh, Papa, it was only a little boy and some kittens. (SESEMAN *laughs heartily.*)

ROTTENMEIER: It is no laughing matter, Mr. Seseman. I don't think she's fit company for Miss Clara.

SESEMAN: Well, what do you say to that, Clara?

CLARA: Oh, I love Heidi! Since she came, there's something happening every day and the time passes so quickly. But sometimes she gets very lonely for her mountains. (HEIDI *is seen through archway crossing from left to right. She is dressed in the clothes she wore in Scene 2.*)

ROTTENMEIER (*Catching sight of her*): Heidi! Come in here! (HEIDI *comes into the room slowly.*) Why have you put on those old clothes?

HEIDI: I am going home to my grandfather.

ROTTENMEIER: There, you see, sir? She's running away, and it's not the first time, either. And what is she running away for, I'd like to know? There is absolutely nothing she doesn't have in this house. Isn't that so, Heidi?

HEIDI (*Hanging her head*): Yes, Fräulein.

ROTTENMEIER: You are an ungrateful child!

SESEMAN: Fräulein, I want to talk to Heidi alone. You may leave the room. I'll ring if I need you. (ROTTEN-MEIER *exits.* SESEMAN *takes* HEIDI's *hand in both of his.*) Aren't you happy here with Clara?

HEIDI: Oh, I like Clara. She's so good to me.

SESEMAN: Then why do you want to go away?

HEIDI: I—I— (*She looks down and shakes her head.*)

MADAME SESEMAN (*Holding out her arms*): Come over here, Heidi, and sit beside me. (HEIDI *crosses to sofa and sits.* MADAME SESEMAN *puts an arm around her.*) Now—tell me what's the matter, dear.

HEIDI (*Suddenly bursting into tears*): I just want to go *h-o-m-e!* I can't stay here any longer!

MADAME SESEMAN (*Drawing her close*): There, there, child, have a good cry.

HEIDI (*Sobbing*): Fräulein Rottenmeier told me I mustn't cry.

MADAME SESEMAN: Nonsense, all little girls cry. I used to. I still do. (*Pause.*) So you are lonely for your mountain home, are you?

HEIDI (*Nodding*): Every night I dream—and it's always the same thing. I dream I am back with Grandfather, and I hear the fir trees rustling in the wind and it is all so beautiful. But when I wake up, I am still here.

MADAME SESEMAN: Do you ever feel a pain anywhere?

HEIDI: Yes, something presses here (*Putting her hand to her throat*)—like a big stone.

SESEMAN (*Rising*): Heidi, that is homesickness.

HEIDI: Will it ever go away?

SESEMAN: It will go away tomorrow, I promise you.

MADAME SESEMAN (*Puzzled*): Tomorrow?

SESEMAN: Yes, Mother. Tomorrow I am sending Heidi home.

HEIDI (*Running to give him a hug*): Oh, Mr. Seseman, thank you, thank you!

CLARA: I shall miss you, Heidi.

HEIDI (*Going to her*): I shall miss you, too. Mr. Seseman, couldn't Clara come to visit me?

SESEMAN: I think it might be arranged—later on in the summer. (*The two girls shout with delight.*)

HEIDI: I wonder if cook would bake a dozen nice fresh rolls for Peter's grandmother.

CLARA: I'm sure she would. And I will pack a basket full of presents for anyone you like.

HEIDI (*Whirling around the room happily*): Home— home—home!

CURTAIN

*   *   *

SCENE 4

TIME: *Summer.*

SETTING: *The same as Scene 1.*

AT RISE: HEIDI *is seated on bench, making a wreath of blue flowers.* PETER *enters from left.*

PETER: What are you making?

HEIDI (*Showing him*): A wreath for Clara.

PETER (*Frowning*): Clara! Is she here?

HEIDI: Not yet, but she's coming. I had this letter from her. Listen. (*Taking letter from pocket and reading*) "We leave Frankfurt tomorrow and will be in Dorfli by Thursday." That's today!

PETER: Who's "we"?

HEIDI: Her father and grandmama.

PETER: Oh. (*He starts across right.*) Are you coming to the pasture with me?

HEIDI: I can't, Peter. I want to be here when Clara arrives.

PETER (*Grumbling*): Clara, Clara! She's all you think about. *I* don't count any more.

HEIDI (*Going to him and taking his arm*): Yes, you do, Peter, but Clara is my friend, too.

PETER (*Jerking his arm away*): Humph! (*He stamps off right.* HEIDI *gazes after him and sighs. An Alpine horn is heard from off left. She runs to look off left.*)

HEIDI (*Jumping up and down*): They're coming, they're coming! (*Shouting toward the hut*) Grandfather, come out! (ALM UNCLE *hurries out of hut.* MADAME SESEMAN *enters left, puffing from the climb.*)

MADAME SESEMAN: Well! Here we are, safe and sound. (SESEMAN *enters, wheeling* CLARA *in her chair.*)

CLARA (*Stretching out her arms*): Heidi!

HEIDI (*Rushing to hug her*): Clara! (*Turning to* ALM UNCLE) Grandfather, here are Clara, and Mr. Seseman, and Madame Seseman! (ALM UNCLE *shakes their hands.*)

ALM UNCLE (*To* CLARA): How happy we are to have you here, Clara.

CLARA: I'm glad to meet Heidi's grandfather. She has told me so much about you.

MADAME SESEMAN: What a beautiful mountain top you live on! No wonder Heidi was homesick.

CLARA: There are so many flowers everywhere. If only I could get out and pick some!

HEIDI: I have picked some for you. See! I made you this crown of gentians. (*She places wreath on* CLARA's *head.*) Hail to Queen Clara! (*She curtsies and they both laugh.*)

CLARA: Oh, Heidi, I want to see all the things you told me about! I wish I could stay here with you instead of at the hotel in Dorfli.

ALM UNCLE: Why not? Heidi would love to have you.

CLARA (*Eagerly*): Papa—Grandmama—may I?

SESEMAN: If the Alm Uncle wishes it.

ALM UNCLE: Indeed I do, sir!

MADAME SESEMAN: But the trouble, the inconvenience—

ALM UNCLE: No trouble at all. I will look after Clara myself.

SESEMAN: How kind you are! We'll have a bed sent up from the village.

CLARA: Heidi, may I sleep where I can look at the stars the way you do?

HEIDI: In the hayloft, yes! Grandfather will carry you up the ladder.

ALM UNCLE: Let us go inside and see if Clara will be comfortable up there. (SESEMAN *pushes* CLARA *to door of hut, then he and* ALM UNCLE *make a seat of their hands and carry her into hut.* HEIDI *follows, then* MADAME SESEMAN, *who closes door behind her. After a moment,* PETER *sneaks in right.*)

PETER (*Shaking his fist toward hut*): Now Heidi will never go up to the pasture with me. (*Going to wheel chair*) She'll always be pushing *you* around with that Clara. Oh, I hate you! (*He kicks chair.*) I wish you'd go tumbling down the mountain. Yes, you! (*He kicks chair again.*) I'd like to see you go bumpity-bang down over the rocks. (*He stands still, thinking, then tiptoes to the hut door and listens. Carefully he wheels chair off left, giving it a final violent shove. A loud crash is heard from off left.*) There it goes! (*He leaps into the air, shouting with joy.*) Now she'll have to go home! Now she'll have to go home! (*He bounds off right.* HEIDI *comes out of the hut.*)

HEIDI: What's all that noise? Why, where is Clara's chair? Grandfather, Clara's chair is gone! (ALM UNCLE *and* SESEMAN *come out, carrying* CLARA *as before, followed by* MADAME SESEMAN.)

ALM UNCLE: Gone? But we left it right here.

MADAME SESEMAN: Perhaps the wind has blown it away.

HEIDI: Oh, dear, if the chair has rolled down the mountain, we'll never find it.

SESEMAN: It may have rolled only a little way. Alm Uncle, let's have a look. (*They seat* CLARA *on bench and exit left.*)

MADAME SESEMAN: Stay here with Clara, Heidi. (*She exits after the men.*)

CLARA: What a shame! I suppose I will have to go home if I haven't any chair. (HEIDI *sees* PETER *peeking around a corner of hut.*)

HEIDI: Peter, come here! (*He comes forward reluctantly.*) This is Clara, Peter. Have you seen anything of her wheel chair?

PETER (*Innocently*): I've been up in the pasture.

CLARA: What shall I do without my chair? I won't be able to go anywhere on the mountain.

HEIDI (*Suddenly getting an idea*): Clara! You might walk!

CLARA: Walk! I couldn't do that.

HEIDI: Yes, you could. Peter and I will help you.

PETER (*Starting away*): I have to tend to my goats.

HEIDI: Peter, come back here this minute!

PETER: Won't!

HEIDI: You have to. I can't do it alone. (PETER *crosses to* CLARA'*s right side,* HEIDI *is on her left.*) Now, Clara, put one arm around Peter and the other around me and when I count three, stand up! One—two—three. (HEIDI *and* PETER *lift* CLARA *to her feet. She cries out.*)

CLARA: Oh, I can't do it.

HEIDI: Of course you can. Now put one foot before the other.

CLARA (*Slowly taking a couple of steps*): Look, Heidi, I can do it! I can take a proper step!

HEIDI: Try to walk by yourself.

CLARA: No, no, I'm afraid!

HEIDI: Try, Clara, try! I'll stay close by you. Walk to the tree stump. (*Falteringly* CLARA *shuffles over to stump and sinks onto it.*) Oh, Clara, you did it! Won't your father and grandmama be surprised! (*Voices are heard off left.*) Here they come! Sit tight, Clara, and when I give you the signal—*walk!* (ALM UNCLE *and the* SESE-MANS *enter.*)

ALM UNCLE: Well, we found the wheel chair. It was at the foot of the rocks, broken into a hundred pieces.

HEIDI (*Cheerfully*): That doesn't matter. We won't need it any more.

MADAME SESEMAN: Won't need it? What do you mean, child?

HEIDI: Stay where you are, please, all of you. Now, Clara—show them. (HEIDI *helps* CLARA *to stand. The* SESE-MANS *exclaim in protest but make no move. Slowly* CLARA *walks to them and falls into* MADAME SESEMAN'S *arms.*)

MADAME SESEMAN: Clara, my darling Clara! (*They sit on the bench.*)

SESEMAN: How is this possible?

CLARA: It was Heidi. She—and Peter—*made* me walk.

HEIDI: She made herself walk. She took the risk—and won.

CLARA: Now I can go to the pasture with Heidi and Peter every day. (*She smiles at* PETER *who has been standing apart near the hut. He starts to slink away.*)

ALM UNCLE (*Speaking to him sharply*): Peter! It was you, wasn't it?

PETER (*Hanging his head*): Yes.

ALM UNCLE: *He* was the wind that sent the chair rolling down the mountain, and he knows he'll be punished.

MADAME SESEMAN (*Rising*): We mustn't be too hard on the boy. After all, we robbed him of Heidi, his dearest companion. Fortunately, it has turned out for the best, for without her chair, Clara has learned to walk. But you will never do such a thing again, will you, Peter?

PETER (*Earnestly*): Oh, no, ma'am—and I like Clara, almost as much as Heidi.

MADAME SESEMAN: Good! Now tell me, what is it you'd like to have more than anything else?

PETER (*Without hesitation*): A penny!

MADAME SESEMAN (*Laughing*): That is not an extravagant request. (*She takes a bright new silver piece from her handbag.*) Here are as many pennies as there are weeks in a year. (*Giving it to him*) A penny a week for Peter.

PETER: As long as I live?

MADAME SESEMAN: Yes, boy, I shall put it in my will. (PETER *yodels and leaps into the air.*)

HEIDI (*Grabbing his hands*): Come on, Peter, let's dance for Clara! (*She and* PETER *start to do an appropriate folk dance, as the curtain closes.*)

THE END

Hansel and Gretel

from Grimms' Fairy Tales

Characters

HANSEL
GRETEL
GERTRUDE, *their mother*
PETER, *their father*
CUCKOO (*Offstage voice*)
SANDMAN
WITCH
GINGERBREAD CHILDREN

SCENE 1

SETTING: *A room in Hansel and Gretel's cottage.*

AT RISE: HANSEL *is sitting at table, center, making a broom.* GRETEL *sits in rocking chair at right, singing as she knits a stocking.*

GRETEL (*Singing*):
"Susy, little Susy, pray what is the news?
The geese are running barefoot because they've no shoes!
The cobbler has leather and plenty to spare,
Why can't he make the poor geese a new pair?"

The songs in this play are from Humperdinck's opera, *Hansel and Gretel.* Simplified versions can be found in many children's song books.

HANSEL (*Throwing aside his work impatiently*): Oh, stop singing, Gretel! How can you sing when we're both so hungry?

GRETEL: It helps me to forget that we're hungry.

HANSEL: Nothing can make me forget. I've been hungry for days!

GRETEL (*Sympathetically*): I know, Hansel. If only Father could sell his brooms!

HANSEL: Brooms, brooms! I'm sick of brooms! It's a wonder I don't turn into one.

GRETEL (*Trying to cheer him up*): Then you could make a fine living for us, entertaining the country folk at the Fair. Hansel, the Talking Broom! (*She laughs.*)

HANSEL: You can laugh, Gretel, but ours is a hard way to live, and you know it. Nothing to eat but black bread, and not even enough of that to feed a sparrow.

GRETEL (*Gently scolding him*): Hansel! (*She puts knitting on table and goes to* HANSEL.) Don't you remember what Father always tells us? "When our troubles are more than we can bear, our heavenly Father will hear our prayer."

HANSEL: Yes, that sounds very fine, but we can't eat pretty sayings. (*He goes to door.*) Oh, I wish Mother would come home! (*He opens door and looks out.*)

GRETEL: She has gone into the forest to gather wood for the fire.

HANSEL: What's the use of having a fire when there's nothing in the pot to cook?

GRETEL: If you will stop complaining, I'll tell you a secret.

HANSEL: A secret? Is it a good one?

GRETEL (*Going to the cupboard*): Come here and find out.

HANSEL (*Following her*): What is it?

GRETEL (*Holding out an earthen pitcher*): Look here in this pitcher.

HANSEL: Fresh milk!

GRETEL: Our neighbor brought it over this morning.

HANSEL: See how thick the cream is on top. Let's taste it! (*He dips his finger into the pitcher, then licks off the cream.*)

GRETEL: Hansel, what are you doing? You ought to be ashamed of yourself, you greedy boy! (*She sets the pitcher on the table, and* HANSEL *tries to dip his finger into it a second time.* GRETEL *gives him a sharp rap on the hand.*) Take your finger out of there! Get back to your brooms.

HANSEL: Not me! Come on, let's dance! We have a pitcher full of milk, and I want to celebrate.

GRETEL: But our work isn't done.

HANSEL: We'll do it later. Come on! (*They move bench near door to clear a space for dancing.*)

GRETEL (*Singing*):
"Brother, won't you dance with me?
Both your hands now give to me,
Right foot first, left foot then,
Round and round and round again."
(HANSEL *tries to do the steps.*)

HANSEL (*Singing*):
"I would dance, but don't know how,
When to step and when to bow,
Show me what I ought to do,
So that I may dance like you."

GRETEL (*Singing*):
"With your feet you tap, tap, tap,
With your hands you clap, clap, clap,
Right foot first, left foot then,
Round and round and round again."

HANSEL (*Doing the steps as he sings*):
"With your feet you tap, tap, tap,
With your hands you clap, clap, clap,

Right foot first, left foot then,
Round and round and round again."
Oh, what fun! I like dancing and having a good time
better than anything else in the world! (HANSEL *locks
arms with* GRETEL, *and they skip around in a circle,
faster and faster, laughing and shouting. Suddenly the
door opens and* GERTRUDE *enters, carrying a bundle of
sticks. She trips over bench and drops wood.*)

GERTRUDE: Oh! (*The children run to her assistance.*)

GRETEL: Mother!

HANSEL: Are you hurt, Mother?

GERTRUDE (*Sharply*): What's going on here? Put this bench
back where it belongs. I nearly broke my leg on it.

GRETEL: We're sorry, Mother. (*Children replace the bench
as* GERTRUDE *picks up sticks and carries them to the
fireplace.*) Is this how you work when I leave you—
dancing and singing? Now show me what you've done.
(*She picks up* GRETEL's *knitting from table.*) Haven't
you finished this stocking yet, Gretel? (*To* HANSEL) And
you, lazybones—how many brooms have you made?

HANSEL (*Guiltily*): Not any, Mother. I was so hungry—

GERTRUDE: What! Not even *one*? (*In exasperation*) I'll
make your idle fingers fly! (*She reaches for broom, and
accidentally knocks over milk pitcher. Children scream.*)
Oh, heavens, the milk! (*She picks up pitcher.*) All
spilled out—not a drop left. (*Setting pitcher on table*)
Now what will we have for supper?

HANSEL: Don't worry, Mother. I will go into the woods
and pick strawberries for supper.

GRETEL: I will go with you. (*She gets a basket from the
cupboard.*)

GERTRUDE: Wait, children. Before you go, you must promise me you will be home before dark. The forest can be
dangerous at night, and I'm afraid you will lose your
way if you stay out too long.

GRETEL: Don't worry, Mother. We will be back before dark. (*To* HANSEL) Come, Hansel, let's hurry. (*Children run out the door.* GERTRUDE *wipes up spilled milk with a cloth, then sits wearily in the rocker.*)

GERTRUDE: Heaven send me help! My children are starving, and I have nothing to give them. Oh, how tired I am! (*She leans back, closes her eyes, and falls asleep. After a few moments,* PETER *is heard singing in the distance.*)

PETER (*Offstage; singing*): Tra la la la la, tra la la la! (*He appears at the window and looks in, flings open the door. He enters with a market basket filled with food. Seeing* GERTRUDE *asleep, he hides the basket under the table, then tiptoes to* GERTRUDE *and shakes her.*) Wake up, wife! I'm back!

GERTRUDE (*Waking with a start*): Oh! It's you, Peter. (*Rising impatiently*) Well, what have you brought us?

PETER: Good luck and laughter, little Mother.

GERTRUDE: *Good* luck! Do you call it good luck, coming home empty-handed? And as for laughter—

PETER: Laughter is a fine thing to have in this house where there's so little else.

GERTRUDE: You have an easy time of it, I must say. No cares, no worries! I'm the one who keeps this house.

PETER: Well, well, so you do, Gertrude. Now let's see what we have for supper tonight.

GERTRUDE: It will be a very simple meal. (*She holds up the milk pitcher.*) The milk is gone. (*She points to pot in fireplace.*) The pot is empty—so is the larder. In fact, dear Peter, there's *nothing* to eat, and plenty of that. So you can have as big a feast as you like. There will be no dishes to wash.

PETER: Cheer up, wife! Look here! (*He picks up basket.*) I've brought home the horn of plenty! (*He sets basket on table and begins to display its contents.*)

GERTRUDE (*Gasping in amazement*): What do I see? Potatoes—butter—flour! Sausage—eggs—apples! (PETER *hands her a small package.*) For me? (*She smells it.*) Why, it's *tea!*

PETER (*Dancing about the room with* GERTRUDE *as he sings*):
Tra la la la, tra la la la!
Won't we have a jolly time?
Tra la la la, hip, hip, hurrah!
We'll be eating all the time!
(*Suddenly, he stops short and looks around room.*) Where are the children? Hansel and Gretel—where are they?

GERTRUDE: They went into the forest to pick strawberries.

PETER: Into the forest! Are you mad?

GERTRUDE: I made them promise they would be home before dark.

PETER (*Opening door*): Look out there! It's almost dark already. They'll never be able to find their way home. They'll be lost for certain!

GERTRUDE: We must go and look for them. (*She runs out.*)

PETER: I pray they are safe! (*He exits after* GERTRUDE.)

CURTAIN

*　　*　　*

SCENE 2

BEFORE RISE: *There is a log on stage, before curtains.* GRETEL *enters, making a crown of buttercups. She sits on log and sings.*

GRETEL (*Singing*):
"There stands a little man in the deep, dark wood;
He wears a purple cloak and a small black hood.

Do you know him, standing there
Silently, without a care?
Do you see him standing in the deep, dark wood?"
(HANSEL *enters from right, carrying basket of straw-
berries.*)

HANSEL: Look, Gretel, my strawberry basket is full to the
brim!

GRETEL (*Rising*): Oh, won't Mother be pleased!

HANSEL: What's that you're making?

GRETEL: A crown of buttercups. Don't you think it makes
a lovely crown? (*She tries to put it on* HANSEL's *head.*)

HANSEL (*Backing away*): Yes, but not for a boy. It's a
girl's crown. (*He puts it on* GRETEL's *head.*) There you
are, Gretel. You are queen of the wood. (GRETEL *sits
on log and* HANSEL *kneels before her in mock so-
lemnity.*) Queen of the wood, I lay at your feet my
heart and this basket of red strawberries—but please
don't eat them! (*They laugh.*)

GRETEL (*Rising*): We'd better start home, it's getting late.
(CUCKOO *calls.*)

CUCKOO (*Offstage*): Cuckoo! Cuckoo!

HANSEL: Gretel, it's a cuckoo-bird! (*He looks about for
bird.*)

CUCKOO (*Offstage*): Cuckoo! Cuckoo!

HANSEL: There it is again!

CUCKOO (*Offstage*): Cuckoo!

HANSEL (*Answering*): Cuckoo! How are you?

CUCKOO (*Offstage*): Cuckoo!

GRETEL (*Answering*): Cuckoo! Where are you?

HANSEL: There it is! (*As he points overhead, he trips
over log and upsets basket of strawberries.*)

GRETEL: Hansel, look what you've done! You've spilled
the strawberries!

HANSEL: We can pick them up.

GRETEL: No, we can't. They're all crushed and dirty.

(*Shaking head sadly*) Oh, what will Mother say? First the milk and now the strawberries.

HANSEL: Don't make such a fuss! We'll pick some more.

GRETEL: But it's too dark to see them. We shouldn't have stayed here so long. Now we won't be able to find our way home. (*She starts to cry.*)

HANSEL: Don't cry, Gretel. We'll find the way. Look for the path. You look over there (*Pointing off left*), and I'll look over here. (*He points off right.*)

GRETEL (*Timidly*): We might lose each other while we look.

HANSEL: We'll keep calling to each other.

GRETEL: No, Hansel. I want to be with you.

HANSEL: All right, Gretel, we'll stay here tonight and wait until morning to find our way home.

GRETEL: I don't think we'll *ever* find our way home.

HANSEL: Yes, we will. You mustn't lose heart, Gretel. I will take care of you. (GRETEL *points off right.*)

GRETEL: Hansel! What is that?

HANSEL (*Alarmed*): Where?

GRETEL: There—glimmering in the dark! (HANSEL *peers off right.*)

HANSEL: It's only a silver birch tree.

GRETEL: But it's grinning at us.

HANSEL: No, it's not. You're imagining things.

GRETEL: I'm not, Hansel! It's making faces at us—horrible faces!

HANSEL: Then we'll make faces right back. (*Calling out*) You there, fellow! How's this for a face? (*He sticks his thumbs in his ears and wiggles his fingers.*)

GRETEL: Don't, Hansel. Come away! Let's say our evening prayer.

HANSEL: All right. (*They kneel beside log, fold their hands and sing together.*)

HANSEL *and* GRETEL (*Singing*):
"When at night I go to sleep,
Fourteen angels watch do keep;
Two my head are guarding,
Two my feet are guiding,
Two are on my right hand,
Two are on my left hand,
Two who warmly cover,
Two who o'er me hover,
Two to whom 'tis given
To guide my steps to heaven."

GRETEL (*Yawning*): I think I could go to sleep now.

HANSEL: So could I. Let's sleep here. (*They settle down against the log.*)

GRETEL: The trees are singing to us. Do you hear, Hansel?

HANSEL: Yes, they are saying, "Sleep well—sleep well—sleep well." (*His voice trails off, and he closes his eyes. There is a moment of quiet, then* SANDMAN *enters from right with a sack on his back.*)

SANDMAN (*Bending over children and speaking softly*): Good evening. (*Children sit up, startled but not frightened.*) If you should meet the Sandman as he journeys from night to day with his pack on his back, he'll buy your dreams. (*Children jump to their feet.*)

HANSEL: Are you the Sandman?

SANDMAN: I am indeed.

HANSEL: Do you really *buy* dreams? I thought you gave them away.

SANDMAN: Well, I have to get the dreams first—before I can give them away.

GRETEL: That's a fine bag you're carrying.

SANDMAN: And there's something even finer inside.

GRETEL: I'm sure there is nothing ordinary in *that* bag.

SANDMAN (*Loosening the drawstring*): Then take a look, both of you. All you can see is yours. (*He opens bag and pulls out a length of gold and silver material.* HANSEL *and* GRETEL *gasp with delight.*)

HANSEL: What is it?

SANDMAN: It's the cloth of dreams.

GRETEL: How it shines!

SANDMAN: It's shining with all the dreams you've been dreaming, asleep and awake.

HANSEL: Are our dreams as *bright* as that?

SANDMAN: They are, indeed. Has no one ever told you that dreams are the most important things in the world?

HANSEL: Well, no. Mother scolds us for daydreaming so much.

SANDMAN (*Returning the cloth to the bag*): That's because you let your daydreams get in the way of your work. Now lie down again and close your eyes, and you will have happy dreams all the night through. (*The children lie down again.*)

GRETEL (*To* SANDMAN): But I'm afraid to sleep out here in the dark forest.

SANDMAN: Don't worry, my child. The angels will come and watch over you. The blessed light of heaven will shine all around you, and not a creature in the forest will harm you. (*He takes a handful of glitter from a pouch attached to his belt and sprinkles it over the children.*) You have met the Sandman on the road from night to day, with his pack on his back (*He slings his sack over his shoulder.*)—and he gave you back your shining dreams. (*He exits right. If desired, the lights may dim to indicate the passage of time, and "Dream Pantomime" music from "Hansel and Gretel" may be played. When the lights come up again, it is morning.* GRETEL *slowly awakens, yawns and rubs her eyes.*)

GRETEL (*Shaking* HANSEL): Wake up, Hansel! (*He grunts and rolls over.* GRETEL *shakes him harder.*) Hansel, do you hear? Wake up!

HANSEL (*Sitting up*): Cock-a-doodle-doo! It's still early! The day's just dawning. Cock-a-doodle-doo! (*He falls back against the log and starts to go back to sleep.*)

GRETEL: Oh, no, you don't! Get up, Hansel! (*She pulls him to his feet. He stretches.*)

HANSEL (*Looking up at sky*): I've never *seen* such brilliant sunshine! (*He takes a deep breath.*) And the air smells so sweet and fresh. I certainly feel good! (*Looking about*) Now let's find out where we are. (*As he starts to look about, the curtain opens.*)

*   *   *

SETTING: *The front yard of the Witch's cottage. The cottage is upstage center. There is an outdoor oven at right, and a large cage with a padlock on its door left.*

AT RISE: HANSEL *and* GRETEL *turn upstage and stare at the cottage in amazement.*

GRETEL: Oh, Hansel, look! What a darling little house! Why didn't we see it last night?

HANSEL: It must have been hidden by the trees.

GRETEL: I wonder who lives there.

HANSEL: Let's knock on the door and find out. (*They approach the cottage door, and* HANSEL *is about to knock when he stops short.*) Gretel! I think it's a— gingerbread house!

GRETEL (*Sniffing wall of cottage*): It smells like gingerbread.

HANSEL (*Breaking off a corner and tasting it*): It *is* gingerbread!

GRETEL (*Touching the door and licking her finger*): The door is frosted cake!

HANSEL: And the window is made of gumdrops! (*He pops one into his mouth.*)

WITCH (*Inside the cottage*):
Nibble, nibble, mousekin,
Who's nibbling at my housekin?

HANSEL: Did you hear something, Gretel?

GRETEL: Yes.

HANSEL: What was it?

GRETEL: The wind, I think.

HANSEL: Let's eat some more. Have a gumdrop.

GRETEL: Have some cake. (*They exchange sweets.*)

WITCH (*Inside the cottage*):
Nibble, nibble, mousekin,
Who's nibbling at my housekin?

HANSEL: There it is again! (*The cottage door opens, and* WITCH *pokes her head out.*)

WITCH: Good morning, my dears!

HANSEL *and* GRETEL (*Jumping back*): Good morning, ma'am.

WITCH (*Entering and standing between* HANSEL *and* GRETEL): So *you* are the mousekins who are nibbling at my housekin.

HANSEL: I hope it's all right, ma'am.

GRETEL: We're very hungry. We've been lost since yesterday.

WITCH (*Pretending concern*): Haven't you had anything to eat since *yesterday?*

HANSEL: No, ma'am—and before that, nothing to eat at home, either.

WITCH: Dear, dear! (*She feels* HANSEL's *arms.*) Why, there's no meat on your bones at all. I must fatten you up—and the little girl, too. What is your name, my dear?

GRETEL: Gretel, ma'am, and my brother is Hansel.

WITCH: Now, just wait here, both of you, while I get a basket of fruit and nuts. (*She goes into the cottage.*)

HANSEL (*Speaking in an undertone to* GRETEL): There's

something about her I don't like. Did you notice her
eyes?

GRETEL: Yes, they are small and red.

HANSEL (*Frightened*): *Witches* have red eyes!

GRETEL: Let's run away! (*They start to run off, as* WITCH
suddenly appears in the doorway, holding up a twig.)

WITCH: *Stop!* (*The children freeze in their tracks as*
WITCH *chants.*)

Hocus pocus, witches' charm!

Move not, as you fear my arm!

Watch me weave my magic spell,

In my cage this night you'll dwell.

(*She leads* HANSEL, *who is gazing fixedly at the twig,
into the cage and locks the padlock on the door with
a large key hanging from her belt. Then she raises the
twig and releases* HANSEL *from his trance.*) *Ho*-cus, *po*-
cus!

HANSEL (*Looking about cage*): Where am I? What am I
doing here? (*He shakes bars of cage, then sinks down in
despair.*)

WITCH: Oh, don't be so downhearted, my little spindle
shanks. See what I've brought you? (*She takes food from
large pocket in her apron and gives it to* HANSEL
through the bars.) White bread—I made it myself. And
a mutton chop. (WITCH *goes to* GRETEL, *who is standing
stiffly at center, and disenchants her with a touch of
twig.*)

Hocus pocus, elder bush!

Rigid body, loosen, *whish!*

(GRETEL *shakes herself and stands normally.*) Now,
Gretel, you be a good girl and do as I say. Go into the
cottage and set the table for a feast. Bustle along, now,
or I shall lock you up, too.

GRETEL: Horrid old witch! (*She sticks her tongue out at*
WITCH *and runs into the cottage.* WITCH *stands the*

elder twig by the door and returns to the cage. HANSEL *pretends to be asleep.*)

WITCH: Humph! Sound asleep. Well, sleep away, you foolish boy. The less you move about, the sooner you'll be fat. (*She crosses to the oven.*) But I think I'll begin with Gretel. What a dinner she will make! I know what I'll do. I'll get her to peep into the oven. Then I will creep up behind her—one little push—bang goes the door! And pretty soon Gretel will be done to a T! When I take her from the oven, she will look just like a cake, a *gingerbread* cake! (*She notices that* HANSEL *is watching her.*) Oh, so you're awake! Are you any fatter?

HANSEL: No, not yet.

WITCH: Hold out your finger. (HANSEL *pokes out a stick and* WITCH *squeezes it.*) Oh! Flying broomsticks! You're like a skeleton! Open your mouth. (GRETEL *sneaks out of cottage, unnoticed by* WITCH, *and stands behind her, trying to take padlock key from her belt.* WITCH *reaches into pocket and takes out raisins, which she feeds to* HANSEL *as she counts.*) One. Two. Three. . . . (*As she continues to count,* GRETEL *gets key and waves it in air for* HANSEL *to see.*) There! Now let me feel your finger again. Quickly!

HANSEL (*Thrusting the stick through bars*): Here it is, ma'am. (GRETEL *passes key to* HANSEL *behind the* WITCH's *back.*)

WITCH (*Feeling the stick*): Oh-h-h-h! Still like a skeleton! Well, I shan't wait any longer. Skeleton or not, I will roast you today and eat you tomorrow. Do you hear that, Hansel?

HANSEL: Oh, no, ma'am! I won't have any flavor.

WITCH: Oh, yes, you will! (*Calling*) Gretel, come with me, and we'll see if the gingerbread is ready. (*She crosses to the oven.* GRETEL *pretends she has just entered.*)

HANSEL (*Warningly*): Gretel! It's a trick. She's going to push you into the oven.

GRETEL (*Pretending to be interested, as she crosses to* WITCH): I didn't know you were baking gingerbread.

WITCH: Oh, yes, a dozen loaves. Peep into the oven and see if they're done. (GRETEL *opens the oven door and the* WITCH *prepares to push her.*) Is it done?

GRETEL (*Quickly shutting the door*): I don't think so.

WITCH: Is the oven hot enough?

GRETEL: I don't know.

WITCH: Well, get inside and find out. (*Meanwhile,* HANSEL *unlocks padlock, comes out of cage, and creeps up behind* WITCH.)

GRETEL (*Stalling for time*): But how can I?

WITCH: The door is wide enough, isn't it? That oven would hold two of you. Get in, get in!

GRETEL: I don't understand what you want me to do.

WITCH: Ninny! Just stand on tiptoe with your head forward.

GRETEL: I'm such a goose. You'll have to show me.

WITCH: Blockhead! Like this. (*She stands on tiptoe, leaning forward into the oven.*) Just stick your head *way* in and give a good look around. (*The* WITCH *leans halfway into the oven, and* HANSEL *and* GRETEL *shove her all the way in and slam the door shut. The* WITCH *screams. There is a blackout, and thunder is heard. During blackout, fence of peppermint sticks and gingerbread is removed from right side of cottage and real* GINGERBREAD CHILDREN *enter, taking place of fence. They stand straight and stiff, with eyes closed and hands joined.* HANSEL *and* GRETEL *are huddled near cage as lights come up.*)

GRETEL: Look, Hansel—the gingerbread fence! It's made of real boys and girls like us.

CHILDREN: We are free! We are free!

GRETEL: But your eyes are shut. Are you sleeping?

1ST CHILD: Touch us, and we will awaken. (GRETEL *goes from one child to the next, lightly touching their eyes. The children open their eyes and smile, without moving.*)

HANSEL: Why don't they move? (*Suddenly*) I know! (*He takes* WITCH's *elder twig from beside cottage door and waves it over the children.*)

Hocus pocus, elder bush,

Rigid body, loosen, *whish!*

(*The* CHILDREN *break their rigid pose and give a joyful shout. They join in a circle around* HANSEL *and* GRETEL, *dancing and singing.*)

CHILDREN (*Singing*):

"The spell is broken, we are free,

We'll sing and dance and shout for glee!"

(PETER *and* GERTRUDE *enter from left, and* HANSEL *and* GRETEL *run to them.*)

HANSEL *and* GRETEL: Father! Mother!

GERTRUDE *and* PETER (*Ad lib*): Our dear children! Are we glad to find you! We've been so worried about you. (*Etc.*)

PETER: We've been searching for you all night.

GRETEL: But now you've found us, safe and sound. (GERTRUDE *and* PETER *hug children.*)

GERTRUDE (*Looking at cottage*): What a pretty little house!

GRETEL: It's a gingerbread house, Mother, and it belongs to a witch.

GERTRUDE: A witch!

HANSEL: Don't worry, Mother, she's gone.

PETER: Gone? Gone where?

GRETEL: Into the oven!

HANSEL: We pushed her in! (*They skip to the oven and peek inside.*)

GRETEL: Oh, look, Hansel! She's gingerbread clear through! (*They drag out a big gingerbread cookie. All cheer as* HANSEL *and* GRETEL *hold up cookie.*)

HANSEL: Well, old witch, how does it feel to be done to a T?

ALL (*Singing*):
"Now the wicked witch is dead!
Now she's only gingerbread!
She is dead, she is dead,
Now she's only gingerbread!"
(*Curtain*)

THE END

Pinocchio Goes to School

by Carlo Collodi

Characters

PINOCCHIO
GEPPETTO
CANDLEWICK
COACHMAN
BOOBIES
BLUE FAIRY
TWO BOYS
TWO GIRLS

SCENE 1

TIME: *Morning of a school day.*

SETTING: *A schoolyard. A bench stands at left and a see-saw right, in front of curtain.*

BEFORE RISE: PINOCCHIO *skips up the aisle, singing.*

PINOCCHIO (*To the tune of "Wooden Shoe Dance"*):
　　Sing and dance, that's what I like to do,
　　　　Tra la, tra la, tra la!
　　Eat and sleep and play the whole day through,
　　　　Tra la, tra la, tra la la!

GEPPETTO (*Jogging up the aisle after* PINOCCHIO): Pinocchio, not so fast! Wait, Pinocchio, wait! (*He catches up with* PINOCCHIO *on stage and sinks down on the bench, out of breath; wipes his forehead with his bandana.*) Naughty puppet! It's time for you to go to school and learn to think of others as well as yourself. School is the place for you.

PINOCCHIO (*Aghast*): School?

GEPPETTO: Yes, school.

PINOCCHIO: I can't go to school. I haven't any spelling book.

GEPPETTO: No spelling book? Why, I sold my coat to buy you one. Where is it?

PINOCCHIO: I've lost it. (*He turns upstage with a cocky air and, keeping his back to the audience, extends his false nose to its full length.*)

GEPPETTO (*In distress*): Lost it! But I haven't any money to buy you another one.

PINOCCHIO (*Turning front*): That's right, and so I can't go to school. (*He starts to walk away.*)

GEPPETTO: Not so fast, my son. What's happened to your nose?

PINOCCHIO (*Stopping short*): My nose?

GEPPETTO: It has grown longer. (*Shamefaced,* PINOCCHIO *puts his hand to his nose.*) Pinocchio, are you *sure* you lost your spelling book?

PINOCCHIO (*Sitting on the bench and crying, he puts his nose back to its original length*): No, no, papa, I didn't lose it! I wasn't telling the truth. Forgive me, Papa, I'll go to school. (*He takes spelling book from inside his jacket. School children are heard offstage, calling to one another.*)

GEPPETTO: Here come the children on their way to school. Wait here for them. Come, come, cheer up! School isn't such a dreadful place.

PINOCCHIO (*Looking up wistfully*): Geppetto, will I always be a puppet with a wooden head?

GEPPETTO: I'm afraid so, Pinocchio.

PINOCCHIO: But I don't want to be a puppet. I want to be a *boy.*

GEPPETTO (*Astonished*): A boy? Why, that's impossible! I made you from a block of wood, because I was lonely. You're my little wooden son, Pinocchio, and always shall be. (*He gives* PINOCCHIO *an affectionate pat on the head, then exits right.* TWO GIRLS *run on stage from left and go to seesaw. They begin to teeter, singing "Seesaw, Margery Daw."* PINOCCHIO *crosses to center, watching them.* TWO BOYS *enter left, but stop abruptly when they catch sight of* PINOCCHIO. *They point to him and laugh.*)

1ST BOY: Did you ever *see* such a sight? A puppet going to school!

2ND BOY: How can *he* learn anything? His brains are made of sawdust. (*They cross to the seesaw, snickering as they pass* PINOCCHIO.)

1ST BOY (*To* 1ST GIRL): Anna, you're going to have a new schoolmate to teeter with.

1ST GIRL: How nice! Who is it?

1ST BOY: You'll see soon enough.

1ST GIRL (*Getting off the seesaw*): Oh, do tell me who it is.

1ST BOY (*Pointing to* PINOCCHIO): Look for yourself.

1ST GIRL (*Going to* PINOCCHIO *and looking into his face*): Why, you're a puppet!

2ND GIRL (*Crossing to* PINOCCHIO): A *puppet!* (*She examines him from head to foot.*)

1ST GIRL: What's your name?

PINOCCHIO: Pinocchio. (1ST *and* 2ND GIRLS *giggle.*)

2ND BOY (*As he and* 1ST BOY *take strings from their pockets*): Let's make him dance! (*They pull* PINOCCHIO *back to bench and tie strings to his feet and hands.* GIRLS *squeal with delight. At first* PINOCCHIO *is too puzzled to object, but when* BOYS *start pulling his legs and arms up and down, he shakes them off angrily and rises.*)

PINOCCHIO (*Threateningly*): Leave me alone! I haven't come here to be made fun of.

1ST BOY: He talks like a book! (*He pulls* PINOCCHIO's *nose.* PINOCCHIO *kicks him in the shins.* GIRLS *scream and run over to seesaw.* 1ST BOY *howls and dances around center.*) Ow! What hard feet! (2ND BOY *snatches off* PINOCCHIO's *hat.* PINOCCHIO *punches him with his elbows and snatches it back.*)

2ND BOY (*Clutching his stomach*): Ow! What elbows! They're harder than his feet!

1ST BOY (*Limping over to* PINOCCHIO *and speaking with grudging admiration*): Let's call it quits and be friends. What do you say?

PINOCCHIO: I'll respect you if you'll respect me.

2ND BOY: We're no match for you, even if you are only a puppet.

PINOCCHIO: All right, but no tricks.

2ND GIRL (*Running to* 1ST BOY): Have you heard the news?

1ST BOY: What news?

2ND GIRL: A whale as big as a mountain has been seen near the shore.

2ND BOY: Really?

1ST BOY: Let's go and see it. Want to come, Pinocchio?

PINOCCHIO: I'll go after school.

1ST BOY: Do you think the whale will stand there and wait for you?

PINOCCHIO: How long does it take to get to the shore?

1ST BOY: About an hour, there and back. (*School bell rings*)

PINOCCHIO: It's too far. We'll be late for school.

2ND BOY: Oh, we're always late.

PINOCCHIO: Not I! (*He crosses right.*) I'm going to be on time.

1ST GIRL (*Taking his hand*): Me, too.

1ST BOY (*Aggressively*): Don't be such a goody-goody!

PINOCCHIO (*Turning*): What do you mean?

1ST BOY (*Shrugging*): Why study?

PINOCCHIO: What's it to you, if I study?

2ND BOY: Don't you see? If you study and we don't, we pay for it.

PINOCCHIO: And if I *like* to study? What then?

1ST BOY: *You'll* pay for it!

PINOCCHIO: I'm not afraid of you.

1ST BOY (*Closing in on* PINOCCHIO): We're not afraid of you, either.

2ND BOY: Remember, there's only one of you, and two of us. (GIRLS *back away apprehensively,* 2ND GIRL *to bench,* 1ST GIRL *behind seesaw.*)

PINOCCHIO (*To the* BOYS): Cuckoo!

2ND BOY: He's insulted us!

1ST BOY: Apologize!

PINOCCHIO: Cuckoo!

2ND BOY (*Crowding* PINOCCHIO): We'll beat you up!

PINOCCHIO: Cuckoo!

1ST BOY: You'll go home with a broken nose!

PINOCCHIO: Cuckoo!

1ST BOY (*Giving* PINOCCHIO *a push*): Take that, and keep it! (*They scuffle, and* 1ST BOY, *in spite of his advantage in size, gets the worst of it. Bawling*) Wait till I tell the teacher! You'll be whipped and sent home! And I'll be glad of it! (*He exits right with* 2ND BOY. GIRLS *look at* PINOCCHIO *distastefully and scurry off right.* PINOCCHIO *retrieves his spelling book from ground. He goes to the bench and sits down.*)

PINOCCHIO: Oh, why can't I ever do anything right? Sent home from school! What will Geppetto say? (*He puts his head in his hands and sobs.*)

CANDLEWICK (*Sauntering on stage*): Hello, kid, what's the matter?

PINOCCHIO: I had a fight with a boy and now I can't go to school.

CANDLEWICK: What do you want to go to school for? Come along with me to the most wonderful country in the world.

PINOCCHIO: What's it called?

CANDLEWICK: On the map it's called the "Land of Boobies," but we boys call it the "Land of Hooky." It's a perfect country—no teachers, no books and no school on Saturdays.

PINOCCHIO: No school on Saturdays? It's the same here.

CANDLEWICK: Yes, but in the "Land of Hooky" every week has seven Saturdays.

PINOCCHIO: No Monday, or Tuesday, or Wednesday—all Saturdays?

CANDLEWICK: Yes! Why, vacation begins on the first day of January and ends the last day of December.

PINOCCHIO: But what do the people do there all day long?

CANDLEWICK: Oh, they eat and sleep and play from morning till night.

PINOCCHIO: That's what I call a life!

CANDLEWICK: It's *the* life for me. How about you?

PINOCCHIO: When do you start?

CANDLEWICK: Right away.

PINOCCHIO (*Rising*): Are you going alone?

CANDLEWICK: Alone? I should say not! There'll be loads of boys going.

PINOCCHIO: On foot?

CANDLEWICK: How you talk! We'll go in a coach, drawn by maybe a hundred donkeys.

PINOCCHIO: A hundred donkeys! What wouldn't I give to see that coach!

CANDLEWICK: You can. It's coming around the corner now. (PINOCCHIO *looks off left.*)

COACHMAN (*From offstage*): All aboard! All aboard for the Land of Hooky! Through coach, leaving now. No stops at workshops! No libraries! No schools! (COACHMAN *enters, carrying a whip.*) Are you ready, Candlewick?

CANDLEWICK: You bet! (*He exits.*)

COACHMAN (*To* PINOCCHIO): What about you, my fine puppet? Will you come with us, or stay here?

PINOCCHIO: I—I'll go with you.

COACHMAN (*Clapping him on the back*): Good puppet! I'll tell you what I'll do. I'll let you take my place as coachman. That's how much I think of you. (*He gives his whip to* PINOCCHIO.)

PINOCCHIO (*Tossing away his spelling book and cracking the whip*): All aboard! All aboard for the Land of Hooky! (*He races off, followed by* COACHMAN.)

*   *   *

SCENE 2

TIME: *A month later.*

SETTING: *The Land of Hooky. There is a booth center, painted with sticks of candy and ice cream cones. A large bunch of balloons floats gaily from the top, and a donkey motif is in the center. Slogans are scrawled on the walls of the booth:* DOWN WITH ARITHMETIC! DOWN WITH SPELLING! NO MORE SCHOOL! *Street signs are near the exits:* LAZY LANE, *stage right;* BLOCKHEAD BOULEVARD, *stage left. The seesaw and bench from the previous scene remain downstage.*

AT RISE: PINOCCHIO, CANDLEWICK *and several* BOOBIES

(*Boys who have run away to Land of Hooky*) *run on stage from right and left, singing to the tune of "Playing in the Sun."*

ALL: Hi-yi-yi! Let us play a game
Out in the sun.
First we'll go whirling in a spin,
Like tops when spinning they begin,
Then we'll go running all about.
Fun, oh, what fun!
Hi-yi-yi! Now another game,
Tag! You are "It."
You try to catch me if you can,
War-whooping like an Indian,
Then we will play a quiet game
So we can sit. (BOOBIES *break up into two groups, one group sitting on the seesaw, the other on the bench. They play cards, jacks, etc.*)

CANDLEWICK (*To* PINOCCHIO): I'm tired. Let's play marbles. (*He gets a bag of marbles from the booth and draws a circle on the ground, center, with his finger.*)

PINOCCHIO: All right, but first I want some candy. (*He takes two large sticks of peppermint from the booth and gives one to* CANDLEWICK.) Here's one for you.

CANDLEWICK (*Kneeling, shooting marbles at* PINOCCHIO): Thanks.

PINOCCHIO: What a nice life we lead in this Land of Hooky. How long do you think we've been here?

CANDLEWICK: How should I know? A month—a year maybe. What difference does it make?

COACHMAN (*Entering right*): Well, well, my boobies! Still happy and amusing yourselves, I see. They tell me there's a wonderful show down Blockhead Boulevard —absolutely free, with popcorn and lemonade. Fireworks, too! (PINOCCHIO, CANDLEWICK *and* BOOBIES *go off left with whoops of joy.*) Foolish boys! It won't be long now until I have them where I want them. I can see the symptoms already. (*He gathers up the games and puts them into the booth.*)

PINOCCHIO (*Returning*): Oh, oh! (*His hands are clasped to his head, concealing his donkey ears.*)

COACHMAN: Back so soon?

PINOCCHIO: I'm sick, very, very sick.

COACHMAN (*Feeling his forehead*): You have a fever, Pinocchio—Donkey Fever. In a few hours you will no longer be a puppet.

PINOCCHIO: You mean, I will be a boy?

COACHMAN (*Laughing*): Much less a boy. You will be a *donkey!*

PINOCCHIO (*Removing his hands from his head and revealing donkey ears*): A donkey! (*He stamps around, shaking his head and trying to pull off the ears.*) It can't be true! Is there nothing I can do to prevent it?

COACHMAN: Nothing. Boys who are disobedient and refuse to go to school must end sooner or later by becoming donkeys. (*He exits, laughing.*)

PINOCCHIO: Oh, dear! What if somebody should see me? I have to hide these ears some way. This is awful! (*He searches booth and finds a large paper bag which he pulls down over his ears.*) Here's a bag that ought to cover my donkey ears. (CANDLEWICK *enters, wearing an identical bag pulled down over his ears.* PINOCCHIO *brightens a little as he sees* CANDLEWICK.) Hm-m-m, I wonder—Candlewick, will you do me a favor?

CANDLEWICK: Gladly.

PINOCCHIO: Will you let me see your ears? (*He tries to peek under* CANDLEWICK's *bag.*)

CANDLEWICK (*Pushing his hand away*): Before I show you mine, I want to see yours, Pinocchio. (*He tries to peek under* PINOCCHIO's *bag.*)

PINOCCHIO: No, you must show yours first.

CANDLEWICK: No, yours first, then mine.

PINOCCHIO: Why not take off our bags together? (*They lift off their bags and go into roars of laughter, as they pull each other's ears.*) Candlewick has donkey ears! Candlewick has donkey ears!

CANDLEWICK: Pinocchio has donkey ears! Pinocchio has donkey ears! How about a nice dinner of grass?

PINOCCHIO: Not for me! You can have it, if you want, though. (*During the preceding speeches,* PINOCCHIO *and* CANDLEWICK *skip about, pointing at each other, laughing loudly. They go off briefly, each one returning with a donkey tail pinned on. They re-enter.*)

CANDLEWICK (*Bent over, his arms dangling*): Help! Help! Pinocchio!

PINOCCHIO: What's the matter?

CANDLEWICK: I can't stand up any more.

PINOCCHIO: Neither can I! Hee haw, hee haw! (*He goes down on all fours, braying continuously.*)

CANDLEWICK: Pinocchio, is that you?

PINOCCHIO: Hee haw, hee haw!

CANDLEWICK: Will I be that way, too?

PINOCCHIO: Hee haw, hee haw!

COACHMAN (*Entering left*): Well done, boys, you bray well. (*To* PINOCCHIO) Ah, my pretty, of all the foolish boys I have brought to the Land of Hooky, you have made the finest donkey of them all. A circus is the place for you.

CANDLEWICK: But what will become of me?

COACHMAN: You'll soon be a perfect donkey, too. Get out! (*He kicks* CANDLEWICK *offstage, and gets a hoop from the booth.*) Think of it, Pinocchio, a circus! I'll teach you a few tricks. Come, let me see how well you can jump through this hoop. Are you ready? *Jump!* (*He lifts hoop high in the air.* PINOCCHIO *dodges under it.*)

No, no, no, all wrong! You can't get away with that! (*This time* PINOCCHIO *passes to one side of hoop.*) Jump, I said, donkey—*jump!* (*As* COACHMAN *pounds hoop angrily on ground,* PINOCCHIO *tries to leap through it. He catches his foot and falls.*) Get up, you lazy brute, get up! (PINOCCHIO *tries to rise, but cannot.*) Lame, eh? Well, what now? Sell you? But who would buy a lame donkey? No one would give even ten pennies for you. No, there's only one thing to do and that is—(*He suddenly pulls out a pistol and points it at* PINOCCHIO.) to shoot you! (PINOCCHIO *crouches fearfully.*)

BLUE FAIRY (*Shouting from the rear of the auditorium*): Stop! (*She hurries up aisle, wearing a long hooded cape which covers her costume and hair.*) Here are the ten pennies you are asking for this donkey. Take them and be off! (COACHMAN *grabs money eagerly and exits.* BLUE FAIRY *helps* PINOCCHIO *downstage, and curtain closes behind them. The scene is the schoolyard again.* BLUE FAIRY *throws off her cape and raises her wand.*) Pinocchio, stand up and be as you were! (PINOCCHIO *stands upright and removes the donkey ears and tail, then he turns gratefully to* BLUE FAIRY.)

PINOCCHIO: Oh, thank you for saving my life. Who are you?

BLUE FAIRY (*Smiling*): I am the Blue Fairy, godmother of all puppets.

PINOCCHIO: Are you *my* godmother?

BLUE FAIRY: Yes, Pinocchio.

PINOCCHIO (*Pleadingly*): Then please make me a boy! I'm tired of being a puppet.

BLUE FAIRY: If I promise to make you a boy, will you learn to be good?

PINOCCHIO (*Evasively turning away from her*): Don't you think I am? (*His back to audience, he pulls out his nose to full length.*)

BLUE FAIRY (*Shaking her head*): Good boys are obedient, and you—

PINOCCHIO (*Turning front*): But I always obey!

BLUE FAIRY: Good boys like to study and learn a trade, and you—

PINOCCHIO: I study, I study hard!

BLUE FAIRY: Good boys always tell the truth.

PINOCCHIO: And so do I!

BLUE FAIRY (*Looking at his nose, and laughing*): Oh, Pinocchio!

PINOCCHIO: What are you laughing at?

BLUE FAIRY: I'm laughing at your lies.

PINOCCHIO: How do you know I'm lying?

BLUE FAIRY: Lies, my puppet, are soon found out. There are two kinds of lies, lies with short legs and lies with long noses. Yours happen to have a long nose. (PINOCCHIO's *hand flies up to his nose, and he hides his face in his hands as he sits upon bench. In this position, he pushes his nose back to its original length.*)

PINOCCHIO: Oh, must I have a long nose forever?

BLUE FAIRY (*Sitting beside him*): Until you learn to tell the truth.

PINOCCHIO: Oh, dear!

BLUE FAIRY: Well, Pinocchio—do you still want to become a boy?

PINOCCHIO (*Doubtfully*): Yes—

BLUE FAIRY: And will you do all the things I ask?

PINOCCHIO: *All* of them?

BLUE FAIRY: There are only five. (*She counts them on her fingers.*) Obey. Go to school. Learn a trade. Take care of your papa. And always tell the truth.

PINOCCHIO (*Sighing*): All right, I promise.

BLUE FAIRY: Beginning today, you'll go to school every day. (*She rises.*)

PINOCCHIO (*Jumping to his feet*): But what about my

papa? Hadn't I better go home first and let him know—

BLUE FAIRY: Your father has been sent for and will be here shortly.

PINOCCHIO: Oh, you dear, kind Fairy! I'll work! I'll study! I'll do everything you tell me to.

BLUE FAIRY: Then come with me to the pump and wash your face and hands. You must look tidy when you go to school. (*She puts her arm around his shoulder, and they start out right.*)

PINOCCHIO (*Singing*):

I will work so hard and be so good,

Tra la, tra la, tra la!

I'll no longer be a block of wood,

Tra la, tra la, tra la la! (*They exit, and his voice fades in the distance.* GEPPETTO *enters left slowly, sits wearily on the bench and sighs.*)

GEPPETTO: Alas, I have looked everywhere for Pinocchio. Maybe he has gone across the ocean to America. So what is to become of poor Geppetto? Old and alone, with no money or food, I shall starve.

PINOCCHIO (*Off right, singing*):

I'm no longer now a block of wood,

Tra la, tra la, tra la la!

GEPPETTO (*Rising*): That voice! (*He looks about him.*) No one. Oh, Pinocchio, Pinocchio, why did you leave your old papa? Why didn't you come back? Could it be that you are dead? Pinocchio—dead? (*He covers his face with his hands, and sobs.*) Oh, no, oh, no! (*He sits again on bench.* PINOCCHIO *enters right, transformed into a real boy. He is carrying a spelling book under his arm.*)

PINOCCHIO (*Running to* GEPPETTO): Papa, Papa! Oh, my poor Papa! Look at me, it's Pinocchio!

GEPPETTO (*Looking up, dazed*): Pinocchio? Is it really

you? (*He rises and embraces* PINOCCHIO.) Pinocchio, my son!

PINOCCHIO: Oh, dear, dear Papa, can you forgive me?

GEPPETTO: Forgive you? Of course I forgive you. But what is this? Your spelling book?

PINOCCHIO: Yes, Papa. I'm really, truly going to school this time.

GEPPETTO (*Holding him off at arm's length*): Let me look at you. Why, you're a boy! (*They move toward exit.*)

PINOCCHIO (*Joyfully*): Yes, Papa, I'm real. My wish has come true at last! I'm a boy, a *real boy!* (*They exit together arm in arm, as the curtain falls.*)

THE END

Jack and the Magic Beanstalk

An English fairy tale

Characters

CLOVERBELLE, *the cow*	GIANT
JACK	GIANT'S WIFE
MOTHER	GOLDEN HEN
BUTCHER	BOYS
TANNER	GIRLS
HUNTER	FARMERS
OLD WOMAN	FARMERS' WIVES

SCENE 1

SETTING: *The yard of a dilapidated farm. There is a small cottage at left, and a barn at right. A stone wall with a sagging gate runs across rear of stage between cottage and barn. A rough wooden bench stands against the wall up center, and down right is a signpost, pointing off right, which reads: "To the Village."*

AT RISE: *Off left,* BOYS *and* GIRLS *are heard singing* "Come to the Fair." CLOVERBELLE *wanders through gateway and moos mournfully as she shakes her head.* BOYS *and* GIRLS *enter down left, on their way to the Fair.*

1ST BOY (*Turning to cottage and calling*): Hello, Jack!

Jack, are you home? (*The others stop and join in calling.* JACK *hurries out of cottage.*)

ALL: Come to the Fair!

1ST GIRL: There's going to be a puppet show!

2ND GIRL: And strolling minstrels!

2ND BOY: Tumblers and jugglers!

3RD BOY: They say His Lordship will be there!

3RD GIRL: You can have your fortune told for a penny!

JACK (*Laughing*): I know what my fortune will be without spending a penny—even if I had one to spend. Don't wait for me. I'll be along later. (BOYS *and* GIRLS *resume their singing and exit down right.* JACK *crosses to barn and gathers up a handful of hay near door. He spreads it before* CLOVERBELLE.) Here you are, Cloverbelle. This is the last bit of hay in the barn—and there's no better in the house for Mother and me. (*He nods to his* MOTHER, *who has come out of the cottage.*) I'm afraid we shall have to sell you, Cloverbelle. (*The cow shakes her head and moos "No!"* MOTHER *goes to her.*)

MOTHER: What's the matter, old girl? Don't you want to be sold? (*Cow shakes her head again and moos "No!" more emphatically.*) But you will starve to death if you stay here with us. Wouldn't you rather go someplace where there is plenty of sweet grass and clover? (*The cow moos "No!"*)

JACK: I think she's afraid the butcher will buy her. (*Cow nods vigorously and moos "Yes!"*)

MOTHER: Oh, no, she shall not be sold to the butcher!

JACK (*Arguing*): But, Mother, I doubt if anyone else would want her. She's so old and thin—and she doesn't give a drop of milk.

MOTHER (*Sinking onto the bench in despair*): What shall we do? Must we all three starve together? Oh, Jack, we have come to a pretty pass! We used to be so rich when your father was alive. Now look at us—dressed in rags and living in a hut that scarcely keeps us dry when it rains. No money—no food—not even any more hay for the cow. (*She bursts into tears.*)

JACK (*Comforting her*): There, there, Mother, don't cry. I will take Cloverbelle to the Fair and try to drive a good bargain with someone. Perhaps a kindhearted farmer will take her.

MOTHER (*Rises, drying her eyes on her apron*): Forgive me, son. I know you will do the best you can. (*She lays her cheek against cow's neck.*) Goodbye, old friend. It breaks my heart to part with you. (*To* JACK) She was your father's favorite pet. When she is gone, there will be nothing of your father's left. (*She exits into the cottage, weeping.* JACK *gazes after her sorrowfully, then goes to barn for a length of rope which he ties to the cow's halter.*)

JACK: Well, it's off to the Fair we go. Come along, Cloverbelle. (*Cow plants her legs firmly in protest.* JACK *speaks to her in a wheedling tone.*) Do come! We'll hear the fiddles playing and the minstrels singing. We'll see a puppet show. (*Cow turns around and starts for the barn.* JACK *heads her off.*) No, you can't go into the barn! Come on, I say! (*He gives a mighty pull on rope. Cow lurches forward and* JACK *sprawls on ground. Cow sits down.* JACK *gets to his feet, exasperated.*) All right, sit there and starve to death! See if I care. (*He folds his arms and turns his back. Cow tosses her head nonchalantly and moos. Voices are heard off left.* JACK *looks in the direction of the sound.*) Hey! Here come some people on their way to the Fair. Maybe I can sell you right here on the spot. Stand up, will you? (*Cow lumbers to a standing position. A group of* FARMERS *and their* WIVES *enter at left. With them are* BUTCHER, TANNER, *and* HUNTER. JACK *calls out as they en-*

ter.) Cow for sale! Fine cow for sale! Who will buy my cow? What will you offer? (*The crowd stops.* JACK *leads cow to the front of the stage and the crowd begins to poke fun and snicker.*)

FARMER: Ho, Butcher! Look here! (BUTCHER *approaches cow and feels her ribs. She twitches nervously.*)

BUTCHER: What a remarkable animal! How do the bones hold together with no meat between them?

JACK: This cow is not for you, Butcher.

BUTCHER: Don't worry, boy, I won't buy her. (*Aside to the crowd*) If I thought I had to, I'd go out of business! (*Crowd laughs.*) The Tanner can have her. Where's the Tanner? (TANNER *advances from the crowd and inspects cow's hide. Cow shifts about uneasily.*)

JACK (*To* TANNER): I won't sell her to you, either.

TANNER (*Sneering*): And I won't buy her, either! This skin is tanned already, even before it is off the beast. (*Crowd roars with laughter.*)

FARMER'S WIFE: I wouldn't want to taste the milk from that leathery old cow!

JACK: She gives no milk—she is dry.

CROWD (*Jeering; ad lib*): Too old for milk! Too old for meat! Too old for hides! He hopes to sell her! (*Etc.*) (HUNTER *steps forward and examines the cow's horns.*)

HUNTER: I'll pay you ten shillings.

JACK: How much?

HUNTER: Ten shillings and not a tuppence more.

FARMER: Listen to that! He'll pay ten shillings for a skeleton!

HUNTER: The horns are worth it—there's not a crack in the bone. I can make two fine hunting horns. (*Cow jerks her head away.*)

JACK (*Hesitating*): Ten shillings isn't much. Do you promise to give her a good home?

HUNTER: A home, did you say? Oh, she will rest easy out in the woods where I will bury her. Only the horns are worth keeping.

JACK: She's not for you! (*He leads cow away upstage. Crowd moves on, laughing and mocking* JACK, *and exits down right.* JACK *sits on bench, dejected.*) Well, Cloverbelle, we have saved ourselves a long walk to the village. (*Sighing*) There is no kindness in the world. (*The cow moos "Yes, there is."*) There is? Where? (*Cow nods her head toward the pasture behind the wall.* JACK *scoffs.*) The pasture? Hah! It's full of rocks and thistles. Do you call that kindness? (*Cow continues to gaze off up left, and presently an* OLD WOMAN *enters behind wall and walks through the gate.*)

OLD WOMAN: Good morning, young man.

JACK (*Rising*): Good morning, ma'am.

OLD WOMAN: Is your cow for sale?

JACK: Yes, but only for a fair price, and you must not neglect her. She must have plenty to eat and the best care.

OLD WOMAN: If you ask enough, I will buy her.

JACK (*Aside to cow*): The poor thing is crazy, she hasn't a penny to her name. But I'll humor her. Ma'am, the price of this cow is one hundred pieces of gold. (JACK *winks at cow.*) That ought to send her on her way.

OLD WOMAN: Boy, you are a fool! You don't ask enough. (*Cow tosses her head excitedly and moos at* JACK.)

JACK: I should think one hundred gold pieces is *quite* enough.

OLD WOMAN (*Banging on the ground with her cane*): You think, you think! Well, ponder this! If you do not ask enough, I will not buy.

JACK (*Tentatively*): *Two* hundred gold pieces, then? (OLD WOMAN *shakes her head and looks into the cow's face.*)

OLD WOMAN: Poor creature! He does not know your true value. Two hundred gold pieces indeed!

Jack (*Boldly*): How about five hundred—or ten hundred?

Old Woman: Not ten hundred nor twice ten hundred. It is not enough.

Jack: Well, what would *you* ask if you were me?

Old Woman: I'd ask for my rightful inheritance, my fortune.

Jack: All right, I ask for that. Give me my fortune. (*He holds out his hand for payment.*)

Old Woman (*Putting something in his hand*): Here it is, and now the cow is mine. (*She starts to lead cow away through the gate.*)

Jack (*Glancing into his hand*): Hold on, there, you can't have the cow! Not until you've paid for her.

Old Woman (*Coming back*): You have your pay—it is in your hand.

Jack: These *beans*?

Old Woman: Aye, those beans. They are your fortune.

Jack (*Returning them*): Keep your beans, old woman, and I will keep the cow. (*Cow moos and shakes her head.*)

Old Woman: You see? She wants to go with me. Now take the beans (*Forcing them into his hand*)—and plant them.

Jack (*Sarcastically*): Yes, plant them—and starve to death while they are growing.

Old Woman: Plant them tonight, and tomorrow climb the beanstalk and seek the treasures that belonged to your father.

Jack (*Suddenly interested*): Treasures? What treasures?

Old Woman: The purse that is never empty, the hen that lays golden eggs, and the harp that plays whatever you call for.

Jack: My father had those treasures?

Old Woman: Your father was a rich man—as rich as a

prince. But one day a giant stole his three priceless possessions—the purse, the hen and the harp.

JACK (*Puzzled*): Why hasn't my mother ever spoken to me about this?

OLD WOMAN: The giant made your father promise never to tell anyone of the three treasures.

JACK: Then how is it that you know about them?

OLD WOMAN: I am the Fairy Beanblossom. I was your father's guardian and, when he died, I became your guardian. That is why I can help you recover what is rightfully yours. But I must warn you, say nothing of all this to your mother, or my power to protect you will be taken away. Goodbye, Jack, for the present.

JACK (*Anxiously*): You will take good care of Cloverbelle, won't you?

OLD WOMAN (*To cow*): What do you think, old girl? (*Cow moos and nods her head happily.*) There's your answer, Jack. (*She goes through the gateway with cow and exits up left behind the wall.* JACK *stands thoughtfully, weighing the beans in his hand.*)

JACK: What will Mother say when she finds out that I've sold Cloverbelle for a handful of beans? And I can't even tell her that they are magic beans. Well, I'd better get it over with. (*He calls.*) Mother! (*She comes out of the cottage.*)

MOTHER: Jack! Haven't you gone yet? Where is the cow?

JACK: I—I sold her.

MOTHER (*Surprised*): Do you mean you've been to the Fair and back already?

JACK: No. An old woman came along and she offered to take Cloverbelle and give her a good home.

MOTHER: What did she pay?

JACK: Uh—close your eyes and hold out your hand. (*He gives her the beans. She opens her eyes and stares at the beans in amazement.*)

MOTHER: What's this? Beans? Don't tell me you gave away the cow for a handful of beans!

JACK (*Quickly*): They are not ordinary beans, Mother. They grow very fast. We shall have bean soup to eat tomorrow.

MOTHER (*Bitterly*): Aye—cooked in a silver kettle, with gold spoons to eat it with! (*Losing her patience*) Well, *this* much for your precious beans! (*She throws them over the wall.*)

JACK (*Aghast*): Mother, what have you done? You have thrown away our fortune!

MOTHER (*Weeping*): Jack, how could you be such a fool? We are ruined! (*A rippling chord on a harp or guitar is heard from offstage as the beanstalk starts to grow behind the wall.*)

JACK: Mother, look! It's the beanstalk, it is really growing! I told you so! (*He leaps onto the bench and then to the wall.*)

MOTHER: Jack, what are you going to do?

JACK: I'm going to climb the beanstalk.

MOTHER (*Grabbing his legs to prevent him from climbing*): No, no! You will break your neck.

JACK: I want to see what's at the top.

MOTHER: There's nothing at the top.

JACK: Perhaps my fortune is there. Let go, Mother! (*He pulls his legs free and sets one foot on the beanstalk.*)

MOTHER: Jack, don't do it! Come back, come back! (*He starts to climb.*)

CURTAIN

*   *   *

SCENE 2

SETTING: *Outdoor kitchen of Giant's castle. There is an outdoor fireplace at right, and at left the entrance to*

the castle. A wall runs across back of stage between fire-
place and castle. At center there are a large chair and
table.

AT RISE: GIANT'S WIFE *is at fireplace, stirring stew in*
large hanging kettle. Behind the wall, beanstalk comes
into view, growing upward, and then JACK *appears be-*
hind wall, as if climbing off the beanstalk. He climbs
onto wall, then jumps down into kitchen.

JACK: Hello!

GIANT'S WIFE (*Whirling around, startled*): Mercy on us,
it's a little boy! How did you get in here?

JACK (*Pointing*): I climbed up the beanstalk. (WIFE *goes*
to wall, stands on a chest against wall, and looks the
beanstalk up and down.)

WIFE: My, my, what a long beanstalk! I can't see the
bottom. What's down there?

JACK: The earth—my home.

WIFE: Well, boy, if you know what's good for you, you
will go right back down to where you came from—this
minute!

JACK: Why?

WIFE: Do you know who lives here?

JACK (*Pretending ignorance*): No, who?

WIFE (*In a dreadful whisper*): The *Giant!*

JACK: Oh, I've never seen a giant. I've heard wonderful
tales about giants.

WIFE: They are all true, believe me, and the truest tale
of all is that they *eat—little—boys!*

JACK (*Bragging*): Huh! I'm not afraid of any old giant.
Besides, I'm tired and hungry. Won't you please give
me something to eat?

WIFE: Very well, I'll feed you—but after that, you must
go. (*She gets a bowl and fills it with stew from kettle.*)

JACK (*At the table, picking up* GIANT's *knife*): Golly, what a big knife!

WIFE: Put it down. It is very sharp.

JACK (*Obeying*): Are you the Giant's wife?

WIFE: Yes, and if he should find out that you were here and I let you go, he will beat me.

JACK (*Reassuringly*): Don't worry, he won't find out.

WIFE (*Setting bowl of stew on table*): Sit down and eat this—and be quick about it. The Giant is likely to come home any moment now.

JACK (*Sitting in* GIANT's *chair*): Thank you, ma'am. (*Just as he raises spoon to his mouth,* GIANT *is heard stamping off right as he approaches the kitchen.*)

GIANT (*Off*): Ho, Wife!

WIFE (*Panic-stricken*): What did I tell you? It's the Giant! Here, hide in the oven. (*She shoves* JACK *into the oven and closes door; then she runs to table and snatches up the bowl of stew. She is about to dump stew back into kettle when* GIANT *enters. He carries a club and drags an enormous bulging sack.*)

GIANT: Ha! I caught you! How dare you eat your dinner before I've had mine? (*He starts towards her with upraised club, and she empties stew into kettle.* GIANT *stops and sniffs.*)

Fee, fi, fo, fum!

I smell the blood of an Englishman.

Be he alive, or be he dead,

I'll grind his bones to make my bread!

WIFE: It's the lamb stewing in the kettle.

GIANT: Doesn't smell like lamb. Smells like boy.

Fee, fi, fo, fum!

I smell a tasty boy, by gum!

(*He sniffs in direction of oven, and* WIFE *quickly steps in front of it, diverting his attention by pointing to sack he has brought in.*)

WIFE: What's in the bag? Did you bring home much?

GIANT: Not much—only a calf, two hogs, three sheep and twenty rabbits. Put them in the smokehouse. (*WIFE tugs at sack, finally hauling it offstage left. GIANT tastes stew with his finger, and then he catches sight of beanstalk. JACK peeks out of oven.*) Ha! What's this? (*He bellows off left.*) Ho, Wife! (*She hurries in with empty sack which she drops beside wall.*)

WIFE: Yes?

GIANT: How did this beanstalk get here?

WIFE: I—I planted it last week.

GIANT (*Suspiciously*): What for?

WIFE: I thought you might like a pot of baked beans for supper next Saturday night.

GIANT: Bah! What are you trying to do—make a vegetarian out of me? Well, I won't *be* a vegetarian, do you hear? (*He sits at table.*) Bring me the kettle of lamb stew. (*He snorts in contempt.*) Baked beans, indeed! (*WIFE sets kettle of stew before him. He eats stew noisily from ladle. JACK pushes open oven door to watch GIANT eat. WIFE motions him to close it. GIANT looks up.*) Wife, why are you waving your hands around like that?

WIFE: It's a fly—it keeps buzzing around the stew.

GIANT: I don't see any fly. (*He wipes his mouth with the back of his hand.*)

Yum, yum, yum, yum!

That dinner was good, by gum!

(*He slaps his stomach.*) I shall get fat if I'm not careful. Now clear the table, Wife. I want to count my money. (*He takes a red leather purse from his belt.*)

WIFE (*Clearing away the kettle*): Why do you want to count your money? It's always there in the magic purse.

GIANT: Stop yapping! I can't count if you talk. (*He spreads a handful of gold coins on the table.*) Two—four—

seven—eleven—eighteen—twenty-five—(*He gets mixed up and counts on his fingers, then starts over again on the coins.*) Two—five—nine—thirteen—(*He checks the sum on his fingers and is more confused than before.*) Oh, never mind, it's all there, anyway. (*He returns the coins to purse.*) Wife, bring me my harp. (WIFE *takes harp from chest and places it on table.*) Play! Play a chicken reel. I am going to dance with my Golden Hen. (*Lively music is heard as harp begins to "play."* GIANT *goes to the castle door and calls inside.*) Here, chick, chick, chick! Here, chick, here, chick! (GOLDEN HEN *hops out of castle and dances with* GIANT. *At end of dance,* GIANT *chases* HEN *around kitchen, finally catching her and pushing her onto table.*) Now, my little Lucky-Clucky, lay me a golden egg. (HEN *reaches under her wing into a pocket and takes out an egg.*) Another. And another. That's enough. (GIANT *lines up three eggs in a row and pats them.*) One, two, three. Three a day makes twenty-one a week, ninety a month—or is it ninety-three?—or eighty-four? (*He counts on his fingers.*)

WIFE: What do you want with so many eggs? You can't eat them.

GIANT: Mind your business! Go to bed!

WIFE: Not yet. (*She glances at oven, obviously worried about leaving* JACK *alone with* GIANT.) Let's have another tune from the harp.

GIANT: No! Go to bed!

WIFE: At least an encore.

GIANT: No more, I say! *Go to bed!* (*He threatens her with his club, and she runs off right.* GIANT *yawns and stretches.*)

Ho, ho, ho, hum!
I am mighty tired, by gum!
(*His head nods and drops forward on his chest. One*

hand has firm hold of HEN's *feet, the other hand rests on the base of the harp and the magic purse. He falls asleep and snores loudly.* HEN *tucks her head under her wing and also sleeps.* JACK *slowly opens oven door and climbs out. He hits the fire poker accidentally and it clatters to the floor. The noise rouses* GIANT, *and he looks up.* JACK *crouches out of sight behind oven.* GIANT *grunts and goes back to sleep. With great caution* JACK *tiptoes to table. He studies* GIANT *from all sides, scratches his head, and an idea comes to him. He stands behind the* GIANT *and tickles the side of his neck.* GIANT *lifts his hand to scratch himself.* JACK *seizes the purse and slips it into his pocket. He tickles the* GIANT's *neck again.* GIANT *lifts same hand to scratch himself and* JACK *snatches up harp.* HEN *opens one eye and cackles.*)

JACK (*Whispering*): Sh-h-h! I'm only taking what is mine. The Giant stole the purse and harp from my father. He stole you, too. I'm going to take you back to earth with me where you belong. Don't make a sound. Sh-h-h! (JACK *now tickles other side of* GIANT's *neck. The* GIANT *withdraws his other hand which is clasped around* HEN's *feet. She moves away quickly, but in doing so, upsets a mug on the table.* GIANT *starts to wake up.* JACK *whispers to harp*) Play! Play a lullaby. (*Soft, soothing music is heard.* GIANT *is lulled back to sleep.* JACK *gets the empty sack by the wall and, with* HEN *helping, eases it over* GIANT's *head.* JACK *then signals* HEN *to descend beanstalk.* JACK *shoulders harp and follows.* GIANT *awakens, bewildered by sack over his head.*)

GIANT: Help! Take this blanket off my face! I can't see! (*He upsets his chair and tugs at sack.*) Wife! Wife! (WIFE *runs out of castle and removes sack.*) I'll clobber you for this! (*He picks up his club.*)

WIFE: I didn't do it! It was—someone else. A thief, perhaps.

GIANT: A thief? (*He looks on table.*) My treasures—they're gone! Who has taken them? (*Harp music is heard offstage, in the distance.*) Listen! That sounds like my harp. Where is it? (*He traces the sound to the beanstalk and leans over wall.*) There it is! A little boy has stolen it. Stop, thief! You scoundrel, I'll catch you! (*He starts down beanstalk and disappears from view. WIFE shouts down to JACK.*)

WIFE: Faster, boy, faster! The Giant is after you!

CURTAIN

* * *

SCENE 3

SETTING: *Same as Scene 1.*

AT RISE: HEN *stands near wall, looking up beanstalk anxiously.* JACK *is stepping from wall to bench. As he jumps to the ground, he calls toward cottage.*

JACK: Mother! Mother, I'm back! Come out here!

MOTHER (*Hurrying out of cottage*): It's Jack. It's my boy!

JACK: Quick, Mother, the ax! I must cut down the beanstalk.

MOTHER: Why?

JACK: He is after me.

MOTHER: Who?

JACK: The Giant. He will kill us!

MOTHER: Jack, what is happening?

JACK: The ax, the ax! (JACK'S MOTHER *gets it from the barn.* JACK *chops away at beanstalk with all his might.*

The stalk falls with a great crash. GIANT *is heard roaring, and then all is quiet.*)

MOTHER: Mercy on us, what was *that?*

JACK: It was the Giant who lived at the top of the beanstalk.

MOTHER: Tell me all about it.

JACK: Later, Mother. (*He opens the magic purse and, taking out a gold piece, drops it into his* MOTHER'S *hand.*) First, put this in your pocket—and this—and this!

MOTHER: Keep some for yourself!

JACK: But the purse is still full. See? (*She looks into the purse, surprised.*) It's a magic purse. And look there! (*He points to* HEN.) You never had a hen like that one in your barnyard.

MOTHER: A golden hen! Does she lay eggs?

JACK: Does she! (*To* HEN) Lay! (HEN *takes a gold egg from under her wing and gives it to* JACK'S MOTHER. OLD WOMAN *enters through the gate.*)

OLD WOMAN: Good evening, Jack.

JACK: Good evening. Mother, this is the woman who bought our cow.

OLD WOMAN: Yes, and I have brought her back again. What would a farm be without a cow? (*Cow enters through the gate and moos a greeting.*) And now, Jack, you can tell your mother the truth about the treasures you found at the top of the beanstalk.

JACK: Oh, there's plenty of time for that. She hasn't heard the harp yet. Come on, harp, play us something jolly. We want to dance! (*Lively music is heard as harp "plays."* JACK *dances about with his* MOTHER, OLD WOMAN *dances with* HEN. *The cow dances about by herself, as curtain falls.*)

THE END

Rip Van Winkle

by Washington Irving

Characters

RIP VAN WINKLE
DAME VAN WINKLE, *his wife*
JUDY, *his daughter*
LUKE GARDENIER ⎤
KATCHEN   ⎥ *Judy's*
MEENIE, *a girl* ⎥ *playmates*
JACOB   ⎦
NICHOLAS VEDDER, *landlord of the King George Tavern*
DERRICK VAN BUMMEL, *the schoolmaster*
PETER VANDERDONK ⎤ *men of the*
BROM DUTCHER   ⎦ *village*
OFFSTAGE VOICE
HENDRIK HUDSON
SAILORS, *Hudson's crew*
ORATOR
JONATHAN DOOLITTLE, *proprietor of the Union Hotel*
JUDITH GARDENIER, *Judy grown up*
LITTLE RIP, *her son*
TOWNSPEOPLE
CHILDREN

Scene 1

Time: *Early autumn, a few years before the Revolutionary War.*

Setting: *A village in the Catskill Mountains. At left, there is an inn with a sign,* king george tavern, *and a picture of King George III. A British Union Jack hangs on the flagpole.*

At Rise: Nicholas Vedder, Derrick Van Bummel, Brom Dutcher *and* Peter Vanderdonk *are seated outside the tavern.* Vedder *is sprawled back in his chair.* Dutcher *and* Vanderdonk *are at the table, playing a game of checkers.* Van Bummel *is reading aloud from a newspaper. From time to time, a rumble of thunder can be heard in the distance.*

Van Bummel (*Reading*): ". . . and it has been learned that Massachusetts favors a Stamp Act Congress to be held in New York to protest English taxation in the Colonies."

Dutcher (*Looking up from his game*): Good! It's high time we did something about this English taxation.

Vanderdonk: Taxes and more taxes! The English are a pack of rascals with their hands in our pockets.

Van Bummel: There's even a revenue stamp on our newspapers. One of these days the people here in the American Colonies will revolt, you mark my words.

Vedder (*Pointing off right as a merry whistle is heard*): Well, here comes one man who is not troubled by these problems—Rip Van Winkle. (Rip Van Winkle *enters, a wooden bucket in one hand, his gun in the other. He props his gun against the tree trunk, then crosses to the group of men.*)

Rip: Good afternoon, Nick Vedder—Brom—Peter. (*To* Van Bummel) Good afternoon, Mr. Schoolmaster.

(*They return his greeting. There is a loud rumble of thunder and* RIP *cocks his head.*) Just listen to that, will you!

DUTCHER: We're probably in for a storm after this heat all day.

VEDDER: Sit down, Rip. Derrick is reading us the news.

VANDERDONK: How about a game of checkers, Rip?

RIP (*Hesitating*): I don't know. Dame Van Winkle sent me for a bucket of water, but—maybe *one* game. (*He sets down the bucket and draws a stool up to the table, as* VANDERDONK *rises.*)

DUTCHER: Your move, Rip. (*Suddenly* DAME VAN WINKLE's *voice is heard from off right.*)

DAME VAN WINKLE (*Calling from off right*): Rip! R-i-p! *Rip Van Winkle!*

RIP: Oh, my galligaskins! It's my wife! (*Before he can get to his feet,* DAME VAN WINKLE *enters with a broom. She looks at men, then crosses directly to* RIP.)

DAME VAN WINKLE: So this is how you draw water from the well! Sitting around with a lot of lazy good-for-nothing loafers. (*She tries to hit* RIP *with the broom.*) Pick up that bucket, you dawdling Dutchman, and fill it with water!

RIP (*Snatching up the bucket and dodging out of the way*): Hey there, Dame, I'm not an old rug to be beaten with a broomstick.

DAME VAN WINKLE: Well, you might better be. An old rug is more use than you. At least it would keep our feet warm in winter, which is more than you can do. Little you care that your family is starving and the cow is gone.

RIP: The cow gone?

DAME VAN WINKLE: Aye, the cow is gone and the cabbage trampled down. When are you going to mend the fence?

RIP: It rained yesterday—

DAME VAN WINKLE: If excuses were shillings, we'd be rich!

RIP: I'll mend the fence—tomorrow.

DAME VAN WINKLE: Tomorrow, tomorrow! All your work is going to be done tomorrow! (RIP *goes to the well as she starts off right, still talking.*) You show enough energy when there's a husking bee or an errand to run for the neighbors, but here at home . . . (*She exits.* RIP *lowers his bucket into the well. The other men rise to go into the tavern.*)

VEDDER: Poor Rip! His wife has the scoldingest tongue in the Hudson Valley.

VAN BUMMEL: A sharp tongue is the only tool that grows keener with use.

DUTCHER: What would you do, Derrick, if you had a wife like Van Winkle's?

VAN BUMMEL: War could be no worse. I would enlist. (*They all laugh and exit through the door of the tavern.* RIP *turns to leave, then stops and smiles, as children's voices are heard off left.* JUDY, LUKE, KATCHEN, MEENIE, *holding a kite, and* JACOB, *carrying a bow, run in, left, and shout with delight when they see* RIP.)

CHILDREN (*Ad lib*): There he is! There's Rip Van Winkle! (*Etc. They surround him, chattering excitedly.*)

JUDY: Hello, Father, I've brought some of my friends.

RIP: Glad to see you, children.

JACOB (*Holding out bow*): Oh, Rip, there's something wrong with my bow. Every time I go to shoot, the cord slips. (RIP *takes the bow, draws his knife from his pocket and cuts the notch deeper for the cord.*)

RIP: There, Jacob, try that, and see if it doesn't work.

JACOB (*Pretending to shoot*): Yes, it's all right now.

MEENIE (*Holding out kite*): My kite won't stay up, Rip.

RIP (*Taking off part of the tail*): Now it will, Meenie—

and this breeze is just right for it. (*He hands kite to* MEENIE.)

KATCHEN: My mother wants you to plug up her rain barrel, so she'll be able to wash next week.

RIP: Tell her I'll fix it tonight, Katchen.

LUKE: Rip, will you see what's the matter with my whistle? I made it just the way you showed me, but it isn't any good. (*He hands* RIP *a whistle.*)

RIP (*Examining it*): You haven't whittled it right there, Luke. Here, I'll fix it for you. (*He sits on the bench under the tree and begins to whittle.*)

JUDY: Tell us a story, Father!

LUKE: Yes, you tell better stories than anybody in the Catskills. (*The children all gather around* RIP, *sitting on the ground.*)

RIP: What shall it be about?

JACOB: Indians!

KATCHEN: I like witches and goblins best. (*A long roll of thunder is heard.*)

JUDY: Oh, Father, hear that! Hear the thunder!

RIP: Why, don't you know what that is, Judy? That's Hendrik Hudson and his famous crew, playing ninepins up in the mountains. (*More thunder is heard.*)

MEENIE: Oh, what a noise they make!

RIP: Yes, they are jolly fellows. They sail the wide sea over in their ship, the *Half-Moon*, then every twenty years they come back to the Catskills.

JACOB: What do they do that for?

RIP: Oh, old Hendrik Hudson likes to revisit the country he discovered and keep a watchful eye over his river, the Hudson.

JACOB: I wish I could see Hendrik Hudson and his crew.

RIP: Peter Vanderdonk says his father saw them once in their funny breeches, playing at ninepins up in the hills. (*A loud peal of thunder is heard.*) Listen to their balls rolling! That must be Hendrik Hudson himself, the Flying Dutchman! (DAME VAN WINKLE *enters with broom as* RIP *is speaking.*)

DAME VAN WINKLE: So! Here you are, telling stories without a word of truth in 'em! Oh, *I* could tell a story or two myself—about a shiftless husband who does nothing but whittle and whistle. Whittle and whistle! What a job for a grown man! (*She snatches the whistle from* RIP.)

LUKE (*Pleadingly*): It's my whistle! Please don't break it, Dame Van Winkle.

DAME VAN WINKLE: Take it and begone! (*She gives* LUKE *the whistle and he runs off.*) Judy, you go and ask Dame Vedder for an armful of wood. Your father is too busy spinning yarns to split wood for *our* fire. (JUDY *goes off behind the tavern.*) As for the rest of you, go home if you have any homes, and don't keep hanging around here like stray dogs looking for bones. (*She sweeps the children off the stage with her broom.*) Get along! Begone, all of you! Go home now! (*With arms akimbo, she faces* RIP.) Well, what do you have to say for yourself? (RIP *shrugs, shakes his head and says nothing.*) Nothing as usual. (RIP *goes to the tree for his gun.*) What are you getting your gun for? Going off to the mountains, no doubt. Anything to keep you out of the house.

RIP (*Good-naturedly*): Well, wife, you have often told me—*my* side of the house is the *out*side. Where's my dog? Where's Wolf?

DAME VAN WINKLE: Wolf is tied up in the cellar.

RIP: You didn't tie up Wolf?

DAME VAN WINKLE: I certainly did. That dog tracked up my kitchen floor right after I'd finished scrubbing it. Well, if you're going hunting, go, and don't come back until you bring us something for supper. And if you can't bring any supper, don't bring yourself.

JUDY (*Re-entering from up left, her arms full of logs*): But, Mother, it's going to rain.

DAME VAN WINKLE (*Taking the wood*): Pooh! Your father won't get as wet as we will in the house, with the roof leaking and the windows broken. You hurry home now. And bring that bucket of water your father managed to get this far. (DAME VAN WINKLE *starts right, but* JUDY *stays behind with* RIP.)

RIP (*Calling after his wife*): Wife, turn Wolf loose when you get home. (DAME VAN WINKLE *looks back at him angrily, tosses her head, and exits right.*)

JUDY (*Starting to cry as she puts her hand in* RIP's): Father, where will you go if it rains?

RIP: I'll find a place. Don't cry, Judy. Remember your little song? Come, we'll sing it together. (*They sing an appropriate folk song, such as "Rosa, Will We Go Dancing?"*)

JUDY (*Hugging* RIP): Oh, Father, I hope you have wonderful luck. Then Mother won't be so cross.

RIP: I don't blame her for being cross with me sometimes. I guess I don't do much work around here. But I'm going to do better, Judy. I'm going to do all the jobs your mother has been after me about.

DAME VAN WINKLE (*Calling from off*): Ju-*dee!* Ju-*dee!*

RIP: There's your mother. I'd better be off. Goodbye, Judy dear. (*He walks left, whistling for his dog.*) Come, Wolf! Come, boy! (*A dog's bark is heard off left, as* RIP *turns, waves to* JUDY, *and exits.*)

JUDY (*Waving*): Goodbye, Father. (LUKE *enters from right and joins* JUDY *as loud crash of thunder is heard. Startled,* JUDY *clings to* LUKE.) Oh, Luke, listen to that thunder!

LUKE: It's only Hendrik Hudson's men playing ninepins. Don't be scared, Judy.

JUDY: I'm not—that is, not very.

DAME VAN WINKLE (*Calling from off*): Judy! Ju-*dee!*

LUKE: You'd better go in or you'll catch it. Your mother is getting awfully free with her broomstick lately. Here, I'll carry your bucket for you. (*He exits right with the bucket of water.* JUDY *lingers behind to look off in direction her father has taken as the thunder gets louder. Then humming softly to herself, she exits right.*)

CURTAIN

* * *

SCENE 2

TIME: *Later the same afternoon.*

SETTING: *A forest glade, high in the Catskill Mountains. There is a tree stump at right center, and a large bush at far left. This scene may be played before the curtain.*

AT RISE: RIP, *carrying his gun, enters left, dragging his feet wearily. He sinks down on the stump.*

RIP: Whew! That was a climb! All the way up the mountain. How peaceful it is up here. No one to scold me, no one to wave a broomstick. Ah, me! (*He gives a big sigh of contentment.*) I wonder where Wolf is. Wolf! Here, boy! (*He whistles and a dog barks off left.*) That's it, Wolf, sick 'em! I hope we get something this time. We can't go home until we do. (*A loud crash of thunder is heard.*) That thunder sounds much louder up here in the mountains than down in the valley. Maybe it's going to rain after all.

VOICE (*Calling from off, high-pitched, like a bird-call*): Rip

Van Winkle! (RIP *looks around wonderingly.*) Rip Van Winkle!

RIP (*Rising*): That's my name. Somebody is calling me.

VOICE (*Off*): Rip Van Winkle!

RIP: Is it Dame Van Winkle? No—she would never follow me up here. (*Sound of a ship's bell is heard from off right.*) What was that? (*Bell rings again.*) A ship's bell! But how can that be? A ship? Up here in the mountains? (*He gazes off right, in astonishment.*) It *is* a ship! Look at it! Sails all set—a Dutch flag at the masthead. (*Ship's bell is heard again, fainter.*) There, it's gone. I must have imagined it. (1ST SAILOR *with a keg on his back, enters from right and goes to center, as* RIP *watches him in amazement.*) By my galligaskins, what a funny little man! And how strangely he's dressed. Such old-fashioned clothes! (1ST SAILOR *stops at center.* RIP *goes to meet him.*) Hello, old Dutchman. That keg looks heavy. Let me carry it for you. (*He relieves* 1ST SAILOR *of the keg.*) By golly, it *is* heavy! Why did you bring this keg all the way up here to the top of the mountain? And who are you, anyhow?

1ST SAILOR (*Gruffly*): Don't ask questions. Set it down over there. (*He points left to a spot beside the bush.*)

RIP (*Obeying cheerfully*): Anything to oblige. (*There is a commotion off right, and* HENDRIK HUDSON *and his crew enter, capering and shouting. They carry bowling balls and ninepins and a drum.* 2ND SAILOR *has a burlap bag containing drinking mugs thrown over his shoulder.* RIP *turns to* 1ST SAILOR.) Why, bless my soul! Here are a lot of little fellows just like yourself. (*To* SAILORS, *as they gather at center*) Who are you?

SAILORS (*Shouting*): Hendrik Hudson and his merry crew!

HUDSON (*Stepping forward*): Set up the ninepins, men, and we'll have a game. (*Two or three* SAILORS *set up the ninepins at extreme right.* HUDSON *speaks to the* 1ST SAILOR.) You there, fill up the flagons! (2ND SAILOR *opens sack and passes out the mugs.* HUDSON *turns to* RIP.) Now then, Rip Van Winkle, will you drink with us?

RIP: Why, yes, thank you, Captain Hudson. I'm quite thirsty after my long climb up the mountain. (*The mugs are filled from keg.*)

2ND SAILOR (*Raising his mug in toast*): To Hendrik Hudson, the *Half-Moon*, and its merry crew!

ALL (*As they raise their mugs*): To Hendrik Hudson, the *Half-Moon*, and its merry crew!

RIP (*Lifting his mug*): Well, gentlemen, here's to your good health. May you live long and prosper. (RIP *drinks and smacks his lips.*) Ah! This is the best drink I ever tasted, but it makes me feel very sleepy. (HUDSON *and his men begin to bowl. As they roll the balls, the thunder increases.* RIP *yawns.*) Ho, hum! I can't keep my eyes open. I guess I'll lie down—(*Carrying his gun, he goes behind bush at left, and lies down out of sight.* NOTE: *Unseen by audience,* RIP *may go offstage for necessary costume changes and return in time for his awakening.*)

HUDSON (*To* SAILORS): Now, men, let's stop our game of ninepins, and have a merry dance. Then we'll be off, to return again in twenty years. (*One of the men beats the drum, and* SAILORS *dance. At the end of the dance,* 1ST SAILOR *points to bush where* RIP *is sleeping.*)

1ST SAILOR: Look! Rip Van Winkle is asleep.

HUDSON: Peace be with the poor fellow. He needs to take a good long rest from his nagging wife. Sh-h-h-h! (*He places his finger to his lips and they all go about quietly gathering up the ninepins, balls, mugs, keg, etc., then they tiptoe off the stage, their voices dying away to a whisper. The lights may dim briefly to indicate the passage of twenty years, and recorded music may be played. When the lights come up, RIP is heard yawning behind the bush, then he stands up with great difficulty. He limps to center, carrying a rusty gun. His clothes are shabby, and he has a long white beard.)*

RIP (*Groaning*): Ouch, my back! It's so stiff. And my legs —just like pokers. My, my, but I'm shaky! I feel as if I'd grown to be an old man overnight. It must be rheumatism coming on. Oh, won't I have a blessed time with Dame Van Winkle if I'm laid up with rheumatism. Well, I'd better get along home to Dame Van Winkle. (*He looks at the gun he is carrying.*) Why, this rusty old thing is not my gun! Somebody has played a trick on me. (*Suddenly recollecting*) It's that Hendrik Hudson and his men! They've stolen my gun, and left this rusty one for me! (*He puts his hand to his head.*) Another scolding in store from the Dame. (*He whistles.*) Wolf! Here, Wolf! Have those scamps stolen my dog, too? He'd never leave me. (*He whistles again.*) Come on, old boy! Maybe he found it too cold and went home to be warmed by his mistress' broomstick. Well, I will follow after and get my hot welcome, too. (*He shoulders the rusty gun and totters off.*)

CURTAIN

* * *

SCENE 3

TIME: *Twenty years after Scene 1.*

SETTING: *Same as Scene 1, except that the sign above the tavern door reads:* UNION HOTEL—PROPRIETOR, JONATHAN DOOLITTLE. *A picture of George Washington has replaced that of King George III. Washington's name is*

*printed below the picture and an American flag flutters
on a pole above it.*

AT RISE: *An* ORATOR *is standing on a bench, haranguing
a crowd of* TOWNSPEOPLE.

ORATOR: Remember the Boston Tea Party! Remember
Bunker Hill! Who saved this country? Who is the father
of this country?

TOWNSPEOPLE: George Washington! Washington for
President! (*Etc. They sing "Yankee Doodle."*)
Father and I went down to camp
  Along with Captain Good'in,
There we saw the men and boys
  As thick as hasty puddin'.

Yankee Doodle keep it up,
  Yankee Doodle Dandy,
Mind the music and the step
  And with the girls be handy.
(RIP *enters with a troop of children, who laugh and
jeer at him.*)

CHILDREN (*Ad lib*): Look at him! He looks like a scarecrow! Where did you come from, Daddy Long-legs?
Where did you get that gun? (*Etc.* RIP *and* CHILDREN
go to center. 1ST CHILD *stands in front of* RIP, *and
crouches down, pulling on an imaginary beard.*)

1ST CHILD: Billy goat, billy goat! (CHILDREN *begin stroking
imaginary beards until* RIP *does the same. He is
amazed to find he has a beard.*)

RIP: By my galligaskins, what's this?

2ND CHILD: It's a beard, old Father Time. Didn't you
know you had a beard?

RIP: But I didn't have one last night. (CHILDREN *laugh
and mock him.*)

ORATOR (*To* RIP): What do you mean by coming here at election time with a gun on your shoulder and a mob at your heels? Do you want to cause a riot?

RIP: Oh, no, sir! I am a quiet man and a loyal subject of King George!

CHILDREN *and* TOWNSPEOPLE (*Shouting, ad lib*): A spy! Away with him! Lock him up. (*Etc.*)

JONATHAN DOOLITTLE (*Stepping forward from crowd*): Hold on a minute! We must get to the bottom of this. (*To* RIP) Aren't you a supporter of Washington for President?

RIP (*Puzzled*): Eh? Supporter of Washington? (*Shaking his head, wholly bewildered*) I don't understand. I mean no harm. I only want to find my friends. They were here at the tavern yesterday.

DOOLITTLE: Who are these friends of yours? Name them.

RIP (*Hesitantly*): Well, one is the landlord—

DOOLITTLE: *I* am the landlord of this hotel—Jonathan Doolittle.

RIP: Why, what happened to Nicholas Vedder?

1ST WOMAN (*Pushing her way out of the crowd*): Nicholas Vedder? Why, he's dead and gone these eighteen years.

RIP: No, no, that's impossible! Where's Brom Dutcher? And the schoolmaster, Van Bummel—?

1ST MAN: Brom Dutcher was killed in the war at Stony Point.

2ND MAN: And Van Bummel went off to the war, too. He became a great general, and now he's in Congress.

RIP: War? What war?

2ND MAN: Why, the war we fought against England, and won, of course.

RIP: I don't understand. Am I dreaming? Congress? Generals? What's happened to me?

DOOLITTLE (*Impatiently*): Now, we've had enough of this nonsense. Who are you, anyway? What is your name?

RIP (*Utterly confused*): I don't know. I mean, I was Rip Van Winkle yesterday, but today—

DOOLITTLE: Don't try to make sport of us, my man!

RIP: Oh, indeed, I'm not, sir. I was myself last night, but I fell asleep on the mountain, and Hendrik Hudson and his crew changed my gun, and everything's changed, and I'm changed, and I can't tell what my name is, or who I am! (TOWNSPEOPLE *exchange significant glances, nod knowingly, and tap their foreheads.*)

2ND MAN (*Shaking his head*): Hendrik Hudson, he says! Poor chap. He's mad. Let's leave him alone.

RIP (*In great distress*): Isn't there anybody here who knows who I am?

2ND WOMAN (*Soothingly*): Why, you're just yourself, old man. Who else do you think you could be? (JUDITH GARDENIER *enters from left, leading* LITTLE RIP *by the hand. He hangs back, whimpering.*)

JUDITH: Hush, Rip! The old man won't hurt you.

RIP (*Turning in surprise*): Rip? Who said Rip?

JUDITH: Why, I did. I was just telling my little boy not to be frightened.

RIP (*Scanning her face*): And what is your name, my good woman?

JUDITH: My name is Judith, sir.

RIP: Judith? Did you say Judith? (*In great excitement*) And your father—what was his name?

JUDITH: Ah, poor man, his name was Rip Van Winkle. It's twenty years since he went away from home. We never heard of him again.

RIP (*Staggered*): Twenty years!

JUDITH: Yes, it must be all of that. His dog came back without him. I was a little girl then.

RIP: And your mother—where is she?

JUDITH: My mother is dead, sir.

RIP (*Sighing*): Ah, but that woman had a tongue! Well, peace be with her soul. Did you love your father, Judith?

JUDITH: With all my heart. All the children in the village loved him, too.

RIP: Then look at me. Look closely, my dear Judy. I am your father.

JUDITH (*Incredulously*): You? My father?

RIP: We used to sing a little song together, remember? (*He sings a few lines from the folksong sung in Scene 1.*)

JUDITH (*Slowly*): Yes, my father used to sing that song with me, but many people know it.

RIP: Do you remember, Judy, that I told you the story of how Hendrik Hudson and his crew played ninepins in the mountains just before I went off hunting with Wolf?

JUDITH (*Excitedly*): Yes! And Wolf *was* our dog's name! Oh, Father, it's really *you!*

RIP (*Taking her in his arms*): Yes, my little Judy—young Rip Van Winkle once, old Rip Van Winkle now. (TOWNSPEOPLE *talk excitedly among themselves, as they watch* RIP *and* JUDITH.)

JUDITH: Dearest Father, come home with me. Luke and I will take good care of you.

RIP: Luke?

JUDITH: Luke Gardenier, my old playmate. You used to make whistles for him and take him fishing. We were married when he came back from the war.

RIP: Ah, the war. There is so much I have to catch up with.

JUDITH: You will have plenty of time to do that—and you must tell us what happened to you.

RIP: Maybe you won't believe what happened to me, Judy —it was all so strange. (RIP *reaches out a hand to* LITTLE RIP, *who shyly takes it, and they start off left,* JUDITH *following. A loud clap of thunder stops them.* RIP *turns front and shakes his fist toward the mountains.*) Oh, no you don't, Hendrik Hudson! You don't get me back up there again. (*There is answering roll of thunder that sounds like a deep rumble of laughter as the curtain falls.*)

THE END

The Brave Little Tailor

from Grimms' Fairy Tales

Characters

TAILOR	KING'S HERALD
BUTCHER	KING
BAKER'S WIFE	PRINCESS ADELINE
GROCER'S WIFE	LADY-IN-WAITING
BLACKSMITH	GIANT
JAM PEDDLER	BROTHER GIANT
SEVEN FLIES	TOWNSPEOPLE

SCENE 1

SETTING: *The town square. There are five shops, with signs in front of them reading* TAILOR, BUTCHER, BAKER, GROCER, *and* BLACKSMITH. *In front of the Tailor's shop, at right, is a workbench with scissors and other sewing materials. On window sill of shop is large piece of cloth, and smaller strip of bright red cloth; also on sill are fly swatter and plate with loaf of bread, knife, spoon, and piece of cheese on it.*

AT RISE: BLACKSMITH *is hammering on his anvil;* GROCER'S WIFE *is putting fresh vegetables on display;* BAKER'S WIFE *is setting out her pastries;* BUTCHER *is chopping meat; and* TAILOR *is sitting cross-legged on his workbench, cheerfully sewing and singing.*

TAILOR (*Singing*):
　A penny for a spool of thread,
　A penny for a needle,
　That's the way the money goes—
　　Pop! goes the weasel!
　I've no time to wait or sigh,
　I've no time to wheedle,
　Only time to snip and sew—
　　Pop! goes the weasel!
　(*He pricks his finger.*) Ouch!

JAM PEDDLER (*Calling from off left*): Jams and jellies! Jellies and jams! (*She enters, carrying large basket of jams.*) Fine jams for sale! Sweet jellies! Who'll buy? (*She approaches the* BLACKSMITH *and holds out a jar.*) Blackberry jam for the blacksmithman!

BLACKSMITH (*In a surly tone*): Don't like jam. Nor jelly either.

PEDDLER (*Turning to the* GROCER's WIFE): Raspberry, strawberry, grape, and currant. Choose your favorite.

GROCER's WIFE (*Sighing wistfully*): I dare not take any of them, or I shall grow too fat.

PEDDLER (*Moving on to* BAKER's WIFE): Jam for your tarts! Jelly for your doughnuts!

BAKER's WIFE (*Snippily*): I make my own jam and jelly, thank you.

PEDDLER (*To the* BUTCHER): Now then, Mr. Butcher, give your sweet tooth a treat.

BUTCHER: Don't have a sweet tooth. Had it pulled last week. (*He laughs uproariously.*)

TAILOR (*Who has been watching the proceedings with interest*): Come here, my good woman, if you want a customer. (PEDDLER *goes over to* TAILOR. *During following dialogue, other tradespeople quietly go into their shops.*)

PEDDLER: What will it be, young man? Apple? Quince? Gooseberry?

TAILOR: Set your basket on the bench. (*She does so, and he studies its contents.*) Now, let me see. Do you have any plum jam?

PEDDLER: Of course I have plum jam.

TAILOR: How about peach?

PEDDLER: I have plenty of peach. Which do you want— peachy peach jelly or yummy plum jam?

TAILOR: I'll have to sample them first.

PEDDLER: No samples. There's no profit in that.

TAILOR (*Pleading*): Only a *taste?* You won't be sorry.

PEDDLER (*Weakening*): Well . . . perhaps—*if* it's only a taste—(TAILOR *takes knife and bread from window sill and samples all the flavors.*)

TAILOR (*Smacking his lips as he tastes each "sandwich"*): Um—good. Um—better. Um—yes. Um—ah. Um—um. This is delicious. And this and this and this.

PEDDLER (*Slapping his hand*): That's enough! You're eating up my profit. Make up your mind.

TAILOR: It's so hard to decide. But I guess I'll take two of the plum—two teaspoons.

PEDDLER (*Hardly believing her ears*): Two *what*, sir?

TAILOR: Teaspoons.

PEDDLER: Of plum jam?

TAILOR (*Correcting her*): Of *yummy* plum jam. (*He holds out spoon and piece of bread.*) Put them on this slice of bread, please.

PEDDLER (*Indignantly*): I'll do no such thing! The idea of hornswoggling me like that!

TAILOR: But I'm not asking you to *give* it to me. I shall *pay* you for it—even if it costs a whole penny!

PEDDLER (*Sarcastically*): I wouldn't dream of taking your money, you are such a *generous* man! Here, have three spoonfuls—for nothing! (*She dips the spoon into the jar and slaps the jam onto the bread.*)

TAILOR: Oh, thank you! I'll be a regular customer from now on. Come back next Tuesday.

PEDDLER (*Mockingly*): I'll come back on the day you marry the Princess! (*She exits right.*)

TAILOR (*Waving and calling after her*): That's fair enough! (*He skips back to his bench.*) No more sewing! Recess time! Bread-and-jam time! (*Spreading the jam and licking the spoon*) Mm-m-m. A drink of milk would go well with this. I'll go get some. (*He sets the plate of bread on the bench and goes into his shop. The stage is empty for a moment, then SEVEN FLIES enter. If desired, they may enter from audience and may perform short dance. Soon they smell the jam and congregate around the bench.*)

FLIES (*Chanting together*):
Yummy-yum-yum!
Plummy-plum-plum!
Form in a circle
And let's have some!

TAILOR (*Leaning out of shop window and flapping his arms at the* FLIES): Hey! Get away from there! Who invited you? Shoo! Shoo, fly! (*The* FLIES *scatter, then start weaving about the bench again. The* TAILOR *comes out of the shop.*) Shoo, shoo, shoo! Where's my fly swatter? (*He gets it from the window sill and chases the* FLIES *about the stage, swatting right and left but always missing. He trips and falls, and the* FLIES *line up in single file at the bench. They pass slice of bread from one to the other, each* FLY *nibbling at the jam. The* TAILOR *gets to his feet, and grabs bread from the last* FLY.) Now I'll let you have it! Swww-wat! (*He slaps his fly swatter at the line of* FLIES *and they collapse in a heap.*) That will teach you to steal my jam! (*He puts bread back on plate.*) I wonder how many I killed. (*He counts the* FLIES, *his voice mounting with excitement.*) One—two —three—four—five—six—seven! Seven at one blow! Gracious! What a great man I am! The whole town shall know about this. No—the whole world! I'll make a belt and tell the world—seven at one blow! (*He takes strip of bright red cloth from window sill.*) When people see my belt, they will think I have killed seven *men* at one blow. They won't know about the flies. (*He gets a length of cloth from window sill and carefully covers the* FLIES. *Then he sets to work, pretending to make the belt.*)

Thimble and thread and the needle's eye,

No one braver than big little "I".

Sew, little big man, sew, sew, sew,

Two, four, six, seven at one blow.

(*He snips the thread and holds up the belt.*) There! "Seven at one blow." That should do it. (*Puts on belt.*) Now to show the town—*and* the world. (*Strutting about*) Come one, come all! See the brave little tailor! Step right this way, folks! Here he is! The spunkiest little stitcher in the world! (BUTCHER, BAKER'S WIFE, GROCER'S WIFE and BLACKSMITH *come out of their shops. Other* TOWNSPEOPLE *enter from left and right. All look at the* TAILOR *and his belt.*)

ALL (*Reading belt*): "Seven at one blow"!

BAKER'S WIFE: Seven at one blow?

BUTCHER: The little tailor who eats bread and jam?

GROCER'S WIFE: How did he do it?

BLACKSMITH: *When* did he do it?

1ST MAN: *Where* did he do it?

2ND MAN: But he *did* do it!

1ST WOMAN (*Admiringly*): My, my, my, my, *my!* (*Trumpet fanfare is heard and all turn to look off left.*)

2ND WOMAN: What's that?

BAKER'S WIFE: Who's coming?

BUTCHER: It must be someone special.

GROCER'S WIFE: It's the King's Herald.

BLACKSMITH: And the King himself!

1ST MAN: And the Princess Adeline. And they're coming this way! (KING'S HERALD *enters, followed by* KING, PRINCESS ADELINE, *and her* LADY-IN-WAITING.)

HERALD: Make way for His Majesty and Her Royal Highness! Make way! (*All bow.* 1ST *and* 2ND MEN *quickly clear off the* TAILOR'S *bench and set it at center for the* KING *and* PRINCESS. *The* PRINCESS *and* LADY-IN-WAITING *whisper together and giggle.*)

KING (*Turning to them irritably*): What *are* you two giggling about? You know I have an important announcement to make.

PRINCESS: Announcement, Papa?

KING: About the two giants.

PRINCESS: Oh, the giants. (*She exchanges glances with the* LADY-IN-WAITING, *and they start giggling again.*)

KING: It's no laughing matter, Adeline.

PRINCESS: Oh, we're not laughing about the giants, Papa. It's the little man over there.

KING: Where?

PRINCESS: Over there. (*She points to* TAILOR.)

HERALD (*Speaking excitedly*): Your Majesty, do you see what is written on his belt?

KING (*Squinting*): What does it say?

HERALD: "Seven at one blow"!

KING: Seven? Seven what?

PRINCESS (*Tittering, to* LADY-IN-WAITING): Seven frail *ladies* perhaps.

HERALD: Seven *men* rather.

KING: Seven giants—I hope. (*Beckoning to* TAILOR) Come

here, young man. (TAILOR *approaches and bows*.) What is your name?

TAILOR: Stitcher the Tailor, Your Majesty.

HERALD: A tailor such as this should be a soldier of the King.

PRINCESS (*Coyly, flirting with* TAILOR): Indeed he should!

TAILOR (*Bowing to her*): It would be an honor to serve— ahem!—the King.

KING: Good! I will make you a Major General.

PRINCESS: A *major* Major General, Papa.

KING: Very well. (*To* TAILOR) Major Major General, I have a job for you. There are two giants in the forest outside this town. They roam about scaring people out of their wits. They rob and burn and plunder. If you can kill these giants, I will give you half my kingdom.

PRINCESS (*Nudging* KING): Oh, Papa, is that *all?* Aren't you forgetting something?

KING: Er—quite so, my dear, quite so. (*To* TAILOR) Half my kingdom—*and* my daughter besides. Can you do it?

TAILOR: Kill the giants? (*Proudly*) That will be easy. I who have killed seven at one blow can certainly get the better of a mere two, even if they *are* giants.

KING: I will let you have a hundred horsemen to aid you.

TAILOR: Oh, I don't need any horsemen, Your Majesty. I shall go alone to meet the giants.

PRINCESS (*Shaking her head, bewildered*): He must be a truly brave man!

TAILOR (*Crossing to his shop window*): Now I'll just take along something to eat. This cheese will do. (*He stuffs it in his pocket.*) What else? My scissors. (*Putting them in another pocket.*) I may have to cut my way through the forest. There, I guess I'm ready. (*He bows before* KING.) I'm off, Your Majesty, and I won't be back until the giants are dead. (*He marches about singing.*)

I've no time to wait or sigh,

I've no time to dawdle,
Only time to say goodbye—
   Pop! goes the weasel!
(*He exits left. If desired, he may repeat song and exit through audience.*)
ALL (*Taking up the song*):
A kingdom for a spool of thread,
A princess for a needle,
That's a mighty fair exchange—
   Pop! goes the weasel!
(*All cheer as the curtain falls.*)

*   *   *

Scene 2

SETTING: *A clearing in the forest. There is a large tree in the background; stones of various sizes are scattered about. A large rock is at left, and beside it is a toy paper bird.*

AT RISE: TAILOR *enters from right whistling "Pop! Goes the Weasel".*

TAILOR (*Stopping at center*): Phew! I'm tired. I've been walking for miles, and I haven't seen a giant yet. I think I'll rest a bit. (*He sits on the rock but jumps up immediately.*) Whoops! I sat on the cheese! (*Taking it from his pocket*) What a soggy lump it is! (*He places the cheese on the ground beside rock, then notices toy bird.*) Oh, look, a tiny bird! I must have a crumb or two I can feed him. (*Takes imaginary crumbs from pocket and holds them out to bird.*) There! Now I'll put you in my pocket where you'll be nice and warm. (*He puts bird in his pocket and is about to sit down again as GIANT's singing is heard. GIANT enters, carry-*

*ing club on his shoulder. If desired, he may enter from
the audience.*)

GIANT (*Singing to the tune of "Little Brown Jug"*):
Oh, large is big and high is tall,
And I'm the biggest one of all,
Except my brother, he's big, too,
It's hard to tell which one is who.
Ha, ha, ha, he and I,
We're so tall we reach the sky,
Ha, ha, ha, he and I,
Fearsome twosome, my oh my!
(*The* GIANT *catches sight of* TAILOR.) Well, well! What
have we here? A tiny little manikin!

TAILOR: Hello, Mr. Giant.

GIANT: Hello, peewee.

TAILOR (*Cockily*): Don't let my size fool you. (*Flexing
his arm muscles*) I can lick 'em in a fight as well as anybody.

GIANT: Lick what? Lollipops? (*He laughs.*)

TAILOR: It's plain you don't know who you're talking to.
I think you'd better have a look at my belt. That will
give you some idea what sort of man *I* am.

GIANT (*Reading with difficulty*): "Sevvun at one buh-
low." Hm. In that case, let's see how strong you are.
(*He picks up a "stone."*) Let's see you squeeze a stone to
powder—like this. (*He crushes "stone" in his hand, and
it crumbles to pieces.* NOTE: *"Stone" may be made of
styrofoam.*) There! Try that.

TAILOR: Who? Me? Pooh! That's child's play. I can do
better than that. I'll squeeze a stone until it gives milk.
Watch this. (*He picks up piece of cheese and squeezes
it until water drips out.* NOTE: *Cheese may be sponge
soaked in water and wrapped in cheesecloth.*) What do
you think of that, Mr. Giant? Pretty good for a peewee,
eh?

GIANT (*Grudgingly*): Humph! Well—can you throw? I'll throw a stone so high you won't be able to see it. (*He picks up a stone and swings his arm in wide circles, getting ready for the throw. The* GIANT *flings his stone off left, and sound of a whistle sliding up the scale is heard.* GIANT *looks offstage after the stone.*) Up it goes! Up! Up! It's out of sight! Here it comes back, here it comes! (*Sound of whistle sliding down the scale is heard.* GIANT *puts out his hands and totters back and forth getting ready to catch stone. He points off left.*) There! It's going to fall right there! (*He runs off left with his hands outstretched, ready to catch stone.*)

TAILOR (*Calling to* GIANT): Watch out! Watch out for your head. (GIANT *re-enters, holding stone with one hand and rubbing his head with the other.*)

GIANT: Ouch! I guess I was standing a little too close when it came down. (*Rubs his head a bit more; turns to* TAILOR) That was some throw, wasn't it?

TAILOR: Not bad. But your stone did drop back to earth, you know. I'm going to throw one that *won't* drop back.

GIANT: What? Throw a stone that won't fall back to earth? It can't be done.

TAILOR: Oh, yes it can. Watch! (TAILOR *turns his back to* GIANT *and takes bird from his pocket; to bird*) Come, my little bird, now is your chance to repay me for my kindness. (*Turns back to* GIANT) Watch this stone, Giant. (*He stands at left and tosses bird up in the air and off left. Sound of whistle sliding up scale is heard.*)

GIANT (*Looking off left, as if following the "stone"*): Amazing! It's going right up into the sky! And it's not coming down!

TAILOR: What did I tell you?

GIANT: Well, you certainly are a strong little fellow. I must introduce you to my brother. He's around here somewhere, pulling up trees for firewood. (*Calling*) Ho! Brother! Where are you?

BROTHER GIANT (*Calling from offstage*): Here I am. (*He enters, carrying club and a large burlap sack in one hand and dragging a sapling behind him with the other. If desired, BROTHER GIANT may enter from audience.*) What do you want?

GIANT: I want you to meet someone.

BROTHER GIANT: Who?

GIANT (*Turning to the TAILOR*): Who?

TAILOR: Stitcher the Tailor.

GIANT (*To his BROTHER*): Stitcher the Tailor.

BROTHER GIANT: Oh. (*He stares at TAILOR open-mouthed.*) Is that him? That little runt?

GIANT: You wouldn't believe it, brother, but that little tailor can squeeze milk out of a stone.

BROTHER GIANT: What? Why, he's no bigger than a grasshopper.

GIANT: He threw a stone so high it never came down.

BROTHER GIANT: That *is* something!

GIANT: And just read what it says on his belt.

BROTHER GIANT: I can't read. What does it say?

GIANT: "Seven at one blow."

BROTHER GIANT: *One* blow?

GIANT (*Nodding*): Seven, mind you—and there are only *two* of us.

BROTHER GIANT: I think you're right—(*Counting slowly*) one, two. (*GIANT draws his brother aside; TAILOR steps upstage and examines tree.*)

GIANT (*Speaking confidentially*): We must get rid of this little tailor before he gets rid of us.

BROTHER GIANT: Indeed, brother. But how?

GIANT (*Pointing to the burlap sack*): We'll tie him up in that sack and take him home for supper.

BROTHER GIANT: But he's only a mouthful.

GIANT: We'll kill a couple of wild boars and bag some rabbits.

BROTHER GIANT: All right, but let's bag that rabbit first. (*They turn to* TAILOR.)

GIANT: Little tailor, come here! We have something to show you. (TAILOR *approaches warily and* BROTHER GIANT *opens the sack.*)

BROTHER GIANT: Look in here.

TAILOR (*Stopping, suspiciously*): What's in there?

BROTHER GIANT: Nothing is in there yet—but something is going to be. (*To* GIANT) Grab him! (GIANT *lunges at* TAILOR, *but he springs out of reach and darts away.* GIANT *and* BROTHER GIANT *run after him, but he runs too fast for them, and they keep catching each other instead of the* TAILOR. *Finally, they catch the* TAILOR.)

GIANTS (*Singing as they put* TAILOR *into sack and tie it at his waist, leaving his chest and head exposed*):

Oh, large is big and little is small,
And he's the littlest of them all.
We're the biggest—strongest, too,
There's nothing that we cannot do!
Ha, ha, ha, you and me,
We're as smart as we can be!
Ha, ha, ha, you and me,
We're as smart as we can be!

TAILOR: Not so smart!

BOTH GIANTS (*Looking about*): Who said that?

GIANT (*To* BROTHER): You did!

BROTHER GIANT: You did!

GIANT: I didn't!

BROTHER GIANT: *I* didn't!

GIANT: Well, somebody did.

BROTHER GIANT (*Pointing to* TAILOR): *He* did! Shut up, you little pipsqueak, or I'll hit you with my club! (*He*

swings his club and accidentally hits the GIANT. NOTE:
*The Giants' clubs may be made of foam rubber covered
with cloth.*)

GIANT: Ow! You just hit *me* with your club. Be careful
with that thing, brother.

BROTHER GIANT: Oh. I'm sorry, brother. I must remember to be more careful from now on.

GIANT (*Yawning*): Ho, ho, hum. I think all our chasing
about has made me tired. Let's rest for a bit before we
go home.

BROTHER GIANT: Yes. A short rest is just what we need.
(GIANTS *lie down under tree and fall asleep, snoring
loudly.* TAILOR, *who has managed to take scissors from
his pocket, cuts hole in sack and finally frees himself.*)

TAILOR: It's lucky for me I brought along my scissors.
(*Putting them back in his pocket, he tiptoes over to the
sleeping* GIANTS *and sings softly.*)

Ha, ha, ha, he, he, he,

You're not as smart as little me!

Ha, ha, ha, he, he, he,

I'm the smartest of us three.

Now I'll fill my pockets with stones and climb up into
this tree. (*He puts several stones into his pockets, goes
behind the tree, climbs up into it, and drops a stone
onto* GIANT's *stomach.* NOTE: *There may be a ladder
concealed behind cardboard tree.*)

GIANT (*Waking up with a start*): Say, what's the big idea?
(*He shakes his* BROTHER.)

BROTHER GIANT: What?

GIANT: Why did you hit me?

BROTHER GIANT: I didn't hit you. You must have been
dreaming. (*He turns over and goes back to sleep. The*
GIANT *leans back and closes his eyes.* TAILOR *drops another stone on* GIANT's *stomach.*)

GIANT: By thunder, if you haven't hit me again!

BROTHER GIANT: What ails you, brother? I didn't even touch you. Stop dreaming and leave me alone. (TAILOR *drops a stone on* BROTHER GIANT'S *stomach.*) Ouch! What are you throwing at me?

GIANT: Who's dreaming now? I didn't throw anything. Go back to sleep. (*They settle down once more.* TAILOR *drops fistful of pebbles on both* GIANTS. *They both sit up suddenly.*)

BROTHER GIANT: You great ox!

GIANT: You fat elephant!

BROTHER GIANT: It's *you* who are doing the hitting!

GIANT: Oh, I hit myself, do I?

BROTHER GIANT: Yes! And you've no right to go blaming me when all the time you're hitting yourself.

GIANT (*Bounding to his feet*): This is too much! (*He pretends to kick his* BROTHER.) Take that!

BROTHER GIANT (*Hopping up and down*): Owww! So you want to fight, do you? All right! (*Pretending to kick him back*) Take that!

GIANT: Owww! You stupid mule!

BROTHER GIANT: You jumping kangaroo! (*Scowling, they lean toward each other until their noses touch.*)

GIANT: Bah! And bah again!

BROTHER GIANT: Bah-bah to you!

GIANT (*Lifting his club*): I'll crown you with this!

BROTHER GIANT (*Lifting his club*): I'll knock your brains out with this!

GIANT: I'm going to knock you colder than a cucumber!

BROTHER GIANT: You and who else?

GIANT: Who else is there?

TAILOR (*In the tree*): I'm here.

GIANT (*Thinking his brother has answered, to* BROTHER): Of course, you're here—and I'm going to give you a good beating! (*The* GIANTS *pretend to hit each other and finally fall to the ground.* TAILOR *climbs down out of the tree and cautiously approaches the* GIANTS.)

TAILOR (*Leaning over them*): I do believe they have killed each other. Seven-at-one-blow has done it again!

KING (*Appearing at right with the* PRINCESS, HERALD *and* LADY-IN-WAITING): Psst! Little tailor!

TAILOR: Your Majesty! What are you doing here?

KING: Adeline insisted that we follow at a safe distance. Is it all over? Are they really dead?

TAILOR: *Stone* dead! I fixed them for good.

PRINCESS (*Clapping her hands*): Oh, you are so brave!

KING (*Calling out*): Come, good townspeople, come! You don't have to be afraid of the giants anymore. The little tailor has killed them. (TOWNSPEOPLE *enter from right and left cheering the* TAILOR.)

TOWNSPEOPLE (*Ad lib*): Hurrah for the little tailor! Hurray! The little tailor has killed the giants! (*Etc.*)

KING (*To* TAILOR): It is with a grateful heart that I give you half my kingdom and my daughter's hand in marriage. (*He joins their hands together and smiles at them both.*)

PRINCESS (*Gazing at* TAILOR): I shall be so proud with such a hero as my husband.

JAM PEDDLER (*Calling from offstage*): Jams and jellies! Jams and jellies!

TAILOR: Listen! That sounds like the Jam Peddler. I think it *is* the Jam Peddler.

PRINCESS: Jam? Oh, Papa, I want some jam.

KING: Herald, bring the Jam Peddler here. (HERALD *exits briefly and returns with* JAM PEDDLER. *If desired,* JAM PEDDLER *may enter from audience, and* HERALD *may go to meet her in aisle.*)

HERALD (*Holding* PEDDLER *by the arm*): Step this way, ma'am.

PEDDLER (*Pulling away*): Take your hands off me! I haven't done anything wrong.

HERALD (*Firmly leading her toward* KING): The King wishes to see you.

PEDDLER (*Frightened*): The King? Is he going to put me in jail? What for? (*She falls on her knees before the* KING.) Have mercy, Your Majesty!

TAILOR (*Raising her to her feet*): No, no, my good woman. The King only wants to buy some jam for the Princess. You remember me, don't you?

PEDDLER (*Regarding him with scorn*): Remember you? I should say so! Three spoonfuls of plum jam!

TAILOR (*Wagging his finger at her*): No, no! *Yummy* plum jam. It was the best jam I ever tasted. It worked wonders.

PEDDLER: What do you mean?

TAILOR: Well, for one thing, I am going to marry the Princess, just as you said—and we'll need lots of jam. (*Smiling at the* PRINCESS) I think Her Highness has a sweet tooth. You shall be the official jam-maker for the palace.

PEDDLER (*Overwhelmed*): Oh, thank you, thank you!

KING: And now let the celebration begin! Blow the trumpets! Ring the bells! The giants are dead! Long live the brave little tailor!

TOWNSPEOPLE (*Cheering, ad lib*): Hurray for the brave little tailor! Hurray for the tailor and the Princess! Long live the brave little tailor! (*Etc.*)

KING: I hereby declare that the tailor's song shall henceforth be our national anthem. (*To* TAILOR) My good man, will you lead us in the singing of our new national anthem?

TAILOR (*Bowing*): With pleasure, Your Majesty. (*He begins to dance about stage with* PRINCESS, *as he leads singing.*)

I killed seven at one blow,
I'm so strong and able,
I slew a pair of giants, too—
   Pop! goes the weasel!
I've no time to wait or pine,
I've no time to dawdle,
The fairest princess now is mine—
   Pop! goes the weasel!
ALL (*Joining in the singing*):
   A kingdom for a spool of thread,
   A princess for a needle,
   That's a mighty fair exchange—
      Pop! goes the weasel!

           (*Curtain*)

         THE END

Dick Whittington and His Cat

An English folk tale

Characters

KATE, *the cook*
SELY, *a serving maid*
DICK WHITTINGTON
ALDERMAN FITZWARREN
ALICE, *his daughter*
PEDDLER JOHNNY
GIRL
OFFSTAGE VOICES, *for Watchman, Mob, and Bow Bell Voices*

SCENE 1

TIME: *A Friday morning in March, 1380.*
SETTING: *The kitchen of Alderman Fitzwarren's house in London. In the center of the back wall is a hooded fireplace. At left is a sideboard. A table and two stools are placed right center, and a low bench is beside the fireplace.*
AT RISE: *The stage is empty. Outside in the street the sing-song cry of the watchman can be heard.*

OFFSTAGE VOICE (*Watchman*): Six o'clock and a fair Friday morning. Six o'clock and all's well. (*The cry is repeated and fades into the distance. There is a pause, then* KATE *enters left. She bustles over to fireplace, stirs embers with poker, and calls out in a loud voice.*)

KATE: Sely! Sely! (*She straightens up and turns around.*) Still sleeping, the slug-a-bed! (*She crosses down left and shouts through doorway.*) Sely! Get up at once, you lazy good-for-nothing! (*She returns to fireplace, grumbling.*) Plague take the girl! Not a drop of water in the bucket. Not a single stick to lay on the fire. (*She goes to table and turns a basket upside down.*) The egg basket empty. Sely! (*She slams basket back on table.* SELY *runs on left, hastily arranging her dress and hair.*) How am I going to get breakfast ready for His Worship, I'd like to know? Take that bucket to the well and fill it.

SELY: Yes, cook. (*She runs to hearth for bucket.*)

KATE (*Pointing to basket on table*): And bring me every egg there is from the henhouse.

SELY (*Dashing to the table*): Yes, cook. (*She snatches up basket and runs to street door, letting out a scream when she opens it.* DICK WHITTINGTON *staggers across threshold and falls in a dead faint.*)

KATE (*Crossing to door*): Another beggar boy—he's probably been fighting in the streets.

SELY (*Bending over* DICK): He has fainted away. See how pale he is?

KATE: Well, he can't stay here. (*She shakes him.*) Come to, boy, come to! (*DICK groans, then opens his eyes. He looks about in a daze.*)

DICK: Where am I? (*He puts his hands to his head.*) Oh, my head!

KATE (*Triumphantly to* SELY): There! What did I tell you? He *has* been fighting.

DICK (*Struggling to his feet, protesting*): Oh, no, ma'am.

I was set upon last night and beaten up. (*He collapses onto bench.*) Please, may I have a drink of water?

KATE: You'll have to go to the well and get it.

SELY: I'll go! (*She runs out into street.*)

KATE (*Calling after her*): Aye! You'll hop fast enough for a beggar boy, but you can't lift a foot when *I* ask you!

DICK (*Earnestly*): Please, ma'am, I'm not a beggar. I want to work.

KATE: Oh, indeed! And what work can you do?

DICK: I'll work at any odd jobs. I'm strong and willing.

KATE (*Turning away, unconvinced*): Huh!

DICK (*Pleading with her*): Please! I'm so tired and hungry.

KATE: Those who loaf about the streets all night deserve to be hungry. (SELY *re-enters with bucket of water and basket of eggs.*)

SELY: Here's your water, lad. I'll get you a mug. (DICK *takes bucket, and* SELY *goes to table, setting down egg basket and bringing him a mug which she fills with water.*)

DICK (*Taking mug from her*): Thank you. You're very kind.

SELY (*To* KATE): Perhaps, cook, if he just had a bite to eat—a piece of bread and—an egg—

KATE (*Aghast*): An *egg!* Have you gone out of your mind, Sely? Would I be likely to give an egg to a street urchin and His Worship's breakfast not cooked yet? (ALDERMAN FITZWARREN *and his daughter,* ALICE, *enter right.*)

ALICE: Kate! What's all this scolding about? Father and I could hear you away out in the garden. Who is this boy? (DICK, KATE, *and* SELY *all answer together.*)

DICK: If you please, sir—

KATE: Your Worship—

SELY: Mistress Alice—

FITZWARREN: One at a time, one at a time! (*Again all answer together.*)

DICK: It's like this, sir—

KATE: This young jackanapes—

SELY: This poor boy—

DICK (*Bursting out*): I'm *not* a jackanapes! I'm an honest boy from the country.

FITZWARREN: Come here, young man. What is your name?

DICK: Dick Whittington, sir.

FITZWARREN: How old are you, Dick?

DICK: Twelve, sir, and I'm willing to work at anything, if you'll only let me.

ALICE (*Eagerly*): Father, we need a boy in the kitchen.

FITZWARREN (*Smiling at her*): Do we, my dear? (*He turns to* KATE.) Do we, Kate?

KATE: A pin's worth of work I'd get out of that bag-o'-bones!

FITZWARREN: Then feed him up, Kate, feed him up! He'll be a great help to you, if he's well-fed. (*To* DICK) Young man, you're hired.

DICK: Oh, thank you, sir!

FITZWARREN: Come, Alice, we'll finish setting out those tulip bulbs before breakfast. (FITZWARREN *and* ALICE *exit right.* KATE *gets a loaf of bread from cupboard and gives it to* DICK.)

KATE: Here—you can chew on this. And there's some stew in the pot left over from yesterday. Eat it in the scullery, and scour out the pot afterwards.

DICK (*Going to fireplace for stew pot*): Where's the scullery?

KATE: Smell it out with your nose!

SELY (*Pointing left*): It's off there, Dick.

KATE: Never you mind showing him! Get you gone to the baker's and the grocer's and the fishmonger's! (SELY *grabs a market basket from cupboard and escapes through street door.* DICK *exits left as* KATE *mutters to herself.*) If His Worship's breakfast is ready when he wants it, it will be a miracle. I'd better go set the table. That lazy Sely will never be back in time. (*She exits right. Outside the house,* PEDDLER JOHNNY *is heard singing, accompanied by ringing of a handbell, as he approaches from off left.* NOTE: PEDDLER JOHNNY's *song, "Merry Is My Bell," can be found in "Singing and Rhyming," Ginn and Company.*)

PEDDLER JOHNNY (*Entering up left, with a pack on his back, swinging a handbell as he sings*):
Merry is my bell, and merry does it ring,
Merry is myself, and merry do I sing.
With a merry ding-dong, happy, gay and free,
And a merry sing-song, happy let us be!
Come and buy my velvet, kersey and shalloon;
Ribbons for the morning, lace for afternoon. (*He stops in middle of kitchen and looks about.*) Ho, there! Anyone up? Hullo! Kate! Sely! (DICK *appears from scullery, eating bread and sipping soup from ladle.*) Bless me, lad, who are you?

DICK: I'm Dick Whittington, and I've just come from Gloucestershire.

PEDDLER JOHNNY (*With a sweeping bow*): Peddler Johnny, at your service. Ever been to London afore?

DICK: No. They say some of the streets are paved with gold.

PEDDLER JOHNNY: Oh-o, so you've heard about that, have you?

DICK: It's not true, then?

PEDDLER JOHNNY: Why, Dick, there is more gold in a field of buttercups than you'll ever see in the streets of London town. But for all that, London's the finest city in Christendom, and don't you forget it. (*Clapping* DICK *on the shoulder*) I haven't a doubt but you'll make your fortune here. (*The sound of faraway church bells is heard.*) Listen! Those are Bow Bells ringing for the apprentices to start work.

DICK: They sound like the bells at home in Gloucestershire. They shall be *my* bells. (KATE *enters right, carrying an old straw mattress.*)

PEDDLER JOHNNY: Ah! Good morning, Kate! Where is Miss Alice? She has asked to see my ribbons and laces.

KATE: You'll find her in the garden with Master Fitzwarren.

PEDDLER JOHNNY: I'll see you again, Dick. (*He sings.*)
Merry have we met, and merry have we been;
Merry let us part, and merry meet again.
With our merry sing-song, happy, gay and free,
And a merry ding-dong, happy let us be! (*He exits. KATE thrusts mattress she is carrying into DICK's arms.*)

KATE: Here! Carry this mattress up to the attic. That's where you'll sleep.

DICK: Where's the attic?

KATE (*Mimicking him*): Where's the attic? Where's the scullery? Where's this? Where's that? It's a wonder you ever found your way to London! (*She points left.*) Go along that passage to the end, and you'll come to the attic door. (DICK *hurries off with the mattress.* KATE *fills a pot with water from the bucket and, placing several eggs in it, hangs it on a crane over the fire. Then she gets a tray from the fireplace mantel and carries it to the table. Suddenly she is startled by a series of frightened cries coming from offstage.*) What on earth! It sounds like that stupid Dick. (*Footsteps are heard running offstage, and* DICK *enters, terrified and out of breath.*)

DICK: Kate! Kate!

KATE: What is it now?

DICK: Rats!

KATE: What?

DICK: Rats! The attic's full of rats!

KATE: What did you expect? Bluebirds? (*She goes to the cupboard for plates and puts them on the tray.*)

DICK: It was horrible! I opened the door and they ran every which way. I won't go back! I won't sleep up there!

KATE: Either you sleep there or you sleep in the gutter. Take your choice. (*She exits right with tray.*)

DICK (*Hysterically*): I *shan't* go back! I'd rather sleep with wolves or lions. I can't bear rats—with their long tails and sharp teeth—squeaking and scratching! Oh, what am I going to do? (*He sinks down onto bench, shivering with dread. Offstage, there is a commotion which begins with jeers and catcalls and mounts to a steady chant.*)

OFFSTAGE VOICES: Catch her! Catch her! Catch the witch girl! Drown her cat! . . . Catch her! Catch her! Catch the witch girl! Drown her cat!

DICK (*Raising his head to listen*): What's that? (*A scream is heard.* DICK *jumps to his feet.*) That's a girl screaming! (*As he starts for the door up left, it is flung open, and a* GIRL *rushes in, hugging a black cat.*)

GIRL: Hide me! Hide me!

DICK (*Pointing to the doorway left*): Through there! (*He shuts street door and stands with his back against it. The voices grow louder, then diminish.* DICK *opens door warily and looks out. Then he closes door and calls off left.*) You can come out now. They've gone. (GIRL *creeps into the room, holding cat tightly.*)

GIRL (*Pathetically*): I'm not a witch. You don't believe I'm a witch, do you?

DICK (*Gently taking her arm*): Of course, I don't. Come and sit by the fire. (*He leads her to bench, and she sits with the cat in her lap.* DICK *sits beside her.*)

GIRL (*Stroking cat*): They were going to drown her. They say she's a witch's cat, because she's black, but she's not.

DICK (*Scratching cat's head*): I can see that she's not. Is she your cat?

GIRL: No, she's a stray, but if those hoodlums get hold of her, they're bound to drown her. (*Hesitantly*) You— you wouldn't be wanting a cat, would you?

DICK: Indeed I would! But I can't pay you anything for her. I haven't a penny to my name.

GIRL: Oh, that's all right—if you promise to be good to her and feed her.

DICK: Feed her! I should say! She can have an attic full of rats! What's her name?

GIRL: I just call her Kitty. (*The cat rubs against* DICK's *hand.*) Will you look at that! She's taken a liking to you already. Hear her purr!

DICK (*Taking cat*): Kitty, you've saved my life.

GIRL (*Rising*): Well, you saved hers. Turn about's fair play. (*She starts toward street door.*)

DICK (*Anxiously following her*): Are you sure you'll be in no danger?

GIRL: Oh, no. When they see I don't have the cat any more they'll leave me alone.

DICK: If you ever need a friend, come to me.

GIRL (*Smiling gratefully*): I will. Goodbye. (*She goes out. In distance, Bow Bells are ringing.* DICK *stands in open doorway, listening. Then he speaks to the cat.*)

DICK: Kitty, I'm going to call you Bo-belle. You and those bells are the only friends I have in the whole world. (*He closes door and comes down center.*) We'll just have to stick it out together, you and I and the bells, up there in that horrid attic. Are you hungry? How about a big fat rat for breakfast? Or two rats, or three? You come along with me, Bo-belle, and you can have as many courses as you like of rats—and rats—and *rats!* (DICK *exits down left with the cat in his arms, as the curtains close.*)

* * *

SCENE 2

TIME: *Mid-morning, two weeks later.*
SETTING: *Same as Scene 1.*
AT RISE: DICK *is playing with cat, pulling a toy mouse by a string along kitchen floor. Outside, watchman is calling the time of day.*

OFFSTAGE VOICE (*Watchman*): Past eleven o'clock and a fair Saturday morning! Past eleven o'clock and all's well! (KATE *enters down right and stands with her arms akimbo.*)

KATE: So this is how you black His Worship's boots, is it? Get that mangy cat off my clean floor!

DICK (*Picking up the cat*): Bo-belle's not mangy. She's the healthiest cat in Leadenhall Street. And I blacked Master Fitzwarren's boots the first thing this morning. (*He carries cat off left and returns.*)

KATE (*Sarcastically*): And do you imagine your work's done for the day? (*She goes to hearth, removes spit from fireplace, picks up small box of sand and hands both to him.*) Get on with cleaning this spit, and don't be all morning about it. (DICK *takes spit and sand, and sits on bench.* KATE *crosses to table, where a pastry is in the making.*) The Captain of the "Unicorn" will be here for supper, and not even an apple tart ready! (*She puts finishing touches to her pastry in frantic haste.*)

DICK (*Interested*): A sea captain here—for supper?

KATE: Don't sit there gawking! Seagoing men like their vittles, same as anybody else. The "Unicorn" is one of His Worship's ships. She sails with the tide tomorrow.

DICK: Master Fitzwarren is sailing with her, too, isn't he?

KATE (*Glancing off right*): Stop your chatter! Here he comes with Miss Alice. (FITZWARREN *and* ALICE *enter*.)

FITZWARREN: Good morning, Kate, Dick. Where's Sely?

KATE: Scrubbing the scullery, Your Worship. I'll get her. (*She calls off left*.) Sely!

SELY (*Offstage*): Yes, Kate?

KATE: Leave off and come here! His Worship wants you.

SELY (*Offstage*): Yes, Kate! (*She enters, wiping her wet hands on her skirt*.)

FITZWARREN (*Speaking to all*): As you know, tomorrow I sail on the "Unicorn" for the Barbary Coast to trade with the King of Barbary. It is my custom to let each one of my household venture something in my ships, be it only a sixpence or a shilling. Kate, how much have you to lend?

KATE (*Fumbling in her pocket*): I *think* six groats, Your Worship, but I was never a good hand at reckoning. (*She pulls out several coins and counts them*.) Here is one, and that is two—then follows four and five and seven.

FITZWARREN: Hold on! Where are three and six? (*She gives him the coins, and he counts them*.) Here are one, two, three, four groats, and a small clipped piece of gold. I'll enter that, and you shall share in the profits. Sely?

SELY: Four pennies.

FITZWARREN (*Counting coins*): Four—pennies. Now, Dick. Miss Alice insists I let you make an investment, too. Have you anything to barter?

DICK: If you please, sir—nothing.

FITZWARREN: Oh, come now, you must have something. (KATE *catches sight of cat in passageway down left.*)

KATE (*Slyly*): Your Worship, he has a cat. (*She pulls cat into view.* DICK *hurries over and picks up cat.*)

FITZWARREN (*Chuckling*): A cat? We'll have to send the cat then. A sea-going cat is good luck.

DICK: But Bo-belle is the only thing I have in the whole world. If she is gone, the rats in the attic will keep me awake every night.

ALICE: I'll get you another cat.

DICK (*Shaking his head*): Never as good as Bo-belle.

ALICE: Please, Dick. Who knows what may come of it?

DICK (*Pressing his lips together firmly*): No, Miss Alice. (*Cat rubs her head against* DICK, *trying to attract his attention.*) What is it, Bo-belle? (*The cat purrs in his ear.*) You *want* to go? . . . For my sake? . . . Well, if you're so anxious, I suppose I must let you go. (*He gives cat to* ALICE.)

ALICE: Don't you worry about Bo-belle, Dick. She'll be more than a match for the stupid ways of sailor men. Hasn't she taken care of herself—and you, too?

FITZWARREN: Come, Alice. (*With a reassuring smile for* DICK, ALICE *joins her father, and they exit right.*)

KATE (*Taunting* DICK): D'ye think your cat will sell for as much as would buy a stick to beat you with? Most likely she'll come back—stuffed! (*She exits left, followed by* SELY. DICK *sinks down onto bench, depressed.*)

DICK: I can't face those rats in the attic without Bo-belle! I won't stay here! I'll run away—back to Gloucestershire—anywhere—where there aren't any rats! (*Sobbing,* DICK *runs up to street door and wrenches it open.* PEDDLER JOHNNY *stands there, smiling pleasantly.*)

PEDDLER JOHNNY: Whoa there, Dick! Where are you going in such an all-fired hurry?

DICK (*Gasping*): Peddler Johnny!

PEDDLER JOHNNY: What's up, my lad?

DICK: Oh, Johnny, I can't stand it any longer! Kate doesn't like me, and there are rats in the attic, and Bo-belle is being sent to Barbary—

PEDDLER JOHNNY (*Interrupting*): Bo-belle? Who's Bo-belle?

DICK: My cat. I love her more than anything in the world, and now they're taking her away from me.

PEDDLER JOHNNY: There, there, Dick. Don't take on so.

DICK: I'm going to run away!

PEDDLER JOHNNY: Every lad must run away at least once. It's as natural to the breed as fighting and whistling. (*Bow Bells are heard ringing in the distance.*) There go Bow Bells a-ringing. They always sound so friendly.

DICK: It's wonderful to hear them, isn't it?

PEDDLER JOHNNY: Aye. They reach out to you. Times when I've been weary a-peddling on the road, those bells seem to say, "Keep a-going, Johnny, keep a-going."

DICK: I wish they'd tell *me* what to do.

PEDDLER JOHNNY: If you listen closely, maybe they will. (DICK *listens to bells and, in the background, soft* OFFSTAGE VOICES *accompany the rhythmic ringing.*)

OFFSTAGE VOICES: Turn again, Whittington. Turn again, Whittington. (OFFSTAGE VOICES *continue under following dialogue.*)

DICK (*A little excited*): You know—they *do* seem to be saying something—in a way.

PEDDLER JOHNNY: That's right. Put your mind to it. That's what I do.

OFFSTAGE VOICES (*Singing distinctly*): Turn again, Whittington.

DICK: You'd laugh if I told you what they seem to be saying to me.

PEDDLER JOHNNY: Not *me,* lad.

DICK: Well, they seem to be saying—turn again, turn again. Turn again, Whittington.

PEDDLER JOHNNY: You'd better do as they say. I always do.

DICK: It's as plain as anything. Turn again, Whittington.

OFFSTAGE VOICE (*Solo*):

Turn again, Whittington,

Thou worthy citizen,

Lord Mayor of London.

DICK (*Laughing*): I'm hearing things all right. Lord Mayor of London! *Me?*

PEDDLER JOHNNY: You can't account for half the strange things that happen in this world.

OFFSTAGE VOICES:

Turn again, Whittington,

Thou worthy citizen,

Thrice Mayor of London.

DICK (*Marvelling*): Three times Mayor of London! That would be a bit of all right! (*Emphatically*) I'm going to stay right here!

PEDDLER JOHNNY: Bow Bells aren't often wrong.

DICK: Why shouldn't I be Lord Mayor, as well as anybody else? Somebody has to be. I'll show them, I will! (*He puts his arm around* JOHNNY's *shoulder and turns him toward open door.*) Look out there at those church spires shining in the sun! It's the grandest day I know of to be staying in London! (*Bow Bells ring out, as curtain falls.*)

*   *   *

SCENE 3

TIME: *An afternoon, two months later.*

SETTING: *Same as Scene 1.*

AT RISE: DICK *is standing in front of the window, looking*

out and whistling. KATE *is seated at table, laboriously making out a list.*

KATE: Oh, for heaven's sake, Dick, stop that whistling! It spoils my spelling!

DICK: I'm sorry, Kate. I was thinking of Bo-belle.

KATE: Bo-belle! Haven't you forgotten her yet? It's been two months. She's probably drowned in the high seas by now.

DICK (*Turning, distressed*): Oh, don't say that, Kate!

KATE: Here—take this list to the tailor in Threadneedle Street, and mind you're back within the hour.

ALICE (*Calling, off right*): Dick! Dick! (*She enters running.*) The "Unicorn" is in! And Father wants to see you!

SELY (*As she enters from the scullery*): The "Unicorn" back?

DICK: Oh, Miss Alice, is Bo-belle on it? (FITZWARREN *enters right, carrying a large chest.*)

FITZWARREN: Dick, my boy, I want to be the first to congratulate you on your great good fortune.

DICK: What good fortune, sir?

FITZWARREN: The King of Barbary has sent you this chest full of gold.

DICK (*Dumfounded*): But why, sir?

FITZWARREN (*Explaining*): Because of your cat, Bo-belle. The King's palace was overrun with rats, and Bo-belle got rid of every one.

DICK (*Proudly*): Oh, she's a Jim-Dandy of a ratter!

FITZWARREN: And so, Master Richard Whittington, you're the richest lad in London. (*He gives* DICK *chest of gold.*)

DICK (*Awed by the title*): *Master* Richard—?

ALICE: It's true, Dick.

DICK: Oh, sir, if you're really sure it's mine—you must take at least half of it for all your kindness.

FITZWARREN: No, my lad, it's all yours, down to the last gold piece.

DICK (*Excitedly*): I must find Peddler Johnny—and the girl who gave me Bo-belle. I'm going to buy presents for everybody!

KATE (*Meekly*): Even for me, Dick?

DICK: Of course! I don't hold any hard feelings against you, Kate.

FITZWARREN: Spoken like a man, Dick.

DICK: Master Fitzwarren, am I rich enough to be a merchant like you?

FITZWARREN: Yes, indeed, my lad—and have a ship of your own, too.

DICK (*Jubilantly*): All my dreams are coming true. Why, one of these days—

FITZWARREN: One of these days you might even go into politics. You might end up—who knows?—as the Lord Mayor of London!

ALICE: Oh, Dick! How grand you will look, riding in the Lord Mayor's coach, with all the bells in London ringing, and the people shouting in the streets as you go by!

DICK: And you beside me, bowing to them!

FITZWARREN: Here, here, now! Things are going a bit fast, aren't they? You've still a long road ahead of you.

DICK (*Laughing in embarrassment*): Yes, I know, sir.

KATE (*Suddenly exclaiming as she looks off down right*): Hen's eggs that hatch out fish! Look who's here! (*Cat comes in.*)

DICK (*Delighted*): Bo-belle! How did you get back from Barbary, how? (*He sets the chest on table and picks up cat.*)

FITZWARREN: In the "Unicorn," naturally.

DICK (*Bewildered*): But I thought—

FITZWARREN: I was keeping it as a surprise. But, as usual, Bo-belle has taken matters into her own paws.

DICK: But if Bo-belle is here, my fortune will have to go back to the King of Barbary.

FITZWARREN: Not at all. The King of Barbary is well served. He gave payment for one cat, and now he has four.

DICK: How can that be?

FITZWARREN: Bo-belle's kittens. Four ruthless ratters! They were born soon after we left London, and they are now sleeping on silken cushions in the King's bed-chamber. Your fortune is still yours, Dick.

ALICE: Didn't I tell you, Dick, that Bo-belle could take care of herself and you, too? (*Bow Bells ring out merrily, as the curtain falls.*)

THE END

Cinderella

The traditional fairy tale

Characters

CINDERELLA		HERALD
KATE	} *her stepsisters*	CHAMBERLAIN
HESTER		PAGE
STEPMOTHER		DRUMMER BOY
MARTIN, *the gardener's boy*		HORN BLOWER
FAIRY GODMOTHER		LADY-IN-WAITING
PRINCE CHARMING		GUESTS
QUEEN		COACHMAN (*Offstage voice*)

SCENE 1

TIME: *Morning.*

SETTING: *The kitchen of Cinderella's home.*

AT RISE: CINDERELLA *is kneeling before the fireplace at left, sweeping ashes from the hearth and dumping them into a coal hod.* MARTIN *enters up center from outside, carrying a large pumpkin.*

MARTIN: Miss Ella, here is the pumpkin you wanted for the pies. I brought the biggest one I could find.

CINDERELLA (*Rising*): Oh, thank you, Martin. Please put it in the corner over there. You shall have one of the pies for your trouble.

MARTIN (*Setting down pumpkin*): I was glad to do it, Miss Ella. It's a shame the way you have to work in your own house, getting up at five o'clock every morning, scrubbing the floors and polishing and dusting.

CINDERELLA: But what else can I do? My stepmother is mistress of the house, and if I don't obey her, she will scold me.

MARTIN (*Snorting in disgust*): Huh! That old shrew! She and her two hoity-toity daughters who think they're duchesses! They're the ugliest girls I've ever set eyes on. (CINDERELLA *starts toward door up center with the hod of ashes.*) Here, Miss Ella, let me empty those ashes for you. (*He takes the hod from her and is about to exit when the voice of the* STEPMOTHER *is heard from off right.*)

STEPMOTHER (*Calling*): Cinderella! *Cinderella!* (*She enters right and sees* MARTIN). What's this? (*She turns to* CINDERELLA.) Lazy bones, wasting time again, are you? Chattering away as if there were nothing to do.

CINDERELLA: But, ma'am—

STEPMOTHER: Hold your tongue!—and get on with your work. You haven't made your stepsisters' beds yet and there's the mattress on my bed to turn.

MARTIN: I'll do it for you, Miss Ella.

STEPMOTHER: *You* will get back to weeding the garden, and don't poke your nose into what doesn't concern you.

MARTIN (*Facing her firmly*): But Miss Ella *does* concern me.

STEPMOTHER (*Sarcastically*): Oh, indeed!

MARTIN: You treat her like a servant. You dress her in rags, and make her do all the work.

STEPMOTHER: How dare you speak to me like that?

MARTIN: I'm not afraid of you. (*He exits outside taking the hod of ashes with him.*)

STEPMOTHER (*Turning on* CINDERELLA *in a fury*): Don't you ever let him into this kitchen again!

CINDERELLA: He's my friend. (KATE *and* HESTER *are heard calling off right.*)

KATE (*Off*): Cinderella!

HESTER (*Off*): Cinderella!

STEPMOTHER: Answer your sisters!

CINDERELLA (*Calling to them*): Here! I'm in the kitchen! (KATE *and* HESTER *enter, each wearing a dressing-gown which conceals her ball dress.*)

KATE: Why hasn't the floor in our room been swept, Cinderella?

HESTER: And the bed linen changed?

KATE: You haven't mended my stockings!

HESTER: Or ironed my petticoat!

KATE: What have you been doing all morning?

STEPMOTHER: I'll tell you what she's been doing. She's been gossiping with that insolent gardener's boy.

KATE: She ought to be punished, Mama.

STEPMOTHER: Oh, she will be, depend on that.

HESTER: I'm hungry. I want my breakfast. (*She sits at the table at center.*)

STEPMOTHER: Cinderella, get our breakfast.

CINDERELLA: Yes, ma'am. (*She starts to set table with dishes and cutlery from cupboard near door up center. A trumpet sounds outside.*)

KATE: What's that?

HESTER: It's a trumpet! (*They run to door up center and open it.*)

KATE: Look! It's the Royal Herald!

HESTER: He's coming here! Oh, Mama, and we're not properly dressed!

KATE: What shall we do?

STEPMOTHER: Calm yourselves, girls. Perhaps he won't notice. (*The* HERALD *enters, carrying a scroll. He bows.*)

HERALD: Madam and ladies. A royal proclamation. (*He unrolls scroll and reads.*) "Know ye that a grand ball will be given this evening in the royal palace to celebrate the birthday of our most noble and beloved son, Prince Charming. All gentlewomen and gentlemen are hereby invited to attend." (HERALD *bows and exits.*)

HESTER: A court ball! Tonight! I shall dance with the Prince.

KATE: Yes, Hester dear—*after* he has danced with *me*. I shall wear my cerise velvet with the long train, and look beautiful.

STEPMOTHER: I'm sure the Prince will want to dance with both of you, you are such graceful girls. Now Cinderella, you must help your sisters get ready for the ball.

HESTER: Not until she has washed her hands, Mama.

KATE: Yes. Cinderella, you're covered with ashes from head to foot. Go out to the pump and wash. And be quick about it. You have a lot to do before we go to the ball. (CINDERELLA *runs out.*)

STEPMOTHER: Now, let's decide what you'll wear, my loves.

HESTER: I shall wear my diamond tiara and dazzle the Prince.

KATE: I shall wear my ruby necklace. He'll find me irresistible!

STEPMOTHER: Girls, we must hurry. At this rate, you'll never be ready for the ball in time. Come along now. (*She steers them off right.*)

CURTAIN

*   *   *

SCENE 2

TIME: *That evening.*

SETTING: *The same as Scene 1.*

AT RISE: CINDERELLA *is busily ironing ribbons on a board laid across a bench at right.* HESTER *and* KATE *enter right, wearing their ball gowns and carrying jewelry, ribbons, etc., which they drop onto the table. Both girls have hand mirrors.*

KATE: Cinderella, have you ironed my handkerchief?

CINDERELLA (*Giving it to her*): Here it is, Kate.

KATE (*Loftily*): *Miss* Kate to you, if you please. Remember your place, my girl.

HESTER: What about my ribbons?

CINDERELLA: I'm just finishing them.

HESTER: Slowpoke! Hurry up! We'll be late for the ball. (CINDERELLA *gives her ribbons.* HESTER *and* KATE *admire themselves in their mirrors.*)

KATE: Come here, Cinderella, and hook my dress. (CINDERELLA *hooks the dress.*)

HESTER (*Searching through the finery on table*): Where's my fan? I can't find my fan. What did you do with it, Cinderella?

KATE: There it is, right in front of you, where you put it yourself. You need eyeglasses, Hester dear. (*She picks up a bottle of perfume and douses herself with it.*)

HESTER: And you need an ear trumpet! (*She snatches the bottle from* KATE.) I've told you a hundred times *not* to use my perfume.

KATE (*To* CINDERELLA): Well, don't stand there, stupid! Curl my hair. (*She sits at the table.*)

HESTER (*Sitting*): Do mine first.

KATE (*Haughtily*): Yes, you'd better do hers first. My hair is easy to dress because it's naturally curly. (HESTER *picks up ostrich plume and sticks it in her hair.* KATE *snatches it away angrily.*) Give me that plume! It's mine!

HESTER: Now, now, Katie, don't lose your temper. You'll make your face all red. (*She pats her own face with a huge puff filled with white powder.*)

KATE: Well, you're a sight! You look as if you've fallen

into a flour barrel. Fix my hair, Cinderella. (CINDER-
ELLA *crosses to her*.) Look out, you clumsy thing! You're
stepping on my train.

CINDERELLA: I'm sorry, Miss Kate.

KATE: Now brush it off and smooth it out.

CINDERELLA (*Doing so*): I wish *I* could go to the ball.

KATE (*Snorting in derision*): *You!* Go to the Prince's ball!
What would you do? Dance a jig with the andirons?
(KATE *and* HESTER *burst into jeering laughter*.)

HESTER: The Prince would take one look at you and send
you down to the kitchen to tend the fire and see that
the smoke goes up the chimney. (*They laugh again.*
STEPMOTHER *bustles in from right, dressed for the ball*.)

STEPMOTHER: Kate! Hester! Aren't you ready yet? The
carriage is waiting.

KATE: It's Cinderella, Mama. She dawdles over everything.

STEPMOTHER: You lazy girl, wait on your sisters. Quick!
Stir yourself! (CINDERELLA *rushes from one to the
other as they order her about*.)

KATE: Polish my rubies!

HESTER: Dust my diamonds!

KATE: Straighten my plume!

HESTER: Tie my ribbons!

KATE: Buckle my slipper!

STEPMOTHER: Do you know what I heard, girls?

SISTERS: No—what?

STEPMOTHER: They say the Prince will choose the most
beautiful maiden at the ball to be his bride.

HESTER (*Squealing with delight*): Oo-o-o! He will choose
me.

KATE: He will not, he'll choose *me*.

HESTER: Huh! What Prince would marry a *broomstick*?

KATE: What Prince would marry a *pudding*?

STEPMOTHER: Come, come, girls, we're late already. The

ball will be over before we get there. Go out to the carriage without another word.

CINDERELLA: Please, ma'am—

STEPMOTHER (*Impatiently*): Well, what *is* it?

CINDERELLA: Please—may I ride as far as the palace gate and watch the people go in?

KATE: Ride with *us*?

HESTER: In your dirty rags?

CINDERELLA: I could sit outside with the coachman.

STEPMOTHER: Indeed you will not! What would folks say? (*She exits up center with her nose in the air.*)

HESTER: Good night, Cinderella. Sit by the hearth like a good girl and sing the ashes to sleep. (*She and* KATE *exit, laughing.*)

CINDERELLA (*Standing in doorway and waving*): Goodbye! Have a good time! (*She turns back into kitchen, closing the door behind her. She goes to table and starts to tidy up the clutter left by the stepsisters. Suddenly she bursts into tears, sitting with her face in her hands.*) Oh, I wanted to go—I wanted to go so much! (*The sound of tinkling bells is heard.* FAIRY GODMOTHER *enters.* CINDERELLA *does not see her at first.*)

GODMOTHER: Good evening, Ella. (CINDERELLA *looks up, startled, then slowly gets to her feet.*)

CINDERELLA: Who—who are you?

GODMOTHER: I am your fairy godmother.

CINDERELLA: My fairy godmother? I didn't know I had one.

GODMOTHER: You have always had one, my dear. Why are you crying?

CINDERELLA: I want to go to the Prince's ball.

GODMOTHER: Is that all!

CINDERELLA: But I have no carriage and clothes. How can I go?

GODMOTHER: Pooh! What are carriages and clothes to a

fairy godmother? (*Looking around*) Let me see—I wonder, is there a nice big pumpkin anywhere about?

CINDERELLA: A pumpkin? Why yes, there's one in the corner over there.

GODMOTHER: Good! I shall want it for the coach. Take it outside and set it down in the driveway. (CINDERELLA *does so and returns.*)

CINDERELLA (*Excitedly*): What next, Godmother?

GODMOTHER: Why, the horses, of course.

CINDERELLA: Yes, I can't get to the palace without horses.

GODMOTHER: You'll find them in the mouse trap behind the bench.

CINDERELLA (*Laughing*): What! Horses in a mouse trap?

GODMOTHER (*Nodding wisely*): You'll see! (CINDERELLA *looks behind bench*)

CINDERELLA: There are six little mice here, Godmother.

GODMOTHER: Good! Put them out by the pumpkin. (CINDERELLA *takes a small cage outside and then returns.*) Now! A coach must have a coachman. Fetch me the rat trap by the cellar stairs. (CINDERELLA *runs into the hallway and returns with a trap.* FAIRY GODMOTHER *nods.*) That rat will make a magnificent coachman. Out with him, my dear. (CINDERELLA *carries the trap outside and re-enters.*) There now, we're all ready.

CINDERELLA (*Crying out in dismay*): Ready? But what about *me*? I can't go to the ball dressed like this!

GODMOTHER: Well! You might have given me credit for thinking of that, too.

CINDERELLA: You mean you can change people as well as things?

GODMOTHER: My dear Ella, what do you suppose a magic wand is for? Watch! (*She waves her wand over the cupboard door up right. Bells tinkle.*) There now—look in the cupboard. (CINDERELLA *opens the door. Her ball gown is hanging there.*)

CINDERELLA: Oh! Oh, it's beautiful, Godmother! Shall I put it on?

GODMOTHER: You can dress in the coach. It will save time.

CINDERELLA: What shall I wear on my feet? I haven't any slippers.

GODMOTHER (*With mock consternation*): No slippers? My, my! You must have slippers. They are very useful at a ball and a fine lady is always well-shod. Well, I'll do my best. (*She raises her wand and throws a handful of glitter into the fireplace. Bells tinkle again.* GODMOTHER *takes a pair of glass slippers from inside the chimney.*) There you are, my dear—a pair of glass slippers, shaped in the fire and polished by ashes.

CINDERELLA: Oh, how lovely they are! But will they fit?

GODMOTHER: Of course they'll fit. Aren't they magic slippers? They will fit no foot but yours. Put them on and you will dance as light as a feather. (CINDERELLA *slips her feet into them and whirls about the kitchen.*)

CINDERELLA: Oh, thank you, Godmother!

GODMOTHER: And now it's time for me to send you off to the ball. But before I do, listen carefully to what I have to say. Don't tell anyone your name, not even the Prince if he should ask you.

CINDERELLA: I won't, I promise.

GODMOTHER: And most important of all—Cinderella, you must leave the ball before midnight, no matter what happens. My magic spell will last only until the stroke of twelve. If you stay one second after that, everything will vanish. The coach will change back into a pumpkin —the coachman and horses will become mice again— and you yourself will be dressed as you are now, in rags and patches. Remember all this, and listen for the clock.

CINDERELLA: I will, I promise. But now shouldn't I be on my way?

GODMOTHER: Indeed you should! Go and stand in the doorway. (*The* GODMOTHER *raises her wand to the accompaniment of jingling bells and chants the spell, as* CINDERELLA *opens door.*)

Pumpkin, rat and six white mice,
I will change you in a trice.
When I wave my magic wand,
One time up and twice around,
Horses, coach and coachman be!
Jingle, jangle! One, two, three!

(*A golden light appears outside the open door. There is the sound of horses' hoofs and a whinny.*)

COACHMAN (*Offstage*): Whoa there, whoa!

(NOTE: *If stage facilities permit, a cut-out pumpkin coach could be pulled into position outside the door.*)

CINDERELLA (*Looking outside the door excitedly*): Oh, there's a golden coach and six white horses and a coachman with tremendous long whiskers!

GODMOTHER: Presto! Off you go!

CINDERELLA (*Hugging her*): Goodbye, dear Godmother! Thank you for everything! (*She runs out.*)

GODMOTHER (*Calling after her*): Goodbye, Ella! Don't forget! Return before the stroke of twelve.

CINDERELLA (*Off*): I will! Goodbye!

COACHMAN (*From offstage*): Gee *up!* (*He cracks his whip. Fanfare. The horses are heard trotting away into the distance.*)

CURTAIN

*   *   *

SCENE 3

TIME: *An hour later.*
SETTING: *The royal ballroom.*
AT RISE: *The ball is already in progress and the* GUESTS

are dancing a minuet. PRINCE CHARMING *is dancing
with a* LADY-IN-WAITING *while* KATE *and* HESTER
watch jealously from the sidelines, standing beside
STEPMOTHER *who is seated down left in one of the
chairs. The* QUEEN *is seated on her throne on a dais up
right, attended by the* COURT CHAMBERLAIN. *The
music stops and the dancers gather in groups on the
terrace, laughing and chatting. As the* PRINCE *escorts
his partner to her place beside the* QUEEN, KATE *and*
HESTER *rush over to him.*

KATE: The next dance is mine, Your Highness!

PRINCE (*Surprised*): Is it?

HESTER: You promised to dance with me, Prince.

PRINCE: Did I?

STEPMOTHER (*Intervening*): Girls, girls, where are your
manners? Pray forgive them, Your Highness. They are
so young and eager.

PRINCE (*Wryly*): *Eager*—yes, madam.

KATE: My sister is a sweet girl, Your Highness, but she is
too fat to dance really well. Now *I* am slender and very
graceful.

HESTER: Yes, Prince, when you dance with Kate you'd
swear you were dancing with a bean pole.

STEPMOTHER: Now, girls. (*Simpering at the* PRINCE) They
have such a roguish sense of humor, don't you think?

PRINCE: Uh—yes, madam. Won't you and your daughters
go into the garden and see the colored lights? They are
quite spectacular. Excuse me. (*He bows and sits on his
throne beside the* QUEEN. HESTER, KATE *and* STEP-
MOTHER *move away with offended backward glances.*)

QUEEN: A delightful ball, my son. I didn't know there
were so many pretty girls in our kingdom.

PRINCE: They are very pretty, Mother, but they do not
interest me. May I have your permission to retire?

QUEEN: Certainly not! Have you forgotten that this ball is being given in your honor?

PRINCE: No, Mother, and I haven't forgotten that I am expected to choose my bride tonight. But she is not here. (PAGE *runs in up center.*)

PAGE: Your Majesty! Your Highness! A princess is coming!

GUESTS (*Exclaiming*): A princess!

PAGE: She has just arrived in a golden coach drawn by six white horses. (*Fanfare offstage.* HERALD *appears in the center archway.*)

HERALD (*Announcing*): Her Royal Highness, Princess— No-name!

GUESTS (*Murmuring in astonishment*): No name! How odd! She must have a name! (CINDERELLA *enters, wearing her ball gown. All bow low. For a moment, the* PRINCE *seems incapable of moving, then he walks slowly toward her and takes her hand.*)

PRINCE: Your Highness.

CINDERELLA: I'm sorry to be so late.

PRINCE: You are not late. For me the evening has just begun. Allow me to present you to the Queen.

QUEEN: You are most welcome, my dear. (CINDERELLA *curtsies.*) Come and sit beside me. (*While the* QUEEN *engages* CINDERELLA *in conversation,* KATE, HESTER *and* STEPMOTHER *talk together down left.*)

STEPMOTHER: Princess No-name? Whoever heard of a princess without a name?

HESTER: She's very beautiful.

KATE: I don't think she's so beautiful. Her feet are much too small.

HESTER: Yes, now that you mention it, they are. And I never really liked blonde hair.

STEPMOTHER: Let's ask the Prince to introduce us. (*They cross to him.*) Oh, your Highness, we're just dying to meet the Princess.

CINDERELLA (*Coming down from the throne*): Who are these ladies, Prince?

STEPMOTHER (*Answering before the* PRINCE *can speak*): This is Miss Katherine and this is Miss Hester. (*They curtsy.*) And *I* am the mother of these two exquisite girls. (*She curtsies so low that she sits on the floor and has to be helped up by the sisters.*)

CINDERELLA (*Secretly amused*): Haven't we all met somewhere before?

KATE: Unfortunately, no.

HESTER: I'm sure we would never forget such beauty as yours.

STEPMOTHER (*Fingering* CINDERELLA's *gown*): Where did you find such wonderful material for your dress?

KATE: And where did you find anyone who could make such a dress?

HESTER: Only a fairy could have made a dress like that.

CINDERELLA (*With a sly laugh*): How right you are! (*The* PRINCE *has been standing by with growing impatience. He turns to* PAGE.)

PRINCE: Go tell the musicians to play the midnight waltz. Immediately! (PAGE *runs out.* PRINCE *turns to* CINDERELLA.) Princess, will you do me the honor of dancing with me? Your pardon, ladies. (*The music begins.* PRINCE *and* CINDERELLA *waltz together, the only couple on the floor. The guests stand in a semicircle and watch, applauding at the end.*) And now, my lords and ladies, it is time to go to supper. The Queen will lead you to the banquet hall. (*Formal marching music.* QUEEN, *escorted by* CHAMBERLAIN, *leads the way up center and off, followed by* GUESTS, *two by two. Finally* CINDERELLA *and the* PRINCE *are alone.*)

CINDERELLA: Aren't we going to supper, your Highness?

PRINCE: In a moment. First, tell me who you are.

CINDERELLA: I can't tell. I promised not to.

PRINCE: Then you must break your promise. I cannot let you go out of my life tonight without knowing who you are.

CINDERELLA: You must. After tonight, you will never see me again.

PRINCE: Of course I'll see you again! Don't you understand? I love you. I am asking you to marry me and be the queen of my kingdom.

CINDERELLA: Your Highness, you can't mean that!

PRINCE: But I do, I *do!*

CINDERELLA: Suppose I were to tell you that I am not a princess?

PRINCE: It would make no difference. I love *you*—not *what* you are but *who* you are. Even if you were a scullery maid in my own kitchen, I would still want you for my queen. (*The clock begins to strike twelve slowly.*)

CINDERELLA (*With a start*): What is that?

PRINCE: Only the clock striking.

CINDERELLA: What time?

PRINCE: Midnight.

CINDERELLA: Twelve o'clock! I must go!

PRINCE (*Catching her hand*): No! The ball isn't over yet.

CINDERELLA: I must leave! Please let me go! (*She pulls her hand away and dashes to the center archway just as* PAGE *appears to make an announcement.*)

PAGE: Your Highness, Her Majesty, the Queen, wishes to ask you—(*He collides with* CINDERELLA, *who whirls around, and is then blocked by* PRINCE.)

CINDERELLA: Oh, please—I must go! (PRINCE *reaches out his hand to stop her. She turns, and runs toward* PAGE.)

PRINCE: Wait, Princess, wait! (*She runs off past* PAGE.) After her, Page! See if you can catch her! (PAGE *races out after* CINDERELLA. PRINCE *paces about with a worried expression.*) Why did she leave so suddenly? What did I say? What did I do? I can't lose her now! (PAGE *returns, out of breath.*) Well! Quick! Where is she?

PAGE: Gone! Vanished—as if by magic! But she left this behind. (*He holds out a glass slipper.*)

PRINCE (*Taking it*): Her slipper—her glass slipper. It will lead me to her. Page, tomorrow we will take this slipper to every house in the kingdom, and every maiden, rich and poor, shall try it on. And that maiden whose foot this slipper fits shall be my bride. Go and announce it to the Queen—and be ready to start at dawn. (PAGE *exits.* PRINCE *presses the slipper to his heart.*) I will find her! Even if I have to search the whole world over, I will find her and bring her back.

CURTAIN

*　　*　　*

SCENE 4

TIME: *The next morning.*

SETTING: *The same as Scene 1.*

AT RISE: CINDERELLA *is alone in the kitchen, gazing tenderly at the glass slipper which is the mate to the one she lost at the ball. She wears her ragged dress and apron.*

CINDERELLA: Oh, it was such a glorious ball! I was never so happy in all my life. Even if I never see the Prince again, I'll always be able to remember him as he was last night.

STEPMOTHER (*Calling from off right*): Cinderella! (CINDERELLA *hastily stuffs the slipper into her apron pocket as* STEPMOTHER, KATE *and* HESTER *enter, still wearing their ball gowns.*)

KATE: Cinderella! Come mend my train at once! I've

been dancing all night long, and somebody stepped on my train.

HESTER: Comb my hair, Cinderella. I have been up all night, and I am so tired. (*The two sisters sit down.*)

STEPMOTHER: Cinderella, go out and scrub the front steps. They must be spotless when the Prince arrives.

CINDERELLA (*Catching her breath*): Is the Prince coming here?

KATE: Of course he is. Haven't you heard? An unknown princess lost one of her glass slippers at the ball last night.

HESTER: And the Prince has announced that he will marry the girl who can wear the slipper.

STEPMOTHER: He must be head over heels in love with her to go to all this trouble to find her. (*To* CINDERELLA, *who has been listening eagerly.*) Well, simpleton, don't stand there mooning. Get on with your work. Scrub the steps!

KATE: Mend my train!

HESTER: Comb my hair.

CINDERELLA: I can't do everything at once.

STEPMOTHER: If you would get up earlier, everything would have been done by now.

KATE: *You* have no excuse for lying abed this morning.

HESTER: *You* weren't out late at the ball last night.

BOTH (*Jeering*): Don't you wish you had been? (*They burst into laughter.*)

STEPMOTHER: Hurry up, girls, and get ready. The Prince will be here any minute. (*Trumpet sounds outside.*) There, what did I tell you? He's coming! (*The outside door opens and* MARTIN *sticks his head in.*)

MARTIN: Miss Ella, the Royal Herald is here and Prince Charming is with him.

STEPMOTHER: You fool! Take them to the front door. Don't let them come in the back way.

MARTIN: Can't do it, ma'am. They're too close—and anyway, most likely the Prince wants to see Miss Ella. She's the only lady in the house. (*He makes a face at the* STEPMOTHER.)

STEPMOTHER (*Grabbing the broom*): You clear out or I'll take this broom to your back! (*He dodges out.*) Cinderella, go down to the cellar and stay there until the Prince is gone.

MARTIN (*Popping in again*): Don't you do it, Miss Ella. You stay right here and see the Prince. I'll fetch him. (*He darts away.*)

STEPMOTHER (*In a rage, pointing to the hallway*): Go on, Cinderella, and not a sound out of you, do you hear?

CINDERELLA (*Passionately*): No! I want to try on the slipper!

STEPMOTHER: *What!* Are you out of your mind?

KATE: Oh, Mama, get her out of sight before she disgraces us.

CINDERELLA: No! *Please!* (*They all push* CINDERELLA *off right, as she protests vigorously.*)

STEPMOTHER (*Re-entering with* KATE *and* HESTER): Well, *she's* taken care of, thank goodness! Now, girls—get ready. Hester, fix your hair. Kate, brush off your train. (*Both girls do as she tells them.*) And remember, if either one of you can get the slipper on, we'll be living at the court for the rest of our lives. (*The trumpet sounds at the door.*) Quickly! Sit over there on the bench, both of you. (*The sisters just have time to get into position when* HERALD *enters, followed by the* DRUMMER BOY *and* HORN BLOWER, *carrying their instruments. Behind the boys comes the* PAGE *carrying the glass slipper on a velvet cushion.* PRINCE CHARMING *brings up the rear.*)

HERALD (*Bowing*): Ladies, His Highness the Prince honors

your house. (*The ladies curtsy.*) Madam, how many maidens live here?

STEPMOTHER: Only these two, sir—my daughters.

HERALD (*Setting a chair in front of the table*): Will the elder please be seated? (KATE *sits and the* PAGE *kneels before her with the glass slipper in readiness.*)

KATE: It will fit me, I'm sure. It's just my size. (DRUMMER BOY *beats his drum and* HORN BLOWER *blows his horn. This is repeated each time the slipper is tried on.* KATE *forces her toes into the slipper but it will not go on any further.*) You're not holding it straight. Please let go. (*She tugs with all her might, grunting and groaning with the effort.*) There! It's on!

PAGE: No, m'lady, it's only over your big toe.

HESTER (*Gloatingly*): I knew you couldn't get it on. It's my turn now. (*She shoves* KATE *out of the way and takes her place in the chair, simpering at the* PRINCE.) My foot is much smaller than hers. See? (*She thrusts her foot into the slipper to the accompaniment of the drum and horn.*) There!

KATE: It's not on.

HESTER: No, but it will be when I stand on it. (*She stands up and stamps hard.*)

PRINCE: Do be careful! You'll break it.

KATE: It doesn't fit. Her heel is sticking out.

STEPMOTHER: Hush, Kate! It fits perfectly.

HERALD: Let the lady walk across the room.

KATE: She can't do it!

HESTER: I can, too! (*She walks, trying to maintain her balance. Her face is contorted with pain at every step. She manages to cross the room but as she turns back, she gives up.*) I can't, I can't! It's killing me! Take it off, take it off! (PAGE *rescues the slipper as* HESTER *collapses on the floor, nursing her sore foot.*)

PRINCE (*With a sigh of relief*): Thank heaven it didn't fit *them!*

HERALD (*To* STEPMOTHER): There is no one else here to try on the slipper?

STEPMOTHER: No one else, sir.

HERALD: Then good morning to you, ladies. (*As the* PRINCE's *party turns to leave,* MARTIN, *who has been secretly watching the proceedings from the doorway, steps forward.*)

MARTIN: Wait, Your Highness! There *is* someone else.

STEPMOTHER (*Threateningly*): Be silent, boy!

MARTIN: You're hiding her, you know you are!

PRINCE: Who is he talking about?

STEPMOTHER: Nobody, Your Highness.

MARTIN: Please, Your Highness. Wait just a moment. (*He dashes off right and returns shortly with* CINDERELLA.) Here she is, Your Highness. Let *her* try on the slipper.

STEPMOTHER: Her! Why, she's just the scullery maid.

KATE: She couldn't possibly wear it.

HESTER: *She* wasn't at the ball.

PRINCE (*Who has been gazing at* CINDERELLA *with growing recognition*): Are you sure, ladies? I believe she *was* at the ball. (*He leads* CINDERELLA *to the chair in front of the table.*) Please sit down. I will try the slipper on you myself.

CINDERELLA: Thank you, Your Highness. (*The* PRINCE *kneels. She puts out her foot. Drum and horn are played with a triumphant flourish. On goes the slipper.*)

ALL: *It fits!*

HERALD: It fits as if it had been made for her.

PRINCE (*Smiling at* CINDERELLA): It was.

CINDERELLA (*Drawing the other slipper from her pocket*): And here is its mate. (*The* PRINCE *puts it on her other foot and rises, taking her hand.*)

PRINCE: At last I have found you, my princess.

STEPMOTHER: *Princess!*

CINDERELLA (*Rising*): Yes. I was the princess at the ball.

KATE: You? A ragged cinder maid?

CINDERELLA: My fairy godmother sent me. She gave me the dress and the coach and the horses.

HESTER (*Scoffing*): I don't believe it! You don't have a fairy godmother. (*Bells tinkle and the* GODMOTHER *steps into the room.*)

GODMOTHER: You are quite wrong. Cinderella does have a fairy godmother.

STEPMOTHER (*Rudely*): Who is this? I've never seen her before.

GODMOTHER: And you never will again. I come only to the good and kind who need help. But now my task is done except for one thing. I must dress my godchild as befits our future queen. (*She lifts her wand.*)

PRINCE (*Holding up his hand*): One moment, madam. I will take my bride as I find her. Permit me. (*He removes his crown and sets it on the head of* CINDERELLA.)

GODMOTHER: You're a fortunate young man, Prince Charming. See that you deserve her. (*She puts* CINDERELLA'S *hand in his.*) This time I give her to you for always. (*She raises her wand in a gesture of blessing.*) May you both live long and happily ever after. (PRINCE *takes* CINDERELLA'S *hand.*)

PRINCE: And now, I would have an answer. What *is* your name, Your Highness?

CINDERELLA (*Laughing*): Ella—Cinder-Ella.

HERALD (*Leading the others in shouting the acclamation*): All hail to the Princess Cinderella! (*The* DRUMMER *beats a merry tattoo and the* HORN BLOWER *toots a mighty blast, as the curtain falls.*)

THE END

Production Notes

THE EMPEROR'S NIGHTINGALE

Characters: 7 male; 5 female; real and Toy Nightingales may be male or female.

Playing Time: 25 minutes.

Costumes: Traditional Oriental costumes. Stage Manager wears an elaborate Mandarin coat and headdress and carries a fan. Imperial Doctor, Nurse, and Watchmaker may wear special costumes to indicate their professions. Real Nightingale wears drab gray costume; Toy Nightingale wears brightly colored, jeweled garments. Property Man wears black costume and queue. Members of the Court all carry fans.

Properties: Gong and stick; large lacquered property box containing willow tree, cup, saucer, teapot, book, paper flower hung with tiny bells, scroll, clacker, toy carving knife, and comb covered with tissue paper; wire coil; drapery; jeweled casket; key.

Setting: The Emperor's Garden. The stage is set with Chinese screens and curtains. A throne is at center with a tea tray on a stand beside it. At left center is a garden bench. A large lacquered box containing properties is down right. A small platform for the Gong-Bearer is up left.

Lighting: No special effects.

THE PIED PIPER OF HAMELIN

Characters: 7 male; 1 female; 12 or more male or female for children and townspeople.

Playing Time: 25 minutes.

Costumes: Costumes of the thirteenth century. Children and townspeople may wear peasant costumes, and the Mayor and Aldermen may wear more elegant clothing. The Mayor has an ermine robe. The Pied Piper wears a motley costume of yellow and red, and a peaked cap with a feather in it.

Properties: Cupcakes, plums, apples, market basket, pipe, purse, money bags, and valuable objects, such as jewelry, clothes, money, etc., cookies.

Setting: The public square of Hamelin Town. There are stone benches set about, with clumps of shrubbery behind them. The entrance to the Town Hall is at left. The way to the river and mountain is up left. At right, a street leads to the homes of the townspeople. Running across the back of the Square is a parapet which borders the river bank.

Lighting: No special effects.

Music: The Piper may play his pipe, or a record may be used. The music for the songs may be found in *Complete Nursery Song*

450

Book, by Inez Bertail (Lothrop, Lee and Shepard).

ALADDIN AND HIS WONDERFUL LAMP

Characters: 6 male; 4 female; Attendant can be male or female.

Playing Time: 30 minutes.

Costumes: At rise, Mother, Aladdin, Jusuf and Sharah wear peasant dress. Later they change into same type of elegant dress worn by Sultan, Abu and Princess. Slave and Genie wear typical "Arabian Nights" costumes. Magician wears long black cloak and fez. Attendant is dressed as page. All males wear sashes.

Properties: Pole with bag of confetti attached, ring, bag of coins, food packages, empty cloth bag, apple, pear, casket of jewels, necklace, platform, large filled sack, flower, parasol, grapes, supper tray, piece of embroidery, bowl of fruit, tarnished lamp.

Setting: Scene 1: A street in Baghdad. Aladdin's hut with curtained doorway is at right. A broom and basket are beside the doorway and a bench is at left of it. Tree is upstage; at left is cave with iron ring embedded in its door. Flat depicting palace turrets should be available. Scene 2: A room in Aladdin's palace. At rear is a raised terrace on which a lilac tree can be seen. A divan is at stage left in front of a screen, and a table and hassock are at stage right in front of another screen.

Lighting: The cave interior may be brightly lighted.

Sound: Crash of cymbals, thunder, music, footsteps as indicated in text.

RUMPELSTILTSKIN

Characters: 4 male; 7 female.

Playing Time: 30 minutes.

Costumes: Traditional fairy-tale costumes. Elf suit, elf cap, and long gray beard for Rumpelstiltskin; black elf suit for Shadow. Court costumes and coronets for Princesses, Crispen, and Cockatoo. Miller wears white smock over brown trousers. Grizel wears peasant dress, beads in Scene 1; royal dress and a crown in Scene 2. Happily wears a bluebird costume or blue elf suit with cloth wings.

Properties: Handkerchief, sack of flour, cradle. The two bales of straw are square boxes of fine wire overlaid with flame-proofed raffia, with yellow ribbons to attach to spinning wheel; embroidery.

Setting: Rumpelstiltskin's hill and the King's pavilion. The hill is a platform at the back of the stage, with steps at right and left leading to it. The sky is in the background. The pavilion is in the foreground. It is an open space with arches on three sides. The widest arch, at the back, frames the setting of Rumpelstiltskin's hill. The arch at right leads to the palace and the arch at left leads to the garden. A low wall separates the pavilion from the hill. In the center of the wall is a secret door. In the pavilion are a garden bench at left center, a fountain with a circular seat at right center, a stool downstage and a spinning wheel upstage left.

Lighting: Yellow lights should shine behind the bales of straw when the straw turns to gold; a color wheel should be used during the spinning scene; lights should dim and then come up again to indicate passage of time.

TOM SAWYER, PIRATE

Characters: 6 male; 6 female.

Playing Time: 25 minutes.

Costumes: Dress of the late nineteenth century. Aunt Polly wears a simple housedress and apron, and Becky wears a plain school dress. Tom is barefoot and is dressed in dark trousers or knickers, shirt with prominent collar, and jacket. Sid and Joe wear clothes similar to Tom's. Huck wears soiled, shabby overalls and is barefoot. Alfred wears neat, dark suit with shirt and tie, and an Eton cap. In Scene 3, Aunt Polly, Mrs. Harper, and Widow Douglas wear black dresses and hats. Becky, Amy and Gracie are in simple white dresses. Sid and Ben wear "Sunday" suits.

Properties: Barrel; wooden stool; two pans; potatoes; paring knife; books for Sid, Alfred and Becky; two large needles threaded with black and white thread, respectively; two pennies for Tom's pocket; simulated campfire; log; pirate flag; piece of bark; string of fish; handkerchiefs for Aunt Polly and Mrs. Harper.

Setting: Scene 1 is set in Aunt Polly's back yard. The rear of Aunt Polly's house is at left and is enclosed by a whitewashed fence with gate downstage. At right is the Thatcher garden enclosed by picket fence with gate downstage. Below the Thatcher gate is a vine-covered arbor. A barrel and wooden stool are at center stage. Scene 2 takes place at Jackson's Island. A campfire is at center with large log to the left. Scene 3 is the same as Scene 1, with barrel and wooden stool removed.

Lighting: No special effects.

THE ELVES AND THE SHOEMAKER

Characters: 6 male; 7 female; 3 elves (male or female).

Playing Time: 25 minutes.

Costumes: The elves are barefoot and wear ragged, patched clothing. (At the end of the play, they put on their new clothes.) Johann wears a cobbler's apron over his shirt and trousers. Frieda wears an apron over her dress. The other characters wear hats, gloves and long scarves over their costumes to indicate the winter weather outside the shop.

Properties: Wreath, garland, doll, cardboard shoe, needle, hammer, nails, ruler, scissors, doll's shoes, red leather, thread, glue pot, polishing cloth, red shoes (to fit Elsa), wrapping paper, five gold pieces, pieces of leather, four pairs of shoes, three sets of clothes for the elves: shoes, jackets, trousers, shirts, socks and stocking caps.

Setting: The shoemaker's shop. Upstage center there is a counter with empty shelves on the back wall behind it. A lamp is on the counter, and a cobbler's bench with tools on it is near the counter. A curtained doorway at right leads to the living quarters at the rear of the shop. The door to the street is up left, and near it is an empty display window. A bench is set in front of the window. In Scene 4, a decorated Christmas tree is in the shop.

Lighting: In Scene 1, the lights dim as Johann exits and then "moonlight" floods stage as elves appear.

Sound: Cock crowing, clock striking, bells ringing, music.

DUMMLING AND THE GOLDEN GOOSE

Characters: 15 male; 9 female; 4 boys or girls for children; as many girls as desired for Bridesmaids.

Playing Time: 25 minutes.

Costumes: Appropriate peasant costumes for Mother and her sons, Innkeeper and daughters, and Children. Gray Man wears a gray cape and hat. Others wear appropriate costumes.

Properties: Cloth bundle containing bread and cheese, jug, 2 cardboard axes, fishing pole with small fish on the end of the line, a stuffed goose with golden feathers, clothes basket filled with sheets, dishes of food, loaf of bread wrapped in napkin, wild flowers, baskets of berries, wedding cake, basket containing bouquet of roses, long scroll for Herald, 2 gilt chairs, handkerchiefs, two boxes, one labeled "Dry Handkerchiefs," the other labeled "Wet Handkerchiefs."

Setting: A country road. At right is the door of an inn, over which hangs a sign: GANDER INN. Near the door there is a table with two stools. A row of trees extends across the back of the stage. At left is a gnarled oak tree, which stands apart from the other trees, and behind which is hidden the golden goose. There are exits right and left, and through the door into the inn.

Lighting: No special effects.

Sound: Trumpet fanfares, as indicated in script. If desired, recorded music may be played as the procession marches about.

THE THREE WISHES

Characters: 3 male; 5 female; extras for additional Boys and Girls if desired.

Playing Time: 15 minutes.

Costumes: Tree Fairy may wear long gown. Others wear appropriate peasant costume.

Properties: Wooden ax, bag, rubber knife, string of sausages, primrose plants, skillet, ladle, sandwich.

Setting: At opening of play, a log is placed at center stage. Scene 1 is a forest. Trees are at right, left, and in the background. (If desired, Tree Fairy may be hidden behind tree instead of inside it.) Scene 2 is the kitchen of Adam's cottage. At left, there is a fireplace with an iron pot (containing sausages) on crane. A table stands at center, with stools at either side. An open cupboard filled with dishes, and a spinning wheel may complete the setting. Door at right leads outside.

Lighting: No special effects.

THE SAUCY SCARECROW

Characters: 3 male; 8 female; 3 male or female for birds; male and female extras may be added as desired for witches and birds.

Playing Time: 25 minutes.

Costumes: Scarecrow wears fancy coat, breeches, starched shirt, Windsor tie, and straw stuffed in his sleeves, collar, etc. Farmer Barley, Maggie, and Bess may wear peasant clothing; Maggie has a sailor hat and Bess wears heavy boots. Witches wear traditional costumes. Birds wear representative costumes of crepe paper.

Properties: Whisk broom for Farmer Barley; wooden clacker for Maggie; broomsticks, caldrons, and spoons for witches; wire carrier filled with bottles for Witch-Boy; ladle for Cook-Witch; milk pails for Bess.

Setting: Farmer Barley's barley field. A fence, with a wide center gate, runs across the stage and separates the field, which is upstage, from the road, which is downstage. Outside the gate is a rustic bench. There is a wooden support in the field for the Scarecrow, made of two crossed sticks on a base.

Lighting: Lights change from daylight to dusk to moonlight, and back again from moonlight to dawn to daylight, as indicated in the text.

Sound: Crowing of a cock; music for the songs, "Ki-yi-yi-yi" and "April" may be found in *Music for Early Childhood,* New Music Horizons Series (Silver Burdett Co.) and music for "Api-kai-i" may be found in *Listen and Sing,* Enlarged Edition (Ginn and Company). Any appropriate music may be used for the Birds' Dance.

KING ALFRED AND THE CAKES

Characters: 6 male; 3 female.
Playing Time: 15 minutes.
Costumes: Peasant clothes for Wilfrid and his family. Rowena wears a cloak over her dress on her first appearance. Appropriate court costume for Cedric and Ulfstan. King Alfred wears hooded cloak over his minstrel's costume. He has harp slung over his shoulder, and wears crown hidden under his hood when he first appears.
Properties: Broom, board with cakes, rake and hoe, spatula, two milking pails, sack.
Setting: The kitchen of a Saxon farmhouse in Somerset, England.

A rough stone fireplace is at right, and downstage of fireplace is a cradle. A long bench, table and smaller benches, and low stool make up the furnishings. On wall beside door is a bracket holding an unlit torch. Wilfrid's spear hangs on upstage wall, and farm implements may stand in one corner. On one wall are pegs for hanging up cloaks. Door at left leads to storeroom, and upstage door leads outside.

Lighting: No special effects.
Sound: Sounds of baby, as indicated in text.

THE APPLE OF CONTENTMENT

Characters: 4 male; 5 female.
Playing Time: 30 minutes.
Costumes: Manikin Redcap is dressed in a red elf suit and wears a red stocking cap with a silver bell at the end. Christine wears a ragged and patched dress and heavy shoes. Willa and Nilla are dressed in full skirts with pockets, peasant blouses and bodices. Dame Tinney wears a long, simple dress. Tree of Contentment has a brown costume with green leaves attached to her head and arms. King wears royal robes and a crown. Page and Herald are dressed in traditional court costumes.
Properties: Fishing pole, money pouch, and large black seed (this may be a lump of coal) for Manikin Redcap; old boot; basket of bird feed for Christine; comb for Willa; hair ribbon for Nilla; branches for Tree; several apples covered with gold foil and with string loops attached to stems; trumpet for Herald; pouch for King, 4 handkerchiefs, one wrapped around a round stone, another around weeds.

Setting: A meadow near the home of Dame Tinney. Extending across the back of the stage is a ground-row of grass which represents the bank of a brook. At right, there is a large rock; behind the rock is a bucket of water that may be used for wetting Manikin's cap. A clump of bushes is at left, with a bench close by.

Lighting: No special effects.

THE SWINEHERD

Characters: 5 male; 9 female.

Playing Time: 20 minutes.

Costumes: All except Prince wear appropriate royal costumes. The Princess and Maids wear long, full skirts. The Prince wears ragged clothes and carries a rattle and crown in his pocket.

Properties: Handkerchief, small ornamental box which contains red rose, bird cage covered with silk scarf and containing toy bird, small cooking pot hung around with tiny bells and rattle hung around with tiny bells.

Setting: A corner of the Emperor's orchard. A stone wall across the back separates the orchard from the imperial pig sty behind it. A cherry tree bends over the wall at center. There is a grape arbor at left. An apple tree is at right with a rustic bench underneath. Exits are at right and at left, through arbor.

Lighting: No special effects.

Sound: Pigs grunting, bird singing, recording of "Ach, du lieber Augustin" accompanied by bells, as indicated in text.

RAPUNZEL

Characters: 3 male; 7 female.

Playing Time: 30 minutes.

Costumes: The Witch wears a black robe, and the Prince has an appropriate royal costume. Others wear peasant dress. Rapunzel has blonde hair, with a long braid.

Properties: Watering can, trowel, glue, paint pots and brushes, doll, dark and blonde doll's wigs, doll's pinafore, bassinet, book, oversize scissors, knapsack, rope, sewing basket.

Setting: Scenes 1 and 2: The Witch's garden and the front yard of Franz's cottage. The garden is at left, and is separated from the yard by a stone wall which extends part way down center and ends in a high iron gate. The wall continues along the back of the garden. In the center of the garden is a bed of lettuce, and oddly shaped rocks and flowers are scattered about. In Franz's yard are a bench and a work table, which is strewn with material and tools for making dolls. Down right is a sign: FRANZ—DOLLMAKER. Exits are at left, up right and down right. Scene 3: A tower room. A casement window, through which characters enter and exit, is on the right wall. There is a hook beside the window. Nearby is a table and a stool, and at left is a cot.

Lighting: Lights dim and come up at the end of Scene 3.

Sound: Birds singing, thunder, as indicated in text.

THE MAGIC NUTMEG-GRATER

Characters: 4 male; 5 female; male and female extras.

Playing Time: 25 minutes.

Costumes: Karl, Elsa, Frau Stropken, and the playmates are dressed in peasant costumes. Frau

Welzel and Lena wear rich-looking long dresses, fancy hats and gloves. Heinrich wears a long smock; Heidi, an apron over her peasant costume. The beggar is in rags. Tinker Hans is dressed in oddly-assorted clothes, with saucepans, frying pans, cake tins and trays hung from his neck and waist by lengths of twine. Ladles of every kind are stuck into the band of his broad-brimmed hat.

Properties: Pots, kettles, brazier and bag of tools, for Tinker Hans; penny, for Frau Stropken; tea kettle, for Elsa; nutmeg-grater, with four strings attached to the handle (any type of grater will do); easel, small canvas and paint-box, for Heinrich; milk-pail, for Heidi.

Setting: The stage represents a town square in old Germany. Frau Stropken's garden is in the foreground. There is a rustic bench at right, under a tree. A low wall runs across the back of the stage, with a gateway at center. At left is a trellised arbor leading to Frau Stropken's cottage.

Lighting: No special effects.

Sound: The sound of a harp is heard offstage, as indicated in the text.

CHRISTMAS EVERY DAY

Characters: 5 male; 4 female.

Playing Time: 25 minutes.

Costumes: Kindheart, Tinsel and Tassel wear appropriate fairy and elf costumes with Christmas decorations added. In Scenes 2 and 3, Abigail wears a night-gown, Robin wears pajamas, and Mr. and Mrs. Phillips wear dressing gowns. In Scenes 4 and 5, the Phillips family wears everyday clothes. Jenny and Jim wear everyday summer clothes.

Properties: Scene 1: letter in envelope. Scene 2: four stockings (one containing a jackknife; one, a fruitcake Santa; one, a wrapped potato; and one, wrapped lumps of coal). Scene 3: the same filled stockings; a blindfold for Abigail; wrapped Christmas presents for Mr. and Mrs. Phillips; letter. Scene 4: shopping list for Mrs. Phillips; bills for Mr. Phillips; newspaper pattern for Jenny; paper bag containing raisin "torpedoes" for Jim; two boxes of candy cane "fireworks" for Robin; doll and toy gun for Abigail; letter. Scene 5: Noisemaker for Robin.

Setting: The living room of Abigail's home, decorated for Christmas. There is a fireplace at center of the rear wall, with four stockings hanging from the mantelpiece. At left, French windows lead to a side porch. At right, an archway opens on the front hall. There is a divan left center, an easy chair and small table, right center. In Scene 4, the French windows are open to indicate summer.

Lighting: If possible, in Scene 1 the stage should be lit only by light coming through the French windows until the Elves turn on the lamps.

Sound: Offstage noises (bells ringing, whistles blowing, people cheering) at beginning of Scene 5.

THE TWELVE DANCING PRINCESSES

Characters: 4 male; 13 female; extras as dancing partners for princesses, if desired.

Playing Time: 30 minutes.

Costumes: Appropriate court costume. The princesses wear ball gowns or dressing gowns over their dance dresses, as indicated in text. Irene's gown has laced bodice, and she carries magic key in her pocket; King has large key in his pocket. Charwoman wears apron. Felix wears simple tunic and boots; later, he wears magic cloak.

Properties: Magic key, worn-out slippers, small switch for Page, parchment, scrubbing brush and bucket, basket containing twelve pairs of slippers with name tags, goblet of milk, necklace, hand mirror and powder puff for Belinda, brooch, hairpins, brush, two hair ribbons, handkerchief for Lenora, key and handkerchief for King.

Setting: Scenes 1, 2, and 4 are set in a room in the King's palace. A folding screen is set before entrance to the princesses' bedroom, up left. A couch with pillows and blanket on it is upstage, and near it is a small table with a vase of flowers. Door to the hall is at right, and above it is a hatrack with an elaborate plumed hat and a velvet jacket hanging on it. In Scene 1, at rise, the Prince's boots are beside the couch. Scene 3 is set in the enchanted garden. A sparkling tree with leaves shaped like diamonds is at center. A pedestal at left holds an urn filled with long blades of silver grass, and a golden rosebush is at right.

Lighting: Lights may flicker when Charwoman casts spell to clean palace floor, if desired.

Sound: Cock's crows, clock striking twelve, soft music, waltz, polka, as indicated in text.

Puss in Boots

Characters: 6 male; 2 female; roles of Puss, Page, and Lion may be played by boys or girls.

Playing Time: 25 minutes.

Costumes: Traditional royal dress for King, Princess Gabrielle, and Marie. Louis wears plumed hat and elaborate courtier's costume with ruffles and lace on front of jacket. King carries gold-headed cane. Puss wears cat hood and boots, and Lion may wear hood representing lion's mane. Ogre has a beard and wears tunic and trousers. Page wears plumed hat, colored tights, and a velvet cape. Oliver, Bernard, and Pierre are dressed in shabby peasants' clothes.

Properties: Toy mouse on wire or string or mouse puppet for Scene 1; cloth bag with leather boots; gold-headed cane; extra courtier's suit; tablecloth; picnic baskets with picnic food, etc.; bag of game. Rubber mouse with long tail for Scene 2.

Setting: Scene 1: A meadow near an old mill which is visible in background. If feasible, mill may be turning. A stone wall runs across rear of stage, with a gate in it, at left of center. At right of gate, a full sack of grain leans against wall. A path leads off right to highway, and off left to Ogre's woods. At right there is a clump of shrubbery. A rustic picnic table and benches are right of center, and a tree stump and rock at left. Scene 2: Entrance hall of Ogre's castle. A very large armchair with a high back stands at right, in front of a tapestry curtain. Room also contains low table. A door at right leads outside, and door left leads to rest of castle.

Lighting: No special effects.

Sound: Knocking on door, squeak of mouse, blare of trumpet, lively music.

THE RELUCTANT DRAGON

Characters: 3 male; 1 female; 10 or more male and female extras for children and villagers.

Playing Time: 30 minutes.

Costumes: Children and villagers wear peasant costumes. St. George wears golden armor and a white cloak with a red cross on it. He wears a red-plumed helmet. Horace wears a beautiful, shiny dragon costume with bright green scales at the top and lighter green scales below; he should be able to wave his long, scaly tail when he walks.

Properties: Picnic baskets and sandwiches, handkerchiefs, bark, charcoal, stool, sword, spear with a little white pennon which has a crimson cross on it, square of flannel and small bottle.

Setting: An English hillside. A backdrop shows green, rolling countryside, with a hint of old gray cities on the horizon. At left is the opening to Horace's cave; at right is the path to the village. Upstage center is a long platform with rocks on it, representing the hill.

Lighting: No special effects.

THE LITTLE PRINCESS

Characters: 3 male; 9 female.

Playing Time: 30 minutes.

Costumes: Dress of the 1890's. Sara and the other students wear party dresses in Scene 1. Later, Ermengarde wears an attractive dress, and Sara wears old and ragged clothes. Later she wears the new slippers brought by Ram Dass. Becky wears ragged clothes throughout, and in the last part of Scene 2 wears a faded, patched nightgown. Miss Minchin wears a severe, dark-colored dress. Ram Dass and Chanda wear Indian clothing. Mr. Carrisford wears a suit.

Properties: Large doll, bird on string, crumbs, pile of books, tin box with food and lace paper lining, old trunk, lantern, wood, lamp, satin quilt, scatter rugs, tray of food, dressing gown, pad of paper, pen.

Setting: A dreary attic room, in need of repair. A door, right, leads to the stairway. There is a window in the back wall. The furniture is old and rickety: a narrow iron bed with a pillow, a thin blanket and a ragged patchwork quilt, a kitchen chair and table, a wood stool, a clothes tree, a rocking chair, and a washstand with a cracked bowl and pitcher. Against the left wall is a small fireplace with grate.

Lighting: Lights should be dimmed to indicate night. Hidden below the grate there may be a small red light or flashlight which can be turned on to simulate a fire. Also, there should be a small flashlight in lantern which may be turned on.

Sound: Music during Scene 2, as indicated in text.

THE SLEEPING BEAUTY

Characters: 6 male; 12 female.

Playing Time: 20 minutes.

Costumes: Fairies wear long gowns and carry wands. Woodcutter and his grandchildren wear peasant costumes; Woodcutter has a hat. Others wear appropriate court costume.

Properties: Gold rattle, velvet cushion, 5 gold flowers.

Setting: Scene 1 takes place in the throne room of the palace. Down left is the royal cradle; up right is a small table with five gold flowers on it. There are thrones up center for King and Queen. Door at left leads to interior of palace; door at right leads to entrance hall. Scenes 2 and 3 are in a tower of the royal palace. A bed, covered with rich velvet, is up center. A stool and spinning wheel are at left; an old chest is up right. Skeins of brightly colored yarn may be hung about the room. Exits are at right and left.

Lighting: No special effects.

Sound: Excerpts from Tchaikovsky's "Sleeping Beauty" may be played if desired. Fanfare, church bells, as indicated in text.

HEIDI

Characters: 4 male; 7 female.

Playing Time: 35 minutes.

Costumes: Swiss peasant costumes for Alm Uncle, Peter, and Barbel. Alm Uncle carries a long wooden staff. In Scene 1, Heidi wears a light summer dress. Dete has on a plain dress and carries a handbag. In Scene 2, Heidi wears a Swiss costume and Dete wears a fancy dress and a hat piled high with artificial flowers and fruit. The Sesemans and Fräulein Rottenmeier wear appropriate city clothes. Heidi's dress in Scene 3 is similar to Clara's. She later changes into her peasant dress. Tinette wears a maid's uniform, with cap and apron. Tony is dressed in ragged clothes and barefoot. In Scene 4, Madame Seseman carries a handbag containing a silver coin.

Properties: Bundle of clothes, coins, carved wooden spoon, branches of autumn leaves, jug, feather duster, packages wrapped in gift paper, hand organ, covered basket, small bundle made of

table napkin, wheel chair, wreath of blue flowers, letter, rolled-up paper snake.

Setting: Scenes 1, 2, and 4: A space in front of the Alm Uncle's hut, high up on the Alm Mountain in the Swiss Alps. The hut is at right, and a rustic bench is up center. A tree stump is down left. An exit right, behind the hut, leads up the mountain to the goat pasture, and an exit left leads down the mountain to the village. There is another exit through door of hut. Mountain peaks and sky are in the background. Scene 3: The drawing room of the Seseman home in Frankfurt. A fireplace with mantel is at left, and near it are an armchair and a small table. At right is a sofa with a coffee table in front of it. Up center is an archway, through which the hall can be seen. An exit right beyond the arch leads to the front door, and another exit at left beyond arch leads to the rest of the house.

Lighting: No special effects.

Sound: Sound of yodelers, goat bells, Alpine horn, cat's meow, doorbell, loud crash, music of hand organ, as indicated in text.

HANSEL AND GRETEL

Characters: 3 male; 3 female; offstage voice for cuckoo; as many boys and girls as desired for Gingerbread Children.

Playing Time: 30 minutes.

Costumes: Colorful peasant costume. Sandman carries sack and has pouch of glitter attached to his belt. The Witch has key on her belt, and has white bread, "mutton" chop, and raisins in pocket of her apron.

Properties: Broom for Hansel; knitting for Gretel; bundle of sticks; dust cloth; market basket containing potatoes, butter, flour, sausage, eggs, apples, and package of tea; crown of buttercups; basket of strawberries; drawstring bag; twig.

Setting: Scene 1: A room in Hansel and Gretel's cottage. Door is at left, and beside it are brooms of various sizes, leaning against wall and hanging on pegs. Upstage is a window, with a cupboard beside it, containing an earthen pitcher of milk and a basket. There is a fireplace at right with a pot hanging in it. A rocking chair is in front of the hearthstone. At center is a table with a bench and stool. Scene 2: A clearing before the Witch's cottage. Before rise, a log may be placed on stage. Curtains open revealing gingerbread cottage, with a door of frosted cake, and a window of gumdrops. There may be a cookie and sugar plum trim. At right corner, cottage joins a peppermint stick fence with gingerbread men as posts. At right is an oven, containing large gingerbread cookie, and at left is large cage with stick inside and padlock on door.

Lighting: If desired, lights may dim, and there may be a blackout, as indicated in text.

Sound: Accompaniment to songs, "Dream Pantomime" music, and thunder, as indicated in play.

PINOCCHIO GOES TO SCHOOL

Characters: 6 male; 3 female; any number of additional males for the "Boobies" and extra school children.

Playing Time: 15 minutes.

Costumes: Traditional storybook costumes.

Properties: Bandana, spelling book, hat, two sticks of peppermint, donkey ears, donkey tail, paper bag, for Pinocchio; pieces of string, for boys; whip, hoop, pistol, for Coachman; bag of marbles, donkey ears, donkey tail, paper bag, for Candlewick; cards, jacks for Boobies. For the expanding and contracting of Pinocchio's nose, a roll of film cut and attached to a false nose can be pulled out and pushed back to give the proper illusion.

Setting: The first scene, played in front of the curtain, is the schoolyard. A bench is at stage left and a seesaw at stage right. The second scene is the "Land of Hooky." There is a booth, stage center, painted with candy sticks and ice cream cones. A large bunch of balloons is on top, and slogans, as indicated in the text, are written on walls of the booth.

Sound: The songs "Wooden Shoe Dance" and "Playing in the Sun" may be found in *Rhythms and Rimes,* Enlarged Edition, Ginn and Company.

JACK AND THE MAGIC BEANSTALK

Characters: 5 male; 4 female; 1 or 2 male or female for cow; as many extras as desired for Girls and Boys, Farmers and Wives.

Playing Time: 30 minutes.

Costumes: The women wear long, old-fashioned dresses and aprons. Old Woman carries a cane and has beans in the pocket of her apron. Jack and Giant wear rough tunics and trousers. Giant has a purse containing gold coins tucked in his belt, and carries a club. Hen's costume is bright yellow and has a hidden pocket to carry golden eggs. Cow's costume may be for either one or two persons; it should have horns. Boys and Girls wear festive clothes and others wear appropriate costumes to represent their occupations.

Properties: Hay, rope, beans, large sack, purse, coins, harp, golden eggs, cane, club, ax, large dishes, big cardboard knife, spoons, ladle.

Setting: Scenes 1, 3: Yard of a dilapidated farm. The cottage is at left and the barn at right, and a stone wall with a sagging gate runs across the rear of the stage between them. A rough wooden bench stands against the wall up center. There is a signpost down right which points off right and reads: "To the Village." The road to the village extends across the front of the stage. Scene 2: The outdoor kitchen of the Giant's castle. The entrance to the castle is at left, and at right is an outdoor fireplace and chimney, with a side oven large enough to hold Jack. A wall runs along the rear of the stage. A huge kettle hangs on a crane in the fireplace, and a metal fire poker leans against the fireplace. A chair and a table set with oversized eating utensils and dishes are at center, and against the wall is a chest containing the harp. In both scenes, the beanstalk is seen growing behind the wall, as indicated in the text. There are exits right and left.

Lighting: No special effects.

Sound: Music of the magic harp, played offstage, as indicated in text. This may be played on a guitar, if recorded harp music is unavailable.

Rip Van Winkle

Characters: 11 male; 5 female; as many boys for Sailors and girls

and boys for Townspeople and Children as desired. Offstage voice may be male or female.

Playing Time: 30 minutes.

Costumes: Appropriate 18th century dress, for all except Hudson and crew, who wear suitable 17th century costumes. When Rip awakens, his clothes are shabby, and he has a long, white beard, and his gun is old and rusty.

Properties: Newspaper, pocketknife, bucket, broom, armload of wood, kite, bow, whistle, two toy guns, ninepins, balls, large keg, sack containing mugs, drum.

Setting: Scenes 1 and 3: A village in the Catskill Mountains. The village tavern is at left, and nearby are chairs, a stool, and a table with a checkerboard on it. At right, near a tree, is a well with a bench beside it. There are exits right and left, and another exit through the door of the tavern. In Scene 1, the sign on the tavern reads: KING GEORGE TAVERN, with a picture of King George III. A Union Jack hangs on a flagpole nearby. In Scene 3, the sign reads: "Union Hotel —Proprietor—Jonathan Doolittle." There is a picture of George Washington, and an American flag flies from the flagpole. Scene 2: A forest glade, high in the Catskill Mountains. A tree stump is at right center, and a large bush is far left. If desired, the scene may be played before the curtain. An exit is at right, and another at left, behind the bush.

Lighting: Lights may be dimmed in Scene 2, to indicate passage of time.

Sound: Thunder, dog's bark, ship's bell. If desired, recorded music may be played in Scene 2, as indicated.

The Brave Little Tailor

Characters: 7 male; 5 female; seven boys and girls for Flies, four boys and girls, or more, for Townspeople.

Playing Time: 30 minutes.

Costumes: Appropriate royal or peasant costume. Tailor's jacket has pockets in it.

Properties: Hammer and anvil, vegetables, tray of pastries, meat, toy knife, and chopping block, basket of jams, two clubs made of foam rubber, burlap sack, sapling.

Setting: Scene 1 is the town square. There are five shops, with signs in front of them reading, TAILOR, BUTCHER, BAKER, GROCER, and BLACKSMITH. In front of tailor's shop, at right, is a workbench with scissors and other sewing materials. On window sill of shop are large piece of cloth and smaller bright red strip for tailor's belt (words SEVEN AT ONE BLOW may already be written on belt); also on sill are fly swatter and plate with loaf of bread, knife, spoon, and piece of cheese on it (cheese may be sponge soaked in water and wrapped in cheesecloth). Scene 2 is a clearing in the forest. A large tree, which may have ladder concealed behind it, is upstage; "stones", which may be made of styrofoam or papier-mâché, are scattered about. A large rock is at left, and beside it is a paper bird.

Lighting: No special effects.

Sound: Trumpet fanfare, whistle sliding up and down scale, as indicated in text. If desired there may be musical accompaniment for songs.

Dick Whittington and His Cat

Characters: 3 male, 4 female; extras for offstage voices. A real cat may be used for Bo-belle, a child dressed as a cat may play the part, or a toy cat may be used.

Playing Time: 25 minutes.

Costumes: Medieval costumes. Girls may wear long dresses or blouses and long skirts; boys may wear tunics and tights. Dick wears ragged clothes; Kate, Sely, Peddler and Girl wear simple clothes; Fitzwarren and Alice wear more expensive-looking clothes.

Properties: Poker for fire, egg basket, bucket, eggs, loaf of French bread, stew pot, market basket, handbell, ladle, peddler's pack, straw mattress, tray, dishes, fireplace spit, box of sand, pastry, kitchen bowls, coins, chest of gold, toy mouse.

Setting: The kitchen of a medieval house. In the center of the back wall is a hooded fireplace. Against the left wall stands a sideboard or cupboard. A table and two stools are placed right center and a low bench is below the fireplace, at left center. There are three entrances: left of the fireplace is a doorway leading to the street, and entrances left and right lead to the servants' quarters and the master's quarters. Right of the fireplace is a mullioned window set in an alcove.

Lighting: No special effects.

Sound: Church bells. They should be played loudly or softly as indicated in the text.

Cinderella

Characters: 7 male; 7 female; male and female extras for Guests; male offstage voice for Coachman.

Playing Time: 35 minutes.

Costumes: Consult any illustrated edition of "Cinderella" for appropriate costumes. When they first enter, Kate and Hester wear dressing gowns over their ball dresses, so that the dresses cannot be seen. In Scene 2, the Stepmother, Kate and Hester appear in ball gowns. Cinderella appears in her ball gown in Scene 3; in Scene 4, she is again in her ragged dress and apron (which has large pockets in it). The Fairy Godmother has a wand and handful of glitter.

Properties: Scene 1: broom, coal hod, large pumpkin, dishes and cutlery, scroll for Herald. Scene 2: iron, ribbons, board, jewelry, hand mirrors, bottle of perfume, ostrich plume, puff with white powder, cage, trap, handkerchief, fan, curling iron, dust cloth, ball gown for Cinderella (inside cupboard), glass slippers (inside chimney), wand for Godmother. Scene 4: broom, drum, toy horn, glass slipper on velvet cushion.

Setting: Scene 1: The kitchen of Cinderella's home. At the left, there is a fireplace. Downstage of the fireplace is a stool. At the center, rear, a door leads outside. Left of the door is a window. Right of the door is a cupboard. Another door upstage in the right wall opens into a hallway. Downstage, set against the right wall, is a bench. There is a table right of center with three chairs. Scene 2: Same as Scene 1. An ironing board is laid across the bench. Scene 3: The royal ballroom. There are archways at back leading out onto a terrace. There are entrances right and left. A dais with two thrones is upstage right of center. Three or four chairs are placed at intervals against the left wall with flowers on stands between them. The space in the center of the room is clear for dancing. Scene 4: Same as Scene 1.

Lighting: When the "coach" is ready outside the door, a golden spot might shine there, as indicated in the text.

Sound: Offstage trumpet, tinkling bells for Fairy Godmother, sound of horses and coach and cracking of whip, music for ball, striking of clock.